SPACEMEN 3
& The Birth of **Spiritualized**

SPACEMEN 3
& The Birth of **Spiritualized**

Erik Morse

OMNIBUS PRESS

LONDON / NEW YORK / PARIS / SYDNEY / COPENHAGEN / BERLIN / MADRID / TOKYO

Exclusive Distributors
Music Sales Limited,
8/9 Frith Street,
London W1D 3JB, UK.

Music Sales Corporation,
257 Park Avenue South,
New York, NY 10010, USA.

Macmillan Distribution Services,
53 Park West Drive,
Derrimut, Vic 3030,
Australia.

To the Music Trade only:
Music Sales Limited,
8/9 Frith Street,
London W1D 3JB, UK.

Every effort has been made to trace the copyright holders of the photographs in this
book but one or two were unreachable. We would be grateful if the photographers
concerned would contact us.

Typeset by Galleon Typesetting, Ipswich.
Printed by Creative Print & Design, Ebbw Vale, Wales.

A catalogue record for this book is available from the British Library.

Visit Omnibus Press on the web at www.omnibuspress.com

To Roger and Nicholas Rodney in memoriam
And (dare I say it) For All The Fucked Up Children Of
This World

CONTENTS

ACKNOWLEDGEMENTS

IN ENGLAND AND EUROPE:

MY EDITOR CHRIS CHARLESWORTH, OMNIBUS PRESS AND MUSIC SALES LIMITED for playing with fire, PETE KEMBER AND ANITA for far too much to acknowledge here, JASON PIERCE AND JULIETTE for backstage shenanigans, WILL CARRUTHERS AND HELEN for being cheeky and for sandwiches, PETE BAIN for use of portions of his own writings and alternative p.o.v.s, ROSCO ROSWELL for alternative raiment, PAT FISH for proving ace musicians can still study at Oxford, CHARLIE PRITCHARD, JONNY MATTOCK for driving me around Northampton in the rain, MARK REFOY for entertaining any and all LGM questions, GOFF RODERICK for his mania, GERALD PALMER for yet another view, STEVE KALIDOSKI for helping me reach that view, GRAHAM WALKER for techno bits, PAUL ADKINS, GAVIN WISSEN for showing me around Rugby, TIM MORRIS for upstairs discussions at YP, NATTY BROOKER for a surprise appearance, STEVE EVANS, ALAN MCGEE for taking time out of his busy schedule, DAVE BARKER, SONIA BOVIO, CLIVE SOLOMON, DAVE NEWTON for Britain in the Eighties, IAN GOODCHILD for his wealth of archival bits, IAN EDMOND for numerous other bits and bobs, MARK LASCELLES for great stories and good e-conversation, CHRISTOPHER ROSE for S3 live tapes, GRAHAM HOLLIDAY, NIGEL CROSS, EDDIE PREVOST, VINITA JOSHI, ROBERT HAMPSON for not hanging up until I mentioned Spacemen 3, STEPHEN PASTEL, STEPHEN LAWRIE for sonic memories, RICHARD FORMBY, RICHARD ADAMS, MARK CLIFFORD for allowing me the distinct pleasure of entering the world of Seefeel just for a moment, RICHARD D. JAMES, FIONA @ BELLA UNION, DAVE PEARCE for twilight phone rants about feedback, Nick, and Syd, CLINTON HEYLIN, JOHN PERRY for his honest and personal observations, MILES, DAMO SUZUKI, TONES SANSOM @ TRIAD, LAURENCE VERFAILLIE for memories of The Mary Chain, CHRIS SHARP @ 4AD, STEVE GREGORY @ FIERCE RECORDS, PETER BRUYN for translations, ROB YOUNG @ THE WIRE, ALEX NEEDHAM @ NME, ANGELA AND DOUG WHITBREAD for opening up their home and kitchen, THE KIND STAFF OF THE BELLS INN PUB IN TANWORTH-IN-ARDEN for my somniferous visits to Nick's home, THE STERN LADIES OF THE RUGBY LIBRARY

IN AMERICA:

STACE/FACE for love in spite of authorship, MUM AND DAD for love in spite of receivership, J. A. NEAL, my grandfather, from his penchant for Robert Frost sprung my first experiences with "ambience", VICTOR BOCKRIS for insight compassion opportunity and redaction as well as four years of Burroughs and Warhol quizzings, JOHN CALE for Ezra Pound and for mentioning Brian and Lou, SIMEON COXE for my very first interview, ALAN VEGA for patience despite being my second interview, DEAN WAREHAM for putting up with Galaxie questions, LAWRENCE CHANDLER AND MARTHA SCHWENDENER for putting up with my drunkenness (twice), LESLEY @ BEGGARS, SIMON REYNOLDS for advising on all things blissed out, FRED MILLS for pointing me in the right direction, COREY DUBROWA for all things shoegaze, JONATHAN VALENIA, BYRON COLEY for a great phoner and trying to get Thurston for me, MARK ARM for America in the Eighties, PETER TRAHM, KIM GORDON for trying to get Thurston for me, JAMES CHANCE, RANDALL NIEMAN, NICK KRAMER, CHRIS BARRUS, FRANK GIRONDA @ LOOKOUT! MANAGEMENT, LONG GONE JOHN @ SYMPATHY FOR THE RECORD INDUSTRY, GREG SHAW @ BOMP RECORDS, R. J. REYNOLDS & RENE JUNOT for severely cutting short my life-expectancy, JIM AND NANCY ENDMAN & FAMILY for crustless quiche and afternoon LA whimsy, HOLLINGSWORTH CAMP-BELL a.k.a. JAKI LEVY for animation and compassion despite my indie snob-bery, TERRY WAGNER a.k.a. rock'n'roll bodhisattva for introducing me to Spacemen 3, DEREK WOODLEY a.k.a. gearhead for travelling between the nocturnal and diurnal, DAN HUNT for his inspiring divinations of Everett McGill that forever kept me laughing, JERRY SWIFT @ Peddler's Co-Op, Conroe, TX, for invoking the spirit of the Sixties in the 00s, BRYAN&ERIN individually captivating but duo-ed divine, JONATHAN for the sound of con-fusion, JEN&SARAH&MELANIE for making Stacy so happy, CAROLYN, JUAN AND CHUCK @ Biography Bookshop, NY, NY, for part-time sympathy, ALL THERAPISTS PAST AND PRESENT for the perfect prescrip-tion, CHRIS STRAAYER AND ALLEN S. WEISS for scholastic *jouissance*, HALLOWED PROPHETS OF THE INDIE-ROCK TRINITY @ Other Music, Kim's, and Rebel Rebel, NY, NY

"ULTIMATELY WE, AS PART OF THE ORGANIC UNIVERSE, ARE PRINCIPALLY ANALOGUE DEVICES."

SONIC BOOM, in an interview with Andrew Stevens 2002

PERSONNEL

SONIC BOOM: guitars, vocals, synthesisers, samples, feedback, tremolos, drones

JASON: guitars, vocals, keyboards, harmonica

MARK REFOY: guitars

BASSMAN: bass vibrations

WILL CARRUTHERS: bass vibrations

TIM MORRIS: percussion

NATTY BROOKER: percussion

ROSCO ROSWELL: percussion

JONNY MATTOCK: percussion

GEAR (RADIOPHONY)

GUITARS:

VOX STARSTREAM TEARDROP SEMI-ACOUSTIC (WITH INBUILT PALM WAH, FUZZ, TREBLE/BASS BOOSTER, REPEATER, E-TUNER, AND TONE CONTROLS)
EKO (VOX) ACOUSTIC
TURKISH CAZ/SAZ
BURNS JAZZ GUITAR
VOX STARSTREAM XII
FENDER JAGUAR
FENDER TELECASTER
FENDER THINLINE
GIBSON THUNDERBIRD
GRETSCH COUNTRY GENTLEMAN
RICKENBACKER 6-STRING
RICKENBACKER CAPRI 360
MARTIN ACOUSTIC

EKO ROCKET
EPIPHONE OLYMPIC
EPIPHONE CASINO

SYNTHESISERS AND KEYBOARDS:

EMS VCS 3 MK 1
EMS VCS 3 MK 2 (MODIFIED)
EMS SYNTHI AKS (MODIFIED)
EMS SYNTHI A (MODIFIED)
EMS DK2
EMS 49 X 49 MATRIX
NEW ATLANTIS DIGI-TRIX DIGITAL 16 X 16 MEMORY
  PATCHING MATRIX
OSCAR MIDI VERSION
EDP WASP
MOOG OPUS 3
ROLAND MC202 CV SEQUENCER AND SYNTHESISER
KORG EA1 VIRTUAL MONO SYNTHESISER
CASIO VA10 VOCODER, PITCH SENSOR AND SPECIAL
  EFFECTS KEYBOARD
FENDER RHODES
VOX DUALMANUAL SUPER CONTINENTAL
VOX UNIVOX VALVE MONOSYNTH
NEW ATLANTIS KRAAKLE BOX
CASIO CZ101 SYNTHESISER
YAMAHA TX81Z FM TONE MODULE
HAMMOND ORGAN AND RHYTHM ACCOMPANIMENT
  UNIT
RIYAZ PROFESSIONAL ELECTRONIC TAMBOURA
ALESIS AIRSYNTH
SUZUKI OMNICHORD SYSTEM 200M
  (MIDI OUTPUT FROM SONIC STRINGS)
LONGWAVE ELECTRONICS MK1 THEREMIN
FARFISA COMPACT
FARFISA ORGAN
ROLAND D20

EFFECTS:

YAMAHA SPX90 MULTI FX PROCESSOR
DIGITECH S 200 MULTI FX / VOCODER

DIGITECH S 100 MULTI FX / VOCODER
BOSS RRV 10 MULTI TAP REVERB
BOSS DE-200 DIGITAL DELAY WITH TRIGGER FUNCTION
BOSS TU-2 TUNER
EVANS SE-810 SUPER ECHO TAPE DELAY/SPRING REVERB
DANELECTRO BACK TALK REVERSE ECHO
PETERSON TRIGGERED ENVELOPE
    (WITH BACKWARDS GUITAR, STEEL GUITAR,
    SYNCED TREMOLO PEDAL) PROTOTYPE
NOBELS TRX TREMOLO
VOX REPEAT PERCUSSION PEDAL
VOX TREBLE/BASS BOOSTER PEDAL
VOX TONE BENDER
VOX VOLUME PEDAL
VOX AMPLIPHONIC OCTAVOICE 1 (CLARINET)
VOX OCTAVOICE 2 (BRASS)
PSYCHOSONIC SUPER-FUZZ (CUSTOM)
ZVEX FUZZ PROBE
ZVEX SEEK-WAH
COLORSOUND WAH
COLORSOUND SUPA WAH
BOSS BF1 BASS FLANGER (MODIFIED)
BOSS DD3 DIGITAL DELAY
DOD DFX9 DIGITAL DELAY
ARION DDM-1 DIGITAL DELAY
GUYATONE TD1 TUBE DISTORTION
LOVETONE BIG CHEESE FUZZ
KAY FUZZ TONE
SCHALLER DISTORTION
MORLEY EVO 1 OIL-ECHO
MORLEY PFA 11 PHASER
WALCO SOUND-A-ROUND (REPEAT PERCUSSION)
EAGLE ELECTRONICS SPRING REVERB/DISTORTION
TRANSFORMERS PITCH SHIFT/MODULATOR (CUSTOM)
STARMAKER VOICE CHANGER/ FREQUENCY SHIFTER
    (CUSTOM)
WALCO FEEDBACK DESTROYER
TRANSFORMER VOICE SYNTHESISER
MEGAMOUTH WARPR FREQUENCY SHIFTER (CUSTOM)
RAT DISTORTION
DRONES
FEEDBACK

AMPLIFIERS:

H&H TRANSISTOR AMP (INCLUDES REVERB AND
  SUSTAIN)
VOX CONQUEROR 35 WATT HEAD, WITH VOX CABINET
  (INCLUDES TREMOLO, FUZZ, MRB, TOP BOOST AND
  REVERB)
VOX FOUNDATION 50 WATT BASS/LEAD HEAD, WITH
  VOX CABINET (INCLUDES VOX FUZZ, TONE X AND
  M.R.B.)
VOX BUCKINGHAM 35 WATT AMERICAN HEAD
  (INCLUDES TREMOLO, FUZZ, REVERB, TOP BOOST,
  TONE X AND M.R.B.)
DOOBIE 15W PRACTICE AMP
MARSHALL AMP
REALISTIC 15W PRACTICE AMP

GEAR (PHARMACON)

STIMULANTS:

AMPHETAMINE SULPHATE
METAMPHETAMINE
COCAINE HYDROCHLORIDE
PRO PLUS PILLS

DEPRESSANTS:

CANNABIS
HASHISH
SINSEMELLIA
LIBRIUM (CHLORDIAZEPOXIDE HYDROCHLORIDE)
VALIUM (DIAZEPAM)
XANAX (ALPRAZOLAM)
PROZAC (FLUOXETINE HYDROCHLORIDE)
PAXIL-SEROXAT (PAROXETINE)

ANALGESICS:

DICONAL (DIPIPANONE)
HEROIN (DIAMORPHINE)
MORPHINE SULPHATE
PHYSEPTONE (METHADONE)
PALFIUM (DEXTROMORAMIDE)
OMNOPON (PAPAVERETUM)
VICODIN (HYDROCODONE)
OXYCONTIN (OXYCODONE)
PETHIDINE (DEMEROL)

HALLUCINOGENS:

LSD (LYSERGIC ACID DIETHYLAMIDE)
PSILOCIN
PSILOCYBIN
MESCALINE
MDMA (METHYLENEDIOXYMETHYLAMPHETAMINE)
AMYL NITRITE
BUTYL NITRITE
BUTANE
DMT (DIMETHYLTRIPTAMINE)

INTRODUCTION

Launching The Dreamweapon
Or, An Alternative History Of
Transparent Radiation

The *Melody Maker* decreed 1988 to be the greatest year ever for rock music. 'It rained hard all year and it washed us away,' was the claim. And despite the admittedly exaggerated and absolutist tone that can be standard issue for the music press in the UK, the evidence at hand would seem to prove the statement. In America, the charge was led by Sonic Youth, who completed a New York City trilogy with *Daydream Nation*, to unanimous applause. Fellow New Yorkers Swans rode their own noise-rock crest with the sacrosanct *Children Of God* and their menacing live album, *Feel Good Now*. B.A.L.L. spun dirty guitar and stuporific songwriting on their Beatles "Butcher"-sleeve parody *Bird*, while D.C.'s anarcho noiseniks Pussy Galore pursued superlative squall with their explicit *Sugarshit Sharp* and *Dial M For Motherfucker*. Up in Boston, Galaxie 500 displayed their love for The Velvet Underground and adoration for collegiate naïveté with their debut album *Today*, Dinosaur Jr. unveiled their first anthem 'Freak Scene', and The Pixies' *Surfer Rosa* merged a visceral death rattle with a soft quivering melancholia.

With call-and-response fervour the English indie-scene produced an equal multitude of classic recordings. A. R. Kane released the *Up Home* EP with its swell of echoed atmospherics and dub-inflected deep soul. Kevin Shields finished shedding what remained of early period, indie-jangle My Bloody Valentine, and suffused the sound of a Jazzmaster tremolo with a reverse reverb effect, concurrently causing ears to bleed and bodies to drop with 20-minute live versions of 'You Made Me Realise' and an album, *Isn't Anything*, that finally fulfilled the horror-schmaltz of the band's cinematic namesake. An afterbirth of copyists would soon fill the Creation roster: Slowdive, Ride, The Telescopes, et al. Meanwhile, The Jesus and Mary Chain had reinvented themselves as melodious purveyors of scintillating pop on *Darklands*, and made the bold decision to cut ties with maverick manager and Creation founder Alan McGee, symbolically terminating the reign of Creation's "anorak music" culture. Ultra Vivid

1

Scene and Talk Talk investigated more textured atmospherics stretching The Cocteau Twins and The Durutti Column deeper into the ether. Those stalwart guardians of jangle-pop, The Smiths, had fragmented at the previous year's end, allowing guitarist Johnny Marr to pursue his bourgeoning interest in Electronic. Soon enough the guitar would become completely excommunicated by an influx of samplers and Roland drum-machines. White-labelled acid-house anthems would hasten to extinguish what remained of trad-rock's cult of personality. The collaboration and collective anonymity of the DJ and producer would soon swallow the snarling and/or glib character of the indie "star". Where had hero-worship gone? Where were the faces and voices to humanise the astral sounds? The year fell on the cusp of a noise revolution.

Spacemen 3 were orbiting it all. . . .

In August of that year, 1988, a quiet summer evening greets the denizens and amblers of Hammersmith down along the Thames River. The Waterman's Art Centre is screening Wim Wender's *meisterwerk*, *Wings of Desire*, drawing a queue of smartly dressed locals who push toward a PA's crackled announcement of show times. Suits and skirts scramble through the oversized entryway, across the plush foyer, and toward the screening room. The wall on the immediate left is comprised completely of a translucent glass exposing the serpentine twists of the Thames below. The bar sits in the centre of the large open room, where several suits putter about waiting for evening cocktails but with slightly bemused expressions. For between the two large marble columns that seem content to frame the scene, a cadre of young musicians ready their music-making machines and wait patiently to begin.

Plugging his teardrop-shaped Vox Starstream into an antiquated Vox Conqueror, the lithe, inscrutable alchemist Sonic Boom (a.k.a. Pete Kember) coaxed a pulsing, almost alien sound from his guitar. The tone had a certain warm crackle displaced by cool aquatic drifts of reverb as the vibrations appeared to modulate from wave to particle and back again. Soon the oneiric tones began echoing off both sides of the wall and recombined with the ever-flowing pulsations from the Vox to form completely new waveforms. A lukewarm ooze of sound covered the lobby. Sonic continued to sit crouched over his guitar determined to plug into the drone zone.

Meanwhile, Jason Pierce, by now sitting beside Sonic with his Fender strapped across his shoulder, inserted subtle melodic permutations atop this thick radiophonic stream. The licks burned quickly and then descended from within the mushroom-shaped drone, only to appear again with each rhythmic advance. Bassist Will Carruthers sat atop his amplifier surveying the scene: the handful of kids cross-legged before them, followed by the inebriated milquetoasts and cinephiles who seemed less than pleased with the distraction. This was one of Carruthers' first gigs as a Spaceman, and, frazzled on a concoction of nerves and fuzz, he'd forgotten to plug the lead of his Gibson Thunderbird into the amp. Oblivious to such trivialities, he soldiered on, his bass lines reduced to faint clicks of the plectrum. Steve Evans, a Rugby local and Spacemen compatriot, crouched to the side, droning his guitar on a single chord and watching the elongated queue of filmgoers. Andy Jackson stood near the thin cluster of punters sporting an unwieldy tape-recorder. He'd bootlegged innumerable indie gigs in previous years but had rarely encountered such an eerily disorienting exhibition of drones and tones, yet alone in such an unconventional setting.

Businessman and Spacemen impresario Gerald Palmer stood off to the side gazing at the oddly hypnotic spectacle. Sonic and Jason puffed on a vast quantity of rolled cigarettes between guitar-parts. Smoke 'n' riff. Smoke 'n' riff. Palmer's patent distaste for the horrendous din matched the sentiments of nearly every punter idling at the bar. He'd approved the gig for the band but, after witnessing the unruly reception, second-guessed his decision. A few drunken suits cursed from the bar, as an ambience of mounting resistance threatened to neutralise an increasingly voluminous electric blanket. The sounds began to shape themselves to the architecture of the lobby, erecting a slab of multivalent textures and intervallic tones, until heads began to spin and bowels rumble.

Seated nearby was Pat Fish, The Jazz Butcher guitarist, who'd accompanied The Spacemen to the Art Centre with plans to join them after an intermission. But it quickly became evident to him, as he sat among the unruly punters at the bar, that a mutiny would be far more likely than a second "set".

> PAT FISH: You see, there was a plan and then there was what actually happened. And it was fucking beautiful, but in this setting it was really, really annoying people. It was quite loud in the room. And there's like all these middle-class people coming in to see some German film or something, ya know. And tempers were beginning to fray.

Ten minutes into what had been billed as 'An Evening of Contemporary Sitar' and the first riffs of Spacemen 3's 'Honey' zoink from the gelatine drone, succeeding quickly from a tense ascendance of guitar pings. Jason counters with ringing phrases, bits and bobs of 'Come Down Softly To My Soul' accelerating into a near lock groove before evaporating into the surrounding hum. *Repetitio ad infinitum.* Sonic's guitar slurps the Vox amp in a natural phase, as a straw might a dark cola. The repeater-delay binds nucleoids of audible energy (hitherto anonymous ripples in space) together as random moments in time. *Repetitio ad nauseam.*

Fifteen minutes in, Sonic and Jason build to a climax and effortlessly cascade to a blurbed hissing. A few relieved stuffed-shirts peer up from their glasses at the bar and toward the bathetic rumble of feedback. The noise slows to a steady pulse. Heads shift around: "Are they fuckin' done yet?!" But then the faint clicks of guitar ignite and mushroom once again, pounding soft flesh ever louder. Someone huffs: "Shut up you fuckin' twats!" Layered between Sonic's vibrating 'Honey' riff and Jason's modular rotations, the PA's crackled transmission announces last-minute seating for *Wings Of Desire* in the adjacent theatre.

> PAT FISH: And, round about the sorta 30-minute mark I guess, I went to the bar to get a drink. And I swear to God that what I'm going to tell you is gospel truth word for word. I was at the bar and there's these two old boys about 40 or 50 drinking their beer. And they were obviously totally disgusted with the music, ya know. And one said to the other, "To think that Elvis died for this!"

A stiff and starched member of The Waterman's Art Centre management desperately sought out Palmer in the dwindling crowd. Gerald nodded pleasantly as the fatigued woman paid the necessary £100 fee and smiled politely toward his band as if to say, "Worth every penny, huh?" The manager responded by offering two more £50 notes if they stopped.

They didn't. Rather, after pausing for a final interruption from the intercom, whose petulant whine draws the bulk of the waiting crowd into the theatre, The Spacemen mantra continues. After a full 45 minutes, Sonic contents himself with the sound-solution dribbling before them, and gingerly signals the band, as they close diminuendo to a faint hum of electric current. There are a few claps of recognition, though mostly from acquaintances, who like the dyspeptic gawkers, look on with equal relief.

> PAT FISH: This lad who was in charge of the bar came up. He had this immaculately pressed blue and white striped shirt and tie. He was a real dandy. Comes up to Sonic and goes, "Um, I'm afraid our patrons don't particularly appreciate your particular form of minimalism." It was just the way he put it. He was obviously a bit scared. It was a scary thing what they had just done. It was a really scary thing. People did not do that in London. Least of all in a crowd of people just milling about trying to go to the theatre. So we went

4

back to the dressing room, which had no windows at all, it was like a cupboard. And we went in there and you can imagine what those buggers were like, I mean they were chain-smoking dope all the time. And we just stayed there until round about the time we would have finished the second set. Then we went back to Rugby. And yeah that's all I got to do all day, and maybe look big and threatening enough to scare off the blokes who wanted to punch Sonic. It was really weird. People were really taking offence at it. And at the time it was quite a stressful experience to be there although the music was very beautiful. It was odd when the record came out and people were going, "Oh the serenity." Had you been there you wouldn't have felt that way about it specifically . . . it was a bit more like, "Pack up the kit and we'll get out of here alive lads!"

Christened DREAMWEAPON, this 1988 performance by Spacemen 3, although clocking in at less than an hour, stands as both a dividing point and consummation of a lineage of anarcho-musico "non"-events contained within a bloodline that binds all movements in the underground back to the close of the previous century and inextricably links the sounds of the musical vanguard with the words of its poetic *provocateurs*. In fact, if Debussy was, at his most seminal, the sonic exposition of Mallarmé's literary scores, then one century later Spacemen 3 developed a progressive experiment into analogue alchemy that not only references this past, but also illustrates with sound the increasingly fictitious/astral social-fabric explored in the white-hot ovens of Burroughs' *Nova Trilogy*, the thermodynamic ambience of Pynchon's 'Entropy', DeLillo's *White Noise*, Philip K. Dick's *Ubik*, or J.G. Ballard's *Crash*. The infatuation with DREAMS, magnified so vividly by the 19th-century Symbolists, had by the end of the late 20th century become a scientific fetish devoted to the mechanised worlds of inner- and outer-space. The two greatest obsessions of the second half of the 20th century had become WEAPONS and DREAMS, marked by two lasting *memorabilia* courtesy of Spacemen 3's terrestrial home of Rugby: the jet engine and the hologram.

The first DREAMWEAPON was launched some 20 years previously, when Lou Reed, John Cale, Sterling Morrison, and Angus MacLise first performed at Jonas Mekas' Film-Maker's Cinemateque amid a saturation of slide-projections, short films, and spoken poetry. Reed would feed the signals of his Gretsch guitar through a similar maze of fuzz boxes and speed/tremolo controls, producing 16 notes for every note he played (literally, a sheet of sound) while Cale would seduce the screeching feedback from his viola against the mesh of his Vox amplifier. Weaponry had become the spectacle. A new "underground" lifestyle began with the emergence of a popular/classical crossover. The Velvets became the reference point for all post-Sixties mixed-media experimentation and rock'n'roll cool, their influence reaching as far as the backwaters of Rugby and The Spacemen.

HIROSHIMA

In his essay *On the History of Radiation . . .* Gerburg Treusch-Dieter posits that the conception of matter irreparably changes in the 20th century following the development and use of radioactive material, namely with the detonation of the first atom bomb over Hiroshima and the Chernobyl meltdown. According to Treusch-Dieter, matter begins to dematerialise and radiate through transparent means. Its origins and destinations become identical, as matter begins to seek it's own catastrophe through reversal: 'it brings forth nothing, let's everything decay.' Matter has first encountered the DREAMWEAPON.

ARTAUD

Shortly after the conclusion of the war, Antonin Artaud – poet, philosopher, and schizophrenic – prepares his ultimate diatribe against Western culture in *To Have Done With The Judgement of God*. This last major project involves a dramaturgical rant on French radio that is eventually refused transmission. Shortly thereafter, Artaud succumbs to a silent bout of rectal cancer. Strange as it seems, some contend that Artaud's radiophony might have contributed to the development of his cancer, equating the decomposition with the radioactivity of amplified sound. And amplified sound is thereby associated in its catastrophic effects with those still-living victims of Hiroshima who were silently decomposing in the aftermath. The DREAMWEAPON takes its first casualties.

Artaud was the first post-war oracle, con-man, madcap, and alchemist of nuclear style – defined by Deleuze as the "pure auditory": "To find oneself again in a state of extreme shock, clarified by unreality, with, in a corner of oneself, some fragments of the real world." Though his genealogy might be traced back through his forebears – the Gothicism of Poe, the derangement of Rimbaud, the obsessive transvaluations of Nietzsche, the war-torn tragedy of Apollinaire, the eccentricities of Roussel, the picaresque Genet, the ballistic *futurism* of Marinetti and Russolo's *intonarumori* – Artaud was the first post-nuclear, plastic-fantastic psychotic to solicit an absolute submersion into *style*. Artaud became a referential indulgence in the repetition of "thatness", "throwness", ad-space for Heideggerian existentialism. Artaud Le Momo ("the fool") nuked madness into pop brut: identity as performance. Wired to an electric console, the depressed cleft of his skull became a tremolo-machine, his mouth a sampling machine, the rigid tremor of his limbs producing a riff-machine. His incarceration at Rodez secured his status as rock's first burnout and his maddened death from rectal cancer proved the gap between schizophrenia and radiation to be ever closing. As Allen Weiss points out in his exploration of Artaud, ". . . the implications of feedback reach beyond the strictly musical, as in the notion of a self-feeding system seeking its own catastrophe, its own sonic destruction – noise may be coaxed or pressured toward music or silence." Just as Artaud's body had been irradiated and mutated into a cancerous landscape, his mind had endured the same radiation and mutated into a landscape of schizophrenia.

A deep, denuded landscape settled on the grooves of muscle and bone . . .

> ARTAUD: The body under the skin is an overheated factory,
> and, outside,
> the patient glistens,
> he shines,
> from all his pores,
> burst open.
> Like a landscape
> by van Gogh
> at noon.

ROCK'N'ROLL

From the gorging bowls of post-War culture, the first sign of the DREAMWEAPON emerges: Bo Diddley's quaking tremolo on his eponymous debut and the shimmering sounds of The Ventures' surf-adelica; The Yardbirds' fuzzy sitar-guitar on 'Heart Full Of Soul' or Keith Richards' rhythm on 'Satisfaction' crackling from a VOX AC30 amplifier. It was the cacophonous rumble of ammunition, effectively radioactive in its ability to cause involuntary gyrations in the muscles and mutant deviancy in the afflicted. Its energy resided in its crunching repetition, its apparently simplistic serialism melded with the melodic permutation of freewheeling blues-licks. And in its volume.

KEITH RICHARDS: Rock'n'roll hit England like Hiroshima!

. . . The sound of the shell, its impact on the solid earth, was recorded and spliced by the earliest pop-modules, zapped onto a recently developed magnetic tape (ANALOGUE) that would irradiate the planet. A new weapon detonated upon the corporeal battlefield: a ripple of the six-string, frazzled pops of a machine-gun – the wailings of falsetto, the primal scream of a recently debauched amputee – the piercing thud of a drum-stick on a tight snare the death-rattle of the Luftwaffe igniting Manchester – the sounds of dismemberment forged from blood and current. Voices generated into desire. Sound generated into radiating waves. The combination of radiation and pop, from its composite pulses generates an envelope of schizophrenia: the concept of rock'n'roll.

LAMONTE & THE VELVETS

LAMONTE YOUNG: In order to have a concept of the measurement of time it is necessary to have a concept of periodicity. If we assume that the measurement of time is dependent on periodicity, then we might also assume that in determining the relationship between two or more frequencies the human mechanism can best analyze information of a periodic nature which, in the case of information transmitted by the auditory neurological network, would include only those sets of intervallic relationships satisfying the condition that every pair of frequency components can be represented by some rational fraction, inasmuch as only combinations of these harmonically related frequencies generate periodic composite waveforms.

At nearly the same moment, LaMonte Young, in collaboration with Marian Zazeela (vocal drone), Angus MacLise (hand drums), Tony Conrad (amplified violin), and John Cale (amplified viola) transforms this sound into a science. He rejects 12-tone equal temperament and redirects his energies to just intonation, amplification, and Richard Maxfield's sine waves. With his investigations into perfectly tuned pitch in *Trio for Strings* and *The Well-Tuned Piano* and his use of sine wave generators and amplification in *Drift Studies,* Young treated sound as an atomised diagram of vibrations, frequencies, and periodicity. Just as importantly, Young developed a style of Apollonian blues, rooted as much in the avant-garde soundscapes of Cage, Stockhausen, and Schaeffer as in the repetitive chords and primal wailings of W. C. Handy, Robert Johnson, and John Lee Hooker. Masked though it was in the cerebral homeostatis of "ambience".

LAMONTE YOUNG: Current psychoacoustical research and the assumptions of place theory and volley theory suggest that when a specific set of harmonically related frequencies is continuous or repeated, as is often the case in my music, it could more definitively produce (or simulate) a psychological state since the set of harmonically related frequencies will continuously trigger a specific set of the auditory neurons which, in turn, will continuously perform the same operation of transmitting a periodic pattern of impulses to the corresponding set of fixed locations of the cerebral cortex.

The uranium released over Hiroshima is discovered in the composite waveforms of sound: a luminescent flash of vibrations, the implosion of the senses, the enveloping wash of static-laden wind, the mutant aftermath. Sound becomes radiophony. Radiophony becomes a weapon.

JOHN CALE: When we formed The Dream Syndicate I needed to have a strong sound. I decided to try using guitar strings on my viola, and I got a drone that sounded like a jet engine!

Cale fused a pop-minimalism aesthetic while spending late nights listening to country and rock 45s at Tony Conrad's apartment on 56 Ludlow Street, NYC. What remains is avant-rock legend: Cale stumbles upon a struggling songwriter called Lou Reed and they conceive a unique sound combining the ear-splitting sound of electric viola and organ drones with sugary-sweet melody and black-leather lyricism. By February of '66, they simulate their own "lightning-war" at the Film-Maker's Cinematheque as a part of Andy Warhol's *Uptight* showcase, astounding the few punters fortunate enough to be present, and thereby conflating any differences that remained between radiation and pop.

ELECTRIC WARRIORS

The lineage continues as the DREAMWEAPON permeates popular-culture and infects those poets who increasingly become yet another component in a large electromagnetic circuit. Marc Bolan categorises the plight of these damned electro-troubadours engaged in a lighting-war of sonic-weaponry, by ascribing them the rank of ELECTRIC WARRIOR. With all of the necessary gear at their disposal, these pop mercenaries endure nightly gigs of tortuous sonic-blitz and radioactive *hummm* with high casualties.

GILLES DELEUZE (lampooning the psychoanalyst): Leave your desiring-machines at the door, give up your orphan and celibate machines, your tape recorders and your little bike, enter and allow yourself to be oedipalised.

Syd Barrett missed a scheduled Pink Floyd recording for BBC's *Saturday Club* on July 28, 1967, and reappeared the following week, evincing a body-without-organs, and projecting the ever-so alienating Stare. The Binson echo-unit he so obsessed over had finally frazzled every outlet, every connective flow, leaving a tallowed recording surface iridescent as it was with the chalky cum-grey of Brylcreem.

Alexander Spence rode high on the wave of Moby Grape's success until a concoction of hallucinogenics and arcing guitar licks lead him into the arms of an Electric Witch. She was known only as Joanna – seductress, femme fatale, post-feminist – an incomparable succubus among rock groupies (Yoko was simply cartoonish in comparison). As Queen Mab she lured Skippie into a gothic abode of black-magic and alchemy. From the spirited hijinks of 'Omaha', Skip quickly slipped into a Dionysian trance and left us with the screams of his eponymous dirge 'Skip's Song': a weekend excursion into New York upon a dimethyltriptamine-christened flotilla.

The United States of America was an unacknowledged electro/psych collective bubbling up from UCLA in late 1967. Oddly named and envisioned by experimental 'drop-out' Joseph Byrd, USA managed to compose and record traces of as-yet unheard drones and burbles in their self-titled magnum opus, *The United States of America*, before disseminating in a radioactive wind. Hieroglyphs of their abductions are preserved on the vinyl: the screams of singer Dorothy Moskowitz fading into a Durrett Ring Modulator in 'The Garden Of Earthly Delights' or Byrd's mantra "I think it's over now, I think it's ending . . ." over humming keyboards on 'Coming Down'.

Poor Roky Erickson wailed like a coyote from inside the bowels of his Texas cell, his body an electric slide-machine. The doctors seemed hopelessly confounded; they never listened to *Easter Everywhere*, weren't aware that Tommy Hall's electric jug is a lysergic-trick nestled deep within Roky's throbbing gristle. Iggy Pop engaged in an identical THROB upon the slag-heaped stages of Detroit until the self-same rhythmic monotony of Scott Asheton's bass-vibrations caused him to slit the better part of his viscera to expose the machine within. But wait . . . Dig Iggy's stained corpse and radiant eyes transfixed toward SPACE wherein Sun Ra founded a new colony of music and Simeon (the machine and the man are one) noshed from *Silver Apples Of The Moon*.

SIMEON: After a concert in New York we had a gasping and

10

tearful fan rush up to the stage and tell us that 'Dust' had made her levitate! When you put two low notes together that are not quite in tune with each other they set up a natural pulse. Our bodies are composed of many rhythms, different in each of us, and when these low pulsating drones have the time to start influencing our naturally occurring rhythms, strange and sometimes beautiful and sometimes frightening things happen. There's no question about it. I have had people tell me they had everything from bowel urges to orgasms from my drones. But that girl who levitated beats all.

Of the many conceptual highlights occurring within this late psychedelic period, one stands out: a late night in '67 when less than a hundred punters, unfazed by the light-weight psych-kitsch of Lennon/McCartney, stumbled over to the Grande Ballroom in Detroit to witness Sun Ra and his Arkestra jam with the MC5 to the wash of the Magic Veil lightshow. Similarly, Jimi Hendrix had jammed with John McLaughlin and planned collaborations with Gil Evans and Roland Kirk before his untimely overdose in 1969. Predating his foray into *Bitches Brew*, Miles Davis had immersed himself in Sly Stone, studied the theories of Stockhausen and snorted coke backstage with Iggy Pop. Behold the free-jazz/minimalism crossover: Eric Dolphy's Fluxus performances, LaMonte Young's predilection for Don Cherry and Ornette Coleman, the acid-visions of Albert Ayler and Pharoah Sanders. By '71 Stockhausen converted to this experimental-pop dogma (and the jazz/rock/electronic transubstantiation) upon witnessing a sacramental performance by Sun Ra.

The electro seduction ebbed accordingly, from the transparent lunar forces to the green worlds below: Eno's gallery of sound-sculpture to the quaking man-machines of Germany and Can's death-disco to the Lower East-Side vomitariums click-clacking to Martin Rev's patented synth-schlock. Only Alan Vega staved off the imposing threat of intergalactic abduction with his rootsy homage to Elvis and Roy Orbison. The Ancienne Belgique, June 1978: as Suicide, Rev and Vega hot-wired a rioting mob of Belgians literally to dismantle the stage and all of the noisemakers. Surreptitious bootleggers transcribe and document the bloodshed as *23 Minutes Over Brussels*:

ALAN VEGA: Things started getting really crazy and somebody called the cops or something. And the next thing I know they're flying in there with riot gear and tear gas and shit . . . And I'm standing there right offstage laughing my ass off watching this whole thing. It's like a war-zone: people running and falling over each other, gas all over the place, equipment getting fucked up, everything.

11

The roots were sewn for the Electric Warrior to proceed back to the soil and underground: the first casualty, the Apollonian dreamer Jonathan Richman who is cemented behind the studio wall. Alex Chilton's last séance in Memphis divined the possessed souls of Stax channelled through the syrupy tongue of a Liverpudlian in *Third/Sister Lovers*. Rocket From The Tombs returned to Cleveland from SPACE without Peter Laughner (sadly lost on re-entry) but from the survivors: the skittering pulses of Alan Ravenstine's synth blurbs over David Thomas' vocal warbling and Pere Ubu's two-guitar Beefheart-style aggression recounted the tragedy in *The Modern Dance* and *Dub Housing*. The Gun Club and The Cramps followed the same dusty road to Hell, divining Robert Johnson and Russ Meyer along the way with the funereal buzz of an electric slide-guitar.

CHERNOBYL

Lester Bangs forecast the tragedy at Chernobyl a full decade in advance when, in a trademark amphetamine-laced rap on Kraftwerk (see translation: power-plant) that would eventually find canonisation in *Psychotic Reaction*, he penned his musings on the future of distortion and the human variable.

> LESTER BANGS: In the beginning there was feedback: the machines speaking on their own, answering their supposed masters with shrieks of misalliance.

As if the words of a medieval prophet cum-alchemist had filled Lester's chunky passages during one of his soporific binges, the admonition of rock'n'roll's own Ezekiel – replete with inchoate images of doom – warned of the progression of sound-technology, synthesis, and radioactivity. Lester underlined one important difference inherent in the synth (and by extension, nuclear energy): the concurrent flash-point would occur from the inside, a wired machine built upon the natural phenomenon of radiation but enclosed in a progressively technical system, a structure developed by man that would collapse into a chaotic melt-down of radiophony.

> LESTER BANGS: Gradually the humans learned to control the feedback, or thought they did, and the next step was the introduction of more highly refined forms of distortion and the artificial sound, in the form of the synthesiser, which the human beings sought also to control. . . . we see at last the fitting culmination of

this revolution, as the machines not merely overpower and play the human beings but *absorb* them, until the scientist and his technology, having developed a higher consciousness of its own, are one and the same.

A decade after Bangs' commandments, the second major radioactive event occurred: the Chernobyl meltdown. Not since the obliterations at Hiroshima/Nagasaki had nuclear technology proven its potential for eradication on such a grand scale. The crucial difference separating the two events being the alternative stratagem instituted by the DREAMWEAPON at a point in which it demanded its own freedom. In fact, the meltdown had come from *inside*, an act of terrorism in that the machine had subverted its superior in order to liberate itself. To liberate itself from the very mechanism that ensured its continuity, as if to simulate its very demise. But illusory in that energy cannot be eradicated, only transformed or transferred. In actuality the DREAMWEAPON had escaped to the ether without recourse to body (cancer) or mind (schizophrenia) and complete self-sufficiency.

The event evinced a decade that Baudrillard claimed was the apogee of history, a distortion of time's sphericity, in which the slope of events began to run in reverse. The curve of music and history runs analogously according to Baudrillard: as the stereophonics of sound-technology erase the aura of musicality, so too does the conduction of instantaneous media expose the simulated effects of any historical event. Effects and technology invade the original compositions of music until what remains is the ecstasy of its reproduction and dissemination. "Songs" rapidly transform into multi-"tracked" pastiche bloated with phase-tones, gates&triggers, delayloops, chorus/flange: quantum permutations along the frequency spectrum: the verticality of timbre and texture made electronic.

> JEAN BAUDRILLARD: . . . that famous feedback effect which is produced in acoustics by a source and a receiver being too close together and in history by an event and its dissemination being too close together and thus interfering disastrously. . . .

Musicality becomes the "perfection of its materiality", and transmits itself through the transparency of an (ether)eal reversal. An infinite series of synth-machines . . . The DREAMWEAPON is a machine-like echolalia, the schizo-desire of deterritorialisation reverberating in the stylised consumption of pedals and knobs. The recording device standing alongside a vibrating organ-device producing the material of homeostatic "this"ness: EXcess. A stage littered with the *bricolage* of Mini-Moogs, VCS3s, Vox, Fenders, *ad nauseam*. And radiophony becomes this matter in reverse gear. Music itself mutates toward the DREAMWEAPON.

Unnerved by this millenarian realisation, rock'n'roll recedes into the underground. It holds up in bunkers, fleeing from the radioactive tide it has unknowingly released upon the world. It begins hoarding every available relic, any piece of obsolescent machinery, every scrap of history in the vain hope of retaining a vague conception of identity. In order to thwart the end (or the illusion of the end), rock'n'roll enters a blanketed period of nostalgia and revisionism. It fuses the fragmented pieces of the past onto its own material body with aid from the *pharmacon:* medicinal machines, syringes, sensory devices. Fallout from above causes the body of rock'n'roll to descend into the underworld, to become an underground.

It is at this moment that a new cadre of Electric Warriors begin exploring this energy and the DREAMWEAPON once again: The Jesus And Mary Chain, Spacemen 3, The Rain Parade, Opal, My Bloody Valentine, A. R. Kane, Sonic Youth. Historical events and rock'n'roll conflate to identical origins: the collapse of the Berlin Wall might have been transmitted by the rumbling quake of Spacemen 3's 'Revolution' or MBV's 'You Made Me Realise'. Or concomitantly, the fall of the Soviet Union at the beginning of the Nineties may have occurred from the consummation of this laborious alchemy of sound, namely the opening roar of The Valentines' *Loveless*. It wouldn't be too far-fetched to imagine a handful of German indie-kids from both sides of the wall aiming unwieldy stereo-speakers toward the graffiti-inked edifice and blasting 'Revolution' at slight delay causing a natural phase and the first faint trembles of collapse. Or for that matter, the surreptitious stream of military vehicles suddenly bursting onto the Kremlin grounds with the seismic quake of MBV's 'Only Shallow' fuming from a PA jerry-rigged atop a Soviet-built tank. What irony, you say? Upon hearing The Velvet's *Loaded*, Lester Bangs had predicted just such a reaction. He'd found the pulse, only prematurely. But his prognostication had at last found its resolution.

DEFINING THE DREAMWEAPON

The DREAMWEAPON was at work everywhere, functioning smoothly at times, at other times in feedback and tremolo. It breathes, it heats, it eats. It shits and fucks. Everywhere *it* is machines, with all of the necessary couplings and connections. A drone-machine is plugged into an energy-source-machine: the one produces a flow that the other interrupts.

Hence we are all drones: each with his little machines. For every drone-machine, an energy-machine: all the time, flows, and interruptions. Syd Barrett has a Binson echo-unit in his ass. A sonar anus. And rest assured that it works: Syd Barrett feels something, produces something, and is capable of explaining the process theoretically. Something is produced: the effects of a machine, not mere melody . . .

The DREAMWEAPON is firstly an excess. It is a simultaneous surface – slick and spermatozoid (a harmonic block of oscillating space) – that exudes beyond its coordinated boundary. It is "chrono-geneous" – momentary – a melodious decomposition of history. A history of movements and migrations, the spilling of time over territories, and the recordings, inscriptions of these open spaces into localised systems of recognition.

The DREAMWEAPON occurs alongside . . . it is the amplified constriction of a mechanical propulsion. Which is to say that it is generative as well as limiting, a radiophonic tide. It is the deterritorialising flow reverberating from inside . . . in consumption, digestion, excretion. "The retained elements do not enter into the new use of SYNTHESIS that imposes such a profound change on them without causing the whole triangle to REVERBERATE," quoth Deleuze. The dreaded Oedipal triangle: guitar/bass/drums, but underneath it lies the salvation of fuzz. Robert Moog's entire family sleeps on the soft bedding of stereo mesh. The patching of a tone from an analogue synth. It begins with the oscillators, which produce waves fed into a labyrinth of tonal modulators. It ends with magnetic tape or digital codices.

The DREAMWEAPON is a luminescence, if such sensual disparities bear the uncanny glint of an alchemist crouched over his mutation, enchanted by golden slumbers, or the evanescent revelations of an acidhead gyrating to a particle accelerator.

The DREAMWEAPON is a psycho-topological Event, the amplification of a multipliticious *hyle*, but with a skin (of the social, physical, acoustic): a temporal modulation with a spatial thickness. It is a non-visual vibration that skims the tactile surface, a series of institutional codices, locating the nodules of an outlet – a connective flow modulating within the interstices of swallowing, shitting, ejaculating organelles. Synaesthesia is not delusion; it is the oscilloscope of the riffing psychotic.

The DREAMWEAPON is neither a direct representation of the fluctuating body nor the indirect representation of the social body, but rather a sonic material that forms an organic continuum. It is the homeostatic tremolo (generative stasis) produced from the oscillations of an infinite series of cavities.

With the conjunctions of inter-subjective spaces, the DREAMWEAPON returns as modulations of the pathway, transversal indication of this, that, and the other: the emigration of glissando, tremolo, phasing. Inclusive identities on tour in space. This is where the "chrono-genous" receives coordination, localising sound as points of departure or termination. Triggers of cosmogony. The DREAMWEAPON transgenerates inscriptions of melody along these points of Deleuzian intensity: the recordings are etched into the warm, gooey swath of wax as feedback of production.

The DREAMWEAPON: to produce *again* but as anew. For droning is like schizophrenia: a process and not a goal, a production and not an expression. Neither the product nor the intention, but rather the *production*. Neither the subjective nor the objective, but the *movement alongside*. It is this vectoral concurrentness which allows for the re-production again, a re-demonstration that mandates the DREAM-WEAPON be not simply a repetition in time – time as a quantised measure of quality – but rather a regenerative innovation that invariably falls back upon the original through a folding-over, a patchwork of intensities. But not from an inherent lack, the basis of any correspondence theory of meaning; rather from the ecstasy that flows between the two, an indeterminate, an unthought, that floods over into the real with saccharine melody and desire. The original (the product) is an inscription, a burning, a cutting, a recording of the production (in fact a reproducing) linked, or rather feeding back along the interstitial patches of a synth-machine.

The DREAMWEAPON will index rather than represent, vocalise rather than speak – to quote Deleuze, it *goes about its own business* – inducing mere appearances alongside a world *in-itself*.

The DREAMWEAPON wants only what it wants.

The DREAMWEAPON is the oscillation of desire . . .

'Space Trash . . . Jason Speaks (Kind Of . . .)'

The DREAMWEAPON is firstly an excess. It is a simultaneous surface — slick and spermatozoid (a harmonic block of oscillating space) — that exudes beyond its coordinated boundary. It is "chrono-geneous" — momentary — a melodious decomposition of history. A history of movements and migrations, the spilling of time over territories, and the recordings, inscriptions of these open spaces into localised systems of recognition.

C. 1991

FROM AN OPEN LETTER TO *OUTER LIMITS* FANZINE

Spiritualized would like it known that we have made no active contribution to Outer Limits issue number 1. Although we are all for an official Spacemen 3 fanzine the contents page alone reflects the overall ethos of the magazine. Although I would never want to deny or diminish my involvement in Spacemen 3, any working partnership or friendship has now ended therefore an objective and comprehensive biography of Spacemen 3 has become difficult — history as I remember living it differs wildly from how Pete sees it and writing the history of the band as it actually was would have resulted in pages of farcical contradictions. Having any involvement in this magazine condones his bullshit and fuels the misconception that Sonic *was* Spacemen 3. Sonic has had many opportunities to speak about Spacemen 3 to the music papers and has used this space to trash my involvement and for his own self glorification so for us to be involved in this mag is kind of crazy.

By contributing to Outer Limits we establish some kind of inextricable link between ourselves and Sonic Boom prolonging an already drawnout and futile association.

Any link was through Spacemen 3, that is over and although comparisons are inevitable I do not want to actively sustain any links with Sonic Boom outside of that. . . .

Spacemen 3 were a great band but it is finished and for myself Spiritualized is the future.

CHAPTER ONE
Big City

In the autumn of 1982, Peter Kember (alias Sonic Boom[*]) and Jason Pierce (alias J. Spaceman[†]) met for the first time at Rugby Art College, an unimposing institution off Lower Hillmorton Road. Within the town's modest music scene, Sonic had actually already befriended Jason's elder brother Simon, a new-wave fanatic, before he knew Jason. As Sonic and Jason began talking between classes, there appeared common threads of curiosity between them: music, drugs, and boredom. Sonic immediately sussed in Jason a shrewd personality that often compensated for lazy underachievement. Observed Sonic, "Jason was very talented. In Art College, we used to skive off the whole time, you know, to mess around, write songs, listen to music, get high. He only turned up to class one day in three; his attendance record was the worst of anyone. But he still managed to turn in two-thirds of the work, and he got the highest grade by, like, two grades above everyone else in the class."

Sonic began dropping by Jason's home to smoke dope and listen to LPs. Jason lived in a modest post-war bungalow with two brothers (one elder, one younger) and his mother: his parents divorced very early on in Jason's childhood, and his father had relocated to the North, leaving Jason's mother to raise their three children alone. The family's lifestyle was restricted as a result. Jason's strictly religious father had been a firm disciplinarian, and while his departure may have affected Jason and his brothers financially, it might have also come as a relief once the children grew into rebellious adolescence. To make ends meet, Jason's mother took on a job at the Citizens' Advice Bureau, where she earned a wage just comfortable enough to support the family.

Jason had a novice record collection, LPs mostly inherited from his older brother Simon, but Sonic was pleased to see Velvets, Clash, and

---

[*] Prior to settling on the pseudonym Sonic Boom around 1986, Kember used the names Peter Gunn and the Mainliner. For the purposes of this book, Kember is referred to as Sonic Boom throughout.
[†] Pierce took up the pseudonym J. Spaceman in the 1990s. For the purposes of this book, he is referred to simply as Jason, which is how most people knew him during his time with Spacemen 3.

Stooges covers littering the floor. While Sonic impressed Jason with his vast knowledge of The Cramps, The Gun Club, and the Velvets, Jason converted Sonic to the minimal thump of 'Search And Destroy' and the maniacal styling of rock'n'roll *enfant terrible* Iggy Pop. In fact, on one of the sparse, vanilla walls of Jason's bedroom was a poster of the spangled and androgynous Osterberg, half-naked and lusting like an animal, circa *Raw Power*. Jason swooned, "Even before I heard the music, I was so into the image [on the *Raw Power* cover] of this guy and the audience."

The pair would snort from a can of lighter fluid to The Cramps' *Songs The Lord Taught Us* and The Gun Club's *Fire Of Love*. As the buzz kicked in, the sounds of dissonant slide-guitar and reverb swelling from 'TV Set' or 'Sex Beat' captured and translated these synaesthetic trips into vibrant psychic visions. Neither said much during such inebriated bouts of stereophonics, but the electricity between Sonic and Jason took on a tele-pathic weight of its own. When Jeffrey Lee Pierce crooned, "She's like heroin to me/ She's like heroin to me/ She's like heroin to me/ She cannot miss a vein!", the two boys stared at each other in wide-eyed fantasy. It was as if the music had been written completely for them, two provincial English kids. As if the secrets behind Pierce's howl or Bryan Gregory's guitar were being transmitted through coded messages directly from New York via Jason's turntable. "That first Gun Club album is absolutely amazing," Jason enthused. "It's an album that I can never remember reading a review of, an absolutely phenomenal record that was missed. You don't get references to it in modern music."

The hidden palimpsests of these psychobilly bands not only provided a dirty, homespun alternative to increasingly over-produced *Top Of The Pops* fare, but they also provided pathways to the past. "The Cramps didn't make out that they were totally unique," Jason continued. "They were telling their audience about Fifties rockabilly, about Hasil Atkins and Ronnie Hawkins and Sixties psychedelia. You know, they were talking about these weird people making odd records – and a lot of my friends were into it."

"We discovered the blues together," Sonic insisted. "Things like Muddy Waters and the early Chicago electric blues, and we were blown away by it. Like, 'What the fuck?!' The same with Howlin' Wolf and Bo Diddley. We just instantly both recognised something about it, just the language within it that appealed to us. To us, it was a language we wanted to speak and converse in."

The bubbling chemistry between them was nearly palpable. When Jason picked up his ratty electric and played with flawless precision, Sonic was gob smacked. Music was the vehicle and weed was the force, but as they spoke more and more of their futures, they were enmeshed in each other's dreams in a way that could be expressed only in the fractured tones of the records that served as soundtrack. They treaded lightly on the subject of a musical conjunction at the beginning, but Jason certainly took to Sonic's minimal conceptions with the same passion in which Sonic recognised Jason's natural flair for his instrument. The confluence of cannabis smoke and young men's dreams would birth a deep and, for the time being, impenetrable partnership. All they wanted was to make music of their own, music for and about drugs, and music to take drugs to. What else was there to do in Rugby anyway?

The small town of Rugby, in the county of Warwickshire, lies approximately 100 miles north of London along the M1 route to Birmingham. The Rugby off-ramp wraps around the motorway and spits out along the A428, a sparse country road leading to Northampton and Althorp in the east and Coventry and Rugby to the west. Along a patch of verdant country slopes sits a gargantuan industrial complex of newly constructed white buildings, a facility for storing any number of hideous bits of factory-developed gizmos, or maybe producing them, or shipping them: it's hard to discern from the exterior.

Immediately outside the town of Rugby lies the small village of Kilsby, a series of quaint and slightly decrepit suburban houses surrounded by a sweep of open fields dotted with towering radio masts. Evidently used during the Cold War by the military to communicate with submarines and artillery units at great distance, Rugby had the misfortune to be high on the list of nuclear targets by the evil Red Empire and was thus a cauldron for CND rallies during the Seventies and Eighties. The A428 turns into Hillmorton Road at the entrance of the town and cuts a diametrical swathe through the centre of Rugby, separating the large hill upon which it rests from the summit and the large three- and four-storey homes to the south and the careening slope and more modest terraced houses to the north. Rugby is orbited by a collection of small villages, including Brownsover with its row after row of downmarket council houses to the immediate north and, to the extreme south, the commodious detached homes of Dunchurch.

The town centre is a thin network of cobblestoned walkways that wind between the series of one-way roads and which, as of late, resemble so many other town centres of 21st-century England with their Woolworth's stores, Sainsbury's supermarkets, Orange mobile-phone outlets and refurbished pubs. The clock tower stands at the Y-shaped intersection of throughways, the setting of town celebrations, street fairs, and jubilees. A hundred yards further stands Saint Andrew's Church, its spire rising nearly 200 feet, the tallest building within the town limit.

Onward and around a hodgepodge of pubs, fish and chips stands, and a newly constructed "mini"-mall sprawls a lush park, pregnant with the floral trappings of well-tended gardens and the rich soil of the Black Country. The pathway slants downward and back to row upon row of terraced homes, levelling out by the train station, which lies at the bottom of the hill nearer the working-class section of town. Rail track and electrical lines thrust outwards, towards Coventry in one direction and Northampton in the other, abandoned industrial units and coiled bric-a-brac littering the landscape in either direction.

From those terrestrial forces that would zap or plunge Jason Pierce and Sonic Boom onto simultaneous wavelengths, the "magick" began immediately on 19 November 1965. Although they did not befriend each other as children, the two boys were born on the same day and grew up in similar circumstances only a short distance apart. Sonic also had two siblings (a brother and a sister), and through his adolescent years lived in a modest council house near Coventry Airport. Much of his extended family on both sides made Coventry their home, working in the bustling auto factories throughout the Forties, Fifties and Sixties, earning a handsome living thanks to the strength of the car industry unions. Sonic's mother and father had both attended area art colleges in their youth and, following the birth of their first son (who, like Jason Pierce's older brother, was also christened Simon), applied for jobs in the work force to support their growing family. Sonic's father, Tony Kember, entered the textile industry, working at a middle-management position and earning a modest sum in the beginning. When Sonic appeared on the scene, two years after Simon, the family had a secure if austere life.

Sonic spent a large portion of his childhood wrapped around the family hi-fi, listening to his parents' collection of Sixties pop and early Brit-psychedelia. Although his mother and father were not musicians, they cultivated an early love for rock'n'roll in their children, and Sonic recalls whiling away his childhood to the sounds of Buddy Holly, The Everly Brothers, The Beach Boys and The Beatles. Sonic's father would often record *Top Of The Pops* on a reel-to-reel tape-recorder, and Sonic listened to the playbacks over and over again. An acoustic guitar had been passed down to the family by an uncle and, ratty and poorly strung as it was, Sonic and Simon would often pick it up and try to belt out something they'd heard on the television. Jason also picked up his first acoustic guitar when he was seven, but, unlike Sonic, he took to it with the affinity of a prodigy. He later had guitar lessons to hone his skills, but even at an early age he showed signs of mastering the instrument.

Sonic's father prospered in textiles and branched out as an entrepreneur, purchasing a wool mill in Bradford and turning a tidy profit. Thus, after spending much of his childhood in council and manor houses throughout the Midlands, Sonic and his family relocated from the serial modesty of Coventry to the upper-class village of Dunchurch. Famed for its proximity to Ashby St. Ledger's, where the 1604 Gunpowder Plot was reputedly formulated by Guy Fawkes, Dunchurch was a small enclave of mansions and estates reverberating with the history of insurrection. The Kembers moved into a grand home south of Rugby, where Sonic attended a nearby prep school called Bilton Grange – boarding away from home in his final year – before moving on to Rugby, the noted Public School, in the autumn of 1979.

Living away from home offered Sonic his first taste of independence, and he accepted this new freedom with open arms. By the time he entered Rugby's Tudor House dormitory, he'd discovered the surfeit of pleasures that awaited a privileged teenager in the shadow of punk. "I had a good time there, you know," Sonic said. "It was fairly surprising how much freedom you got. There's a lot of access to the town, so there was a lot of room for disappearing and going down to the pub for a couple of hours."

Pete Bain (alias: Bassman[*]) was also born in Rugby, spending his early childhood in a neighbouring village but soon moving back into a middle-class home in the town. His father travelled frequently on business, leaving Bain and his mother alone together for prolonged periods of time. His parents divorced when Pete was 10 and he continued living with his mother, who became increasingly volatile in the absence of her husband, indulging herself with sports cars and spending most evenings away from home. Despite the turbulence surrounding his family life, Bain enjoyed the innocent moments of childhood, plunging into pop-culture and music. He had an old Dansette record player on which he constantly shuffled 45s of The Beatles and The Beach Boys. He loved watching television, and found he was partial to *The Banana Splits, Joe 90* and *Batman*. Every week he made a point to watch *Top Of The Pops*, where he first encountered the Seventies' glam phenomenon and became a David Bowie convert.

Willie B. Carruthers faced a similarly tempestuous family life when he moved from his home in Leicestershire to Rugby at the age of 12. His parents were also divorced, and the division took a heavy toll on Will's youth. His ambition didn't arc much beyond weathering necessary education at Lawrence Sheriff Grammar, where he was in the same year as

[*] Bain took up his pseudonym around the same time as Pete Kember became Sonic Boom, in 1986. For the purposes of this book, he is referred to as Bassman throughout.

Jason's younger brother Adam; Carruthers left school after his 'O'-levels and joined the working masses.

The Silver Jubilee in 1977 was a national event unlike anything Britain had experienced since Queen Elizabeth's coronation, a celebration of pride in the monarchy and in traditional values. On the surface, the whole country basked in a glow of patriotism, with parades, banners and ceremonial speeches, and Rugby was no exception. The town centre was festooned with multicoloured ribbons and royal posters, and its shops offered every possible trinket, button and toy.

On the other side of the tracks, however, there were kids growing up in Rugby – and elsewhere – who couldn't give two shits about pledging loyalty to Queen and country. While the Silver Jubilee entranced the mainstream, punk rock cut a simultaneous swathe through the country, hitting like-minded teenagers right between the eyes with its minimalism and outrage. Rugby's kids loved it too. The Sex Pistols album *Never Mind The Bollocks* articulated succinctly what it was to come of age in the late Seventies, and John Lydon's sneering howl over simple Chuck Berry-style riffs converted thousands upon thousands of young men from across the provincial waste of Britain to pick up an electric guitar and wail away.

Sonic and Jason were only 11 when punk invaded Britain, but they were both swept away with the tide. Sonic's older brother Simon played one punk album after another on the family turntable, introducing Sonic to the glut of bands that formed in The Pistols' wake. In between, Sonic would play Sixties records, The Kinks, The Troggs and the Stones, and he soon realised that these eras of music, though separated by a decade, shared a common simplicity. Bassman took an old valve radio to his bed one night and tuned into John Peel's show, the vanguard for late-night rock'n'roll experimentation, and heard the witty DJ drone on about his recent encounter with mud and beer cans at an outdoor rock festival. Peelie concluded his rant by opining, "Well, everybody's got their problems," and then cueing up the Pistols' 'Problems'. Bassman was mesmerised and took to the radio show with religious dedication.

Rugby's lone outlet for would-be teen punks was an ex-serviceman's club in nearby Hillmorton called Kiddie's Corner. On Monday evenings, the ramshackle hall, normally filled with dipsomaniacal working-stiffs, was transformed into an all-ages discotheque, attracting bored teenagers from all around Rugby. The DJ stood on a decrepit dais, spinning classic Seventies hits and disco numbers to hundreds of kids, a conglomerate of spiky-haired punks, gelled teddy-boy types, and every other sub-species of pubescent hooligan. The young punks would bring their own records along and badger the DJ to play them between his regular rotation of

AOR and dance-tracks, which he'd often accommodate, bathing the hall in the sounds of The Sex Pistols, The Clash, and The Buzzcocks. Bassman frequented Kiddie's Corner, as did several other punks including future bandmates Gavin Wissen and Tim Morris. They often saw each other across the room but hardly spoke, their tough punk affectations belying their soft-spoken, shy adolescence. When Morris finally crossed the dance-floor to invite Bassman and Wissen to a jam at his home, both boys agreed with a squeaky enthusiasm.

Simon Kember jumped into various local punk-bands and Sonic often tagged along to rehearsals, watching them stumble through their Blondie-meets-The Pistols repertoire. He picked up some simple chord positions, and one of the guitarists taught him a few rudimentary riffs and licks. He purchased his first electric guitar the next year, a cheap Les Paul knockoff, and learned a few Kinks and Sex Pistols songs, including the catchy riff to 'Submission'. He tried working out a few basic compositions on his own, and found he enjoyed the weird textures fizzing from his puny practise amp. Contented with his rudimentary playing skills, he fashioned simple one-chord pieces and droned away. After lengthy exercises in E, he decided the sounds had a strange similarity to the industrial din of nearby factories, or the hum of prop-planes that flew frequently over Rugby en route to the nearby air base in Coventry.

Rugby School, the stalwart institution of the town and focal point of outside interest, was founded by a successful local businessman, Lawrence Sheriff, in the 16th century as a free grammar school for local children. In 1750 the school moved from Rugby centre to its present location in the southwest of the town; its intended socio-economic diversity waned as the school diverged from the town that surrounded it and from which it took its name. (It was a full century later before the present Lawrence Sheriff Grammar School was founded on Clifton Road.) Rugby School quickly became a monument of bourgeois prestige, and symbolic of the English "public" (i.e. private) school system. This was due, in large part, to the reforms instituted in the 1830s by Dr Thomas Arnold, famed head-master and self-appointed executive of moral correction. As described by Lytton Stachey in his *Eminent Victorians*, Arnold's purpose in rejecting his predecessor Dr John Keate's method of anarchy/despotism, prevalent throughout all public-education at the time, was to instil a rigid moral code based on self-correction and hierarchy. The Headmaster insisted, "When the spring and activity of youth is altogether unsanctified by anything pure and elevated in its desires, it becomes a spectacle that is as dizzying and almost more morally distressing than the shouts and gambols of a set of lunatics."

As public schools turned more openly to this emphasis on "gentlemanly" conduct and social mores, Rugby School took on its current reputation as an upper-class institution for young men born of wealth and privilege on the road to careers as politicians, diplomats, aristocrats, plutocrats, and, indeed, even as upper-crust criminals.

Like all public schools Rugby espoused the "house" system whereby groups of boys were allocated to certain 'houses' for domestic and sporting purposes. Tudor House was an expansive dormitory located immediately adjacent to the school grounds and, during Sonic's first term, the four-storey building housed about sixty-five boys, most of whom, to his recollection, were all musicians-in-training with expanding record collections. Sonic hung out with an older sixth-former called Frank Douie, a strange Rhodesian character, who often let Sonic borrow his old six-string acoustic, on which he would rattle away between classes. Another student, Chris Heath, who was infamous among the Tudor boys for his nearly encyclopaedic collection of records and tapes, would lend Sonic albums he had strewn across the dormitory.*

Tudor House ascribed to more progressive policies than most other dormitories at the school, although the House Master, John Smith, had a reputation for sporadic cruelty. Most of the Tudor boys referred to him as Pisso. Smith lived in a small cottage adjacent to the Tudor building and only visited the dormitories and studies on Sunday mornings for formal inspection. As per Dr. Arnold's legacy, all of the dormitories at Rugby were run from "in-House", with executive duties levied on a group of sixth-form students called "The Six", chosen by the Housemaster, and regal oversight by "The Levee" and Head of House, chosen by the Headmaster of Rugby School. "Anything in-House would be kept in-House," recalled Sonic. "So you'd have to be caught a lot and be a real pain before they passed anything on to the Housemaster." Accordingly, pupils at Tudor House would spend most of their evenings pissed out of their heads or stoned while The Housemaster would turn a blind eye. That is, as long as the studies were properly cleaned before inspection.

Anomalous features of the House included a downstairs smoking-room (even though smoking was forbidden on school grounds) and a rehearsal room in the cellar, where bourgeoning rock bands would meet to practise. Sonic spent much of his first term watching other bands rehearse, and inspecting the equipment they stored in the cellar. "There are some very aware people there – some were turning out acid on sugarcubes in the science labs in the Sixties," commented Sonic in a 1988

---

* Chris Heath would go on to an extensive career as a music journalist.

Melody Maker interview. "Each house up there gets a music paper, you know, they read the music press, not *Tom Brown's Schooldays*, while they're warming the loo seat for the fagmaster . . ." The variety of instruments enlarged his perception of making music, and he'd often steal down to fiddle with the different electronics, including a Korg MS20, his first experience playing a synthesiser.

During this first term at Tudor House, Sonic enlisted as a fag for members of The Six, a voluntary but common practice for younger pupils to work under the tutelage of the older students. The fag would tend to the older boy's daily needs, taking responsibility for the shittiest tasks: cleaning up, making breakfast, getting coffee, substituting at roll-call, keeping the study tidy, procuring spirits on the weekend in his stead. Sonic was happy to fall into the subordinate position, as with the ritualised minutiae of fagging came the benefits of acquiring friends in higher places. The fagmasters to which Sonic was indentured, two students called Jerry Clegg and Horace Hadrill, treated him well and covered for him on his occasional runs to the pub.

It was also during this first term that his older brother Simon, also attending Rugby School, introduced Sonic to Suicide's debut album. Sonic was fascinated by Martin Rev's glitchy drum-machines and skint bleeps swirling behind Alan Vega's rockabilly drawl. Sonic 'borrowed' the album from his brother, and played it constantly. It would remain a massive influence on his musical fantasies.

Until 1978, reissued editions of classic, obscure rock recordings were not widely available in the UK. Compared to today's massive sweep of compact disc re-releases, Internet databases with a plethora of MP3 material, and the fetishist compilations of entire back-catalogues, the contents of much Sixties and Seventies psychedelia, exotica, and electronica were not only rare but also practically unknown. It was only through the celebrated dedication of record fanatics like Lenny Kaye and Greg Shaw in America, and Geoff Travis and Andrew Lauder in Britain, that stores and record labels intent on harvesting the past were able to blossom. By the late Seventies British labels Rough Trade, Stiff and Radar were reissuing material from bands like The Electric Prunes, The 13th Floor Elevators, and The Red Krayola to young record-collectors looking far beyond 1977. These same labels were releasing new artists almost as fast as they could find them, and the earliest moments of post-punk provided small victories for the bourgeoning indie-spheres of England. Responding to the rampant incongruities between the growing post-punk biospheres and the stifling parochialism of the established music industry, Cherry Red-guru Iain McNay, in collaboration with

Record Business magazine, founded an independent chart in order to reflect accurately the popularity of the hottest releases from these "minor" labels (Mute, Factory, Postcard, Small Wonder, etc.), thereby outlining the future of post-punk and simultaneously dichotomising the worlds of indie- and mainstream-rock.

The first resurgence of psychedelia, an embrace of both the idealism and musical verve of the late Sixties, manifested itself throughout Britain at the dawn of the Eighties. Liverpool spawned Echo & The Bunnymen and Teardrop Explodes, London birthed The Psychedelic Furs and The Sound, and both Robyn Hitchcock's The Soft Boys and Paul Weller's former mod revivalists The Jam matured and locked on to a heady late Sixties groove. Yet for a period at the beginning of the Eighties the guitar, the most sacrosanct of pop icons, looked to become a relic in favour of portable, easily controllable, keyboard synthesisers. In his cultural critique, *Industrial Evolution,* Mick Fish commented, "In London the whole post-Bowie world was about the flouncey trouncey world of The Blitz Club and the nascent Culture Clubbers, while in Birmingham it was centred around the hedonistic narcissism of Duran Duran . . . In London it was all too easy to become lost in the incestuous music business world. With A&R men flapping around, a band like Spandau Ballet could easily lose sight of its objectives before it had even started. After the 'anybody can do it' mentality of punk, a form of cultural elitism was creeping in. A whole new brash bunch of image conscious youngsters had bounded upon the scene. They didn't want revolution or rock'n'roll. They just wanted to party." However, the battle lines were not always easy to recognise. Synth-pop upstarts Depeche Mode were seen by many "indie kids" as indicative of all that was worst of the "Blitz Kid" culture, and yet they signed to that most ardent of independent labels, Mute Records, on a mere handshake. The success of Depeche Mode's early pop hits ironically helped provide the financial foundation for the entire independent distribution system.

Still, with such synthesised frivolity dominating the mainstream, the psychedelic punks were forced to operate from underground. Glaswegian transplant and rock'n'roll *bon vivant* Alan McGee endeavoured to fuse a psychedelia/punk hybrid philosophy based on one-part The Creation and one-part The Buzzcocks. As had so many other Britons turned on to the maniacal sludgery of The Sex Pistols circa '77, McGee had played in his own punk-band (The Laughing Apple), but soon realised his musical talent could not match his ambition. Nevertheless, inspired as he was by the entrepreneurial flair of Iain McNay (Cherry Red), Geoff Travis (Rough Trade), Tony Wilson (Factory), and Dan Treacy (Whaam! label and The Television Personalities), McGee built upon a small network of the like-minded through fanzines (*Communication Blur*) and indie-clubs (Communication Club, later The Living Room). Meanwhile, The Jam's single 'Start' and the reissue-label Edsel's release of The Creation's *How Does It Feel To Feel* prompted McGee to investigate the rich history of Sixties psychedelia, which he concomitantly took to heart. Channel 4 had inadvertently helped champion this small indie-revolution by re-running old episodes of *The Avengers* and *The Prisoner* in the latter months of 1982. It appeared that even regressive TV producers were co-opting the pop-art images scattered on Treacy's record sleeves and McGee's fanzine articles.

A small coterie of psych-fetishists frequented McGee's Saturday evening 'happening' in the upstairs room of a pub on Conway Street, a scene which centred around Dan Treacy and Ed Ball, Jerry Thackray, Dick Green, and any number of forgettable groups dedicated to jangle-punk, pop-art, and the guitar. From this forge would be melded Creation Records and the clearest declaration yet of the Sixties' return to the Eighties.

"My favourite band at the time were The Television Personalities," said like-minded jangle-phile and future Fire chief Clive Solomon. "It was through a mutual love of this band that I first connected with Alan [McGee] and Alan openly acknowledges that The Television Personalities were the biggest influence on him in forming Creation." Solomon had also spearheaded his own Sixties tribute with the opening of The Groovy Cellar, another London nightclub that preceded McGee's Living Room, dedicated to playing classic pop, psychedelia, and anything else invoking a Swinging London, Carnaby Street flair. The only tunes played at Groovy Cellar came from a hi-fi: The Byrds, The Doors, Dusty Springfield, The Zombies, Walker Brothers, American garage-punk, *et al.* "It was a massively successful club," says Solomon, "and I didn't put bands on there, because they wouldn't have attracted anything like the same size of audience." Spacemen 3 would only cross paths with McGee and Solomon at the conclusion of the Eighties. But at decade's dawn, when Britain housed possibly thousands of bedroom indie record labels and a countless number of garage-rattling school-kids, yobbish pub-rockers, rude-boys, amphetamine-blitzed air-guitarists, and none-hit wonders, the networks between Rugby and London were few and far between.

The fragmentation of all these various subcultures in Britain resulted from the fallout of the major punk groups of the Seventies. By the time The Sex Pistols performed their last show in San Francisco in January '78 and John Lydon began his move towards avant-funk and reggae with

Public Image Limited, the youth of the country was already staking out new musical divisions based on exclusivity rather than unity. The explosion of 1977 had done much to consolidate the young boys (and girls) of Britain, and with its disintegration (or transformation in the case of The Buzzcocks and The Clash), musical trends proliferated with the rise of local "scenes" revolving around a network of independent labels and the foundation they provided.

Youth culture changed so much as a result of the '77 punk-rock *Götterdämmerung* that, under the weight of its massive appeal, a unified country of followers splintered into shards by '78. Without the rallying cry of a band like The Pistols, the youth culture split into myriad different tribes ascribing to dozens of ideologies and subcultures. Much as the magic year of 1966 had inflated by '67 into a worldwide phenomena and fell back into itself by '68–'69, the last two years of the Seventies "underground" were fraught with shifts in ideology and musical "scenes". Such was the antagonism that punks who once pogoed together grew apart, one side espousing the ultra-left Rock Against Racism, the other attending ultra-right Oi!/National Front rallies.

The national bent towards violence was punctuated by the multiple slayings of Peter Sutcliffe, known as The Yorkshire Ripper, who attacked and killed 13 women in the Leeds and Manchester areas before being apprehended in the spring of 1980. The North had not suffered such a widespread panic since the days of Myra Hindley and Ian Brady. The hysteria in Yorkshire was doubly frightening because the media-sensation began shortly after the conviction of Peter Cook, The Cambridge Rapist, who attacked nine women while fashioned in a head-to-toe bondage suit. Post-punk's disintegration spawned a violence that differed from its punk predecessors not in intensity (punk was equally violent) but in its expansion from the clubs to the streets and from beyond the metropolitan areas to the backwaters. And the style wars that spilled over into the riots in London, Bristol, Liverpool and Manchester at the beginning of the Eighties were equally prevalent in small towns like Rugby.

In the early Eighties, the Midlands spawned its own unique distillation of a "Back-to-the-Sixties" mentality. "The Midlands was an odd area of the country, because it covered such a large area and different parts developed different scenes," explained Oxford promoter Dave Newton. "The West Midlands threw up Sabbath and Slade in the Seventies, and punk seemed to completely pass the area by." Following the release of Franc Rodham's film-adaptation of *Quadrophenia* in 1979 and the ascension of The Jam, many of the Midlands' punks abandoned the gobbing, safety-pinned ethos of '77-style punk for a '66 mod-boy image, dressing in dapper suits and running between Birmingham and Brighton on their recently purchased Vespas. Groups of greased teddy-boys emerged astride their motorbikes, and from their ranks split derivative gangs of rockabilly punks, both of whom despised the more dapper mods and would often chase them down winding country roads or motorways.

The influence of reggae and Sixties-pop also germinated in the bourgeoning ska/two-tone movements of Coventry and Birmingham, producing a new subculture of rude boys in porkpie hats and mohair, rolling fat spliffs to the Skatalites and grooving to Toots & The Maytalls. Coventry's Special AKA and The Selecter, Birmingham's The Beat and London's Madness created a radically popular scene, and even bands of questionable authenticity like Birmingham's UB40 jumped in head first, scoring an early hit and securing a productive future in the UK and America. The post-punk gothic craze centred heavily in Northampton-shire, which spawned Bauhaus and Love And Rockets (although to see the near-picturesque village where Peter Murphy lived as a child, one might wonder from where 'Bela Lugosi's Dead' originated; the mono-chromatic gloom of Moss Side it was not). Goth's roots were also evident in the introspective punk of *Unknown Pleasures*: the morose lyrical obses-sions of Ian Curtis sweeping over Bernard Albrecht's VU-influenced guitar and Martin Hannett's "industrial" production. Joy Division, A Certain Ratio, and Vini Reilly, in conjunction with the Manchester and Sheffield labels (Factory, Doublevision) contributed much to the nocturnal jackhammer of goth, but retreated to the squelch of synths and the recurring motif of the "man/machine". By the time The Cure hit it big with their diluted and angsty pondering, Bauhaus had collapsed and the preciously morbid sub-genre settled into British cult-dom and American radio novelty.

Convergence Records provided Rugby's own nucleus of post-punk hipsterism and obscuro. A small independent shop on Regents Street, near the town centre, Convergence was owned by a local merchant called Simon Franklin, who attracted pubescent musos riding the '77 tidal wave by stocking the shelves with hard-to-find punk singles and rare Sixties reissues. Franklin made weekly trips to London's Rough Trade and Small Wonder to maintain an *au courant* inventory. Record shelves in Convergence often displayed The Red Krayola's psychedelic classics next to The Slits' feminist funk and Spizz Energy's psycho-punk. New-wave bootlegs were particularly plentiful. Franklin only opened his Regents Street doors between four in the afternoon and half-five, to a rabid crowd of public and grammar schoolboys hungry to fondle the cardboard sleeves and flip through the latest seven-inchers. Conse-quently, Convergence was one of the few haunts where rich villagers and poor townies convened without a scuffle. Jason, Sonic, and Bassman all frequented Franklin's shop early in their teens, though they chose to skip the introductions.

As Sonic explored all of this old material at the record shop, he also discovered an interest in the visual arts. He'd serendipitously come across the animated, panchromatic stylings of pop art while studying at Rugby School. He was fascinated with the comic-book zaniness of Lichtenstein, the gargantuan novelty of Oldenburg, and the nocturnal innocence of Warhol. Like many aspiring "artists" at an awkward age (Sonic recalls feeling like an alien for most his life), he was drawn irrepressibly to Warhol's strange image: the pale figure, the white wig, the black boots, all accoutrements of mid-Sixties New York cool. He bought a copy of *POPism: The Warhol Sixties*, when it was published in 1980, and contented himself by reading passages written by this odd icon, about sex, drugs and rock'n'roll. Though he'd never heard of The Velvet Underground before, he was most intrigued by the sections Warhol devoted in the book to these elusive musicians. The anecdotes revolving around Lou and John's "fuck-off" attitudes and the descriptions of the Velvets' sonorous experimentation hinted at something that for Sonic would be a revelation. During one of his many visits to the local record shop he spied a copy of the Velvets' first album, the bold cover adorned with an extra-large banana, and purchased it. From that moment on, he only wanted to play rock'n'roll.

Sonic smoked his first joint at a Specials gig in Coventry when he was 14. He'd wandered backstage before the show and met up with Rico Rodriguez, an Afro-Chinese trombonist for the 2-Tone band whose roots were firmly in Jamaican ska. Rico was in the middle of rolling a fat joint and Sonic approached him matter-of-factly with the request: "Can I get 2s up?" Rico gazed over at the lumpy prepubescent who looked even younger than he actually was, and laughed. He finished rolling and took some heavy hits, while Sonic looked on, feeling ignored. But Rico surprised him by passing the joint over and allowing Sonic to finish it off. Rico could only laugh at the young schoolboy who seemed to be taking such prodigious care of his cannabis. Sonic wandered out into the audience and watched The Specials show with drug-induced awe.

Growing up, Sonic recalled first hearing the "drug-lecture" when his mother delivered it to Simon before the elder Kember sibling left for Rugby School. The discussion only served to pique his interest immediately, and while Sonic's brother did not take to drugs much beyond typical teenage experimentation, Sonic was massively hungry for it by the time he entered Rugby School in the late Seventies. And when his parents got wind of their son's earliest transgressions, they were not at all amused. "I'm sure as the familial black sheep, they half expected me to dabble," Sonic explained. "Obviously, they didn't encourage me in that, but they were also very fair and open to debate about the 'reality' versus the 'myth' of usage when they noticed I was doing more than smoking a few joints. No parent relishes their children becoming addicted to drugs."

"I bypassed sniffing lighter gas and took to dope," Bassman recalled, of his introduction to Rugby's plethora of drugs, "which nearly everybody did. Rugby was awash with it, and some very fine stuff too: Nepalese temple balls, sticky black resin from Afghanistan, red Leb and crumbly soft Moroccan hash. Getting stoned had an immediate effect on my perception of music." Bassman's first experience with hash came during his stint at the GEC factory, where he was apprenticed after finishing trade school. The General Electric plant was a haunting monolith, dank and ruinous, though it was the largest industrial complex in Rugby and funded many of its residents throughout the Seventies and Eighties. Bassman spent long hours in the assemblage plant, quite unsure of what had led him here and how he was going to get out. When a fellow worker offered him a bit of hash as an alternative method of coping with the job, Bassman welcomed the gesture and smoked it down quickly. The change was near instantaneous. "After a smoke I actually liked the environment," he continued. "It was a fascinating place: the huge drone from all the machines; the casings for steam turbines weighing two hundred tons hung suspended in the air. There were giant machines grinding away at metal."

Will Carruthers came by way of his substances with much the same curiosity and awe. As a child, he used to sneak into the kitchen cupboard and guzzle his mother's home-made blackberry wine, mistaking the elixir's inebriating warmth for its delicious taste. The veil was only ripped from his eyes years later when he gulped down several pieces of space cake and vomited all over himself. As poor as his first experience with pharmacology proved, he found the glassy-eyed, limb-twisting hum of mind-alteration intoxicating, and he quickly gobbled down whatever rogue substances he could procure. Will realised he'd been lied to all his life about drugs. He wanted to know what else was untrue.

Butane was another favourite cheap high for young kids stuck in the English backwaters. It was easy to get from any local tobacconist, not only cheap but also legal for all intents and purposes, and provided an interesting cross-effect of a psychedelic and opiate high. Sonic began experimenting with it during his short tenure at Rugby School and found it to be a curious but rather volatile introduction to the world of hallucinogens. "It was kinda buzzy like alcohol, but tended to induce fairly horrific and very real hallucinations," insisted Sonic. "I have particular memories of being attacked by a berserker Viking . . . and believing it. I nearly had a heart attack from shock. Then there was the weird 'animals' that started to appear." Sonic often sneaked out of Tudor House after hours or skipped classes to grab a quick sniff.

The concoction of his earliest musical and drug endeavours had, by the beginning of 1980, transformed Sonic from a well-meaning student to a rebellious musician. He spent much of his time skiving off courses at Rugby School, and auditioning new records stoned out on weed and butane. His introduction to the new decade came in a miasma of grating guitar and empty canisters of lighter-fluid, raising alarm among his school superiors of his rapidly declining conduct and results. The closed-door policies of the House did not apply after nine o'clock, when late-night stragglers would have to slip through Mr Smith's cottage to enter the dormitory. Sonic was often caught smoking or sneaking out of the House after-hours to hit up local pubs. On a number of occasions, Sonic was sought out by the Head of House for various offences and beaten in front of the assembled boys, in accordance with House policy. These violent confrontations proved to be altogether reminiscent of Lindsay Anderson's late Sixties anti-establishment biopic *If . . .*, the fantastic tale of philosopher-punk Mick Travis and his bloodied squabbles with College House's prefecture. Much like Travis' commitment to techni-colour hijinks and regicide, Sonic had proven to be a thorn in the buttock of authority. In one instance, Smith himself cornered Sonic with a thick, wooden broomstick and rained blows down on him in painful recrimination. "I was caught swearing at a teacher, and he beat me with this full-length broomstick," laughed Sonic. "And he hit me twice with it. It was so painful I stood it twice. And then I turned around and yelled at him, 'Fuck Off!' He just walked out of the room. For some reason he just accepted it and let it go at that."

Musicians around Rugby put in their bid to establish a local 'scene', but it was an onerous task. Rugby wasn't sufficiently populous to host regular tours and its lack of proper venues (apart from occasional one-offs in pub back rooms) meant most aspiring bands skipped over to Coventry in the west or Northampton in the east. At the time, the town hosted its answer to the politico-pop of The Fall or Scritti Politti with Russian Jazz, a quasi-socialist group dating back to the mid-Seventies, and a goth-influenced group, Indian Scalp, formed by competent chord-driven guitar players. Jason would walk down to the Charlesfield multi-function room in the centre of town (the site of their night-long jam sessions), with axe in hand, ready to play. It was at these marathon rehearsals and dope sessions that Bassman first ran into Jason Pierce. "I knew Andrew Fountain, nicknamed Stick, and Steve Milligan, who were both members of Indian Scalp," Bassman said. "We all worked at the GEC. And we shared a loathing of the place, and an interest in music. Russian Jazz also rehearsed there, both bands knew each other well as most of them came from the Bilton area of Rugby."

While attending Lawrence Sheriff School, Jason had acquired his first electric guitar after a neighbour, Roy Ward, offered it to him as a gift. He showed natural talent almost immediately, learning chords and scales and repeating tunes easily by ear. Ward had a musical history of his own, drumming for Birmingham-based 10 c.c. derivatives City Boy, and singing back-up for Tight Fit, a novelty outfit who'd had a number one hit with the African folk song 'The Lion Sleeps Tonight' in 1982. Ward occasionally tutored Jason, instilling in him a musical confidence. As Jason spent more and more of his time and effort with Indian Scalp, his ability to play complicated chord progressions and funky grooves improved, impressing many of the onlookers who would wander in and out of the rehearsal space. Recalled Bassman, "Jason was quite into Indian Scalp; his style was a little funk orientated, though he maintained, in later years, that he just played Stooges' riffs."

Jason's solid playing was matched only by his unusually eccentric fashion sense: he'd wear strange mismatching layers of clothing that he'd proceed to shed during long onstage rehearsals, and his brown plop of hair would be dyed odd colours, slicked-back, or sculpted into a spiky Terry Hall-style. "He'd slick back his hair with some strange home-made concoction that would solidify and look rather like lard," said Bassman, smiling. "This was a constant source of amusement to us." Jason had a lean, pubescent frame that stood just short of six feet, though he appeared shorter due to his introverted posture. His face looked somewhat exotic and statuesque, with a thick rounded chin and probing, icy eyes. Young women – and young men – were drawn to his charming features and soft-spoken personality. "Anyone who knew him back then knew him to be very intelligent and kind of full of himself to a certain extent," Sonic recalled.

While Jason took to learning the vast complexities of the guitar between skiving off classes at Lawrence Sheriff, Sonic honed his musical interests from nearly the opposite direction. Sitting in his small dormitory at Tudor House, a mile from Jason's grammar school, Sonic would while away his evenings smoking weed and listening to The Sex Pistols, The Cramps, and The Gun Club. Stoned out, he would concentrate on the sounds of Jeffrey Lee Pierce's guitar sliding back and forth with the slap-back echo and spring reverb filling the speaker of his turntable. His obsessions with the "sound spectrum" had done little to prompt his guitar playing beyond basic chords and a few rudimentary blues scales.

But whether it was sheer laziness, cannabis torpor, or intentional, he decided it was all he needed to know.

It was through his love for rockabilly and punk, and access to the only hip record store in town, that Sonic launched into his own retro-Sixties epiphany, discovering the pre-punk barrage of American psychedelia. Beyond the usual suspects – The Velvet Underground, The Stooges, MC5 – he also found The Thirteenth Floor Elevators, The Electric Prunes, The Godz, and Red Krayola to his liking, classic bands that had explored the simplicity of drug-fuelled blues and had all but been forgotten. It was primal music that went right to the heart of the blues, whether it was the acoustic rambling of Robert Johnson or the electric romp of John Lee Hooker. Sonic had found the very origin of his obsession.

Unfortunately, as his love for rock'n'roll and good times increased, Sonic's conduct and reputation at Rugby waned. On several occasions he was caught smoking and drinking – a practice that was strictly forbidden – and the sixth formers at Tudor unleashed innumerable punishments upon him, including a fair number of beatings, in an attempt to keep Sonic's transgressions within the house. But the faculty and staff of the school became increasingly aware of his rowdy behaviour, ensuring that the Housemaster and Headmaster would punish him. Sonic and a few of his mates were in the habit of climbing out of one of Tudor House's upstairs windows during late-night runs to pubs or off-licenses. On one occasion, the group was staggering back to Tudor at sunrise after a night of drinking only to be caught by a local constable. They were dragged en masse to the police station and the Housemaster was summoned from his sleep to accompany them back to the house.

Sonic's volatile status at Rugby School finally came to a head during his second term of '81. Shortly before taking his 'O'-levels, the Head-master phoned his parents to notify them of Sonic's poor conduct. The School's opinion in the matter was blunt: they felt Sonic should with-draw from classes immediately. In addition to his tardiness, poor grades, and numerous reprimands, Sonic had recently been caught sniffing butane on school grounds, reason enough for a prompt dismissal. Somehow, after much cajoling, the Kember patriarch was able to convince school officials that Sonic could remain until his exams were completed. At the end of the term, he left Rugby School with the express admonition that he not return to campus for the following two years – the duration of his intended time in the "Sixth Form". The Headmaster was concerned that Sonic's reappearance might further corrupt his friends and former classmates, leading them down the same path of failure. Sonic mused, "I guess I just didn't want to be at school anymore."

The problems caused by Jason's chronic truancy and Sonic's scholastic excommunication, which appeared to bode so unfavourably for their futures, made their encounter in the cramped classrooms of art college all the more fortuitous. Having found a promising outlet for collaboration before they could sink into the mire of West Midlands complacency, neither Jason nor Sonic could resist envisaging their forebears Reed and Cale at Pickwick or Jagger and Richards on Spielman Road. Sitting under a plume of rancid smog and fantasising in the vacuum of 1982, they supposed themselves humble musicians seized by the gravity of history and weaved into rock'n'roll's religious shroud.

CHAPTER TWO

For All The Fucked Up Children Of This World We Give You Spacemen 3

1982–1985

Despite his desire to work with Sonic, Jason continued rehearsing weekly with Indian Scalp and front man Stick, who remained unaware of his guitarist's butane binges and plans for the future. Sonic's recent appearances at the band's rehearsals and his evident chumminess with Jason failed to set off alarm bells as to his imminent defection. In fact, Sonic attempted to insinuate himself into Indian Scalp's fold by agreeing to help pay for a pending demo tape. He briefly took on what some saw as a managerial position with Indian Scalp, although his motives for doing so raised suspicion among those in and around the band. It was also at these rehearsals that Sonic first encountered Bassman, who immediately took notice of the tall, lumpy kid hanging out with Jason. Although they were anything but best mates, Bassman often chatted to Sonic over the course of the band rehearsals, and observed both Jason and the new kid spending lots of time hanging out in Stick's Ford Consul sniffing butane from the front seats. For his 17th birthday, Sonic staged a gig for Indian Scalp at his party, and also shelled out his promised portion of money for the demo.

"On Pete Kember's birthday I went round to his house," Bassman recalled, "and in the drive was a brand new red mini metro car. It was a present from his parents. With this new-found mobility his life changed radically. Before he must have spent a small fortune on taxis, but after he could bomb around Rugby whenever he wished." Sonic's wheels also allowed him to drive beyond Rugby's perimeter to score dope, which he found in rich abundance amid Birmingham's seedier nightlife. On Monday nights, prior to Indian Scalp's weekly rehearsals, Sonic zoomed the 80-mile round trip to the Bee Hive pub, where he'd load up on hash for himself and the musicians back in Rugby. "The Bee Hive was full of dealers," Sonic recalled. "Like 40 or 50 guys, at least, shoving big lumps of dope and weed and all different types of hash in your face. And I had to

38

sort of fight my way through it to get to the inner sanctum and score the good stuff." Sonic returned to the Rugby rehearsal room with thick, brown clumps which he passed out, until everyone was properly stoned for an all-night jam session.

It was also during these Monday evening rehearsals that Sonic struck up a friendship with Dave West, an older musician who lived in a flat in nearby Brownsover. West was an amiable stoner with connections to the more unseemly characters of Rugby's strung-out drug culture. Sonic spent a lot of time between the Charlesfield rehearsal space and West's flat, chain-smoking dope and listening to records. On other days he'd drive over to Jason's home to strum guitars and sniff butane. Anything to escape the minutiae of Dunchurch.

During an evening of levity in Brownsover, Sonic first experimented with psychedelics when West offered him mushrooms. They sat in the living room of the decrepit old flat where West began rotating records on the turntable as the trip began to unfold. Sonic felt a strong sense of déjà vu and a flood of overwhelming emotion. West put on Laurie Anderson's *Big Science* and Sonic was blown away by the rotary drones emanating from the speakers. This experience was to be a revelation for the young musician. Sounds ebbed and flowed from inside his skull. Echo & The Bunnymen's *Crocodiles* followed with full effect. By the time Sonic heard the reedy swell of clarinet on Chris Barber's 'Petite Fleur', he broke down and began crying, he thought it so beautiful. After the drug slowly began to wane, he headed home, where he felt a resurgence of déjà vu grip his body, an overpowering and bleak sensation of child-hood regression. Sonic recalled, "I was just blown away – just totally wigging out. It wasn't until I started trying mushrooms, acid, amphet-amines, heroin, and various pills around this time that I became aware of the wider possibilities of drug exploration. I felt psychedelics played quite a large part in forming my opinions and helping me come to terms with the human condition."

In late '82, Sonic left for Europe on a solo hostel tour, travelling throughout France before crossing over to The Netherlands and check-ing out Amsterdam's red-light district. Sonic had scored a large amount of hash and cocaine, and procured acid tabs called ET (after the popular film). "Pete took LSD and saw Jesus on the wall in the hostel shower room and smoked as much dope as he could manage," said Bassman. Of the experience, Sonic insisted, "I did a lot of soul searching. I found that aspect of acid very useful and very good at cutting to the chase of the matter. I think acid expanded my capacity for wonder and therefore for knowledge and also self-understanding." So much had Sonic enjoyed the acid experience that he brought a few tabs back for himself and Jason, and wholeheartedly began proselytising his friends into the psychedelic experience. "I soon turned on Pete Bain and Jason and everyone else I was with," Sonic said. "Jason and Pete Bain had had some varied experiences with hash previously, but neither had tried psychedelics before I was hanging around with them." Bassman spied the changes in Sonic instantly, and, so much was his wide-eyed curiosity, he gleefully joined in the psychoactive merriment. "Acid was in a way the catalyst that sent The Spacemen into orbit," he insisted. "It was undoubtedly a life changing event, that we all discovered it around the same time. The frequency was maybe once or twice a month; it certainly was not a regular drug of choice, due to the way it scrambled your brain."

> SONIC: "I recommended mushrooms to Pete Bain after I had them, and some time after he took some at a jazz/funk gig and passed out. Pete was never massively into psychedelics. He did trip with us a few times later and had a much better time. He seemed to dig them as far as I could see."

Jason took a tab of ET acid with Sonic one afternoon shortly after his return to Rugby. To enhance the experience, but inevitably complicating it, Sonic offered Jason a tiny bit of heroin to smoke beforehand. The buzzing couple walked through the middle of town and ended up at the house of a notorious character, Roy Morris, a local drug-dealer whom Sonic had befriended during his earliest excursions to score dope. Morris' home, a spooky terraced house, was testament to years and years of tripping inhabitants. They could literally feel the psychedelic palimpsest as they walked inside. As the smack caressed their bodies, they each took a tab of acid and waited for it to take effect. For most of the 12-hour inner-flight Jason and Sonic sat in the front room of the house. An attempt at listening to *Dark Side Of The Moon* was pre-empted when one of them ripped the record from the turntable in disgust, and then Sonic put on an Electric Prunes album and soaked it in. For Jason, the trip became a bit bumpy at times, as he shifted rigidly from the multivalent highs and lows.

"Jason didn't seem to get on with psychedelics too well," remembered Sonic. "That first trip he had, every time he got 'doubt' from a plateau in the acid, he would turn to me and say, 'Hey! Stop doing that.' Like I somehow could control it." Sonic and Roy had to help guide Jason through the heavier moments, as it was apparent he was having difficulty manoeuvring through it himself. "But it's hard to explain," Sonic added. "We both seemed tuned in to similar frequencies and liked similar stuff. When Jason started playing Muddy Waters and John Lee Hooker records, we both seemed to get the same feeling and buzz."

JASON: "I think good music is the same kind of experience as a drug experience. The bad thing is when people start making drug music, or acid rock, because invariably they sound pretty shitty on drugs. A lot of acid rock sounds horrendous to me on acid, whereas stuff like Buddy Holly or Screamin' Jay Hawkins, now that's acid music."

BASSMAN: "We were quite militant about the drugs thing. We were prepared to stick our necks out. In those days we'd smoke a joint anywhere, buses, trains, anything, y'know, we just didn't care. We were just stupid, we thought it was brilliant – mushrooms, a bit of acid, stuff like that."

Not long after that, Will took acid for the first time. Set and setting being the most crucial factor in a young teenager's romantic visions of the "acid experience", Will swallowed a tab during a late-night excursion to a local fairground with some mates. He felt it kick in as he lay down in the open night air, watching the condensed curls of his breath float upward and refract the garish colours of the carnival lights. Though he wasn't sure where it was coming from, someone put on The Stones' 'Jumpin' Jack Flash', and he was instantly converted. Will had heard the song a million times before but never like this. The feeling was an indescribable collection of music snapshots that rushed into his head. It was youth. It was rock'n'roll. It was rebirth conveniently synthesised into a tab.

Things were generally looking up for Indian Scalp. Stick took Bassman and Jason along in his Consul to a Bauhaus gig where they cornered some members of Southern Death Cult and convinced them to listen to their demo tape. Whether or not they were impressed was moot. Goth was the hip sound and Indian Scalp hoped to cash in. It was only then, much to the chagrin of Stick, that Jason walked from the band and decided to cast his lot with Sonic. "Jason just wanted to do what I wanted to do more than he wanted to do what this other guy Stick and Indian Scalp wanted," Sonic explained. "I think Stick resented it ever since. I'm sure he resented it – like I stole Jason away. But Jason left totally of his own volition."

Now Sonic made his rounds down at Jason's house nearly everyday. With the shady business of Indian Scalp behind them, they set about working on both the concept and sound of their prospective collaboration. Between them, they only had three shitty guitars (one of which was an acoustic) and a single practice amp, which they took turns playing on. "Jason used to have a really horrible Japanese Hondo thing that he had from Indian Scalp – beautiful player but it looked horrible," said Sonic.

In the most vague of terms, they'd agreed the new band would incorporate the hypnotic simplicity of the Velvets, the caterwaul of The Stooges, and the perverted reverence of The Cramps. Toxicity bred voluminous fantasies.

Jason often played around with scales and chord progressions while Sonic droned away searching for a particular sound that seemed to elude him. Within weeks, they'd built up a small roster of potential sounds, directions, and roughly hewn songs, including their earliest stab at The Stooges-meet-The MC5, 'OD Catastrophe' (interchangeably referred to as 'TV Catastrophe'). Jason screeched along to Sonic's skronk with lyrics from *The Idiot* and *Lust For Life*, fusing different vocal melodies over the top. It was only after several listless jams that musical inspiration came from the unlikeliest of sources. "One day, when I was playing around 'OD Catastrophe' down at Jason's house," recalled Sonic, "I was on the guitar just jamming about and his brother was shaving, and the sound of the harmonic mixture of the music and the razor, the drone of it, was just really great. I figured, 'Well that's it, I need to get that sound – to have the fuzz of the razor!'"

The two avid record collectors created an early maxim for themselves from hours and hours of non-stop listening. It was only after delving into every procurable copy of The Elevators, The Electric Prunes, The Who, The Velvets, and Otis Redding (whom Sonic had a particular fondness for) that they stumbled upon a description of their "sound", which they termed "acid soul punk". Heavy and seemingly contradictory, for Jason and Sonic it summed up not only the music they wanted to create but also the environment and lifestyle from which the sound proceeded. "We knew that it worked together," Sonic said. "One of us could come up with something and the other one could find something to go with it. I was much more minimal, much more textural; I liked anything that had one note all the way through it. And Jason helped keep the music, well, musical. He was the Lou Reed to my John Cale. We found that sound between us early on and we decided to get in bass players and drummers to fill that out."

The important question of naming themselves, a sobriquet that would easily sum up their "acid soul punk" philosophy, became the next step on their agenda. Sonic suggested "Xmen" after happening upon the visage of Wolverine in the popular comic strip. He liked the cartoonish "pop" of the mysterious character, and thought the name would lend an enigmatic element to the aspiring band. The name didn't stick for more than a week, though, and finally he and Jason both agreed on 'Spacemen' (minus the article "The") because it was a perfect summation of the sounds they aspired to create. "Space as music. . . ." Jason recalled, "The idea of space just seemed to fit in with what we were doing. It seemed like we were spacemen, like we weren't doing the things that made it easy to slot into normal life in Rugby."

Tim Morris' parents had a large home in the nearby village of Kilsby, where Tim, Gavin Wissen, and Bassman would scramble up to the spacious attic and rehearse their own sloppy Sixties garage-punk until late into the evening. Tim was somewhat central to a number of germinating Rugby bands due to his ample practice room and understanding family. Several different groups would show up on his doorstep with guitars in hand on any given day, hoping to get the nod to trek up the stairs. Once inside, they'd plunk down their gear, smoke dope, and thrash away until Tim's father would come up in the evenings and chase everyone out. Calling themselves Noise On Independent Street (named for a garage where the group would stop off for fags and sweets before rehearsing), Tim played open-tuned guitar, Bassman banged on a drum kit, Gavin sang, and sometimes-musician Dave Jones played bass. Gavin had secured a copy of *Nuggets*, Lenny Kaye's collection of obscure Sixties garage from America, which they all listened to obsessively and tried to emulate with their shoddy gear. The band didn't last much beyond a few rudimentary jams before Bassman "lost" his drums. In fact, his mother had thrown them out.

In place of a kit, Bassman purchased a ratty blue bass, glittered and spangled as if it came straight from the glam era. He didn't know how to play it, but he thought it looked ace as he sat in his bedroom thrashing it until his fingers bled. By this time, Tim had traded in his guitar for a drum kit, and when word got out, more and more kids started showing up at his house hoping to pull a much-needed drummer into their "band". Consequently, Tim played in any number of rag-tag groups who filed in and out during the day. Sonic and Jason showed up at Tim's as well, and the three of them jammed a few times before Bassman visited one day and nominated himself as the bassist of the band. The first roster was complete.

"Pete came round to give me some lessons – he taught me a simple rock'n'roll riff and explained the principles of blues," Bassman said. "This was useful, but Sonic's playing was hardly beyond beginner. I can remember the first rehearsals, you know, could just be anarchic. Just stupid. Just kids being silly." Sonic and Jason rattled through a half-dozen shambolic numbers, including covers of Iggy's 'Fun Time' and 'Funhouse', The Cramps, a few rockabilly originals, and 'OD Catastrophe'. With a rhythm section in tow, Sonic's drone experiment expanded into a noise opus, with Jason screaming 'TV Eye' vocals throughout. Even at these earliest stages, Sonic enticed ear-splitting feedback from his gnarled gear, placing the head of his guitar up against the amplifier. The vibrations travelled down the neck, rather than through the air, creating a thundering pulse Sonic controlled and manipulated laying down heavy on the tremolo arm. Bassman stood near them, crouched over his bass and strumming an open note, and Tim pounded his drums with sloppy ferocity. "I was tremendously impressed with the first few rehearsals," Bassman continued. "Pete used a phaser pedal that gave his guitar a jet engine sound, and my bass sounded like a V2 bomb droning in the distance. I mean, this was the prototype sound – the embryonic Spacemen."

> JASON: "It was just two guitars, bass and drums, but it seemed like this music was coming through the roof . . . it was like, what the fuck is this?!"

> SONIC: "Even after the first practice it was obvious that there was something really there."

With its first line-up, the four-piece Spacemen rotated rehearsals between Kilsby and the Charlesfield rehearsal room in the town centre. "Tim was drumming for three bands at one time, so he was probably practising three nights a week or something," recalled Sonic. "It probably got a bit nightmarish there." The band was eventually evicted from Tim's attic after all the noise became too much to handle for his parents. Tim's father sternly commented, "I have some memories of Spacemen 3. They used to 'rehearse' in our family house and cause some concern as to who and what was coming and going on the rear staircase!"

When the band plugged in and began droning away, it was like a holy racket of Luftwaffe bombers incinerating the English countryside. But onlookers were not impressed. Most of the guys at Charlesfield from Indian Scalp and Russian Jazz looked at The Spacemen with a mixture of pretension and hostility. No one could fathom why Jason walked from potential success for this poxy Stooges rip-off. Gavin explained, "There was this thing about Indian Scalp – at the time it was the sort of dancey, gothic thing that was going on. And Jason was a fucking good guitarist. Then with The Spacemen thing, he was only playing two chords and nobody understood it." Most of the blame fell squarely on to Sonic's shoulders.

Sonic and Jason's effete good looks and their inseparable relationship provided grist for the rumour mill. Ugly comments based on innuendo and third-hand gossip flowed from the rehearsal room and between local musicians. "When we really first got together right at the end of Indian Scalp there were rumours about homosexual activities between Pete and

Jason or Jason and somebody else," Bassman recalled. "There was that slight rumour. I'm not even sure if there was any credence to it. At the time it was just stupid rumours." The accusations of a sexual relationship also proceeded from a common prejudice against Rugby School students and their "perverted" sexual mores. Gruesome and erotic tales of molestation, sodomy, and orgies had long proliferated from this pleasure dome of the rich and idle. Bassman agreed: "Sonic went to Rugby School where homosexuality was allegedly so rife, it should have been featured as a part of the curriculum . . . In my opinion, it was the kind of weird bullshit that produced fuck-ups like Sonic." While gay sex experiments were indeed common in the cramped and highly charged atmosphere of British boarding schools, the degree of shame this produced outside the School's walls was cruel and unrelenting.

"Bisexuality held a place of disgrace below that of even homosexuality in a small town like Rugby," Sonic explained. "But as that would appear perhaps bigoted, our blatant drug-use would be the stick most people wanted to beat us with. That or my education." Any sexual tension in the first days of The Spacemen was relegated to Jason's hot-blooded urges to shag young girls about town. "Whether Jason had relationships with other guys, I can't say, but I never had a relationship with him," he added. Sonic's amorous inclinations were much more enigmatic and muted. His natural curiosities and romantic nature had pushed him into numerous adolescent relationships during his stay at Rugby School, where he'd found himself attracted to both women and men. Sonic insisted he was very open to Jason and his other band mates about his sexuality, despite choosing to tread lightly on the subject. "I don't think I ever hid anything from anyone," he said. "I guess the answer is 'yes' – that they knew. I never hid anything from them. But I don't think I was necessarily the only one in the band to have those thoughts anyway."

After rehearsals, Sonic moved between friends' flats on his constant quest to avoid home life in Dunchurch. Quick pop-ins would always turn into twilight marathons of drug-consumption and vinyl binges, as inebriated discussions between the young musicians took on the air of a psychedelic salon, where participants feasted on obscurantism and excess. To the stoned-out few who had been cursed with the stigmata of psychedelia, it was a vibrant moment of self-discovery and decadence. "The time spent in council houses, just listening to The Stooges, taking magic mushrooms and driving around in cars was kind of what we did behind the scenes," said Bassman. "What we did in our lives. This is how our lives evolved. One time we all had some mushroom tea, and the plan was to go to Warwick University to see The Folk Devils. We all trooped out in a psychedelic state. Before we set off I thought Pete bumped the nasty neighbour's car. It set everyone off panicking. I thought I saw his curtain move and expected him to come out at any minute. 'Go! Go!' we shouted but Pete was blocked in by a friend which exacerbated our panic. We shot off and headed in the direction of Warwick at very high speed. But we had only gone a couple of miles when Pete said he couldn't go on because of all the naked women in the road!"

In another spirited twilight excursion, Sonic took Jason, Bassman and several stragglers to catch an ageing Nico perform in a Birmingham club. En route on the M1, Sonic passed around small portions of opium, which everyone gleefully swallowed. They blagged their way into the club and into a hidden alcove where Jason and Sonic exchanged smokes of hash to the droning sounds of harmonium. As Nico cooed her trademark "Marlene Dietrich-fed-through-an-IBM" rendition of 'It Was A Pleasure Then' the group nodded out into a dreamy narcosis. Hours later on their awakening from opium dreams, they narrowly escaped being locked in the club's cavernous space for the night. Such comical hijinks were regular occurrences during The Spacemen's headier days.

"Until a certain point our pursuits had been relatively benign," said Bassman. "But we were growing up in a town that had the nickname Drugby, a place which, because of its location on the railway and close proximity to London, was on the dope dealer supply routes." Due to massive underground marketing throughout the Seventies, the junk (heroin) lifestyle that once centred only on the small, hip enclave of London's Kings Road had proliferated to council estates in every major metropolitan city and to the remaining provincial towns by the early part of the Eighties. Under Roy Jenkins as Home Secretary, starting in 1968 the Labour Government effectively terminated the licensed avail-ability of prescription heroin (and thereafter substituted the methadone "solution"), and the drug's importation and sale submerged into the alternative worlds of the black market. Trade routes from the East pro-vided varying types of gear with differing consistency and quality to be administered based on a purity scale: pale Turkish junk, Chinese Rocks or Persian brown junk.

Thus did the Home Office's addict register balloon from a few hundred to many thousands. Even the most socially conservative com-munities in the Midlands were not unaffected by the quantum leap in junk use. With a recession across the country and unemployment reach-ing an unprecedented 20 per cent in many urban areas during the early Thatcherite years, small towns like Rugby proved particularly susceptible to drug culture. Many teenagers moved from school directly to the council houses, which were a hotbed for junk. "Possession of drugs was highly illegal back then," reported Bassman. "There were a lot of taboos. It was a period of time where you had AIDS and hepatitis doing the rounds. There was a lot of intravenous drug use and it was on the rise. People dying of overdoses."

Because Rugby lay at the nexus of both road and rail routes between London and Birmingham, and within easy reach of Coventry and Oxford, the town's status as a distribution centre for both legal and illegal substances enhanced its reputation as a dependable source for junk. "It's dead centre in the country, so it's basically a distribution town for every-thing," Jason said. Even with its diminutive size and population, Rugby had an intricate network of smack dealers and hundreds of addicts by the early Eighties. Junk use was such a grave concern that Rugby became one of the first provincial communities to open a methadone clinic.

Shortly after his earliest experiences with acid and mushrooms, Sonic began habitually dabbling in heroin, cocaine, and amphetamine, along with a whole range of prescribed multicoloured uppers and downers. During his protean excursions into heroin, he'd score a bag – about an 1/8th gram – and smoke it slowly down over a two-day period, retaining a near limitless buzz without nodding out. Jason would sometimes take part, and they would often investigate different concoctions of heroin and amphetamine, while blasting music at ultra-high volumes to induce strange harmonic perceptions. Particular albums became linked with the drug cocktails that most accentuated their textures, and turntables and tape decks would be cued accordingly. The Velvets (especially the latter-period *Live '69*-era) were best experienced through the glaze of heroin, whereas The Stooges' *Raw Power* was the ultimate speed album. The Elevators, The Electric Prunes, and other Sixties garage-punk was thoroughly amplified by acid.

Because the nature of heroin was exclusivity and status, and its use and proliferation based as much on the attraction to an alternative lifestyle as the morphine-receptors ringing deep in the brain, junk's seduction was stylish as well as bio-chemical, ideological as well as romantic (the netherworlds of Burroughs, the Victorian "petit"-history of the Deca-dents, the leathery sexiness of Lou Reed). Heroin, then as now, bred sub-terranean collectives mushroomed on the pleasures of chemical design with the self-importance of outlaws. In these circles, alcohol was the demon, and Sonic himself stopped drinking as he discovered these groups and scored more and more regularly. And his curiosity led him to the spike . . .

The needle subculture represented a small but extreme portion of the junk population in Britain. In the immediate punk tradition, "banging" junk involved a specific line of users starting with Iggy Pop, through

Johnny Thunders, and Sid Vicious, the habit then spreading through a ventricled genealogy of '77 punk-bands. Of course, Iggy's dirty habits could probably be traced back to his introduction to the Velvets, the original NYC sirens of the spike. Contrary to the heroin mystique, most junkies in Britain rarely, if ever, burst through the membrane of intravenous use. Unlike the New York junk scene, where the minimal strength of white-heroin (2–3 per cent) made needles a common thread of street-use, the London scene contained pure brown heroin (anywhere from 20–70 per cent) that made banging largely unnecessary. For the expanding sub-population of shooters throughout the Eighties, there was a mysterious division between themselves and habitual non-shooters (one of those inexplicable elements of style inherent to every subculture). Banging junk was either considered to be the most extreme in the beginning stages or the most desperate in the latter stages.

"I found the whole thing – injecting – to be quite frightening," Sonic said. "I had a real fear of needles growing up, and I couldn't stand watching these people shoot up." Yet despite his apparent phobia, Sonic soon learned the proper method of injecting from others floating around these cliques, abandoning his reservation toward needles and refusing to look back. In his words, he found banging "frighteningly easy to do." It was a straight-shot, efficient and clean (if works were replaced regularly). The shot came on fast and would last him for the day. And the sensations from shooting smack bordered on the ineffable: the orgasmic rush, a vast tickle racing up the arm and welling into a fabulous embryonic warmth throughout every corner and crevice of the body, followed by utter relaxation as the brain broke down the compound into its morphine components and sent the cerebrum blinking and buzzing like a carnival midway. Unlike any number of synthesised hallucinogens or amphetamines, heroin produced a completely natural and organic buzz, so much so that Sonic felt his body completed rather than altered. He nodded out and experienced the somnambulant bliss so vividly enumerated by opium-eaters and morphine-users of the past; the descent of Morpheus into diurnal shooting galleries; the confluence of poison and medicine described as the *pharmacon*. Sonic explained, "I had long waking dreams, where, while totally awake, I 'dreamt' conversations and events, and then was quite shocked when someone spoke, pulling me instantly back to a totally different (but real) scenario. It's an undeniably beatific feeling, and the dreams . . . The dreams from early usage of opiates were sublime in the extreme."

Sonic could easily afford the necessary £10 to procure about a hundred syringes on the black market. And for the time being, copping junk was relatively inexpensive and easy in Rugby. By injecting smaller doses – he'd bang half a bag, the effects of which would last throughout the day – Sonic could spread out his use and conserve his gear. He scored quarter gram bags for about £20 without burning a serious hole in his pocket.

The price of junk had risen steadily in Britain from the late Seventies onward due to an influx of higher-grade gear and the sharp leap in demand. From its massive importation in '76–'77, the cost of a gram increased from about £10–12 to about £80 in the early Eighties. To defray the cost, heavier users would score up to a quarter-ounce, saving around £30 a gram. That is, if one had the dosh. The steep climb was fortunate for many young kids on the dole who could afford to dabble but couldn't maintain a habit for any length of time.

It was after another late-night drinking binge at a mate's house on Cambridge Street that Willie took to banging his speed. He walked in drunk to find a local sitting in the kitchen with a set of needles cooking up. When he offered to share, Willie plopped down and set about his gear. But he was so drunk that he hardly felt the shot go in. For the next few hours he wandered aimlessly around the house in a paralytic trance. The feeling vaguely reminded him of being a headless chicken. But he liked it regardless. "It was so dangerous, but I kinda liked it," Will smiled. "I liked that dangerous thing you know. It was a nice feeling doing something bad. So that lasted for about six months, till I lost my job in Birmingham and nearly my mind, you know. And then I came back to Rugby and moved into a house of ill repute. I went on the dole. I always had my guitar. It was the only fucking constant thing I carried around with me."

After months of staggered rehearsals, which had produced a trademark sound but had done relatively little to expand The Spacemen's songbook, the band secured their first gig at a house on Watts Lane in Hillmorton. The host's name was Turkey, and the gathering was advertised as Turkey's Wild Party. The day of the gathering, Sonic, Jason, Bassman and Tim met up at a friend's house, skinned up properly, and took to listening to *Raw Power* repeatedly for hours to stoke their fires. Sonic kept waving around a giant wooden knife and fork, although no one quite knew what it symbolised.

When they drove up to the house that evening, they were shocked at the drunken maelstrom awaiting them. There were all manner of people spread out on the front garden, yelling and screaming. A couple was fucking in the bushes. Nearby neighbours were threatening to call the police. A keg of beer the band had brought along as a gift vanished immediately. When the band attempted to take the "stage" they discovered it was actually a small glassed-in conservatory, which made them feel more like a caged exhibit than a rock-band. The space was so small that it barely housed the four musicians plus the gear. As it happened, the band didn't have to suffer very long. The gig was cut short.

> BASSMAN: "I was kneeling down with my ear to the bass amp trying to play 'I Wanna Be Your Dog'. Then I saw a dark blue trouser leg, and looking up I saw it was a policeman. As I carried on playing, I was watching his lips. Finally I sussed he was saying, 'Turn it off!' The police did us a favour turning up, because I don't think our repertoire went beyond three or four songs."

Although the "gig" ended in shambles, Sonic took advantage of the bust's free publicity and pasted posters all around the town centre, securing another gig at a biker's bar called The Exchange. The band drummed up a little pre-performance buzz, getting a large crowd of friends, including Jason's elder brother and his new-wave crowd, to attend. But from the beginning the show went poorly: Sonic and Jason were wracked on downers, leaving them shaken and sorely out of tune. The crowd dispersed before the shambling band even finished. When they attempted to manoeuvre through a long version of 'TV Eye', it all fell apart. In disgust, Bassman ripped the word "SPACEMEN" off his bass, but Jason was thrilled at the controversy. In a drunken frenzy, Jason yelled over to Bassman, "We're gonna be big. The audience walked out on Alice Cooper's first gig too!" After the show, a number of well-wishers approached Sonic and sneered, "I've never been so insulted in my entire life."

After much cajoling, the band somehow convinced the bar's owner to give them another chance, and a few nights later they returned for a per-formance to a much smaller crowd. A couple of locals and a few musi-cians and friends tripping on acid shuffled below the stage. A synth player called John Ritchie sat behind the band playing strange noises and effects as they launched into a 20-minute rendition of 'TV Eye'. The small crowd loved it. Sonic worked howling layers of feedback from his ampli-fier down the neck of the guitar and to the buzzing pick-ups. The bar vibrated with radiophonic plasma as Jason sneered Iggy's lyrics over the top. It was The Spacemen's first success.

But as quickly as moderate success slanted upward, changes threatened to dissolve the band before it properly got off the ground. By the follow-ing autumn, Jason had finished his courses at Rugby Art College and decided to attend another school in Maidstone, which would leave him absent from Rugby – and thus Spacemen – for most of the week. "When we had first started doing Spacemen, I didn't even know if Jason wanted to take it seriously," Bassman explained. "Jason went to Art College, and I didn't know if that was the last we'd see of him or not." Fed up with college, Sonic left after his courses and began working for a local estate agent called Cartwright, Holt, and Sons, as part of a government-sponsored apprenticeship, where he earned a paltry £25 a week. Bassman quit his factory job at the GEC and signed on the dole, moving out of his mother's home and into a Brownsover council house with another local artist and a schoolmate of Tim's, Natty Brooker.

With Jason absent, Bassman became unhappy with what he saw as Sonic's assertive personality. But Sonic instantly dismissed Bassman's intentions to "democratise" The Spacemen. The idea of composing a song "by vote" didn't appeal to the domineering guitarist. He knew that the band belonged solely to himself and Jason with everyone else merely hugging the cusp. Sonic complained, "Pete Bain used to think I was full of shit and had too much say in everything. That it was taking the piss that I just wanted to play one or two notes. That it was moronic, or it would be better if we did more musical stuff, which was always what me and Jason were against."

When Gavin mentioned his plan to form another band, The Push, to Bassman and Tim, they both saw an opportunity to jump ship from Sonic's fledgling group. Sonic was less than pleased at their defection, but even he admitted that Jason's life appeared to centre on his time at Maidstone. By the time Bassman and Tim walked away from Sonic, The Spacemen found its replacement drummer in Natty, who had listened to a number of early rehearsal tapes at the Brownsover house and agreed to stand in for Tim.

Natty came from the nearby town of Daventry and was, to all who witnessed his antics in the early days, a crazed, almost possessed character. "For me Spacemen 3 began with Natty, even though the band existed before," Bassman recalled. "Natty was just the guru. He was like Salvador Dali. I mean Natty was kind of what Ringo Starr was to The Beatles. Can you imagine The Beatles without Ringo Starr? Natty is and always will be a true artist. He was very much a free spirit, and a person who can only create." Natty's tastes in literature and music erred toward the obscure, which made him instantly akin to those collectors around him. His affections for Delta blues, soul, and the screwball antics of Captain Beefheart gave him an almost curatorial status among his friends. Much of his musical knowledge he passed on to Bassman, Sonic, and Jason. "[Natty] used to tape this radio show that played a lot of roots and blues music," added Jason. "[He] introduced me to John Lee Hooker, jazz, and very early, pre-Stax, Staple Singers." Though he wasn't a musician, such a problem didn't appear to separate his abilities from anyone else's.

He'd borrow a drum kit from someone and thud away with a tribal, Angus MacLise-like beat that fulfilled what Sonic and Jason were looking for.

Rehearsals continued sporadically until, to everyone's surprise, Jason reappeared regularly on weekends. Sonic's week was a tiresome preview of straight life in the West Midlands. He'd arrive early in the morning dressed in suit and tie, and spend his entire working day lurking around the offices of Cartwright, Holt performing residual tasks. He discovered his only escape was his car, and he'd volunteer for any assignments out of the office: showing houses to clients and/or shuttling paperwork back-and-forth from branch offices. When he found that he was making more money from mileage expenses than from his weekly dole-sized wage, Sonic convinced friends to call the office regularly as potential customers, at which point he'd agree to meet said "customers" and actually spend the afternoon cavorting with his chums. After doctoring the mileage on his petrol bills, he'd make two or three days' wages for skiving off.

Dishonest or not, it was all part of the strange system of government-sponsored programmes that ran rampant throughout the UK in the early Eighties. Unemployment soared astronomically in the early years of Thatcher's reign, and although much of it was a result of the neutered Labour Party policies that preceded them, her Conservative government allowed the figures to mushroom before striving to improve them. The policies would only change during ensuing years, when the Government-instigated sweep toward privatisation would leave many of the old programmes redundant and send unionised workers screaming for Thatcher's head on a plate. Until then, myriad programmes proliferated, with local councils attempting to regulate money and proceedings.

The Youth Projects (YP) building in Rugby, which ran a print works and provided odd jobs and low wages for unemployed locals, was a part of this unregulated system. The local government agreed to its establishment after a mass of unemployed workers squatted in a building in the centre of town, demanding money and jobs, and as a result YP set up a government-subsidised printing company. "It was a good way to reduce the dole queue," remembered Will. It was almost inevitable that it became a haven for shifty and shady characters that floated between the odd bit of work and the dole office. After finishing up his term at Maidstone, Jason took a part-time position at YP, working at the printing station, where he and Sonic used materials and machines for advertisements, posters and handbills, all designed to jump-start the band once again.

The Push had taken advantage of their unfettered time by continuing to rehearse and securing a few early gigs in nearby Northampton at The

Black Lion pub, another biker hang-out which hosted local up-and-comers and weekly brawls. The three-piece also brought in lead guitarist and singer Mick Hurdley (because they liked his shoes, according to Gavin), who lasted about six months before his crimped, gothic flair and onstage antics infuriated everyone. After sacking him, they resumed their original fuzzy-garage guitar/bass/drums style, recording a short four-song demo in Coventry. The band's primitive garage-punk thump drew in local beer swilling yobs and middle-class straights by the fistful, easily exceeding The Spacemen in popularity. "The fact that The Push became a popular band on the local circuit rubbed salt into Pete's wounds," Bassman claimed. "He never accepted The Push and would rubbish us at any opportunity, our demo, our gigs, continually dismissing us as a dodgy band.

"Despite The Push being a thorn in his side, I still saw quite a bit of Pete," he continued. "He was still living with his parents, so he always needed a place to enjoy his high. Our place was just another house to crash out in." Sonic's honeymoon with heroin had graduated into heady cocktails of junk rotated with a mixture of banging amphetamine and swallowing acid, which he'd chase with a rainbow of prescription pills to mind-warping, virtually psychotomimetic effect. To his credit, he kept it relatively under control, scoring infrequently and using without tipping his family off despite living at home. However, when Sonic's parents did learn of his exploits – his mother came across a cache of needles he'd stowed in his room – they demanded he check into Saint Andrew's hospital, a Northamptonshire clinic for addiction. Sonic referred to it as a "Looney bin" – its corridors were filled with addicts and drug-induced schizophrenics – and rightly so, as getting off heroin was the furthest thing from his mind. He agreed to attend to appease his family, checking himself into the voluntary three-week drug programme.

Sonic found that he hated the clinic as soon as he heard the doctor's antiquated "help-me-help-you" spiel and suffered the first slight pangs of heroin withdrawal. Between group discussions and therapy, the lanky teenager roamed the hospital grounds with a motley crew of speed freaks and psychotics, bumming joints that had been smuggled in. During one required writing session, he penned an essay describing his attraction to drugs along with the straight world's perceptions of users (later to take song form via Jason in 'Walkin' With Jesus'), predictably confusing the doctors. Sonic noted apologetically, "I got into trouble when I found that mushrooms grew in massive amounts in the hospital grounds and inadvertently set a fried speed freak back a few weeks. I regret that. I never liked to turn people onto drugs who weren't suited or were addictive." Sonic quickly realised that the quickest way out of the hospital was to smile, nod, and say all the right things. For his reward, he'd receive an occasional dosage of Librium and sinsemellia. On his release, Sonic assured the counsellors and doctors he was finished with heroin. Nothing was further from the truth.

By the early months of 1984, Spacemen gigs were still a rarity, encompassing a few local performances in the backrooms of pubs, where guzzling patrons would complain of the racket and young punters would mill around as an excuse to get high. Set-lists at the time usually comprised a variety of Velvets, Stooges and electric-blues covers, as well as a few rough originals with a decidedly rockabilly rhythm, including '2.35', 'Things'll Never Be The Same', and the closing monster 'OD Catastrophe'. Jason took on all the vocal duties, as well as lead guitar, while Sonic provided drones, feedback, and occasional licks. The three-piece played at the Saracen's Head Pub, across from Rugby School, at a backroom event called The Experiment, but by its second week, the club was closed and The Spacemen were once again gig-less. On rare occasions, the band ventured out towards the local network of bars, crypts, and house parties, including trips to Coventry and a debut at The Black Lion in Northampton that ended with typical confusion.

Undaunted, Jason, Sonic and Natty continued composing catchy, multicoloured posters with which they'd litter the walls of Rugby and Northampton. Tasks were allotted between the three members, and the rush of DIY activity verged on the modest sufficiency of a small business. Much of the band's PR expediency came when Sonic took a job at his father's company following the end of his sponsored time with Cartwright, Holt & Sons. His fortuitous employment gave him much free time, which he spent in the building's printing room, drafting and designing posters and advertisements for the band. He and Jason worked for hours and hours on end, creating panchromatic "Pop Art" and trippy Sixties designs which Jason would print up at YP. Jason would pick the lock on his mother's telephone after she left for work, and both boys spent the day making massive call-outs to well-known regional promoters, scrapping for any support gig they could muster. Finding a constant setting for rehearsals, scheduling shows, buying new gear and fly-postering, both guitarists tackled these obstacles with almost militant determination.

It was during one poster-campaign that Natty composed a particularly catchy slogan – "ARE YOUR DREAMS AT NIGHT 3 SIZES TOO BIG?" – which stuck with everyone. Because there were three members and it was the third line-up, Sonic and Jason agreed to amend their name to Spacemen 3, hoping that this would portend a new phase for the struggling band. Other early advertising endeavours included the Velvets-inspired "SEARCHING FOR YOUR MAINLINE" caption with matching syringe-logo and a "VELVETS/STOOGES/STONES" genealogy. If the band was banking on drumming up local support, what they got from the townsfolk was a mixture of cluelessness and hostility. Fly-posters would be torn off right and left. And few supporters would show on gig night.

> JASON: "We made a poster for one show that read: 'Velvets? Stooges? Stones?' We thought if we put those references on it, someone would be walking around and say: 'Yeah, I've got to have me a bit of that tonight.' One person turned up. We cleared halls. It never got to this mythical rewrite where we suddenly took off."

> SONIC: "The only person that came was my uncle. The local environment for gigging, I mean there was no scene at all. We used to get about 10 people at our gigs and we knew all of them."

> WILL CARRUTHERS: "I'd turn up at the pub for these gigs. The Spacemen were interesting, but it was very unformed. They just suffered from not having their shit together."

Spacemen 3 had done fewer than 10 gigs when the three band mates walked into Sheriff Sound Studio to record their very first set of demos. From their earliest rehearsals, someone had always plunked down a tape deck and chronicled all their jams, songs and wayward noises. After hours and hours of playback, often at extremely high volume, and with the aid of psychedelic chemicals, Jason and Sonic had collected a prospective list of songs which they took with them to record.

Dave Sheriff's Rugby studio was actually just another terraced-house that sloped down to the train station along Railway Terrace. The front den of the home had been converted into a makeshift control room, the mikes and wiring descending into the cellar where the recording area was set up. The band spent the bulk of the first day recording in the basement, where the ceiling was so low that Sonic found it difficult to manoeuvre his six-foot-two-inch frame, and resorted to crouching or sitting through the session.

They recorded their earliest version of 'Things'll Never Be The Same', Jason's first original composition, in a decidedly Cramps/blues style, with Sonic playing a frazzled, overdriven slide-guitar *à la* Jeffrey Lee Pierce against Jason's simple blues licks and reverbed voice. The faint sizzle of Natty's cymbals added an electric current from beneath the crunch of guitar, and the deliberate swell of rhythmic overdubs displayed The Spacemen's protean attempts at layering contra-distinct textures despite the derivative sounds. Jason took all of the lead duties, jumping between

blues scales and power chords on his vocal cues, adding a musical verisimilitude to the drone-based din. Sonic used a unique series of
power-chords based solely on the top three strings of his guitar. Often, he
tuned each string in sympathy to the others, and the thick strum of sound
would drone away on a single note. "Jason was always the one doing the
more musical side of it," Sonic said. "Jason was capable of doing that. He
was one of those guitarists that could cover both ends. And Jason was a
very good guitarist, considering we only ever had two guitars in the
band, and I was always doing the sound-based textural stuff."

They followed with a stab at Jason's '2.35', an ode to angel-headed
hipsters out to cop in the 'Waiting For My Man' vein. Sonic spun out a
catchy riff with a deep, echoey skeleton guitar over a trad blues rhythm
while Jason crooned of his withdrawal pangs. The track suffered a little
from the guitars occasionally falling out of time with one another, as if in
their youthful exuberance (and ignorance) neither could quite feel the
other out. But the song's bubbling, ionic textures more than compensated for its primitivism, as if the hollow thuds of black space and the swirl
of electric-blue guitar were spinning from the charcoal depths of an old
78-rpm.

Jason also debuted a primitive rendition of 'Walkin' With Jesus'. He'd
worked out the track's earliest choruses by transposing some of Sonic's
errant writings about heroin. It was a striking incarnation of a Spacemen
3 standard, if for no other reason than for its many future transformations.
Like every song of this first demo, the rhythm was almost entirely concentrated on the beat of the drum, with little room to swagger. "A lot of
early Spacemen stuff was like The Cramps meets The Stooges,"
confirmed Jason. He brought out his harmonica to add a raving solo
while Sonic, who thundered away with reverbed slide-guitar to add a
vibrating psychobilly chunkiness, agreed, "We had some of these songs
early on which were fairly poor Cramps imitations: 'Poison Ivy' – guitar
and all, except it didn't compare with The Cramps by a long way." More
importantly, with references to Christ, smack, death, and the overarching
theme of a sinister piety, 'Walkin' With Jesus' presented the first example
in The Spacemen (and specifically Jason's) oeuvre of the heroin/mystic
fusion. The theme recurred in a cover/version of Dylan's traditional
'Fixin' To Die' (later to re-emerge as Jason's original 'Come Down
Easy'), with tongue-in-cheek emphasis on the title's gear-injected double
entendre. Jason's rendition recreated a gospel-style call-and-response
rave-up, his echo-chamber-ed vocals supplicating, "I'm fixin' to die
Lord, I'm fixin' to die!", while Sonic and Natty's background harmonies
sneered with a juvenile punk whine.

'OD Catastrophe' (named 'TV Catastrophe' on the demo) was less a rock'n'roll song than a ballistic soundscape; over seven-minutes of drones, feedback, pulsing drums, and overdriven guitar in E. With the slow, lumbering climb of electricity, Sonic's first experiment in guitar ambience roared with equal parts MC5 and WW2. As Jason thrashed away to a near static rhythm (imagine the dead calm inside the hurricane's eye) and Natty pounded a continuous Mo Tucker beat, Sonic overdubbed a latticed web of screeching feedback from amp to neck. Guitars buzzed and descended with the unpredictable timing of a kamikaze freak-out, crashing into a shambling decay before rising again. Sheriff's engineer Graham Walker, who worked the tiny mixing board, recalled, "They knew exactly what they wanted sound-wise, to the extent of Jason setting up a rough old vocal PA to get just the right distortion on his vocals. The end result, as I remember it, after about an 18-hour session in airtight rooms with a lot of smoking seemed to be a really dark, loose, swampy sort of blues."

After spending a second day in the den playing back the demos, and adding the occasional guitar and feedback overdubs, they took the finished product and had it copied onto a few hundred cassettes. To personalise the tape, the band added a 10-page booklet, where Jason wrote out the lyrics, Sonic designed the title and drawings (including the infamous syringe logo) and Natty included a poster graphic. The first product of Spacemen 3's religiosity, the title, *For All The Fucked Up Children Of This World We Give You Spacemen 3*, summed up in an explicit phrase the seeming contradictions of punk-cosmonauts tuned into a messianic blues.

Jason and Sonic dropped the blue-boxed cassettes off at Convergence Records, where Simon Franklin agreed to sell them and help put the word out. They posted innumerable copies to different record companies across Britain and The States just for kicks but received no response. Grand dreams of signing to Chris Stein's New York-based Animal label alongside Lux Interior and Jeffrey Lee Pierce went unfulfilled. But back on Planet Rugby, the strength of the demo and the word of mouth it generated allowed the band to secure a few spots at the unseemly and dank biker bar The Black Lion in Northampton, which they played regularly throughout 1984 and '85. *For All The Fucked Up Children* also provided Spacemen 3 with its first printed review, penned at the conclusion of the year by local fanzine writer Gary Boldie. After his first encounter with the band's live set, he effused:

SPACEMEN 3 are three Rugby musicians. The line-up consists of drums, two guitars and a vocalist. They are a band without a bass.
Extensive fly-postering ensured that the members of the Rugby

non-scene (Rugby is not renowned for its fashionable explosions of rebellious youth) were all there. I guess every Flat-top, Bunnyman or Banshee in the area made it along.

Well, how do you describe a music the likes of which has never been in Rugby before? How about Fuzz Guitar Neo-Blues, or Feedback Soul Jazz, or a blend of old-style guitar blues, mixed with the spiky sound of fuzzed electric guitars, and vocals of today's confused mentality?

However exciting those descriptions sound it would be unfair and incorrect to suggest that Spacemen 3 are the biggest threat to a bored music biz since The Sex Pistols. They most definitely need time. The songs, for the most part, are stunningly similar. They need more energy to make them VITAL. The last song was different. A screaming maelstrom (is that the right word?) of feedback guitar, ranting vocals and tribal drumming.

Spacemen 3 are incongruous. They don't look like spacemen. They don't look like Hawkwind (as we had feared they would). At times they sound like a fuzzy B. B. KING. At times, like an early Killing Joke (before they became professionals!).

Seeing a bassless band is a shock. Seeing a bassless band in Rugby is a bigger one.

Maybe Rugby is improving its image as a home of new, inventive music.

It was also at The Black Lion that Pat Fish and his band The Jazz Butcher took their occasional constitutionals for nights of hellraising around Northampton. Though The Jazz Butcher had their start as yet another bucolic post-punk band, they had, by '85, made a handful of solid LPs infused with a Robyn Hitchcock/Morrissey English wit and whimsy, and made some impression on the European market with a tour in Holland and Germany. As their roots were in the Northamptonshire area, The Jazz Butcher acquired David J. with the collapse of Bauhaus, releasing *Sex and Travel* before J.'s departure to form Love and Rockets. By the middle of the year, The Jazz Butcher migrated south to London, where through the aid of Dave Barker's Glass Records, they insinuated themselves into the rapidly expanding Creation scene, and the growing Sixties revival that began to manifest itself more apparently in Islington.

Pat Fish popped back to Northampton sporadically, and would invariably end up at The Black Lion where he'd check out the shambling/garage groups passing through. It was at one of these spontaneous auditions that he had come across the wily antics of Rugby's own retro-punkers The Push shortly before they broke up. Pat liked them, though he was more taken with their kitschy accoutrements and less with their sound.

Fish recalled, "The Push had a real 1964 thing happening. It was like they somehow managed to get the sorta mis-stylings of the British groups of the early Sixties, and translated them into something that was enjoyable to listen to and to look at. I was particularly impressed with Pete Bain because he had a big spangly blue bass, which looked ridiculous. It looked like it ought to be part of a Fifties gas station in America, and he was playing this thing and chewing gum at the same time. And they were just thumping away like The Dave Clark Five, just going 'BABY BABY BABY BABY BABY!'" Fish was also thoroughly bemused with front-man Gavin Wissen's strange, almost satanic stage presence, his howling voice recalled something country-gothic and superannuated. "But Gavin's a great presence on the front and all together they were just very engaging. That night I was well taken with it," he added. Pat couldn't help thinking Wissen's sharp, horned appearance was reminiscent of Bryan Gregory's horrifying addition to The Cramps.

After the show, Pat sat down to have a beer with some locals who ran a fanzine out of Rugby, and he rapped about The Push's set. The seated party assured him of another band from Rugby that were making waves and blowing minds front, left, and centre aisle. According to these piss-heads, Spacemen 3 was like nothing else. Within days, Fish had a front row seat to get his mind blown.

> PAT FISH: "They were extraordinary. They looked kinda intimidating too, 'cause Pete and Jase both were really young at that point. And they were still quite well cared for and very good-looking. So they looked like the last people on earth to be making this noise. They got onstage and sat down and you're thinking 'What's this gonna be? It's gonna be like Vini Reilly or something.' Ya know, these clean young men sitting down. And there was certainly something of the Mo Tucker about Natty. Maybe even more of the Angus MacLise really. And then it began and it was just like, alright . . . they're warming up: 'Oh Christ! Fucking hell!' It was all a bit like that. It kinda dawned on me that it was supposed to be like that."

Through a local Jazz Butcher fan in Rugby, Pat Fish got word to The Push of his interest in taking them on as a support act. An opening slot at London's Rock Garden was a huge step for The Push, who'd advanced quickly from demo sessions to gigs in Warwick and Leicester, but had not performed outside of the immediate West Midlands region. The promise of a London debut held lots of potential for a backwater garage-punk three-piece. In an effort to improve their sound, Tim and Bassman demanded that Gavin throw out his old guitar. Gavin refused. He wanted no part of these antics. "It was just the cheapest guitar I could find, and I just wanted to have a cheap out of tune guitar," Gavin said. Tim and Bassman responded by collapsing into petty whingeing just weeks before the proposed gig. "And I had a bit of a tantrum, told them I wasn't playing in the band any more or whatever. Just being completely childish about it," Gavin continued. Gavin walked away from The Push and the band folded. "It could have been the start of something good for the band," Bassman added scathingly. "At least it would have been our first London gig. I didn't like Gavin for the way he dropped it all with no explanation. I liked him even less when I found out that he had formed another band in our place."

Adding an element of the ridiculous to The Push's silly disintegration, by the time Pat Fish received word that the Rugby band was no more, he hardly gave a toss. *In a battle of the local Rugby bands, there was one clear victor.* After Spacemen 3 had come and gone from The Black Lion, Fish could barely remember why he'd even liked The Push, much less why he'd wanted them in London. As Fish fondly recalled, "I had all these people saying to me that this group out of Rugby, The Spacemen, were just so very different. And I just realised what they said was true: they were like nothing else."

CHAPTER THREE

Taking Drugs To Make Music To Take Drugs To

SUMMER 1985–1986

PRINTED VERBATIM FROM "EAR TO THE GROUND"
FANZINE 3/8/85

By Sean Cook

SPACEMEN 3/ IN THE OUTBRACK – THE BLACK LION,
NORTHAMPTON 3/8/85

In the outbrick came on, late, to obviously promted shrieks and
screams. their prtentious and immaculate set seemed to suggest that
they were playing for their egos rather than for their own enjoyment.
Nevertheless their "crowds of fans" liked them.

The "rival" band Spacemen 3, began with an excellent new version
of '2.35' and continued oblivious to the dissatisfaction of the in the
outbwack worshippers.

The main band played on with a version of The Stooges' "Little
Doll", in which their raw power blew away any previous performances. The set was cut short by in the oiwtuack's inconsiderate
encore, but the last song, "Somewhere In Our Hearts Things Won't
Be The Same", was brilliant and was improved by Peter Kember's
playing. After the SPACEMEN went off having shown how really
good they are especially live.

By the summer of 1985, Spacemen 3's recurring headlines at The Black
Lion pub had expanded the band's followers from a small crew of friends
and users to other curious musicians. Mark Refoy was a young guitarist
from Northamptonshire with an affection for pop melody and an eye
(and ear) toward the now outdated phenomenon of new wave. Refoy
had played in a number of local musical groups before releasing a single
called 'Lady Left This' through Glass Records with a band called The

61

Tempest in 1983. By the midpoint of the decade, he had joined another area punk/goth/sci-fi outfit called The Telltale Hearts and played a few pub gigs along the treacherous Northamptonshire/Coventry circuit. Refoy was well acquainted with Pat Fish from his previous busking and gigging days throughout the catchment, and he often popped into The Black Lion for a pint before sussing out the other struggling live acts.

It was in August when a mate of Mark's, having seen The Spacemen perform the previous month, urged him to have a look at the young Rugby band on their return. "I remember having a drink coming to my lips, and, then the first chord they hit, I stopped, and I just looked around and thought that this was something else," Refoy reported. "It was just that instant." Mark spied the three musicians up on the makeshift dais: Natty hunched over his small drum kit, while Sonic slouched on a stool, thrashing at his guitar, and Jason stood, barely visible, behind the PA stack. "It was like they weren't bothered about saying, 'Look at us! We look like a band.' They weren't saying that, but, by being like that, they drew more attention to themselves," Mark said. And, in fact, both Sonic and Jason were quite self-conscious of their anti-stage posturing. As Sonic commented in a Northampton paper, "We don't prance about the stage. We just sit down and get right into it. No posing. No smiling at girlfriends. No waving to parents. Sitting is so much more relaxing. I can't play standing up especially as some songs are 15 minutes long. We'd have to stop to shake our hands about to get the blood circulating again." In the same article, Jason stated, "We're a very boring band to watch."

Sonic and Jason lumbered through heavily distorted versions of '2.35', John Lee Hooker's 'It's Alright', 'Things'll Never Be The Same', and a prolix 'OD Catastrophe'. Each song ended with a thick sonic rapture, before both guitarists would turn away and begin retuning for the next. These gaps proved powerful in their sheer effrontery to a drunken audience. "There were lots of people there that hated it," Mark continued. "The band was drawing the barriers: it was literally a 5-minute gap, sometimes 10-minute gap between songs, just tuning up or replacing strings. They were so compelling to watch. They were like magicians. It was all shrouded in mystery." The truth, however, was far from magical. Sonic's cheap electric guitar constantly buzzed in and out of tune with obstinate glee, as did Jason's weird Japanese axe. In addition, the two guitarists had experimented with several strange alternative tunings that they'd often have to readjust between each song in order to play drones in perfect harmony.

"But even when they started it wasn't a shambolic start to each song," Mark added. "They seemed to have this complete disregard, as if the audience wasn't there. They had the intensity of Buddhist monks, which in the hands of somebody else would have looked really pretentious, but they were for real." Mark noticed Pat Fish, leaning against the stage, gazing up at The Spacemen with a twinkle in his eyes. By night's conclusion, Pat was completely sucked into the sound. "They were back within a few weeks and so was I," he recalled. "And somewhere halfway through that, I just fucking got it." Pat and Mark would religiously attend Black Lion gigs for the remaining months of '85.

> PAT FISH: I'd talk to Pete and Jason initially and I'd try to position where they were at. And I made all the mistakes. I'd say, "Is this the Roky [Erickson] thing?" Or I'd say, "Is this that Velvet Underground thing or The Mary Chain thing?" And they said they liked The Velvet Underground but weren't trying to be like them. It had nothing to do with that. They were very keen, even at that stage, to be plugged into a line that went back to fucking Leadbelly or Howlin' Wolf!

> MARK REFOY: The blues thing really came out and it was like, "Blues? No, no they can't play the blues. They just play two strings, not even any chords." But a lot of blues is just as simple as The Spacemen. I also remember Pete saying Buddy Holly was one of his favourite artists, and one of his favourite songs was Blondie's 'Heart Of Glass'. So he had a real sort of pop head on as well. Pete just thought that simplicity was the essence of everything.

Bassman and Tim Morris once again found themselves shopping around for groups to play in, while Gavin had begun fronting a psychedelic group The Cogs of Tyme (originally called The High Spirits), a more tripped-out, acid-inspired garage band with Gavin's brother Darren on guitar, a musician called Antony Rogers on bass, and Gavin on keyboards. More frat than the darker psychedelia of The Spacemen, The Cogs of Tyme performed old garage favourites like 'Louie, Louie' and 'Gloria' to blitzed Townies who liked grooving to the edgy but conventional sound.

Sonic still spent many late nights down at the Wissen brothers' flat, dropping acid with Gavin and Darren while discussing the future to the reverberating wall of psychedelic records. Failing to make a go at any area clubs, Sonic and Gavin decided to start up their own weekly gigs at the local Blitz Pub. Sonic organised the event, desperate to make something more happen for The Spacemen, while recognising The Cogs' potential to draw larger crowds. The event was put on in the backroom of the two-storey Blitz pub on Gas Street just off the town centre. Christened The Reverberation Club, The Cogs and Spacemen 3 appeared regularly on Thursday nights in the drab wood-panelled room to a bantam crowd of friends, stoners and weirdoes. The cover charge was one pound. "The Reverberation Club started off being just like a disco," said Gavin. "We'd just take turns playing records, and it would be like . . . it was just somewhere for us to go and get stoned and listen to music really loud." Chairs were dragged in from the pub area and strewn throughout the floor, where the small group of stoners lounged and blissed out to the loud music. Nobody danced. It was much too difficult after swallowing several tabs of acid, a mouthful of downers, and numerous bottles of beer. "Everybody was completely off their tits," Gavin admitted.

With proceeds from the club coming in at a steady trickle, Sonic gathered what money he could and purchased several rigs of obsolescent optokinetic light wheels and disco balls. More than 10 years out of fashion, the strange motorised light-shows, complete with spinning multicoloured effects and cool liquid patterns, were relics of the "dinosaur rock" and disco eras, long since forgotten. But when the candy-coloured bricolage of cogs and sprockets came to life at The Blitz, the vinegary room swirled with lush panochrome – a sensorial overload that proved the perfect setting for tripping out.

The Cogs of Tyme usually opened for The Spacemen, before alternating positions to allow for other local acts. Quite often, the gigs concluded in drug-induced shambles, precipitated by collective noise freak-outs. "At first, it was pretty much just a good time," insisted Jason. "We had this one event we called 'The Mushroom Party', where we filled the room with dry ice and did the free-form thing, let everyone from surrounding towns come, bring their own instruments and play random things." It was evident, from the very beginning, that a wide gulf separated The Cogs and The Spacemen, both in terms of their playing styles and the degree of approbation they received from onlookers. "I mean The Cogs of Tyme were primitive," laughed Gavin, "but The Spacemen took it down to a whole other level – an 'Ugh-Ugh' level – where Pete Kember just played the whole set on one chord. How fucking cheap can you get?! But, then again, how fucking brilliant can you get?!" The Cogs typically drew a much larger crowd (relatively speaking: there was never more than 30 or 40 punters at one time) with their catchy psychedelic boogie, while Spacemen 3 continuously provoked antipathy or apathy from the townsfolk and teenagers who risked attending their sets.

GAVIN WISSEN: The Spacemen would go on and people would say, "They're fucking awful! They're fucking awful! How terrible! What a racket!" We were much more popular because we were just stupid and people could actually get up and dance to us. With The Spacemen, maybe a few people danced completely off their tits. But most people just stood there going, "Oh what a horrible noise!" And, "Look they're sitting down! Why do they sit down?!"

Worst of all were the brawny yobs that showed at The Blitz. Football fans covered in gold chains and leather, they'd often turn up pissed to the gills on cheap lager, heckling and threatening everyone onstage. One evening, the atmosphere turned particularly ugly when a gang hurled empty beer mugs at the band during a lengthy 'OD Catastrophe' encore. Following the show, the yobs skulked about outside The Blitz and jumped Jason, Bassman, Gavin and Darren. Sonic drove his car around in time to catch Bassman pounding one of them with the bass drum. "Oh yeah, Pete Bain used to be a right psycho," Sonic laughed. "He started attacking them all. Gavin and Darren just kept out of it all somehow, and Jason apparently curled up in a ball. But Pete Bain went absolutely mad, and threw one of them through a plate-glass window. He hit another guy with a drum, and, then as the police came, he was chasing one of them up the street."

Most of the returning patrons to The Reverberation Club were kids who had "turned on" digging the light-trip of The Cogs and the deep-hypnosis of The Spacemen. Consequently, many of the same groups appeared regularly at The Blitz, either tripping, speeding, or nodding out against the kitschy light shows and frazzled amps. Because the pub owner looked the other way on these nights, The Blitz became a haven for teenagers craving for chemical escape, bringing camps of differing users and abusers together. "The landlord was actually really quite cool," Gavin laughed. "He just said, 'I don't care what you're doing in there as long as you're getting people in and I'm getting paid.' Of course, we weren't getting that many people in."

One of the few gangs regularly appearing at The Blitz included Will and the other speed freaks from Cambridge Street. They'd come in buzzing on amphetamine and crowd into a corner of the room, laughing and gesticulating, their eyes nearly bugging out of their heads. The factions drew lines almost immediately: the speed freaks steered clear of the acid-heads and smack users, who'd disparage them at every opportunity and vice versa. "There was a little bit of weird antipathy between the two drug camps, kind of a different philosophy, but we didn't give a fuck about that," Will chuckled. "We'd be sitting over there with the speed freaks, but there'd only be like five people in the whole fucking place anyway. So it'd be kinda unavoidable that at some point you'd have to cross over."

Standing out among the slim crowd of townies at The Blitz was Kate Radley, a ravishing, chestnut-haired teenager who grew up near Rugby in a middle-class family of police officers. Kate had played clarinet as a child and attended Rugby High School, the sister-school to Lawrence Sheriff. "It was an all-girls' grammar school miles away from town," recalled fellow student Vinita Joshi. "It took two buses to get there. I hated it because it was so competitive and bitchy." After classes were over, Vinita often popped down to The Blitz on Thursday evenings. "Rugby was such a dull and boring place to grow up in," she continued. "There was no cinema, absolutely nothing to do. I saw The Spacemen at The Blitz many times. I just remember lots of lights and a really old woman collecting empty glasses. I'd lie to my parents about studying at a friend's house and go to gigs." Kate often turned up with Vinita at Reverberation nights and at rehearsals. Jason had already befriended Kate's elder sister, but soon enough his wandering eye and libido fastened onto Kate. "Jason was keen on Kate," said Bassman. "Back in the Indian Scalp days, Kate went out with a punk rocker type for a while. Then she dropped him for this guy Craig Wagstaff." Unfortunately, for Jason, Wagstaff was another local musician and friend to The Spacemen. Thus for the moment Kate Radley remained untouchable.

Evading the rustic legion of Rugby cops became a primary concern for most of the Reverberation crowd, as it had for any local users "graduating" from occasional hash runs to dabbling or peddling in Class A's; trading in opiates or amphetamines levied outlaw status in the increasingly dire political environs of The Midlands, and carried the risk of severe punishment. In an effort to support his own habit and make some extra on the side, Sonic took to trading small quantities of heroin and speed when the opportunity arose. He was not a dealer by any means, but, like most habitual users, sought to work the "middleman" angle between his supplier and un-networked buyers.

Sonic's gig piqued the interest of local authorities when a speed freak, busted for a large quantity of amphetamine sulphate, named the musician as his supplier. The cops cut a deal with their new informant to set Sonic up for dealing speed. It was the classic "hierarchy" strategy and the hope was it would reach to the top of the supply-line like a row of tumbling dominoes.

SONIC: This guy suddenly doubled his order. So I was making a lot of money out of it. It was quite a lot he was buying. I went and picked it up half a mile away and took it back to him and put the money in my pocket. Two days later he phoned to double the amount again – up to like 6 or 8 ounces – it was a lot of amphetamine sulphate. And I said sure, because I didn't know it was him who had been busted. So I said I'd come by with it later on.

A phalanx of unmarked police-cars converged on the drop-off spot, lying in wait, but Sonic failed to appear. In a fortuitous exchange with his supplier hours before the scheduled bust Sonic failed to acquire the quantity of sulphate for the deal. Within days, the police picked Sonic and Jason up on a pub run in the town centre. Booked on the 1/16 bag of hash Jason had in his pocket, they were taken to the police station, where Jason dozed off as the constable took in Sonic for interrogation.

SONIC: I wasn't at all interested. It was like a 30-quid fine or something for hash. But suddenly halfway through the interview they start talking about this large amount of amphetamine, which was a serious crime. And I said, "I don't know what you're talking about. Somebody's trying to set me up here. This is crazy." They said they knew everything about it. And I was shit scared. They said they had photos. I was like, "Oh Shit!" Then it occurred to me that I should see these photos, and it was all just a bluff.

JASON: During the first drug bust they put our names in the local paper. My folks weren't aware of what I was into. In the end, my neighbour told my mum, who hadn't seen the story, that I was in the local rag. She was a bit shocked when she found out why.

In November of 1985, Pat Fish and Mark Refoy drove over to Coventry to catch The Spacemen at Mercia Park Leisure Centre, where a scant audience of just 10 people stood enraptured. At the show's conclusion, Fish took Sonic aside and attempted to interview him for an article he was penning for *ZigZag*, the post hippy monthly by then on its last legs. Sonic and Jason were impressed with the potential publicity, and they also chuckled at Fish's witty charisma. He endeared himself to them immediately. Jason admitted, "We'd been slogging away for three years up until then. We thought no one liked us." The feeling was mutual. "You don't get many 20-year-olds in bands in little country towns who revered Sun Ra, and saw equal value in John Lee Hooker and Kraftwerk," laughed Fish. "Young men aren't normally so broad-minded to understand what it's really about." Fish pointed to the origins of their worldliness in the larger-than-life narcotic myths that surrounded the band even in its earliest days. "I said to Pete, 'What's going on in this town of yours?'" Pat recalled with a smile. "And he just totally deadpanned and said, 'There's a lot of drugs in Rugby . . .' And historically that would appear to be the case, wouldn't it? Taking drugs to make music to take drugs to. And to an extent, they probably got into drugs, because they figured that that's what rock'n'roll people do."

FROM *ZIGZAG*

By Pat Fish

SOONER OR CRATER

Here come your girlfriend's little brother's mates, littered with broken drum kits and telling you *exactly* what they think about EVERY-THING! Of course, you don't expect them to say what you'd hope they would, but they do, and to your (un)surprise they are **The Best Group In The World**. **Pete**, **Jason** and **Gnatty** [sic] (who is) are from Rugby. "There's a load of drugs in Rugby." **What about the riots at your concerts?** "We like to see people enjoying themselves." **I needn't tell you what's on my mind.**

"We hate The Jesus And Mary Chain. We're going to sort them out. They try to make their music sound bad. We try to make music that sounds good." In this they succeed effortlessly. Pete and Jason play very loud guitars, while Gnatty plays like Maureen Tucker, because that's probably the only way he knows. **How many Velvet Underground bootlegs do you own, Pete?** "None." **No?** "Well two actually."

Fancy! So why do you all look like you go on youth hostelling missions? "We do sometimes. Youth hostels are very free places. Great. You can do what you want." Okay.

Other leisure pursuits include the Reverberation Club, which they run with their friends the (*also excellent*) High Spirits, playing "Fifties, Sixties and Seventies punk" under the same very psychedelic lights that glood [sic] the seated Spacemen during their live shows. The club is regular, at The Blitz (*uh-huh?*) in Rugby every Thursday. Their shows, where in the club is effectively dragged into your local bar, are sadly much less frequent, and as yet confined to the not very illustrious Rugby–Coventry–Northampton circuit. Their music, resembling at times vintage Suicide, but with guitars replacing electronics, deserves a wider audience. As Pete says, "People out there want it. They'll love it."

He knows, you see? **But what of this curious electric sitar effect you play, Pete?** "It's called a saz. It's Turkish."
Are you neo–hippies? "No. Well, yes."

Jason and Sonic still spent much of their time together in bouts of communal drug-taking. They'd both hang out at Gavin's flat at the weekends, taking quantities of acid (Jason would still ingest small doses) and listening to LPs. Both were into speed quite heavily and would ingest large quantities of amphetamine before driving out to nearby concerts or spending late-evening hours jamming out songs. But if Jason's earliest experiences with psychedelics had revealed his schizoid-tinged personality, he ignored any of the symptoms. He continued using butane on a regular basis until one horrific trip with Sonic proved his undoing. It was shortly before the recording of The Spacemen's first album that the two sat stoned out sniffing another canister of lighter fluid when Jason wigged out and broke down.

> SONIC: Basically he tripped that the universe was a snake and the snake slowly grew and writhed until it started to encircle itself. As it did so, it ate its tail, until slowly it swallowed itself. He sat there frozen, mortified with terror and confusion. Then I turned to him and asked for the can of gas. At this, tears started to stream from his eyes and he broke down. I jumped up, tripped out on some other vibe, and said, "Shit Jase, what's up man?! What's up ?!" Then he proceeded to tell me the story, and that he was crying because he thought, "How nice of God to let Pete have the last word," which always cracked me up. I guess that's some indication of how close we were back then.

Jason's first experience of *horror vacui* left him mentally exhausted and badly shaken. He complained to others that he started hearing strange voices in his head. Although both Sonic and Jason agreed to stop taking butane, only Jason tapered off much of his heavier drug-use at the time. He realised his body and his mind could not withstand the psychotropic confusion that many of the spacier drugs brought with them. "I guess I was always the most drugged," deduced Sonic. "It became evident that Jason's psyche wasn't up to psychoactive drugs. Jason had his moments, particularly with speed though, and he did a lot of drugs before he got a little fried." After that Jason only smoked small amounts of hash and took the occasional bag of heroin and other downers. Instead, he started hitting the bottle.

As Jason supplemented his intake with more opiates and a dependency on spirits, Sonic introduced a number of different synthetic downers to his best mate. It was during late '85 that Jason, following Sonic's debauched excesses, experienced another potential catastrophe. In the midst of a late-night jam session Sonic offered him a shot of palfium, a pharmaceutical morphine-derivative, which he gladly injected. While the gritty serum pumped through their veins, Sonic whispered, "Oh, it feel so good . . . Oh it feel so fine . . ." against his partner's plucked guitar.

As the sound slowly died away, Sonic looked at Jason, who turned a shade of blue and began to pass out. At the sight of Jason's limp body crumpling onto the floor, Sonic leapt into action, grabbing and dragging his unconscious mate into the bathroom, where he dunked him into the tub and submerged his wilting frame in cold water. Jason's wan, "fishbelly" complexion warmed slowly, until his eyes popped open under the water's crystalline surface. Silent and soggy, the two boys sat huddled together on the bathroom floor. "I did what I could to revive him," Sonic exclaimed. "If you're playing with fire, you've gotta make sure to wear asbestos gloves." Ironically, it was on the same evening they penned 'Feel So Good'.

Meanwhile, Sonic's habits only increased, as he explored more and more uses of synthetic opiates and speed/downer concoctions that he could inject for the desired effect. Scoring heroin throughout Rugby had forged his relationships with a network of dealers and users, and expanded his knowledge of what to get and where to go. There were punk groups on the scene who were infested with heroin and sulphate. Sonic would often tag along with these groups in order to fix and buy odd pharmaceuticals. Owing to his earlier days as a punk running around Bilton and Brownsover, Bassman was also friendly with some of these punks. Now, however, he was disturbed by Sonic's dubious behaviour around these characters. Bassman had gotten burned before: after shooting up amphetamine he'd copped from one of the local punks, he contracted a rather nasty case of Hepatitis B. Having fallen severely ill and turning yellow, Bassman vowed not to involve himself again with the spike.

"The thing is we weren't addicts so there's no point in suggesting that we were junkies," Bassman said. "Sonic was an intravenous drug user whether or not he admits to it himself. The rest of us weren't, and if we ever did it was a huge mistake on all our parts. A huge mistake because none of us would probably be very comfortable with people knowing that we ever stuck needles in our arm. And if we ever did, that's tragic."

It was also in the late winter of '85 that Jason and Sonic decided to record another set of demos, including reworked material from the *For All The Fucked Up Children* . . . recordings and a new list of songs they had composed, rehearsed, and worked into their recent live sets. In a fairly modest period of time, The Spacemen had honed and reconfigured their work massively, jettisoning all of The Cramps' twang and Rockabilly rhythms. Jason was much more aware of their unconventional line-up, especially the band's absent bassist, who could ostensibly bring a much thicker,

70

more fleshed-out "colour" to The Spacemen's music. But Sonic wasn't completely buying this angle: he still adored the shimmering sound of the band's two-guitar blues and lobbied for the three-piece to continue.

Bassman remained band-less after The Push break-up and continued collecting his dole cheque and plucking his bass. To make ends meet, he'd occasionally sell dope around town. He and Natty still roomed together, although they'd recently relocated from the frigid climes of Brownsover to a run-down gaff in Hillmorton. Natty would fill him in with the current comings and goings of the band, including their recent convert in Fish and their plans for recording. It was after a Push gig at The Black Lion that Jason had congratulated Bassman with a phrase that stuck with him: "Jason said, 'You look like a Spaceman, you play like a Spaceman, you are a Spaceman,'" Bassman boasted.

After seeing another show at The Black Lion, Bassman resolved to manoeuvre his way back into the group. He knew Spacemen 3 was IT. They'd come a long way since his exit, while his own alternatives were now slim. To the consternation of Sonic, he and Jason spoke about it at length. In addition to the trance-inducing sound the band had developed with the absence of a bass, Sonic also bore a heavy grudge against Bassman for walking out on him and Jason at their weakest. Neither did his evaluation of Gavin's garage band bode well for his opinion of Bassman. Frankly, despite what Jason had said, Sonic didn't think Bassman could cut being in Spacemen. "The fact that he left Spacemen 3 to join a half-assed fucking covers band – that just says something about Pete Bain," Sonic said. "I think Pete Bain thinks he's fuckin' cool, you know what I mean? He just thought he was the bee's knees, and he didn't like being beholden to other people."

"I was allowed to rejoin the band," said Bassman. "But Pete was reluctant at first. He liked the uniqueness of a bass-less band and he had a point; their skeletal electric blues sound was like nothing else. The band started rehearsing in one of Pete's dad's warehouses: the place was huge but we were all crammed into a tiny office. The atmosphere wasn't good. Pete was openly resentful of my presence and insisted I played at an inaudible level. Although I was back in the band, I knew, because of the past and Pete's grudge, that I would always have to take a fair amount of shit from him."

In addition to adding bass, Jason and Sonic took an afternoon trip over to Leicester to stock up on equipment in an effort to hone their sounds. Jason had been playing with a hand-me-down Japanese guitar and Sonic with a random axe he picked up along the way. They wanted to be choosy – but within a budget – so Jason decided on a moderately priced Fender Telecaster with an H&H amp – replete with tremolo, spring reverb, and gain, roughly modelled after the Vox AC30 – while Sonic grabbed a Burns Jazz guitar and an antiquated Vox Conqueror amp (with speed-control tremolo and distortion) famed for its inclusion in such Sixties recordings as *Sgt. Pepper, Axis: Bold as Love* and *Aftermath.* So would begin Spacemen 3's obsession with retro-analogue electronics.

Mark Refoy made the 40-mile round trip between Northampton and Rugby to catch The Spacemen whenever possible. He'd leg it over to The Blitz for Reverberation events and make his usual appearances at The Black Lion. He and Sonic struck up a rather cordial repartee, but Mark noticed Jason was much less inclined to jump into the typical bois-terous pub conversation. Sonic appeared willing to speak as Jason's proxy. It was only onstage that Jason shone with a muted virtuosity that elevated The Spacemen songbook beyond mere drone-age. Such per-sonality distinctions made these two band mates that much more fascinat-ing, as if one could supply the necessary element the other lacked.

Mark began booking gigs for The Spacemen at The Black Lion, hoping to spotlight the band through word-of-mouth and association with his own band The Telltale Hearts. Sonic and Jason agreed to play with The Hearts at these early shows, although Refoy distinctly remem-bered neither guitarist being thrilled with the band's polished pop glean-ings. Still they made little complaint, content as they were to fill The Blitz with an influx of Northamptonshire fans. Sonic and Jason sat at the bar with Mark after one of The Blitz shows, discussing recording plans. Neither was pleased with the spare trappings and elementary set-up at Dave Sheriff's studio, but there wasn't another inexpensive studio in Rugby where they could bang out some quick demos on a negligible budget. As Mark humorously recalled, "They [the studios] were either too expensive or people were freaked out by their attitude, like copious dope smoking and a very demanding manner." He suggested a small 16-track studio located in his home village of Piddington run by an old school chum and former drummer called Carlo Morocco. Carlo had an old rehearsal shack surrounded by bucolic sprawl, where he and Refoy had jammed for long stretches as teenagers, before Morocco converted the shambling outhouse into a functional studio.

In the closing days of the year, the new four-piece headed over to Morocco's Piddington studio, where they set about a feverish pace of recording for the three-day session. Kember and Pierce brought a long list of new songs and composed a few on the spot. Of their working methods at this second demo session, Bassman claimed, "Sonic and Jason wrote independently, then exchanged ideas, most times outside of the band. I think the great leap forward was due to increased gigging. Sonic was infatuated with Otis Redding and was enthusiastic about his concept of "soul music". Pete's ideas at the time probably overshadowed Jason's, and created an element of competition between them."

The back garden 16-track studio was severely cramped. The atmosphere was not much better than at Sheriff's studio. The band re-recorded '2.35' which flowered with the inclusion of the bass and Sonic's incessant desire to overdub long swaths of feedback. Bassman objected to the sharp "whinnying" effect on top of the track, insisting the feedback was more objectionable than textural. "I thought the feedback running all the way through the song was amazing," said Sonic. "That's kinda what the whole song is about. But Pete Bain didn't like all the feedback, so I had to do two mixes to pacify him." Bassman shrugged in response, "We may have had an argument about feedback, but things like that were not uncommon." The matter was resolved when the band agreed to mix it out on a separate version. 'Walkin' With Jesus', renamed 'Sound Of Confusion', was re-recorded as a fast-paced garage-psych number complete with thick distortion and a sprinkle of Sonic's feedback. Jason's 'Things'll Never Be The Same' was converted from a stiff, bluesy workout into a pulverising one-chord rant, where Jason rocked his wah-wah pedal into signal freak-outs between verses.

As a professed nod to their record collecting roots, and lacking a sufficient log of finished compositions, the Kember/Pierce songwriting team turned instead to a series of covers it was intent on reworking. Sonic suggested a cover of the Redding/traditional 'Amen', a gospel-soul ballad which they recorded in addition to a slightly rewritten 'Hey Man' that would find its way onto the *Sound Of Confusion* LP. Both 'Amen' and 'Hey Man' contained one of the earliest oblique hints of gospel that would come to dominate Jason and Sonic's ensuing work and proved a fine example of plagal cadence and American-gothic 'white boy' blues spilling from the Stax Records/Alex Chilton cross-over. Due to their penchant for Memphis soul and an overriding Otis Redding fetish, 'Hey Man' was of central import to Kember and Pierce. At Sonic's behest the band also recorded an esoteric cover of 'Just One Time' that appeared on garage band Juicy Lucy's 1969 debut. Containing lines evocative of an acid-laden encounter with the ineffable, "The desert sand/ The secret plan/ Lord's own knowledge is in your hand . . ./ Grab a hold and ride that freight/ Be yourself, don't hesitate," Jason's deep reverbed vocal bore faint traces of The Red Krayola and early Pink Floyd. Renaming it 'Mary Anne' The Spacemen version eschewed the original's Barrett-esque pastoralism for a fuzztone mantra. "We took 'Mary Anne' which was a real mellow acoustic number and turned it into a Stooges track," explained Sonic, "because what we wanted was to work on both planes: totally mellow or totally intense. Both methods summed up the different aspects of what we were trying to do." Following his partner's lead, Jason quickly rewrote 'Fixin' To Die' as a blues-based paean to the boredom of 1986, renaming it 'Come Down Easy'.

Even the most realised track, a new composition entitled 'Losing Touch With My Mind', was based on a riff Sonic nicked from the Stones' 'Citadel' off the psychedelic white elephant *Their Satanic Majesties Request*. However, what separated these songs from being mere rip-offs and The Spacemen from being a covers-band in revisionist trappings, was the constant drive on Sonic and Jason's part to rewrite, recycle and reinterpret the music in a way that would allow it – and them – to stand on its own merits, while openly acknowledging the source. Much like their forebears and kindred spirits The Cramps, whose reverent plumbing of Link Wray, Charlie Feathers, and The Rumblers, produced such classics as 'Sunglasses After Dark' and 'Garbageman', Spacemen 3 were less copyists and more congregation. Though most of these earliest songs were yet to be fully accomplished, particular tracks like 'Losing Touch With My Mind' were amazing examples of The Spacemen's method of (un)covering.

Unfortunately, the latter song's key bass-riff caused some arguments between Sonic and Bassman, further exacerbating their fragile relation-ship. After several playbacks, Sonic claimed Bassman wasn't hitting the difficult riff correctly, and chose instead to handle the bass part himself. Bassman was chafed to find Sonic taking over his role for the song. "I think Sonic played Jason's small Burns bass, because he was of the opinion I couldn't play the bass line right," recalled Bassman. "No matter how I played it, he was never happy. Personally, I think it was because he couldn't work out a guitar part for himself." The bassist's dig was a con-fused conjecture to say the least as Sonic appeared on both guitar and bass. As the 'frustrated' guitarist replied, "I do play both parts on that track . . . And I think those kinda things really started to get to Pete Bain. And he had to resolve them in his mind with some stupid little ideas of his."

On one afternoon Mark popped over to the Piddington studio to check on The Spacemen's progress. Refoy peered through the glass from the control-room into an ashen fog that nearly made the band invisible. When Sonic bolted out of the studio to greet him, a rich, cumulous cloud of hash smoke wafted behind him. In just a few short days, the Piddington shack had become a rancid opium den. Morocco was not concerned with production, so both Sonic and Jason often sat in the control-room, smoking joints, listening to playbacks, and adjusting levels accordingly. "We started to realise the importance of trying to handle the production side," recalled Sonic. They rapidly learned their way around the fairly conventional machine, and took over the production throughout the short session time. With freer rein, they played with a few more overdubs, compression, and other track-altering techniques to better locate the simple, textural sounds they desired.

With some time left over for recording, the band laid down several new songs composed shortly before the session. Softer and more pliant in nature, they pointed beyond the harsh garage-tinged psychedelia that had been the band's patented sound, and toward the more fully realised work that appeared with their later albums. "A good portion of what was to be *Perfect Prescription* was already being formulated by that time," Sonic observed.

For 'Feel So Good' Jason and Sonic recorded alone minus the bass and drums to weave a melodious hum of guitar over Jason's soporific vocal and Natty's cymbal overdub. "I remember it was Sonic's first attempt at vocals during this session. He wrote a song called 'Cream In My Jeans'. It sounded corny to me, but he worked it out on the spot, and it became 'That's Just Fine'," Bassman recalled. The song was the first in a long line of Sonic's tributes to the Lou Reed style of speak-singing – a sluggish, Teutonic delivery echoing over drone-guitar – in lieu of Jason's more melodic vocals. Though Sonic's singing capabilities could not compare with Jason's talents, he continued to experiment with lyrical and vocal forms as he became more confident of his abilities. His lazy, street-drawl lyrics "Honey, You look so good/ And you look so fine" offer a kind of simple sexy love song as Jason's guitar climbs ever higher to a glitchy crescendo and Bassman's bass fills the background with a one-note pulse. The song would later be re-recorded during the *Prescription* sessions as an instrumental. Finally, an early cover of 'Transparent Radiation' was also attempted, with the first inclusion of an organ. Another signal of The Spacemen's eventual move to the cumulous textures of keyboard drones, the demoed version is a polyvocaled mesh of Sonic's harmonies dubbed over a harsh, droning guitar.

Owing to the extra spurt of songwriting and recording, the band over-extended their paid time at Morocco's studio. After three days of recording and mixing, they still had not cut the final version onto master-tape, and they spent an extra half-day finishing up at the studio. But Sonic and Jason were short on funds, and Morocco threatened to seize the master until the difference was paid. Although the projected cost was only £110 for the session, no one had the £20 extra it would cost for overtime. As Sonic was the only one not strapped by the dole, he coughed up the complete £130, but not without razzing Jason, Natty, and especially Bassman for not pulling their weight. Jason and Natty promised Sonic an extra fiver when they got their next dole cheques, but

Pete Bain turned scornfully away and bleated, "What do I get for my £5?!" Sonic just stared at his bassist open-mouthed.

On December 19, Spacemen 3 organised their first psychedelic festival in Rugby at the Benn Hall community centre. Calling it Christmas On Mars, Sonic and Jason were able to organise other local bands through connections in the Reverberation Club. In attendance that evening, along with the headlining Spacemen, was Mark Refoy's Telltale Hearts, Gavin Wissen's Cogs of Tyme, Total Contempt, and Magnolia Siege. The stage was bathed in oscillating Technicolor from the luminous gyroscopes and strobes the band had collected at The Blitz. Admission was two quid for each drunk, stoned, and curious local who walked into the auditorium for a night of trips and music. To The Spacemen's chagrin, most of the floor was empty.

> BASSMAN: The gigs became more numerous and we started to cover some ground. Mark Webber [author of "Oozing Thru The Ozone Layer" fanzine] booked us to play his hometown of Chesterfield and promoted many gigs for us after that. We also began playing The Crypt in Deptford, London. This was an actual crypt of a church. It was an all-nighter and without amphetamine you could never last the distance. A professional career was shaping up and now other bands were gravitating towards us, giving us support and helping create a musical movement of sorts.

Natty, Bassman and Jason jumped into Sonic's mini on odd afternoons and raced down the A428 towards Northants with plumes of hash smoke fizzing from the car's cracked windows. The contact high alone ensured even an abstaining passenger would soon be "off their tits" (as the band liked to put it). From the tape console blasted The Stooges, Suicide, or The Scientists, at ear splitting levels, making conversation fundamentally impossible. The front windshield stretched out in front of them like cinemascope. Sonic's car would spin-out, twist and writhe, overtaking one motorist after another at speeds exceeding 100 miles per hour, pulling up to Pat Fish's door in 20 minutes flat. Fish squeezed into the back seat and the car shot back out on the road, towards Northampton and The Black Lion. "I felt old hanging with them then," Fish confided. "I felt like their old uncle. They'd get into Northampton, and they'd want to go somewhere. And so we'd end up at The Black Lion. And frankly, if there's not a gig on, The Black Lion was a pretty dull place. And after about 15 minutes, it would get dull, and one of them would start to skin up, and I'd go, 'NO! You're not in Rugby now!'"

Owing to his ambitious and pushy disposition, Sonic gravitated towards Fish's aged wisdom (Fish was 10 years older than Sonic) and his connections with numerous bourgeoning indie labels. The Jazz Butcher had moved back and forth across several small record companies, before settling on London's one-man operation Glass Records. More than anything, Sonic coveted the cachet of signing with a label. Fish encouraged the young upstart to concentrate on improving The Spacemen and wait for lucrative possibilities, but Sonic was clear: he and the band had waited long enough. Though Pat hesitated about handing over the precious jewel of Spacemen 3 to his label's head Dave Barker, dissatisfied with what Glass had achieved for The Jazz Butcher, he nonetheless took the new demos, entitled *Taking Drugs To Make Music To Take Drugs To*, and agreed to pass them along. In the interim, Barker had received some early press photos of the band down in London, and he immediately locked onto their hip swagger and good looks. They had a mature, aesthetic "cool" that most of the adolescent shambling bands at the time gravely lacked. Although Barker hadn't yet heard any of their music, he wondered if this young band might be exactly what his label needed.

An Essex native and infamous chain-smoker, Barker had worked for Polygram Records Distribution from 1979 until 1983 when he resigned to found his own indie label during the Rough Trade/Cherry Red boom. Though he'd only had experience in the distribution sector (predominantly with graphics) and not in the all-important A&R division, he was able to expand his label rapidly in a short time through connections with the majors, and loose ties with Alan McGee and Clive Solomon in London. Within the first three years of the label's conception, Barker secured The Jazz Butcher and The Jacobites, both potential hopefuls in the mid-Eighties indie-market.

PAT FISH: The whole story of Dave Barker is extraordinary. He used to design record sleeves. And I think he only really started Glass Records so he could do lots of sleeves the way he wanted. He started putting a couple of records out and, more astonishingly, people started buying a couple of 'em. The Jazz Butcher would go down to London to do gigs in little clubs, and there were nights where there were just too many people there. Like, "What's going on?" And Dave Barker would be sitting at a table and there'd be a bloke from the *Melody Maker* with him, and some bloke from another record company. I'd be standing there watching him, thinking any minute now someone's going to tap him on the shoulder and say, "Terribly sorry, Mr Barker, there's been a dreadful mistake." Because Dave – financially especially – didn't have a clue about anything. But he got us into America for Christ's sakes. One bloke in a cupboard. Extraordinary, really, when you think of his achievement. And the truth is, in like 1984, Dave was selling a lot more records than Alan [McGee] was, in a lot more territories than Alan was, with no more basic resources than Alan had himself. And, like, by the summer of 1986, Dave was like sending his little English groups to tour the United States, and he came back having signed Californian groups and put their shit out in Europe.

As if the outrageous narcotic hedonism had not already reached saturation, The Spacemen were destined to meet yet another drug-infused personality in the shape of local head case Goff Roderick. Goff was a major cocaine peddler around town, who made a small fortune from many years of dealing and lived in a large, 15 room Georgian mansion. "He was one of Rugby's drug dealers with a higher profile than others due to his whacked out persona and attitude," said Bassman. "Goff's house was a four-storey townhouse close to Rugby School. It would have had students renting rooms there back in Tom Brown's day, now Goff was a modern day Fagin surrounding himself with a surrogate family of dopers and outcasts." Born in the late Forties in Rugby, he was one of the first heads to bring psychedelics and dope into the town's bourgeoning youth-culture during the Sixties. He'd also had numerous spats with the constabulary, spending time in prison for cocaine possession.

Goff had had brief flirtations with musicians and artists for decades, a carte-blanche entrance to a world of hipsterism that only the drug-culture would afford. His memories of such classic moments extend back to one of his earliest psychedelic experiences, attending a mid-Sixties Pink Floyd gig – with Syd Barrett in tow – a few miles from Rugby's town centre. A thundering rainswept gale poured down on the stage as Goff and the small crowd slogged through cow shit and dodged lightning bolts, stoned off their heads. Goff had spent years and years courting local groups, but he'd never witnessed a Rugby band like The Spacemen until he turned up one evening at The Blitz for a Reverberation event. He walked into the cramped back room of the pub and was gobsmacked at the thundering din echoing from the cheap wooden walls. "And I saw them and I thought, 'Unbelievable!' It was like seeing The Velvet Underground," Goff enthused. But like The Velvets if they'd come from Rugby.

When the evening's show was completed, Goff ascended the small stage to meet and greet his new favourite band. His mad cooing and enthusiasm were quite infectious. Nobody knew what to make of this crazed old sod. "Kate Radley told me he was a millionaire furniture dealer and was into us in a big way," Bassman recalled. Goff chatted with them long into the evening before inviting Jason, Sonic, Bassman and

Natty back to his townhouse for, as Goff recalled, "a mad all-nighter" full of dope, coke, and lysergic dreams. "The first of very many . . ." added Goff. In one of his first vivid memories of the Georgian mansion, Sonic wandered through its vertiginous interior high on sundry amounts of alcohol, cocaine, and mushrooms, only to recognise faint swirls of *Sound Of Confusion* and 'Walkin' With Jesus' commingling from different floors. Having found a salty, middle-aged nutter as passionate about drugs and music as they were, The Spacemen wasted little time nominating Goff Roderick the band's cocaine supplier and unofficial financial backer/ tour-manager/roadie. "It was perfectly natural for younger guys to be under the wing of an older guy," said Bassman of The Spacemen's liaisons with Goff. "With Goff you've got the full package: he was part insanity, part bravado, part charisma."

At the start of the New Year, Natty moved out of the Hillmorton house he shared with Bassman and into a two-storey terraced home on Murray Road along with Jason and Tim Morris. They were all still on the dole at the time, which made rent difficult. But if they combined their monies, along with small bits they made on the side from gigging, they hoped to make ends meet until the first album came out. Natty adorned the first floor with strange artistic collages, and myriad psyche-delic art graced the walls throughout. The Murray Road house was also home to another local called Stewart Roswell (alias Rosco), an itinerant musician who'd been born in Rugby, raised in Africa, and then, as a teenager, re-deposited in his hometown, where he eventually attended and dropped out of Art College. Bred on guitar and bass from the age of 14, Rosco had played in one of Gavin Wissen's early bands, when he began frequenting Murray Road.

"Rosco appeared on the scene and was always a fairly vacuous creature," Sonic said. "I always saw him as being very chameleon-like; he could fit in with different groups of people really easily."

Rosco's fashion-conscious image always seemed to be in flux. He'd been hanging out with a local rockabilly group called The Crazy Cats, who ran a weekly disco in town, wore closely cropped flat-tops and only listened to Carl Perkins, Johnny Cash, and other Fifties Sun Records. Before long Rosco transformed himself into the Eighties trendsetter, donning suave clothes and carefully coiffed hair, embracing new-romanticism with a flashy FRANKIE SAYS RELAX T-shirt. Sonic continued, "Rosco didn't have a clue to what was cool, and how to do something himself, but he could copy us very well." So often did these metamorphoses occur, that the nickname "The Chameleon" stuck, although only behind Rosco's back. "That's strange," Rosco retorted. "I used to have a pet chameleon when I was 12 and I used to have things like lizards for pets. What does that name mean? Like implying the qualities of a chameleon? Something that can change shades or appearance? Yeah, I guess I can do that."

Murray Road became the new epicentre for the band, and a welcome escape for those still attached at the hip to family life. Sonic was still living at his parents' home in Dunchurch, but he'd often spend the afternoons crashed out at Murray Road or popping over to Gavin's flat. "I might spend the odd evening just getting high, but invariably I would take heroin, cocaine, speed, Valium pretty much every day and night," he admitted. Jason didn't seem to mind the company, as they'd sit around strumming guitar or smoking dope. But other residents became tired of Sonic's constant squatting, as if he'd taken over the front room just for a haven to nod out. "You'd see far too much of Pete because Pete lived with his parents at the time he was taking drugs," Bassman remembered. "He used to treat your house like his house. It was a big problem for lots of people. And it really just got to the point where you were just absolutely sick at the sight of him."

Of the many users and connections Sonic made scoring heroin around Rugby, he became particularly close to a young addict called Christopher Fitzgerald. Fitzgerald was a musician from Bilton who'd started the punk group, Protest, with his close mates Ben Robinson and Robbie Smith. As teenagers, they hung out at the local discos listening to The Sex Pistols and The Ramones, and there they all met Gavin, Tim and Bassman. When Tim began hosting rehearsals in his attic at Kilsby, the three of them would often stop by and jam, and Robbie would lend Tim his drum kit to use for the afternoon. Fitzgerald, or Fitzy as most people called him, played bass, while Ben played guitar, and along with Robbie, the three boys started up Protest as their three-chord salute to '77 punk rock. But Protest only symbolised the darker, more errant elements of punk, the Sid Vicious-era, as their gigs often fell apart with Fitzy hardly able to maintain a bass line, and the audience gobbing all over the stage. Though their punk "scene" typically strayed far from the small psychedelic crowd The Spacemen catered to, Sonic became aware of Protest's narcotic notoriety. Fitzy had a particularly bad reputation as a heavy smack user and speed freak. "He was the biggest glue-sniffing, drug-taking . . . I tell you there wasn't a drug he hadn't taken before he met me," Sonic recalled.

Sonic and Fitzy had the same junk dealer and they'd often run into each other while scoring. Once they got to talking, Sonic discovered that Fitzy was sitting on a huge stash of pharmaceutical drugs, including large amounts of Diconal, a morphine-derivative prescribed for pain. The pleasures of Diconal proved every bit as seductive as heroin, producing a

'Walkin' With Jesus' photo session (clockwise from top left): Natty, Bassman, Sonic Boom and Jason Pierce, 1986. (Craig Wagstaff)

Lawrence Sheriff Grammar School, Jason Pierce's *alma mater. (Erik Morse)*

Tudor House, Sonic's dormitory during his tumultuous tenure at Rugby School. *(Erik Morse)*

FOR ALL THE FUCKED UP CHILDREN... : Jason riffs on his guitar during a 1984 rehearsal. *(Sonic Boom Collection)*

PORTRAIT OF A SIREN AS A YOUNG GIRL: Kate Radley at Rugby High School *(Courtesy of Vinita Joshi)*

ARE
YOUR
DREAMS
AT
NIGHT
3
SIZES
TOO BIG?

(Sonic Boom Collection)

Early artwork and gig posters from around 1983 – 1984.

(Mark Lascelles)

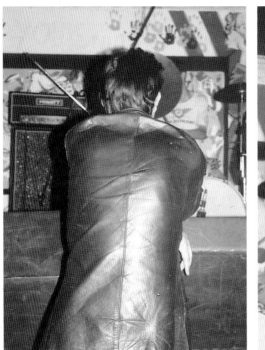

Top left HYPNOTIZED: Pat Fish AKA The Jazz Butcher leans over the stage during his first Spacemen 3 experience at The Black Lion in Northampton, 1985. *(Sonic Boom Collection)*

Top right: Jason sings at a Black Lion gig, 1985. *(Graham Holliday)*

FOR ALL THE FUCKED~UP CHILDREN OF THIS WORLD WE GIVE YOU ⊢SPACEMEN⊣ 3

⊢SPACEMEN⊣ (0788 810185) SPACEMEN ⊢

Spacemen 3 plays Banbury gig with Sonic (on bass), Bassman, Natty and Jason, 1985. *(Craig Wagstaff)*

Present-day photo of The Blitz Pub home to
The Reverberation Club. *(Erik Morse)*

An early Spacemen 3 business card.

SPACEMEN 3
207 RAILWAY
TERRACE
RUGBY
WARWICKSHIRE
CV21 3HU
0788 50231

3

Sonic sings at The Reverberation Club, 1985. *(Craig Wagstaff)*

SPOONFUL OF FUN: Jason's artwork takes a devilish turn.
(Reproduced by kind permission of Mark Lascelles)

LORD, CAN YOU HEAR ME?: Jason, Sonic and Natty pray for a miracle after their first recording sessions. *(Sonic Boom Collection)*

Sonic and Jason look over Rugby from the top of a tower block. *(Sonic Boom Collection)*

Sonic and Jason. (*Sonic Boom Collection*)

relaxed and spacey warmth. Sonic came to relish Diconal and he'd hit up Fitzgerald for it at every opportunity. When Fitzy found himself without recourse to his pain pills, he'd often pop over to his dealer's tenement for junk.

One afternoon a small group of friends stopped by Fitzy's flat on their way from the house of local Russian Jazz member Gary Davis. They'd scored some smack pills from a dealer there and passed a few over to Fitzy who was in need of a fix. He studied the small pills eagerly. At first glance, they looked eerily similar to Diconal, and he decided to save them for later. That same afternoon, Gavin scored a handful of these strange heroin pills and swallowed a few for fun. He had done lots of dope, acid, and magic mushrooms, but this was to be his first and only experience with opiates. Sitting around his flat, he waited for the drugs to take hold, but it wasn't long before he felt faint and sick to his stomach, retching uncontrollably before nearly passing out. He was so gravely ill that he spent the entire afternoon in the toilet throwing up.

Later that evening, Fitzy phoned Sonic to let him know he'd scored a bunch of these smack pills. Sonic had given him a small quantity of heroin earlier in the week, and Fitzy promised to pay him back when he got hold of more pills. Sonic claimed his supply was tapped and he was eager to get more. "He obviously got the shit and called me up about 8 o'clock at night but I wasn't there," said Sonic. "I was meant to be sharing those drugs with him. That had been the intention. He'd called me up to say, 'Hey, I got the shit. Come down.' And I wasn't there so my mum took the message." Fitzy wanted a fix and decided not to wait for Sonic. He ground up the pills, cooked it over a spoon and shot it up.

The next morning Fitzgerald's landlord came around to the tenement where he lived to collect his rent and found Fitzy collapsed on the floor, a needle hanging from his arm. He had overdosed and died during the night, and his body – spread out beneath a poster of Sid Vicious – was pale blue. Sonic came upon the scene later that morning when he popped over to get more Diconal from him. He found the landlord raving frantically about what he'd discovered. "Fitzy's landlord didn't even know what he was into," said Sonic. "He just thought he smoked weed and that was it. And then when he finds him and he still has the needle in his arm and everything – found him fucking blue – it fucking freaked him right out."

Within days, the town was in uproar over the incident: a young man's premature death to narcotics. The situation intensified when the local Catholic Church refused to bury Fitzy's body in the parish cemetery. The coroner had ruled his death an overdose which was classified as suicide according to law. The Fitzgerald family were staunch Catholics and demanded their son's death be ruled a homicide in order to please the clergy. When the cause of death was changed to manslaughter, and the church still refused to inter the body, Fitzgerald's father went in search of the dealer responsible for his son's demise. "His death sent shock waves through our scene," Bassman remembered. "His father started a campaign to expose the person who had given his son the drugs that tragically killed him."

All pushers and users became potential targets for his vendetta. "He just went absolutely over-the-top," added Goff. "He went completely on this mission to get all of the dealers and all of the people that were known to be into drugs and stuff. Everyone used to call him The Vigilante."

Fitzgerald took to stalking out the homes of anyone suspected to be a drug-dealer, including Goff. Although he'd never taken heroin, Goff noticed Fitzgerald parked across the street from his townhouse for long periods of time. The police had long been onto Goff but were eternally frustrated in their efforts to nab him. As Bassman remembered, "Goff would rent out every available room of his house. This gave the Rugby drug squad a difficult time obtaining a search warrant as they had no idea who lived in what room."

Weeks after his death, gossip was still rife over who had killed Fitzy. One particularly insidious rumour that reached Gavin concerned the similarity between the pills he'd been given and the pills that had killed Fitzy. Evidently, Fitzy had used the same pills to fix before his death. When Gavin heard this news, he was freaked out. "It was like, 'Oh Fuck!' It just like scared me to death," Gavin admitted. "Somebody I actually knew took the same thing on the same day as me and died." But what Gavin found most chilling was the identity of the person who'd passed the pills to him in the first place. According to his fogged recollection, a member of Spacemen 3 had been by the very same day trying to unload the mysterious pills. Sonic dismissed the thinly veiled innuendo as speculation and hearsay. "He certainly didn't get the drugs off of me," he retorted. "But," he added, "it's not like I hadn't given him drugs before. I had. And he'd given me drugs. We gave each other drugs, we'd taken drugs together dozens of times. You know, we'd stolen drugs from doctors and chemists and all sorts together. You know a lot of people would probably like to blame a lot of shit on me."

Fitzy's father also took to fly-posting the houses of suspected drug-users with libellous slogans and baited the local police with rumours and innuendos that identified dealers in the area. Stories ran rampant, but no one knew who passed off the drugs that killed Chris Fitzgerald. Suspicions fell on known users and musicians who ran in Fitzy's group, but without any hard evidence, no charges were brought. The town of Rugby came down hard on heroin, leaving local junkies without supply. Until the furore died down, most users migrated to nearby Coventry to score, where smack was still plentiful, cheaper and of higher quality. "Coventry down the road had a far bigger heroin base in them days than Rugby," Goff recalled. "The city was like a rebuilt concrete jungle after the Second World War. And that kind of thing was reflected in the mentality of the people who lived there and the drugs."

It was only after the national media picked up on the story and began sending reporters from London to investigate, that the finger pointing went from mere accusation to witch-hunt. Eventually Fitzgerald claimed local user and Russian Jazz member Gary Davis was the dealer who'd passed on the pills that killed his son. He put up posters throughout the town claiming Davis was the killer, and urging his indictment for manslaughter. Armed with Fitzgerald's slanderous invective, the press had a field day with the story, tackling Davis' reputation and taking snatch photos.

BASSMAN: A news team came to Rugby and they set out to confront Gary Davis, thinking that Gary was someway responsible. I watched the programme when it was broadcast. The reporter tried the intercom of the tower block where the Davis's lived and got a bemused Alun Davis, Gary's younger brother. Gary turned the corner holding a box of cornflakes, immediately the reporter confronted Gary. We all knew Gary was a long-time friend of Fitzy and was in no way responsible for Fitzy's death. But this cocksucker of a journalist was extremely misinformed, so we all were glad when Gary exploded with rage. Fitzy's father was skulking in a car, and Gary spotted him and then turned his anger on him. It really was an ugly period for everybody.

GOFF RODERICK: I think Fitzy's father eventually became an embarrassment to the police as well. Because he was trying to feed a lot of information back to the police and stuff. And I think, at the end of the day, he became an embarrassment to everyone really. It was sad, because I could understand exactly where he was coming from. I used to wave at him every time I went in and out of the house. He was sitting at the car park across from my house, and I just sort of waved at him. Most people just sort of waved him on.

During one of The Jazz Butcher's many trips around the country in '86, Dave Barker finally heard The Spacemen's second demo recordings. He was travelling in the tour bus with the band when someone popped *Taking Drugs To Make Music To Take Drugs To* into the tape deck. "He was umm . . . he was a bit sceptical at first I think," recalled Fish. "I don't know if Dave Barker ever really got The Spacemen or not but he definitely recognised it was worth the investment." Barker didn't quite know what to make of these young boys playing such ferocious music. But he was intrigued enough to start making inquiries when he returned to London.

"There were a lot of those so-called noise bands around at that time, influenced by Sonic Youth, Pussy Galore and The Mary Chain," Barker replied. "But Spacemen 3 had more blues and gospel. Older music influences as well as new. I liked the fact that The Spacemen were into the MC5, The Stooges, and The Elevators, but they went back to the music that inspired those bands and checked out Sun Ra, Howlin' Wolf, Coltrane, blues, gospel and folk. So I think their music had more of a roots influence than people gave them credit for. I don't think the other bands around at that time were so heavily into that." Barker drove to Northampton to scout out a few of their local gigs at The Black Lion with The Jazz Butcher. "My main impression of them live was they took about six minutes between each song tuning up," Barker observed. "And they had the psychedelic lightshow going on throughout this process so it was sort of interesting." Despite his reservations, Barker banked on The Spacemen's good looks and blues-infused noise. He offered them a two album, three-year contract with Glass. Nearly three years after forming the band, Sonic and Jason got their very first shot at recording an album and just maybe making the big time.

'Dreamweapon In Brooklyn, Episode 1 (Drone On . . .)'

The DREAMWEAPON is neither a direct representation of the fluctuating body nor the indirect representation of the social body, but rather a sonic material that forms an organic continuum. It is the homeostatic tremolo (generative stasis) produced from the oscillations of an infinite series of cavities.

With the conjunctions of inter-subjective spaces, the DREAMWEAPON returns as modulations of the pathway, transversal indication of this, that, and the other: the emigration of glissando, tremolo, phasing. Inclusive identities on tour in space. This is where the "chrono-genous" receives coordination, localising sound as points of departure or termination. Triggers of cosmogony. The DREAM-WEAPON transgenerates inscriptions of melody along these points of Deleuzian intensity: the recordings are etched into the warm, gooey swaths of wax as feedback of production.

SONIC BOOM'S EXPERIMENTAL AUDIO RESEARCH
November 2002
North Six Club, Williamsburg, New York

From behind the cramped dais, littered with discarded amplifiers and bits of coil and copper, multi-chromatic halogen lamps dim to a twilight glow. As if simulating the hues of an ulcerated organ rusted to a flaky scab, the oversized crimson backdrop dulled to a hazed brown. A mere hundred heads, plunged into darkness, popped forward in auto-tropic response. Sonic Boom steps across the stage with a slight nod of his bobbed hair, shielding his bloodshot eyes from the overhead spotlights. His svelte, stained blue jeans and wrinkled red windbreaker belie the maudlin theatrics with which he bends down to his assembled rig. In a flourish he spins his back to the punters below and toward his pinball gear with the contorted gravity of Van Cliburn, of Lou Reed, of Mendelev.

The echoed drone ascends slowly from the twists and twirls of Sonic's thin, pale fingers upon his ping-pong modules. Hands, arms, necks writhe toward the source of the electric quake. When the original current reaches its zenith, another squelched *zoink-zoink-zoink* pulses against it, popping the bubbling timbre into a thousand glassy shards. There is a grating din stabbing across the floor, panning from right to left like hundreds of choking lawnmowers engaged in a massive *chop-chop-chop*. The sound drops away as quickly as it registers, germinating into an aquatic blurb: a tidal wall of aquamarine soaking warm, trembling flesh.

A nebulous melody creeps surreptiously into the rapture, twinkling and sparkling like tiny silver flecks shot skyward (or roofward). It takes nearly 45 minutes before every available synthesiser is groaning with dials perched toward auditory sublimation. The 27 different drones hovering near the ceiling commingle, arc, subtend, and homogenise into a glacial effluvium. Synaesthetic mucus dribbles from every pustule and pore. Bodies tumble towards the rear exit; bodies attached to anaemic faces contorted in virulent disgust. Vast sound platelets drift in and out, in and out, crack against the back wall and cascade into charcoaled cavities. Sonic crouches forward over his sound-laboratory, adjusting . . . adjusting . . . until there appears a backward slipstream, like a great reverse phase, and a "pangaeatic" drone drops onto the audience. There is a silence, one silence, two silences, silences measured in quick duration. The electric generators pour out vibrating currents of absolute stillness. It is its own pumping body, its own primitive bacillus, whipping its tentacled frame into the corner. Fifty heads glance at the animalcule. It glances back.

Sonic Boom cuts the power and, with a wave, is gone.

CHAPTER FOUR

Walkin' With Jesus (Sound Of Confusion)

SPRING 1986–1987

At the time Spacemen 3 signed with Glass Records near the beginning of 1986, gigs were still few and far between. Beyond convening their usual weekly assemblage at the Reverberation Club in Rugby, most shows extended not much further than the local Rugby/Northampton/ Coventry circuit. Indie "networks" in the English West Midlands were tentative at best, both for a lack of playable venues and accepting audiences. A band without a record to their credit was essentially left to busking. But hopes were running high in the laboratories of Rugby that all of this would soon change.

In the spring of that year, around the time when Chernobyl was blowing its top and boiling over the Ukraine, the four Spacemen staggered into the Highbury Road studios of Bob Lamb to record their first album for Glass Records. The modest 24-track studio in the King's Heath district of Birmingham had been the setting of UB40's first album *Signing Off*, including the singles 'Food for Thought' and 'King' six years' previously, which might explain why Lamb labelled his set-up "Home of The Hits". But Lamb had had few hits in the years since (he'd been producing independent acts like Glass' The Jacobites) and the pairing did not seem to portend success, at least on the level of a UB40. Pat Fish drove up from Northampton to survey the scene at Lamb's studio and keep some semblance of order and/or hierarchy between Lamb and The Spacemen. "The original idea was that I was to produce the album," Fish said, "but The Jazz Butcher schedule required me to be in Spain halfway through the session. So I just travelled up with the band for the first few days to see that everything was all right." Instead of producing, he set about the dual task of making tea and joint rolling.

Dave Barker had budgeted less than £1,000 for the album, allowing only five days of studio time for the recording and mixing. This prompted both band and producer to work quickly with the minimum of techniques. But with nearly two albums worth of demos at their disposal, some decisions had to be made. It was apparent to both Sonic and Jason that the conceptual lynchpin of this first album was volume and overdriven distortion. Abandoning whatever remained of their earliest trad-blues/rockabilly style, the *Sound of Confusion* album – as Spacemen 3 would call their debut – became a crunching and chugging juggernaut of drone-guitar, arcing with feedback, and dolloped with a modicum of vintage effects. "That album was to be a concept album really," explained Sonic. "The *Sound of Confusion* was like teen confusion in a way. Just starting to grow up a bit and not finding it very easy, and, perhaps because of drugs and stuff, finding some of the trials and tribulations we were going through in those years a bit tough."

Backing tracks to '2.35' and 'Losing Touch With My Mind' were laid down almost immediately. Two of the more raucous numbers in the early Spacemen oeuvre, they seemed obvious choices for inclusion. As on the demos, Bassman refused to work out the bass line to everyone's satisfaction, so Sonic hunkered behind Jason's Burns bass and attempted to elicit the necessary rhythm. Recalling The Velvets' 'Waiting for My Man', Jason's lyrics on '2.35' summed up the twin emotions of discovering one's desperation for drugs only by their absence, along with the frazzled anticipation of scoring. Jason also contributed some ominous reverb from his H&H amplifier, creating an atmospheric "quaking" sound. The intensity of '2.35' climaxed at the end of each verse with the shredding scourge of feedback, as if the creeping addiction swallows the listener into a miasma of desire or alternatively has been quelled by a shot of junk. A highlight of the album, 'Losing Touch With My Mind' was a similar ode to the mindless seduction of Morpheus. With a more rollicking, rhythmic pace than the previous demo, 'Losing Touch . . .' had a thick garage sound and a bit of Hawkwind's metallurgic locomotion. To add a hazier, more ethereal style to 'Losing Touch . . .', Sonic concocted a warping intro using a delay effect feeding back onto itself at faster and faster speeds. The result was the aural equivalent of being sucked into a jet turbine.

Sonic's predilection for the early psychedelia of The Thirteenth Floor Elevators blossomed into a stab at Roky Erickson's throttled 'Rollercoaster', an epic garage-blues ode to love, loss, and psychotomimetic holiness, with a memorable Leary-esque tag-line of "You've got to open up your mind/ And let everything come throughhhhh . . .!" As the original purveyors of the musical term *psychedelia*, The Elevators' 1966 *Psychedelic Sounds* LP, clattering with overdriven rhythm-guitar, death-driven wails, oscillating electric-jug, deep-South paranoia, and "third-eye" imagery, was a radical departure from much of the California good vibes and English whimsy prevalent during the latter part of the decade. And as

The Spacemen lineage tended to avoid all things jangly and/or prog-gish and embraced obscure American retro-hardcore as a part of their "record-collecting" rock, an Elevators' cover seemed not only fitting but obligatory.

"Bob seemed fairly bemused by these tracks, but he was getting it down all right, no problem," said Pat. But just what was in store for Bob did not become apparent until the band's first attempts at 'Rollercoaster'. "We were up at the studio that first day doing the backing track to 'Rollercoaster'," Fish continued. "The lady that ran the office there for Bob kindly made a round of tea, and she came into the control room with this tray. And through the window is Pete Bain, Natty, Jason and Pete doing the backing track and they're doing it without any guide vocal. They've just sat down looking really concentrated, and to any passing observer appeared to have just played E for the last eight minutes. And the lady with the tea tray stopped and gazed through the window, listening for a bit. She looked a little troubled, like she was trying to think of something to say. She watched. And they held grimly to this E. And she turned around to us and said, 'They're really into what they're doing, aren't they?'" Lamb only vaguely nodded in half-hearted support. And to Sonic's recollection, Lamb was anything but responsive to their style. "We did endless live takes, but it just didn't go well," he said. "The atmosphere didn't feel right, and Bob Lamb just didn't click with the vibe."

In addition to The Elevators, Jason and Sonic attempted a cover of The Stooges' 'Little Doll', another nod to the primal one-chord sound that had provided both inspiration and soundtrack to Rugby's pubescent night-trippers. Jason's distended vocal injected little of Iggy Pop's maniacal snarl but his languid, almost apathetic tone created a hollow-ness, implying something far more sinister. The tracks' swirling and bubbled textures, plumped by Jason's wah-pedal, was further high-lighted by removing the bass/drum groove from The Stooges' original. *Forced Exposure* journalist Byron Coley highlighted why the maudlin style of 'Little Doll' indicated The Spacemen's adept method of (un)covering: "Their cover of 'Little Doll' was so ingenious," claimed Coley, "because The Stooges' version was this high-school garage rock, making the vocals completely primary and repressing the riff to the point where it's just completely Neanderthal. The Spacemen 3 version was totally different. For them, the Neanderthal-ness of the riff became the primary focus, and the lyrics were just this submergent kind of meditation. The monolithic riff turned into a kind of mantra giving it a spiritual quality that it didn't have in The Stooges' version. The Space-men took all the elements but put them together in a way that took the sneer out of the song and made it really different. It's completely reversed. And completely British."

The album's variegated title track 'Walkin' With Jesus (Sound Of Confusion)' became Jason's focus for improvement. Sonic had added a chorus bit to Jason's original composition, including two new lines: "Listen Sweet Lord, please forgive my sin,/ 'Cos I can't stand this life without sweet heroin," and " 'Cos if heaven's like heroin then that's the place for me," but Jason was uninterested in cheapening the song with overt smack references. He refused to sing the amended lines for fear of transforming 'Walkin' With Jesus' into a "drug" song, although no one in the studio could doubt the source of the song's existence. "But the song just sounded shit," Sonic insisted. "The vocals were flat or the drone guitar was off pitch. We were really lazy, we should have done a lot more than what we did. A lot of the songs were so fragile in the way that they were made up that if one element was wrong you can just screw it."

Sonic and Jason agreed to record a new version of 'OD Catastrophe' as the album's closing colossus. The two guitarists worked for much of the day recording, re-recording, erecting and perfecting the fuzzed and distorted walls of 'OD Catastrophe''s white-noise. Lamb simply threw up his hands in frustration, endeavouring to differentiate between the sundry takes. Even Pat Fish, ever a keen musician, was gobsmacked. "Me and Jas would do 'OD Catastrophe' for hours and then say, 'Yeah, that last take's the one,' and Pat couldn't understand how the fuck we knew the difference," although Sonic openly admitted, "OD Catastrophe on record never captured it live."

Unlike the previous version on the *For All The Fucked Up Children . . .* demos, Jason chose to work out a derivative vocal based on The Stooges' 'TV Eye' as he had done in the song's earliest incarnations. With a surly council-house drawl, Jason intoned, "Do you see that kid?/ Down on his luck/ Do you see that kid?/ Just spent his last buck/ Well he got an OD catastrophe . . .", a primitive regurgitation of Iggy's invective spiked with the moribund spectre of smack. Jason's most curious line comes with the final verse, "Well do you see that kid?/ Yeah I loved him so/ Do you see that kid?/ Yeah I loved him so," evoking a vague homoeroticism. Sonic explained, "Jason and I had a conversation about one thing in relation to our lyrics. We agreed that we wouldn't specify the drug in a drug song ('Walkin' With Jesus') or the sex of the love in a love song, or try and limit the possible scope of interpretation of our songs. The wise people would always know anyway, right? I can't think of any exceptions other than Jason's 'OD Catastrophe', which seemed like a marginal indiscretion from our earliest era." Although the sexual connotations of the lyric fitted well with the ejaculation of feedback and wah-wah that followed, Jason's profession of love was more likely an elegy for drug casualties.

Mixing began on the fourth day of the sessions, but problems arose when Lamb refused to let Sonic or Jason near the control panel. Although they'd had little rehearsal time and were admittedly naive to the techniques of production, the starkly simple live recordings required an equally minimal mixing. "By that time Jason and I had gotten used to working EQs and faders," hissed Sonic. "And we actually knew better than him what we wanted to do, but Bob wouldn't let us touch the mixing desk or anything." Lamb's unfamiliarity with guitar-driven indie rock led him to choose an odd assortment of fades and textures, with a heavier emphasis on drums and an excessive supply of outboard effects, all of which erred toward a "metalled" edge on playbacks.

> PAT FISH: I was disappointed that there wasn't more top end on most of the tracks. I was also a bit taken aback at what I still call the "Hawkwind noises". These appear to have been the work of Bob, who was eager to please, but a bit off the mark.

Whether it was the overproduction or Jason's inability to lay down a solid vocal, 'Walkin' With Jesus (Sound Of Confusion)' was abandoned despite being the title track. "The song just didn't work for us, it just wasn't happening," said Sonic, "so we had to ditch 'The Sound Of Confusion', definitely one of our better tracks, and which we'd already decided to call the album." As the five-day session concluded, nerves began to fray. Pat Fish, the studio *attaché*, had exited for another Jazz Butcher tour, leaving The Spacemen and Lamb encamped on separate sides of the glass.

Their £800 and week-long recording time spent, the four wayfaring alchemists took one last look at the Birmingham studio and vowed never to suffer such an experience again. The time spent was disappointing at best. "No one in the band thought of that record very well," mourned Sonic. "I think what lets down the first album is the production of it. We felt we'd gone backwards really. We weren't what Bob Lamb tried to make us appear to be." When the four musicians finally set off from Lamb's studio and Highbury Road on the final day, they turned to see Bob running frantically towards the speeding Mini. Everyone laughed at his expense until someone realised Lamb was pointing to the car's roof. Stacked there were the two-inch masters whipping in the wind.

> BASSMAN: The journey back must rate as one of the most terrifying experiences of our lives. Pete's driving manner sometimes

perfectly mirrored his personality and on the road he was often a demonstratively impatient bastard. Harassing drivers to pull over from the fast lane to let him through was a favourite habit. Most times the drivers would get out of his way, but on this occasion a pick-up truck with two builders were the obstacle and they were staying put. Pete eventually got past on the inside and made a rude hand-gesture to them. They started to chase us. As we slowed for roundabouts they leaned out of the cab and lunged at us with hammers. Despite having a much faster car, we could not shake them. We got to Dunchurch when the truck got in front of us and jammed on its brakes, leaving both vehicles to swerve across the road and end up on the grass on the wrong side of the road. I was in the back with Jason; Natty was in the front clutching the pile of master tapes. The builders leapt from the van and charged at us with blunt instruments, saliva running from their mouths. It was one of those situations when time slowed down. The momentary time warp bubble burst when Pete put the car in reverse and floored it, and we shot off backwards to Rugby.

Local musician and photographer Steve Evans snapped *Sound Of Confusion*'s cover photos at the YP building. The short photo "shoot" included quite a lot of hash and a mesmerising panorama of the four Spacemen backed by their patented red and green light show. The bemused and smirking faces staring out from the mist on the front cover epitomised both the album's title and its contents. As a final eulogy for their deceased mate Christopher Fitzgerald, Sonic and Jason agreed to dedicate *Sound Of Confusion* to his memory.

The release of *Sound Of Confusion* in July failed to attract any positive attention from the British weeklies, which was indicative less of the album's qualities than the state of London's insider music scene. In a local interview, Jason stated, "A lot of old Sixties hippies like to see us. They see something in us. They get high to the music. Kids buy the LP, and their parents listen to it. We don't understand why!" Although what kids (or parents) remains a mystery. In fact, there were no blurbs or capsule reviews from the *NME* or *Melody Maker*, only a "promising" mention from the left-field *Sounds*, whose Andy Hurt humorously opined, "*Sound Of Confusion* goes off at half cock. The basic fault here is that they start with a sound and worry about what to do with it after. The first couple of minutes sounded great until someone I assumed to be either Emlyn Hughes, Alan Ball or Aled Jones started singing and I realised it was on at the wrong speed." Cleverly sardonic or not, Hurt's conclusion lays in the real groin popper, "At 45 revs there's an energy present, whereas at 33 we've got the Mary Chain without the choruses. The Purple Things without the guts. Faust could take an outwardly tedious noise and turn it into 13 minutes of captivating, brilliant noise. Spacemen 3 have got to get back to basics."

Morrissey and Marr who were, in the Eighties, the *divi filius* and *major domus* of the indie fiefdom, had been the ones to take the retro-Sixties pop-craze public with The Smiths, stretching and ultimately redefining the parameters of independent-labelled post-punk. Though they were Mancunians by birth and remained there throughout the Eighties, they'd signed with London-based Rough Trade Records, effectively reinforcing the first-city's monopoly on punk/indie (sub)culture. By 1986, The Smiths' blazing popularity, spurred by Morrissey's lyrical/vocal verisimilitude and Marr's mythic guitar-lines, had garnered Geoff Travis' London post-hippy label an inflated power worthy of the majors.

But as The Smiths' star continued to rise, Morrissey and Marr lost the imperative indie credo, generating a vacuum in the British rock underground. A number of Sixties-style retro-pop school kids, taking their cues not just from The Smiths, but also from The Television Personalities, Alan Horne's Postcard label, and elsewhere, galvanised London's indie-rock market in their icons' absence. Spacemen 3 archivist Mark Lascelles recalled this stark ascension of Sixties psychedelia as it hit the streets of London. "I guess it must have been late '85 or early '86 – Goth was massive and I was rather taken with these black clothes that masses of people were wearing. But suddenly I noticed that instead of black crimped hair and white paint on leather jackets everyone went colourful. Similar hairstyles but in bright red, pink, blue, and the clothes lit up in bright coloured patterns on people's leather jackets and bright boots. Everything was psychedelic. I know that acid was making a huge return to popularity and I suppose it might have been its influence. Psychedelia had certainly made a comeback."

A mishmash of derivative retro-bands, content to follow Morrissey and Marr's pop without their incendiary style, filled the indie world. The nocturnal swell of The Velvets' 'European Son' was degraded into the saccharine psychedelia of The Byrds' 'Younger Than Yesterday'. According to David Cavanagh, in *The Creation Records Story: My Magpie Eyes Are Hungry For The Prize*, "The most influential band in this break-off sect, the one that set the tone in sound and attitude was The Pastels [who performed regularly at Dan Treacy's Room At The Top Club in Chalk Farm]. They were, claimed a member of their Edinburgh protégés The Shop Assistants, 'probably the most important band in Britain today'."

Cavanagh continued, "The eminence of The Pastels was based partly on a misunderstanding. Their perceived lack of competitiveness made them the cynosure for younger groups who loved the fact that The Pastels had never sold out." In fact, from The Pastels' luddite technique and "pure-pop" style – the sloppy changes, the inadvertent squeals of detuned guitar, the grammar-school longing in Stephen Pastel's larynx – ensued a proliferation of London-based anorak bands or, as Simon Reynolds referred in his *Blissed Out* essay collection, "regressive" rockers.

According to Reynolds, these "cutie-pop" or C86 bands (so-called for the *NME* compilation tape released in that year) were "a whole range of bands going from Creations' Sixties' classicists like Primal Scream and The Weather Prophets to Scottish Buzzcocks imitators The Soup Dragons, to The Pastels and The June Brides to The Bodines and The Shop Assistants' jangle-thrash to The Mighty Lemon Drops. There were others like Stump, who were very Ubu/Beefheart-influenced, and Big Flame who were somewhat Gang of Four-ish. Basically it was less a genre than a field of possibilities determined by a mixture of influences that were all white, guitar-y, and non-dancey: a mix of the Sixties with late Seventies post-punk, new wave, pop-punk, psychedelia, Romanticism, and druggy oblivion. Because the feeling was that the only way forward was to go back, and the Sixties seemed very alluring."

What all of this meant for the raw, drone-based "American" garage of The Spacemen was a unilateral boycott by the major London papers. Worsening the band's prospects for the future was the near simultaneous move of The Pastels to Glass, which left *Sound Of Confusion* on the back burner. "Spacemen 3 were getting bugger all coverage in the UK press at that time," said *Bucketful of Brains'* founder and *Forced Exposure* critic Nigel Cross. "People were totally self-conscious about what they listened to [in the mid-Eighties]. Worst of all was the new Puritanism/anti-rock movement that started a certain wimpiness British rock has never managed to shake off since. Like most of the Creation bands that were rather twee."

Reynolds concurred: "In the UK, it was The Jesus and Mary Chain, Primal Scream, and the milieu around Creation that really pushed that shift towards rediscovering the Velvets, Spector, Brian Wilson, Love, Byrds, Stones, garage punk." But what they produced sounded unmistakably British (i.e. fey and jangly).

The distinctions between British and American neo-psychedelia were best described as the differences between primitivism and primalism. The Spacemen were wholly unique as an English group who espoused the latter. Consequently, of the few punters who acknowledged and lauded

Sound Of Confusion, most belonged to American-based fanzines of the SST variety. The sounds of American neo-psychedelia emphasised the cryptic margins of avant-rock, incorporating evanescent textures over an immutable bass line, producing a "heavy" metallic ambience, contra-distinct to the sing-song filigree of British psychedelia. While the British music press sang the praises of Alan McGee's band *Biff Bang Pow!* and parsley, sage, rosemary, and thyme, *Forced Exposure* recognised a psych-genealogy extending back to the raunchy-stomp of R&B, cosmic free jazz, and the shit-heaps of hard-rock Detroit.

"What made The Spacemen so great was that they were creating from an ideal state of someone from outside America," said Byron Coley. "But they created a better version of American culture in their imagination than could ever have possibly existed. Because they didn't understand it intuitively, or the context which it fit, The Spacemen over-amplified individual elements and recreated a completely unreal but authentic America." Much like the sources from which they wove their musical pastiche, Spacemen 3 were wholly grounded in the contemporary sounds of experimental Americana. The harsh, drone-based garage-style drew closer ties with Sonic Youth's 1986 release, *EVOL*, a landmark collage of noise and melody rooted in New York's no-wave and post-hardcore scenes. Californians Opal shared a similar penchant for The Doors, feed-back, and heavy-distortion; as did refried acidheads The Butthole Surfers, Dinosaur, Jr., and The Flaming Lips. Accordingly, Coley wrote of *Sound Of Confusion*, ". . . best goddamn psych album to crawl outta the dark since the Flaming Lips debut. Grinding, thumping gtrs do a serious job on the best Stooges SONG ever ('Little Doll'), then they bruise a shitload of other stuff in a similar manner. Makes most recent decent Anglo drug-music sound as fruity as it is. This's more like eating psylocine-laced worms w/Clementine hall at some Austin beer blast in the fall of '65 and teleporting to one of those early MC5 gigs where they'd jam on 'Black To Comm' for an hour while sirens screamed in the streets. These boys are serious crunchers as anyone w/the balls to co-write 'TV Eye' as an 'original''d have to be."

Likewise Jon Storey, contributor to British fanzine *Bucketful of Brains*, gushed, "Jeez, the sonic rush of sound opening 'Losing Touch With My Mind' (and that title alone should give you an inkling of where The Spacemen are at) made me suspect I was gonna be subjected to a 'Silver Machine' rewrite; but it wasn't to be. Instead, an overwhelming tide of heavy-ish feedback dominated gloop issued from the speakers, sorta pleasant it was too – though the carpet is irreparably damaged! Checking out the psychy sleeve reverse and spying a song called 'OD Catastrophe' and the picture became clearer. After 'Hey Man' (not nearly as crass as its title) there's a fuzzed up stab at the Elevators' 'Roller Coaster'. A little lacking in dynamics but it's a passionate performance with some anguished "oh, yeah's" from vocalist Jason – hypnotic or monotonous? It's a fine line and depends on your state of mind. 'Mary Anne' I found quite endearing, in a warped sorta way, and on Iggy's 'Little Doll' The Spacemen up the tempo a little it's not quite as claustrophobic as some of the other stuff here despite the same wall-of-fuzz sound. 'OD Catastrophe' is nine mind numbing minutes of distortion, fuzz 'n' effects that'll have all but the most blitzed running for cover – or the "off" switch! There are four Spacemen (2 guitars, bass, drums) and they've beamed in from Birmingham rather than Uranus, thems the facts! Criticism? Not enough variation in tempo, good effects, fuzz 'n' feedback and nice to hear an English band not afraid to unleash a little power to match their madness, doesn't quite have the naked aggression of, say, the Nomads though. A Jesus and Mary Chain for garage freaks, or something more? Maybe so!"

Sound Of Confusion stalled and almost immediately fell into the dustbin of pop-culture. Sonic placed much of the blame squarely on the shoulders of Dave Barker, whose enthusiasm for the album appeared less than stellar. Pissed at what they saw as Barker's non-existent publicity blitz for *Sound of Confusion*, both Jason and Sonic took it upon themselves to set up the PR-charge, however "grass-roots" their methodology. Fashioning more psychedelic-meets-DIY punk flyers, Jason produced them *en masse*, and Sonic continued "borrowing" phone-time and photocopies from his father to contact area fanzines, to which he posted the new single and the advert-sized posters.

Jason and Sonic were determined to resist the dehumanising offal of the Midlands. Throughout the spring and summer of '86, The Spacemen alternated between playing regular gigs at The Black Lion in Northampton, and occasional one-offs in Birmingham, London, and other metropolitan areas, buoyed by a limited word-of-mouth. In May, they played the Rock Garden in London with The Jazz Butcher, then hustled over to Coventry for a gig. In July, they performed at Dudley's, north of Birmingham, and returned a week later at the Sensateria. In August, they shuttled to Brighton, followed next evening by a show at The Black Lion.

If *Sound Of Confusion* ensured a steady trickle of "paying" performances, very few of the responsive venues exceeded anyone's paltry expectations.

In one of the oddest, a gang of local bikers invited Spacemen 3 to highlight their annual bash at the local Imperial Pub down on Oxford Street. The bearded leather-clad hosts were obviously partial to the metallic road beat of Hawkwind, and hadn't expected the hypno-monotonous drones of 'OD Catastrophe' or the heavy ambience of 'Hey Man' when The Spacemen plugged in. "A sizable crowd had turned up," recalled Bassman. "I guess interest had rocketed with the release of our first album. And we thought a biker audience was guaranteed to dig us." But after shambling through two noisescapes, the gang leader rushed the stage and tore the microphone away from Jason. "He got on the mike and announced to the audience that the committee didn't think we were really cutting it," laughed Bassman, "and there should be a show of hands to decide if we should carry on."

The band looked on wearily waiting for the vote. "All the bikers wanted us to stop," replied Sonic, "but there were tons of people there to see us – our friends and fans – so they were outnumbered. They took a vote and more people wanted us to play so we did."

Sonic and Jason set back up on guitar and cranked up more buzzing skronk, but the music died away almost immediately. "The guy got back up onstage and said the committee was still not happy with the quality of our performance," Bassman remembered. "So they paid us off and a disappointed band and audience went home. Funnily enough, we noticed outside that most of the so-called bikers had turned up on bicycles." Said Sonic, "That was certainly one of the more bizarre moments for us on stage."

Bowing to pressure from the band and hoping to jump-start sales on *Sound Of Confusion*, Dave Barker sent Sonic, Jason, Bassman and Natty back to Piddington and Studio Morocco (they refused to return to Lamb's "Home Of The Hits") to record their first prospective single 'Walkin' With Jesus'. Using their earlier demos as a template, they reworked what was fast becoming their most arduous recording. "We went in to remix 'Walkin' With Jesus' and spent a lot more time than we expected," remembered Sonic. After many failed attempts at recording the single, Jason and Sonic reluctantly decided to use the earlier Northampton demo.

However, much to their credit, they re-recorded 'Rollercoaster' for the B-side, a version that surpassed what they had done previously for the album. A 17-minute sheet of repetitious grit, with equal parts anabolic surge and catabolic drift, the pulsing rhythm gradually insinuates itself into the muscle and bone with hisses of hydraulics and pre-pubescent screams reverberating from deep within the drone zone. If there was a clear indication that *Sound Of Confusion* suffered more from production rather than content, this was it. The first realised statement of intent, 'Rollercoaster' defined The Spacemen's snarling, smoking and chugging noise replete with over-driven guitar, Jason's wah-wah, and a drumless space swollen with symphonic texture. " 'Rollercoaster', on the single, was without real drums," affirmed Sonic. "We did it through a click track, me and Jason playing guitars. Then we recorded 'Feel So Good', and we just decided that we liked the idea of 'Rollercoaster' segueing into that kind of nirvana of 'Feel So Good'." To complete the epic B-side, Sonic took Jason and a tape deck to the Billing Aquadrome in Northamptonshire, where they skinned-up and spent the afternoon riding and recording the sounds of a corroded rollercoaster. After hours of hash-induced giggles and dyspeptic turns on the amusement ride, they fucked off without so much as a good sample. Jason eventually retrieved rollercoaster sound effects from a BBC record and dubbed the sounds over the top.

RICHARD FORMBY (future SPECTRUM collaborator): Although I liked much of *Sound Of Confusion*, it was the 'Walkin' With Jesus' 12″ that really did it for me. I thought it was an extraordinarily good record. I saw quite a lot of their early gigs, and they used to stay at my house when they played in Leeds. The gigs around this point were always hit or miss for them. There was always the element of not knowing what would happen next, and never knowing how long the songs would go on for.

SONIC: Around 'Walkin' With Jesus', Jason and I both got business-like about it. We were gung-ho for it; we knew we had something good. I was constantly writing to people, mailing promoters, doing something for the band. Like we started printing those *Walkin' With Jesus* posters, which used to cost us half-a-pence each – we used to print shitloads of them – and then I'd write to like 50 psychedelic fanzines and offer it to them as an insert. So we were getting full-page colour ads for free and that really helped us get going.

The *NME* responded with its first proper write-up of The Spacemen in its November 22, 1986 issue. Journalist Dessa Fox opined simply, "This is a single that didn't hear the warning from the stage earlier, the one about fake psilocybin now being peddled at the back of the crowd. This single has a sort of holy fool expression on its face. It has boundless energy, and wants to get tactile and meandering with electric guitars. . . . There are long, long guitar passages with sly melodies beautifully sustained, the kind that would be meditative if it weren't for the feedback. Sonic Youth are here in spirit, and maybe even drifting fragments of the Swans. More please. Shocker of the week." *Sounds* concurred with its own congratulatory blurb and 'Walkin' With Jesus' peaked at number 46 on its December 13 indie chart. The *Push, Buzz* fanzine included a short interview with Sonic and Jason, and, after much consideration, concluded, "The band's sound is centred upon a ceaseless, droning beat, punishing and wearing away any resistance, whilst strummed and picked guitars do battle all around. Live, it is a throbbing noise, writhing with effects and fuzz, occasionally bolstered by almost inaudible lyrics. Their desire for experimentation is driving them into fresher, positive areas."

After playing pubs in Birmingham, Coventry, and Northampton throughout the summer, the band travelled to London for their first show at Hammersmith venue The Clarendon in late August, opening for Kill Pop Ugly and The Instinks. *Sounds* critic Ricky Kildare proclaimed The Spacemen mystic diviners of Lou Reed with their "hypnotic ouija board of lengthy but frantic song dramas and two note solos" and a welcome change to the soporific drudgery of London pop. Not to be outwitted or over-hyperbolised, the *NME* printed its own capsule critique of the Hammersmith show, musing, "Spacemen 3 are practitioners in the fine art of repetition; instinctively drawing on the lessons of their forefathers and adding an atmosphere, a mood and sonorous backbeat of their own . . . they take hold of a chord and work every last permutation out of it before calmly working through to the next." Fuck the aggrandising rock sermons: The Spacemen finally made the reputable press!

Owing to the steady trickle of interest generated by 'Walkin' With Jesus', and an increase of shows outside of Rugby, the Reverberation Club became increasingly unnecessary. By the closing months of '86, the band had already put out both an album and a single and were preparing to begin their follow-up. The entire operation took a leap into the next gradient and the lustre of small-town self-promotion had faded. And it wasn't as if the ascent had been anything other than tortuous; the general consensus among local punters was unanimously negative toward the 'un'hooked, somnambulistic, repetitive sound Spacemen 3 would churn out. Sonic would riff away on the same chord for half an hour, Jason would turn his eyes upward, ever so glazed as they were, and sing to no one in particular. They were seated on stools for fuck's sake! To paraphrase wild man Hasil Adkins, "This wasn't no rock'n'roll show!" This was ballistics research for Fluxus junkies. Small towns adored predictability, and red-faced townies loved hummable jingles when getting pissed out of their gourds and kicking some unlucky bastard's face in. The buzzing, screeching wash of an hour-long rendition of 'OD Catastrophe' didn't provide adequate soundtrack for thumping skulls.

But this wouldn't be the first or last time folks in Rugby refused patronage to the upstarts of rock'n'roll. When The Rolling Stones came through town in 1964 to lay down their unprecedented raunch, the uptight audience literally booed them off-stage. Of course, the Stones would get the last laugh. But The Spacemen weren't exactly the Stones. "I just think it was one of those things that nobody likes you in your own town," claimed Gavin. "To be anybody decent you've got to be hated in your own town, and The Spacemen had a strong attitude like, 'You don't fucking like us! We don't care!' And I think it took years for people to catch up."

Both personal and professional attitudes had changed between The Cogs and The Spacemen (although, to be fair, most of the blame was directed at Sonic). Spacemen 3 had finally conquered the local circuit, and the Rugby crowds that had loathed them from the beginning. The Cogs of Tyme, meanwhile, hadn't gone much beyond their roots, but remained more popular than ever at The Blitz. The tension was very palpable between the two groups. "There were lots of bad feelings between us," Sonic confessed. "The Cogs got hung up because we got this record deal and they didn't. The only reason The Cogs of Tyme had a bigger audience in Rugby was because they continued to play there when we started to branch out. I mean that whole scene, we just played lots of cool music to a lot of really uncool people." Resentments came to a head one evening during a Reverberation show, when Gavin strolled in with his girlfriend, whom Jason and Sonic both despised. Gavin was girl-crazy, and he almost always had a local chick on his arm. But his latest acquisition was a feisty and belligerent local called Angela, whose large mouth always turned on The Spacemen, and Sonic particularly. She'd give him hell at every turn, while Gavin stood silently beside her, as much frightened by Angela as laughing at Sonic. As she walked past the two of them that evening, Sonic shoved her and she tripped over onto the floor. Gavin looked toward his falling girl and was livid: he jumped at Sonic, punching him once, and wrapping his arm around his neck. They both fell clumsily to the floor in a slapstick display. "It was just really pathetic, but I guess we stopped doing gigs together after that," lamented Gavin.

Although the two bands stopped appearing together, the weekly shows at The Blitz continued sporadically until the end of '86, when the landlord split town with a few thousand pounds from the New Year's takings and the pub closed down. But relations between band members were irreparably damaged. Owing to the fiery split between Gavin and Sonic, The Cogs of Tyme and The Spacemen temporarily severed ties. Relations at Murray Road became heated, when Tim cornered Sonic during one of his many visits, and berated him for his Machiavellian tactics. Angered at what he saw as The Spacemen's policy of using local bands like The Cogs as stepping-stones for their success and then disposing of them, Tim blamed Sonic for the band's paltry successes in the face of Sonic's greed. "I was just astounded at him really," said Sonic, "but it was a reflection of some of the petty crap that was going on in Rugby. Just because we got most of the gigs outside of town and The Cogs of Tyme didn't."

Soon after the spat, Tim moved out of the Murray Road house, leaving Jason, Natty and Rosco with a larger house than they could afford. They relocated to a smaller terraced house on nearby Oxford Street. Rosco and Jason had bedrooms upstairs and Natty converted the front room for his sleeping quarters, decorating the whole ground-floor with National Geographic cutouts. The white walls would be covered with a jumbled montage of Third-World natives and exotic animals.

Natty increasingly showed amazing displays of artistry but he also began acting very strangely, subscribing to a hippie ethos few around him understood. Though he'd always been considered an eccentric character, Natty's comportment at the Oxford Street house was inexplicable even by his standards. Natty was taking loads of hallucinogens at a rapid pace, leaving him frazzled for long periods of time. His belongings were strewn all over the floor in a chaotic hodgepodge. Of his psychotomimetic behaviours, Bassman explained, "Natty seemed to have his own really well-defined sense of what he liked, and when he found drugs like LSD and magic mushrooms, they were Natty's gateway. He loved it." Natty stopped showering and refused to wear shoes. Occasionally he would stride into Oxford Street after a long absence with flowers littering his wild and unkempt hair. Nobody was sure if he'd put them there or if they'd just spontaneously rooted themselves in his bushy mane. He'd taken on a kind of lupine aura around his friends. Though his drumming talent was always questionable, Sonic became concerned when Natty continued tripping up with his bass drums. His refusal to wear shoes had caused his playing ability to suffer. At least from Sonic's perspective. "If you're not going to be bothered enough to wear shoes to play drums, then there's no room for you in the band," Sonic said when he cornered Natty. The drummer simply shrugged in response. "Pete found it hard to discipline him," Bassman insisted. "He resented the fact that Natty was just a natural nonconformist, the most creative of all of us."

BASSMAN: Pete was spending almost every waking hour crashed out at Oxford Street and this finally took a huge toll on everybody because we got sick of the way he took control over our own living spaces. It got fucking unbearable at times. Especially for Natty. Pete found Natty impossible to control and finally pushed him out.

SONIC: This was totally untrue. It represents the views of someone who wasn't partaking in the same drugs or lifestyle. Natty and Pete Bain had the same birthday, and they both had the same mentality. When they came up with some dumb idea, they stuck to it.

"That was a really strange time," Rosco recalled of his early days at Oxford Street. "That was just about the time Pete Kember completely lost the plot. He turned into a vicious bastard." In a noctambulous rampage, Natty disposed of his precious clutter, ripping all the graphics off the walls and painting the entire ground floor white. He covered the walls, the windows, even the screen of the front room television in an ivory slurp. Taking on the contrary aura of a shrooming ascetic, he sat silently in the front room, bathed in monochrome. "Natty's room was usually just total fucking chaos, and then suddenly he went through this really minimal phase where he had absolutely nothing and everything was just white," Sonic recalled.

Natty suffered quite enough of Sonic's incessant bickering, and he tired of playing with the band. His history was littered with the tendency to move on when the first signs of boredom gripped him, and Spacemen 3 was now more onerous than rewarding. Natty's eccentric artistry had finally drawn him out of the only successful band he'd played with. He told Sonic and Jason he was leaving, and asked Rosco to take his place. Rosco laughed, "Natty just said, 'I don't want to do it,' and I told him, 'I don't really want to do it either,' but I *couldn't* do it. I didn't know how to play drums." Rosco had never played the drums but, after some apprehension, decided to take up the empty stool. "I can't remember whether Rosco even had a drum-kit," confessed Sonic. "But Rosco famously used to *borrow* people's equipment. Then he'd sell it. He used to pinch gear all the time. I don't know how he could play drums. But he was good at copying." Rosco joined Sonic, Jason and Bassman onstage for his first gig at Birmingham's Barrel Organ. Though his drumming was hardly up to snuff, everyone agreed to keep him on until someone better came along. Rosco would occupy the drummer's seat for the next two years. "Rosco actually played really well after a fashion," Sonic reluctantly admitted. "He could do lots of Keith Moon and Ginger Baker sort of stuff. But he could never sustain it."

Although Glass Records was Dave Barker's enterprise in name, much of the label's day-to-day tasking was handled by a young South Londoner called Josh Hampson,* an aspiring musician and part-time petrol station attendant. "Josh was my assistant," explained Barker. "He looked after the mastering, booked gigs, and ran the office when I was away on tour. He also brought The Pastels to Glass who sold more records than Spacemen 3 did at the time." It was during his time away from Glass that Hampson started up a jangly psychedelic band called John Aged 4½ in Croydon. Reputed to have had three bassists and numerous drummers, Hampson's band fused some limited experimental textures with a pop-sensibility more akin to early Pink Floyd. The band didn't go much beyond a few local stages and, despite his connection with Glass, Barker failed to see Hampson's potential as a signable talent. Long before he met up with Spacemen 3, Hampson became a bit of a Sixties freak, immersing himself in the bourgeoning shambling scene in London and running The Jazz Butcher fan club. "I first met Josh in '84, when he started coming to Jazz Butcher gigs," Fish said. "He was into The Kinks, wore cardigans and had sideburns. After a while, he was always around, he was always the keen lad who would stand in front. And he got that job working with Dave Barker. And it was just the two of them in there."

After signing with Glass, Sonic occasionally popped down to London to visit Barker, and he'd often meet Hampson. "Josh came along to lots of Spacemen gigs, probably first saw them playing with our lot," Fish said, "and he got well into it." Sonic and Josh began to hang out more regularly, trading ideas and musical tastes. Hampson, being a few years younger, naturally deferred to Sonic in matters of music, but Sonic was duly impressed with the teenager's enthusiasm. The Spacemen stopped off at Hampson's flat to crash out after several late-night shows in London. During one of these evenings Sonic turned the chemical dilettante on to acid and began showing him some of his investigations into guitar manipulations including the use of a Vox Conqueror with its antiquated effects. Sonic explained, "He used to come to all our early gigs around London. To a certain extent, we had the same tastes as this guy, but he was also into a lot of poppy shit like Syd Barrett, which I don't dig." Barker disagreed with Sonic's assessment, claiming, "I know Robert [Josh] was more into free jazz and electronic noise stuff: Miles, Albert Ayler, stuff like that . . . I remember his pre-Loop band sounding pretty much like that before either of us ever heard Spacemen 3. I mean that they had the same sources: Velvets, Stooges, MC5, Elevators, et cetera."

* After attaining cult success in the band Loop, Josh Hampson became known as Robert Hampson. For the purposes of this book, he is referred to as Josh throughout.

PAT FISH: I had a jam at Josh's house in the summer of '86. Going down from the Glass offices all the way back to Croydon where he lived. I remember he had a bus pass and it actually said Sterling Morrison on it. And we just had a couple of guitars jamming away, and, after about 10 minutes, I just thought: 'This is ridiculous. We're just doing The Spacemen: I'm impersonating Sonic and he's impersonating Jason.' And he was. I mean, he was steeped in it.

When Josh Hampson announced his intentions to form Loop (apparently named for John Cale's obscure mid-Sixties tape-loop composition of the same name) Sonic and The Spacemen agreed to take his group on board as an opening act for their first few gigs. Bassman recalled, "First of all Pete got very chummy and a little bit sycophantic about Loop." Agreed Dave Barker, "Early on, Pete and Robert [Josh] were pals." Josh's three-piece, including Neil Mackay on bass and girlfriend Becky on drums fell in well with The Spacemen vibe. On December 18, Sonic and Jason reconvened at The Benn Hall Community Centre along with Mark Refoy's Telltale Hearts, acid-punk group The Purple Things, local-beginners The Darkside, and Loop for the second Christmas on Mars. As with the previous year's psychedelic festival in Rugby, the crowd did not extend much beyond the regulars at The Blitz. But attention that evening was directed less on the thin crowd than towards more sinister things.

"I remember the first time I saw Loop at the show in Rugby," recalled Mark Refoy. "We [The Telltale Hearts] walked into The Benn Hall, just getting ready like all the other bands, doing soundchecks or whatever. And some band was doing a soundcheck on the stage, but I couldn't tell who it was, because I was standing right at the back of the hall and I'm short sighted. But I heard them play and thought it was just The Spacemen doing a soundcheck. And then I got nearer and saw there was a girl on drums, and I thought maybe they had got a girl in the band, because the guy sitting down near her was just a dead-ringer for Jase. But as I walked up to the stage I realised it wasn't The Spacemen, but some other band called Loop." It seemed Loop had suddenly taken on a performing persona and musical style that was unusually similar to the riffing minimalism of their mentors, playing what some saw as blatant "covers" of The Spacemen's fuzzy/tremoloed songscapes. "At the time I think it was purely affectionate," said Pat Fish, "purely that Josh thought it was great music and he wanted to play some. But I've got to say that it's absolutely true, Loop ripped them off." The principal distinction between them and Spacemen 3 was that, in short order, Loop was to be massive.

A few roads away on Cambridge Street, Will Carruthers' squat was suffering a narcotic rampage. Everyone in the house had turned to shooting speed regularly, many to a regimen of daily injections. Because incoming dole cheques were immediately handed over to score more speed, or lager, or the occasional loaf of bread, the absence of rent money had the landlord banging on the front door constantly. Nobody inside cared, so no one bothered to answer the door. The house fell into irreparable squalor. "The whole place got wrecked," Will reported. "It was all bad drugs and nasty things. It got to the stage where you wouldn't find a clean spoon in the kitchen. I mean I'd go down there to eat breakfast and all the spoons were black, you know, from people banging amphetamine." Worse still was the row of empty cupboards and the hunger pangs that gnawed at Will's stomach when the effect of sulphate wore thin. The "katzenjammer-ed" squad of sallow and lank speed freaks buzzed into Sainsbury's and began loading their pockets with scraps of food from the shelves. Unfortunately Will's shaky and sticky-fingered prestidigitation bordered on the laughable bumbling of Tommy Cooper, and he was nabbed by a security guard while struggling towards the exit with a clove of garlic and a box of Maltesers. The game was up.

"I just drifted out about then," remembered Will. "That whole house just got too fucking weird for me. It got more and more seedy after a while." Rumours abounded of bad sulphate that was hitting speed freaks all over Rugby, causing sundry diseases and death. "There were people around town – heavy intravenous drug users – who lost limbs and shit," he continued. "Injecting pills became very big. But the chalk in them caused the veins to block up and you could lose your hand or arm to gangrene." Will was increasingly reaching the end of his tether with speed. He wanted out desperately. "I stopped injecting when I saw these three blokes trying to bang this bad amphetamine," Will explained. "And as they heated it up, it turned into jelly in the fucking spoon. But they still tried to inject it. They were still so desperate to get it in their veins, they were going to put this jelly in their fucking arm. That was it for me.

"I started knocking around with musicians, because I still had my guitar," he explained. Will started playing in a loose, on-again off-again group with Natty, and he'd often spend his days hanging out at Oxford Street. "I started mixing with those guys down at Natty and Jason's house, and I started going to their gigs a bit more," Will added. "I just wanted to get in a band." His time there was an escape, however fleeting, from the hellish conditions that he suffered just up the road. Sadly, what he and Natty attempted in a band quickly degraded into a psychedelic free-form bluesy mess. Their cannabis drenched jams erred toward crazy freak-outs but little of the musical debris resembled anything close to a song. After spying Sonic nodded out in the front room on several occasions, Will pondered if his temporary liberation was just a matter of jumping out of the frying pan into the fire.

CHAPTER FIVE

Transparent Radiation

1987

With the turn of the new year came a seminal period for Spacemen 3, a moment when any and all shambling, amateurish trappings were to be shed, when the decorous garnish of "retro/garage/punk" was abandoned, and in its place was served something deep and organic and sweet, an ineffable lyric penned by Mayo Thompson himself. The Reverberation Club was past history, and all immediate ties to Rugby severed for the possibilities of London, country, and continent. Spirits were higher than the sun, as Sonic and Jason prepared for their *meisterwerk*, *Perfect Prescription*. All in all, it was a bucolic pub band's wet dream. *Perfect Prescription* would define Spacemen 3's musical and collaborative zenith, and hoist Jason and Sonic to the successful precipice from which they would plunge.

In January the band retired to Paul Adkin's VHF Studios for the now infamous six-month session of hash smog, radiophonic effluvium, and behavioural excess that might well bring a menacing smile to the ossified corpse of Georges Bataille. The 8-track VHF Studios was adjacent to a sheet metal works and a garage on Arches Lane, located in the industrial "no man's land" between Rugby and Brownsover. The VHF building itself had the distinct feel of a bunker. It was an 888 square feet concrete block structure with exposed interior brick and wood painted grey and red in a Hessian style. The inside was a large empty shell of a room in which Adkins had installed a soundproof studio and control-room, leaving an L-shaped anteroom for lounging. Upstairs was a storage area full of electronics and obsolescent gizmos. Adkins was a musician with an electronics background who had spent years dipping in and out of home recording. Having built VHF around '85 to further explore his interests in recording and production, he'd often travel to and from his home in nearby Daventry to work on demos and backing-tracks for local bands. Adkins also worked out a contract with a radio DJ to record and produce radio jingles and voice-over commercials.

Sonic and Jason learned of the studio's existence through previous studio engineer Graham Walker, who had recently relocated from

Sheriff's studio to Adkins' VHF. When Walker heard that the band was looking to record around Rugby, he suggested they use VHF where Paul was eager to bring in young bands. Walker volunteered to engineer the album and recommended that Sonic and Jason buy block time from Adkins. The band walked into the studio with gear in hand, eager to begin working through demos as they negotiated a long-term deal.

Some of the earliest attempts at recording at the 8-track studio yielded demoed versions of 'Take Me To The Other Side', 'Transparent Radiation', 'Walkin' With Jesus', and 'Things'll Never Be The Same', some of which radically differed from the final album versions. Christening the recordings the "Out Of It" Demos, referring to a sizable importation of Thai weed that coincided with their inception, the band also demoed 'Starship' (MC5 cum Sun Ra), 'I Want You Right Now' (MC5 cum The Troggs), 'Ode To Street Hassle' (Lou Reed), 'Call The Doctor', and a second version of 'Come Down Easy' (it was '87 by now). Already the mood and direction of the bourgeoning recordings was one (mind) bent on experimentation, mutation and alteration. As happened with The Spacemen, the slow steady ascendance of any band from its juvenile roots to its prime was a geological study of time, friction and pressure. The incendiary spark was unidentifiable, however spectacular the resultant fallout: four Spacemen skinning up and descending deeper into FXs. "Paul bought a Yamaha SPX90 digital effects processor at this point," Walker continued. "Initially, whilst the band were all crashed on beanbags with the Thai, headphones and a live mike in the room, I began putting the SPX90 through its paces to see what it could usefully do. When used sparingly it could thicken a mono drone sample and give a pseudo-stereo effect or, when suffering an attack of the Thai giggles in the headphones, the extreme settings got well . . . silly."

> SONIC: They're one of the first things I can remember us recording at that time. It's us lying on the floor laughing through echoes and stuff. Basically there were four people just giggling. Thai weed giggling at the sound of our own laughter going through echoes!

The two songwriters squatted in the recording room playing different bits of gear they'd pulled from the attic above. Jason located a cheap, learner's Farfisa organ and took to it instantly while Sonic adjusted the spring reverb on his newly purchased Fender Jaguar to get a crispy, surf sound. "Pete was discovering a lot of new things around this time," claimed Bassman, "and finding an amplifier with a tremolo effect on it was a bit of a revelation for him." Sonic pressed down a single key on the Farfisa fed through the high-speed tremolo control on his Vox Conqueror. A beautiful electronic pulse bled through the entire studio.

Jason also began experimenting and altering his own vocals in order to better suit the tranquil, gospel-ish atmospheres of the recordings. He had never attempted to modify his gruff Iggy-style timbre as it had suited the early Spacemen material and was *de rigueur* with the Sudden Death Cult-style Goth of Indian Scalp. But with the protracted length of time in the studio, and the deluge of dope that stained his gristle, Jason added a soft melancholia to his voice, where it had only snarled and fumed in *Sound Of Confusion*. He started singing through a small vocal PA with speakers in order to perfect a muted and shadowed vocal persona while retaining the necessary J. J. Cale-style rawness. "I think we had a lot of time to experiment in the studio with *Perfect Prescription*," recalled Sonic. "And, at some point, Jason realised he could sing in different ways. He got the chance to experiment with it and try to sing in lower and quieter voices." The product was a Delta-blues/punk hybrid voice that would fill the album with differing tones, adding a multivalent resonance to many of the tracks.

While everyone was eager to jump into recording, they quickly realised the antiquated trappings of VHF would, in fact, need upgrading. Abbey Road it was not. "The recording equipment was only an 8-track but geared towards high-quality voice recordings on European broadcast standard open-reel tape," remembered Walker. "The microphone cupboard included a Neumann u87i, a pair of AKG C414bs and a d12, as well as the usual sm57s and 58s. Monitoring with DT100s and NS10s. Outboard effects included Drawmer gates and compression, Roland digital reverb and an early digital delay/sampler. The heart of the studio being a 24-channel mixer wired with a 16-track tape loom for when 16-track machines had previously been hired in."

Adkins was eager to comply and a deal was hammered out between himself and Glass Records to overhaul VHF to 16-track in return for an upfront lump sum that would provide the band "unlimited time" to use the studio. "Advance payment was negotiated with which Paul purchased a 16-track recorder with autolocator and timecode sync, as well as an Accessit autopanner/tremolo box," recalled Walker. "These items permanently upgraded the studio to 16-track, ready for the *Perfect Prescription* sessions but, foolishly thinking I'd receive payments later by being named on the recording, I didn't negotiate any payment for myself for the following six months of work."

Jason and Sonic had long since quit their fledgling jobs and dug themselves a niche inside the control room where they would smoke, eat, sleep, and work for the next several months. On days when the studio was available, Sonic would leave in the afternoon to pick up Graham, and swing by Oxford Street to grab Jason before heading down to the studio.

They piled into the control room, listening to playbacks and working on the odd song, chain-smoking dope along the way. Someone would set up the Reverberation light show, comprised of glistening mirrored balls and fluorescent orbs which would paint the interior in strange red and green hues. From inside these contraptions, the whirring motors emanated drones that would often find their way onto the recordings.

Pete Bain and Rosco would turn up later in the evening usually to check the progress and work out some of their parts before leaving again in the late evening. Both songwriters would continue to work all hours, playing the various bits on guitar or singing and then altering lyrics. Often they'd crash out on a couple of old mattresses lying about the studio as they listened to the day's recordings. "What I remember most about those long nights was getting hot cheese sandwiches from the bakery opposite the studio at about four in the morning," Graham recalled. Joked Sonic, "So we sat around and said, 'Aw fuck . . .' I lost half an ounce of dope one day in the studio, it was that fucking crazy. We just sat around for days and days and days, often not doing anything except listening to stuff." Sonic was using more bags of junk by the inception of *Prescription* although he remembers rarely shooting-up in the studio. He found speed surprisingly non-conducive to late-night sessions and Jason had abandoned it following earlier bumpy experiences. They disciplined themselves according to certain drug regimens, though both found working under the influence of dope essential to their song craft. "We didn't do anything if we had no drugs, though that rarely happened," he added. "The drug experiences and modes were massively influential on our musical writing and our lyrical subject matter."

JASON: The idea that you can take drugs and do music is out there, it's just not on. It's really bad science, isn't it? . . . But it's like saying the greatest psychedelic music was made by people with frilly shirts. It all goes with the romanticism of a rock'n'roll idealism, but there's so much bad music made by people on drugs.

SONIC: Jason stopped taking heavy drugs around *Perfect Prescription* time. Actually, earlier than that, but particularly around that time. I mean he took opiates after that, but he didn't take psychedelics for quite a while.

PAUL ADKINS: They really hadn't made too big a deal about it, but I think I was a bit heavy-handed from the start – laying down the law that I didn't want drugs in the studio – I tried to avoid that, which is partially why Graham ended up doing a lot of the early sessions. I just expected to be raided every week if it was known that they were there.

GRAHAM WALKER: It sort of went unsaid that Paul didn't want to know. If we'd got busted in the studio . . . he knew absolutely nothing about the drugs.

For the earliest recordings of 'Take Me To The Other Side' Sonic twiddled with a crunching riff while Jason began improvising vocals based on lyrics Sonic had written earlier for another composition. Although Sonic was taken aback at what he saw as Jason 'borrowing' his lyrics, he loved the way Jason improved them to make the vocal fit. Sonic also added a second, minimal riff that echoed against the drone-drone and unzipped into the central riff. Through the sludgy hum of electronics, Jason scatted out impromptu choruses including, "I put a spike into my vein/ Things'll never be the same . . .". Opening for Glaswegians The Shamen in January in the tiny upstairs room at Rugby's Peacock Pub, the band debuted 'Take Me To The Other Side'. Performed live, the song was a powerful cocktail of distortion and tremolo, drowning out any errant voices. Consequently, this earliest version was also purely instrumental, verging more on an extended effects freak-out à la Syd Barrett's 'Interstellar Overdrive' than a four-minute pop song.

Next, the band turned to a demo of The Red Krayola's 'Transparent Radiation'. They worked the cover through from a version that Sonic located on International Artists' *Epitaph For A Legend*. Unlike the more widely recognised album version, the epitaph version was a stripped-down guitar/bass/vocals affair that Sonic attempted to work out with himself on vocal and Jason on lead guitar. Due to his inexperience in transcription, Sonic mistakenly left out the fourth chord. There was another problem early on when no proper lyric sheet could be found. Careful to create a version worthy of the original, and unable to decipher the esoteric and slurred lyric, Sonic phoned Mayo Thompson at London's Rough Trade for a read-through. "I told him I wanted to check the lyrics to 'Transparent Radiation' because we were covering it and he didn't remember the song," laughed Sonic. "Over 10 years later, I met him in Los Angeles and he said that he loved my version. He liked the way we'd taken it from four chords to three chords. At the time we didn't really know."

Jason updated 'Come Down Easy''s lyrical hook from the original Northampton demo to correspond with the '87 version, and fiddled with a number of subtle transformations until he perfected his new arrangement. With a weave of acoustic guitar churning out a trad-folk/blues complete with Bassman's descending bass-runs, Jason croons of *fin de siècle* paranoia and boredom, imploring for divine relief. But his simultaneous desire to dance, shake, writhe with his lover (a woman or a drug is indecipherable) and experience Dionysian possession introduces a paranoid rush of excitement. Jason's echo-laden vocal building to the frenzied yell of a Southern Baptist moved by tongues of fire. His jittered body having lost all sobered autonomy, he's uncertain whether he will ever come down. Trapped in the religious crisis of total drug-possession, he screams for Intervention ("Jesus Christ I was only shakin' . . . Lord!") only to fade out on the verge of schizoid breakdown (or conversion).

For the 'Walkin' With Jesus' and 'Come Down Easy' demos, Jason switched to acoustic guitar, adding a Stones-ish feel to Sonic's use of heavy tremolo. Both 'Walkin' With Jesus' and 'Come Down Easy' also hinted at similar strides each musician had made following the Northampton sessions to excise the fuzzy garage-rock and shuffling rockabilly rhythms from their earliest compositions. Emphasis was placed less on a horizontal method of kicking-out the rhythms and more on a vertical layering of multiple textures and sounds. In much the same way, 'Things'll Never Be The Same' was transformed into a rotating wash of feedback and wah-wah, which Sonic modulated by hand as he sat on the studio floor. Jason worked much of his guitar parts through backwards and dubbed slushy distortion on top, creating a thick, plodding wreckage of Fender. Still dissatisfied with the final product, Sonic varispeeded the track – a production homage to the late, great studio wizard Joe Meek – to tighten up the plodding tempo.

> JASON: That's the period of The Spacemen that I was very into doing. It was the first time that I wasn't writing songs that were based on anybody else's songs. 'Walkin' With Jesus' was purely about what I was doing, and I was kind of shocked to see the lyric written down. Same with 'Things'll Never Be The Same'; it was the first time I thought, "Yeah I really want to do this. I really want to write songs." That's a cool record; I really like it.

> SONIC: It was just that we were getting to be better musicians working with each other.

Since procuring a bootleg copy of the MC5's *Kick Out the Jams* (difficult to come by in the early Eighties), Sonic had been an avid Motor-City fanatic. He and Jason had since come to idealise and mimic the Five's status as revolutionaries of the late Sixties, when musicians immersed in free jazz, the European electronic avant-garde, and dirty rock'n'roll, began seriously studying one another for inspiration. The Spacemen endeavoured to capture this secret moment in musical history with their rendition of the Five's gutter-rock stab at Sun Ra's 'Starship'. Heaving with layer upon layer of noise over a repeated riff, nearly bulging out at the seams as it chugs toward complete textural saturation and rhythmic freak-out, 'Starship' is 15 minutes of signal-to-noise embolism digesting and refluxing Detroit hard-rock, cosmic jazz-improv, and the electric entropy of Musica Electronica Viva. "'Starship', the MC5 song, we arranged," Sonic said. "The end of it has every drop of feedback I could get out of the guitar, and the final thing was I chucked my guitar into the middle of the room. It's one of the last sounds on the thing, there's some more of Jason's guitar going, but there's quite a definite 'plonk' at the end as you hear my Jaguar fall in the studio."

In February, amidst the controlled chaos of the germinating album, the band broke briefly from the *fumière* at VHF to play a few gigs, including a return to the Hammersmith Clarendon on the 13th of the month to play support for The Pastels ("they were too busy working at the library to be a band," Sonic recalled) and The BMX Bandits ("we thought they were a kind of joke"). The wide breach between such shambling anorak-pop as crooned in Stephen Pastel's 'Oh Baby Honey', and The Spacemen's one-chord monster 'OD Catastrophe' was never so evident. "A forthright extremity," claimed a *Melody Maker* journalist in a March piece done on Spacemen 3. The Mary Chain's Jim Reid and Douglas Hart appeared in the crowd for what was probably their first ever Spacemen show, an interesting meeting of two legendary underground bands. Recalled Laurence Verfaillie, Creation's head of PR during the late Eighties and long-time girlfriend to Reid, "Jim was a huge Spacemen 3 fan. I remember when he went to see them and, when he came back, all he could talk about was how great they were."

The Jesus and Mary Chain had made headlines in 1984 when Alan McGee dragged them down from East Kilbride and put them on at The Loft, where they fooled their way through Syd Barrett's 'Vegetable Man' before trashing their gear and rekindling a lost love for feedback. The *NME* caught wind of the story and wrote them up as a second-generation Pistols. The Mary Chain's ensuing tour ended in nightly riots, though incitement appeared to come more from the Reids' onstage taunting than the uproarious levels of guitar ballistics. In fact, as the fervour spread ahead of the band, the Reid brothers would barely shamble into their first "song" before violence would erupt from the audience. Much like the apocryphal yarns that mushroomed from Dylan's electric debut at Newport '65, The Mary Chain riots took on mythic status that ultimately outgrew the band. As Oxford promoter Dave Newton recalled, "The Jesus and Mary Chain were an event.

'Upside Down' was just one of those earth shattering records that come along once in a lifetime. I think the story behind The Mary Chain was more press-worthy and their gigs were chaotic and often riotous. The name courted controversy and they seemed to bring danger and excitement to everything that they did." None more evident than in the Reids' early B-side 'Jesus Suck', and wildly unconventional *Psychocandy* LP, which solidified their reputation as Pistols-like iconoclasts, twisted and twirled by their own McLarens, namely Alan McGee and Geoff Travis.

"We were going for years before the Mary Chain even started," claimed Sonic in a 1988 *Forced Exposure* interview. "Mary Chain hit 'Upside Down' and everybody says we sound like Jesus & Mary Chain – it's quite infuriating after being ignored for so long. I didn't listen to *Psychocandy* for at least a year after that – but since I played it, I do believe it's one of the classic albums of the Eighties." Jason was equally perplexed by the comparisons made between both bands, "I couldn't see any similarities to what we were doing. I've since come to love *Darklands* but I still don't get the first one, and I still don't think it mirrored what we were doing at all."

Moreover, while the temptation may be to classify The Jesus and Mary Chain with Spacemen 3 simply for their similar investigations into "noise", and their simultaneous recognition of musical subculture as ciphers of the past, the two bands' roots only seem to converge at the totems of The Velvet Underground, The Stooges, and The Beach Boys. The Mary Chain divagated into the strange netherworlds of Einsturzende Neubaten and The Wedding Present alongside the Sixties über-harmonies of The Ronettes, while The Spacemen based much of their minimal crunch on the rambling holler of Chess legends Muddy Waters and Bo Diddley and down south to Memphis soul. "I don't think the Mary Chain had the lyrical relevance to me personally," added Will. "There was something a little more real about Spacemen 3, you know what I mean?"

To some degree, the debate may come down to the more diversified record collection, but each band's genealogical traces punctuate the crucial difference. While The Mary Chain seemed to relegate feedback the role of musical *sine qua non*, an end in itself, The Spacemen chose to elevate its effect beyond mere novelty as a means of making connections. "As transfixing as Spacemen 3 gigs were, there was never a chance of the PA being smashed up by the crowd when the band walked off after only playing a 12-minute set of pure feedback!" Dave Newton added. "Obviously The J&M Chain were going to get the press coverage. Musically I think that the Spacemen 3 influence was more subtle. The Mary Chain was all about *Psychocandy*. Although they managed to then move forward and make some great albums, *Psychocandy* was their moment. Spacemen 3 probably had a greater influence on other musicians but The Jesus and Mary Chain were far more visible." To put it another way, by the time Spacemen 3 began recording *Perfect Prescription*, The Mary Chain were already ossified at their peak. While the appearance of *Psychocandy* had captured a certain controversial blitz in the papers, The JAMC's lack of consistency had long since outweighed the novelty. The Reid Brothers had gone into a kind of paranoid self-exile following the album's release, propelled by a schizophonica of feedback, riots, and cheap lager.

At the end of the month, Spacemen 3 supported The Folk Devils at The Old Five Bells, a cavernous ballroom-sized pub on Harborough Road in Northampton. Perhaps bolstered by the raging Goth scene in the immediate area, the venue had grown in popularity with eastern Northamptonshire youth and was hosting bigger and bigger acts. Club promoter and business entrepreneur Gerald Palmer had done much to attract The Spacemen to his venue.

Palmer grew up in the south of Wales, near Cardiff, to a Jewish mother and gentile father who was a career serviceman in the Marines. Gerald had only the requisite education provided by an area state school but learned much of his business acumen from his maternal grandparents during summer holidays to their home. He left home after 'A'-levels, travelling to the Far East and Australia, where he first attempted to manage local rock bands in Perth (home to Kim Salmon and Scientists) and dabbled with mushrooms and hash in Asia. Having settled back into English life and the Northamptonshire village of Titch Marsh (very near the site of his father's childhood home in Oundle) in the early seventies, he endeavoured putting his erudite business sense to the test. In the ensuing years Palmer founded and ran a small network of incorporated ventures, including an industrial cleaning company, Albright Cleaners Limited, a chain of take-away restaurants throughout Cambridgeshire, and a site-services repair and building company eventually titled Palmer Holdings Limited.

But Gerald remained fascinated with the music business and simultaneously hustled between daily maintenance of his companies and evening work as a promoter. Under the titles Head Music, Trooper Promotions, and Kamikazi Promotions he'd promoted hundreds of concerts around the Midlands and East Anglia since the early Seventies, from Stamford and Lincoln to Hemel Hempstead and from Coventry to Cambridge. He had networked his promotion activities between tour-managers, bands, and club-owners, throughout the prog-rock, punk, and post-punk period and into the Eighties, during which time he'd put on every band from The Enid to The Clash to Theatre of Hate. By 1984,

Gerald's attention was drawn to The Old Five Bells, a ramshackle pub on the outskirts of Northampton, which had suffered a steady decline in venue promotion despite its massive function-room and austere environment. The pub owner was eager to strike a deal in order to bolster business and Gerald was able to negotiate a favourable lease that allowed him complete *carte blanche* on the Five Bell's function space. He consolidated a large portion of his concert promotions at the pub while raking in all of the door fees and a cut of the bar. Large gigs would draw crowds beyond capacity, prompting bouncers to squeeze hundreds of extra punters against the back wall. Soon The Old Five Bells became one of the hottest clubs in Northamptonshire and yet another financial score for Palmer. "Musically and artistically, I think it was very successful because we did have a lot of formative bands that did become very successful in the late Eighties," said Gerald of The Five Bells. "I mean, you name it and when they were starting out this was a venue they played at." Pat Fish recollected the sudden surge of hit acts appearing in Northampton at the time. "There were a couple of seasons of fashionable-ish underground bands in '87. We even got Tom Verlaine, for heaven's sake. And The Jazz Butcher opened for Robyn Hitchcock around then. The promoter, of course, was Gerald."

With all the support acts that came in and out of the clubs over the years, Palmer kept abreast of the bourgeoning Eighties indie-rock scene, though he didn't fancy himself an Allen Klein or Malcolm McLaren and hesitated about crossing the line between promotion and management. Not that Palmer didn't exude the part. His six-foot, two-inch, 15-stone frame gave him the striking presence of a club bouncer and instantly attracted him to the wispy and wilted indie rockers. Tapes and seven-inch records would flood his office, all from young musicians desperate for gigs. "You have these bands who think you have all the answers," Gerald cited. "You're a promoter. They're young, naive, immature, and inexperienced. And they say, 'We're looking for a manager. Are you interested?' And that's generally how it starts." Palmer had been approached for management positions by a whole host of young indie bands, including The Folk Devils and My Bloody Valentine, as they toured through their earliest incarnations.

Owing to this glut of inquiry and free music, Gerald took only polite interest in Spacemen 3 when Sonic shoved copies of *Sound Of Confusion* and 'Walkin' With Jesus' in his hand during a forgettable evening of music at The Five Bells sometime in late '86. When Gerald finally got around to playing the records, he was not impressed with the noisy, garage-derivative sound and "shelved" the two albums. He'd heard faint whispers about the local Rugby band's tumultuous and incendiary performances but he was soon to hear much more. "Pete would ring any promoter looking for gigs," said Gerald. "And he pestered and pestered. He was prodigious in his output. He pursued not just me but everybody, I think. He was very persistent and ambitious. He was by far the most ambitious, in terms of Pete and Jason. At least on the surface anyway. Jason was very quiet and enigmatic. He didn't really speak very much. Pete was the one I got to speak with. That's how we first met, even before they were recording *Perfect Prescription*."

Gerald finally acquiesced after Sonic's frequent phone calls bordered on supreme irritation, and he booked them for a handful of support slots starting at the end of '86. When Spacemen 3 strolled into The Old Five Bells for the first time, Gerald was instantly struck by their hip, slightly dishevelled appearance. Sonic and Jason had features almost like male pin-ups, the former a tall, aristocratic 20-year-old with a crew-cut who was a dead-ringer for Jeremy Irons, and the latter a slightly shorter but no less striking kid with a dark and hirsute flair. His opinion of Bassman and Rosco was less favourable but he was impressed by how organic Spacemen 3 appeared: they just looked like a band. And they looked fucking cool.

Their cool and calm demeanour belied their shambling and jumbled performances, and Gerald turned stone-cold after he witnessed Sonic and Jason sit through a short set, with a near 10-minute interlude for re-tuning. The thick flood of noise and drones on record did not translate well into live performance. Or so thought Gerald upon first inspection. "They only did a half-hour set, maybe 40 minutes as a support act. I was not particularly impressed. There was a novelty factor for the audience, because they sat down. They were playing their guitars seated, and they were totally stationary. They were totally immobile. Not particularly entertaining. Not particularly good. I'll admit it went over me completely the first few times." On these evenings, Gerald had in tow a group of five young men, who he payrolled as gophers, roadies, and a general entourage of sorts. They'd hump the gear in and out for the headlining band and work the door, in addition to sharing their thoughts on the opening acts. When he asked the group's opinion on The Spacemen, Gerald claimed the unanimous response was, "They all hated the band. They thought they were absolutely goddamn awful. And my opinion was that I wasn't far behind them at that stage."

"Gerald openly confessed to disliking us, he made this known right from the start," recalled Bassman, who eyed Palmer with a mix of chagrin and dread. "He just smelt money and wanted a share, as simple as that. He was a slightly intimidating figure: tall, bald, Jewish, with a moustache. He reminded me of a stereotypical villain." Gerald was intrigued by

Spacemen 3 despite their poor debut. Especially by Sonic and Jason, who according to Gerald, were just so damned arrogant: in their shuffle, their non-existent stage performance, their musical tastes, and their "fuck-off" attitudes. Through the beginning of the following year, he brought The Spacemen over to Northampton on many occasions, scouting their progressing and optioning other talents along the way.

> PAT FISH: One night I went to see The Spacemen opening for the Folk Devils at The Five Bells. I was stopped at the door when I told them my name for the guest list. I was told to stay put; I wondered what I had done wrong. Then Gerald appeared and said he loved The Jazz Butcher and wanted to be my manager. I didn't really have a band or a record deal at that point, nor was I in any hurry to get one really, so I didn't have much need of a manager, least of all some bloke from the middle of nowhere whom I had only just met. I figured that if I needed help in the business, I knew enough people on the scene in London. And Hamburg. And New York . . . you get the picture. Why should I involve myself with some businessman from Corby, of all places? That was the way I was feeling. But he wouldn't let it lie. I had just come in off the street, remember, and I was keen to see The Spacemen. As they started to set up, I said to Gerald, "You want to manage this lot, mate. They've got something going on right now." Basically, I was trying to turn away the conversation so that I could watch the band in peace, but sometimes I think about that remark and wonder what I did back there.

Plans were also in the works for a short jaunt across Europe in March. Unlike the UK and America, the Continent had had a long history of welcoming, even adoring the shambling bands despite their unpolished and raucous adolescence. Sonic had tripped over to Holland in '85 to check out the network of clubs, in hopes of building up a roster of venues in the absence of any tour management. Of course, he'd also looked into places to score with aspirations to hit upon the near mythic chemicals solicited in Amsterdam. While on the prowl, he'd come across a strange pub called Mazzo, a massive "members-only" club that was, in reality, a cocaine speakeasy. The decadent old Dutch parlour was a perfect candidate for a Spacemen show. And the owners agreed to host the band. Meantime, *Sound Of Confusion* caused a small but palpable buzz in Holland, and through word-of-mouth and radio time, Sonic procured an agent called Gunter, from Dutch-based Circa-Do, to organise the small tour.

Throughout the end of February and the first of March, Sonic and Jason reconvened at VHF between tripping out and signing on, to skin-up and put down more tracks. Drug consumption had reached such excesses during late-night recordings that they took to stashing caches of hash inside the studio. On one particular occasion, Sonic stowed a large sack of hash inside the wall, only to find it missing the next evening. The band took the better part of a day tearing the room apart without a trace of the bag. Had they already smoked it and forgotten or did someone in The Spacemen have sticky fingers?

Relations between the musicians was manageable, although to some present it became more and more apparent that Sonic was asserting his leadership over a band that had begun as a democratic collective. Not to be misconstrued: The Spacemen had not based their organisation on any socio-political principles; they weren't reading Althusser or Gramsci between takes. That post-punk phenomenon had died out years before when Scritti Politti decided to hang up their socialist trappings and gorge on the sweet excesses of pop. But like any zero-point D.I.Y. rock band formed from a group of provincials, some expectation of equality was to be expected. At least the rhythm section thought so.

Such conflict arose as a result of Sonic's reworked 'Ode To Street Hassle' demo, evidently a steadily mounting pressure exerted by the songwriter's behaviour as *de facto* sole producer and director towards the rest of the band. Bassman was generally displeased with the increasingly larger role Sonic began to play, punctuated by his Lou-Reed "tribute". "I wasn't impressed with 'Ode To Street Hassle'," recalled Bassman. "This was the first Spacemen album with Pete singing . . . and he used a soft spoken delivery that compensated for his limited range. I didn't like his vocal, and I thought the title of the song was too sycophantic. After voicing my opinions, Pete responded with his usual bitchy attitude which resulted in a confrontation."

"His input was so minimal musically, it's unbelievable," said Sonic of Bassman's contributions. "The only person who probably did even less was Natty, you know, and Rosco, who apart from playing the drums, rehearsed occasionally. That was all they did. In fact, most of the time Pete Bain used to sit in the corner of the studio sulking. That was his role: to sit and sulk." But Bassman's complaint pointed to a much larger problem in the pecking order of the band, as he claimed Sonic almost single-handedly took over the sessions to the band's – and especially Jason's – detriment. "Sonic had a bigger part to play," continued Bassman. "Previous to that he had tried doing some writing which was fine. Some of his songs were good, but he wasn't as consistent as Jason. It was something he had to work on. But *Perfect Prescription* was the album that he decided to complete on his own, so he started singing a lot of songs and giving a lot of direction. I was always more inclined to work with Jason. I just didn't think that Pete should have so much say. It was all ego . . . For Sonic it was just like, 'I want to be Brian Wilson.' Fucking Brian Wilson! He would just get so obsessed with certain things. I was falling out with him and it got to be very difficult for me during those sessions really."

At the beginning of March, the band got together to rehearse their set-list for the imminent 10-day tour. On March 6, they played the Hackney Empire Theatre in London as the third instalment in a series of X parties (also at Hackney's Club Mankind) thrown over the course of the previous year and which would become the inspiration for Sonic's magnum opus 'Ecstasy Symphony'. The band travelled to London to play these gigs for a promoter called Big Steve who organised late-night, multi-act events, drenched in psychedelic accoutrements and kaleido- scopic light shows. Though Ecstasy was floating around the perimeter of the London scene and the festival's eponym hinted at its usage, most of the spaced-out partygoers were on dope and acid-derivatives and not MDMA. Ecstasy had yet to ascend to national recognition in Britain.

It was also at these parties that Sonic and Jason seriously incorporated the sitar and saz into their play lists, a foretaste of their later 'Indian Summer' and 'Dreamweapon' material. Jason noodled about on the sitar, playing five-stringed dulcet licks that sympathised with the drone strings and jangled over the mesmerised audience. Sonic countered on the elec- trified saz, sliding along a pentatonic scale on the top pair of strings as the bottom two-pair reverberated on one chord, creating a ringing drone in A. Although the exotic instrumentation was first used in Spacemen shows only as a novelty (Sonic would play saz on 'Things'll Never Be The Same'), the eclectic platform for the X Parties and 'Indian Summer' allowed Sonic and Jason to work out extended, Eastern-inflected drone-pieces that they would perform throughout '87 and '88. *Forced Exposure* writer and Spacemen 3 zealot, Nigel Cross, recalled an early Indian Summer gig in Chalk Farm. "It was definitely one of the best Spacemen 3 gigs I ever saw – incredibly hypnotic like being in some opium den in Istanbul or somewhere – both druggy and very exotic!"

The band and sound-engineer Graham left for Europe, as had so many groups before them, in a sparsely comfortable tour van, chauffeured by a hired hand for the 10-hour drive to Flemish country. The tour com- menced in Antwerp, Belgium, on March 10, at the "1000 Appeltjes" youth centre, a rather drab looking pub with a slipshod stage. Their debut was solid and the patrons appeared hungry for the cacophonous sludge echoing from The Spacemen's amplifiers. "The group started one and a half hours late with a warming-up they called 'Starship'," wrote a reviewer from *De Morgen*. "Probably an impression of the MC5-song with the same name, but you never can tell . . . It was mostly wild fuzzing and suicidal fast guitars." The night ended on a sour note, however, when Sonic discovered a less than honest punter had pinched several sheets of newly penned lyrics from his guitar case. But appropriation is the highest form of flattery.

The van wound its way through Den Haag for a show at Paard the following evening, then hustled across country for shows at the Vera Club in Groningen and Eindhoven, Holland. Dope was in abundance once the van entered the Dutch townships. "I didn't really notice who was taking what, but the phrase 'de-criminalised, not compulsory' comes to mind," said Graham. After a day of respite, the band played a show in Brussels on the 15th at the Anciens Belgique (site of the infamous "23 Minutes Over Brussels" concert), where they attracted a modest cadre of supporters, who sported handcrafted Spacemen 3 T-shirts. The band performed solidly, bolstered by a searing combination of songs, including 'Starship', 'Come Down Easy', 'Mary Anne', 'Walkin' With Jesus', 'Rollercoaster', 'Things'll Never Be The Same', 'Take Me To The Other Side', 'OD Catastrophe', and a fine version of 'Losing Touch With My Mind'. These songs would become staples of Spacemen live shows for the next two and a half years. After the performance, the club owners treated the band to free liquor well into the morning.

The tour concluded in Amsterdam on March 16, with the band slashing away as a Technicolor projection-show whirled across Mazzo's cavernous belly. That night they crashed at their promoter Gunter's flat in the middle of the city's red-light district. The situation got a bit crazy when Graham disappeared during the night and failed to return. Said Graham, "I'd nipped out for some fresh air as I couldn't sleep, but then couldn't find the tiny little doorway leading back up to the flat. In fact I couldn't even find the right street as they all looked exactly the same." An inebriated Bassman nearly went spare when he discovered the sound engineer missing. Meantime, Sonic scored some smack and nodded out on the stove, grilling holes into his jeans and nearly setting fire to the apartment. The next morning Graham reappeared in the doorway, and the touring party loaded back into the van. Having made their debut outside English soil a success, they drove back to England with cocaine-sizzled dreams for the future.

> BASSMAN: The first gig we had back in the UK was at the Club Dog in London. I think after the tour Pete may have gone back to Amsterdam, maybe to take some more drugs, then back to Rugby. And he was due to meet us at the London gig, but he got busted back in Rugby so we played it as a three piece. The performance

was neither good nor bad. I remember being severely chastised by Pete for using his amplifier, piece of shit that it was.

The Rugby cops busted Sonic during their routine stakeout of a local dealer they were hoping to nab for heroin distribution. He'd just popped out from the front door of the terraced house when the police converged. In his jacket pocket was a small bag of morphine and a smoke of Turkish hash he'd brought from Amsterdam. The cop gave Sonic a toothy grin as he pulled the cache of white powder up to his face, adding a contemptuous, 'What's this?' Sonic grabbed the bag from the cop's hand and attempted to swallow it before he was thrown against the car and handcuffed.

> SONIC: Eventually I got a Class A and a Class B for that one. They took me to court. They really wanted to use me to prove that this guy was selling heroin. But for some reason that day he'd got some pharmaceutical morphine. And they were annoyed as fuck that they'd only got morphine and it wasn't heroin. It's still a Class A. But they just didn't consider it to be such a good catch. Very small amount they got on me. And I wouldn't testify against him in court. So I told them I had it before I even entered the property.

The band returned to The Old Five Bells to support goth-rockers Fields Of The Nephilim on March 22. Gerald Palmer played it coy with the Rugby boys as they sat at the bar after their set. Sonic recalled Gerald pumping him with subtle compliments and promises like, "You lads could go far with the right help," weaving insinuations into sparkling ribbons. But Jason and Sonic weren't interested in selling off their project to an uptight businessman and they politely declined his invitations at the time. Gerald remembered the suggestive pressures originating from The Spacemen camp rather than from his side. According to his recollection of events, Sonic and Jason invited Gerald to Rugby and into VHF during studio sessions and over to Sonic's manorial home in Dunchurch for drinks and chat. The subject of management was broached a number of times during visits and phone discussions between the three but without resolution. Bassman and Rosco were rarely informed of these discussions and a deep divide began to set in between the rhythm section and the songwriters with a potential manager in the middle.

"I really did not want to manage this band," Gerald confessed. "And they wouldn't listen to anything you would say. They wanted to do what they wanted to do." Gerald wasn't sold on their anti-stage presentation and seemingly anti-audience antics. To him, all the song interruptions and onstage tunings were tantamount to turning your back to the crowd.

Great for legends but not for ticket sales. "People were paying to see them," he continued. "And they didn't want to pay money to see someone string up for 10 minutes. Or sat there in silence for 10 or 20 minutes." Gerald was not convinced, but Sonic persisted: "We kept getting gigs up there at The Old Five Bells, and I guess people started responding to it. We went down well in Northampton from The Black Lion days onward, so I guess Gerald got more interested."

On April 23, Sonic and Jason convened their third and final Rugby area psychedelic festival at Benn Hall Community Centre. Coined Easter Everywhere after The Thirteen Floor Elevators' second album, it was the most successful and well attended of The Spacemen's local shows. Mark Refoy's Telltale Hearts, The Darkside, fellow droners The Perfect Disaster, London hopefuls Loop, and members of The Inspiral Carpets all turned up for an evening of psychedelics, light shows, and floating operas. "I remember going down to that gig at the Benn Hall," smiled Will. "It was just like WAH-WAH-WAH; all of the sudden, there was some power there The Spacemen didn't have before, do you know what I mean? It was like the songs just gelled and came together. They had found the sound, and they were just fucking awesome!"

The band had found fellow space travellers and enthusiastic support in many local musicians and area bands, who were equally awed by the loud, bracing swagger of the young Rugbians. "At one of our first outings to Sheffield, The Inspiral Carpets opened up playing at least four of our own songs in their set!" boasted Bassman. "Clint Boon explained that they were big fans and played the whole of *Sound Of Confusion* before every performance. The Inspiral Carpets were one of the most honest bands on the scene, with that typical down-to-earth, tough Northern attitude. Many bands we played with were regarded with animosity, until we came across staunch allies like The Inspirals and Perfect Disaster." The animosity between bands had solidified in the personage of Josh Hampson and his work with Loop. These Spacemen 3 acolytes opened for their exemplars down at the Hammersmith Clarendon the evening after Easter Everywhere. The atmosphere was tense, to say the very least. Bassman witnessed the disintegration, "Problem was Josh was using the same guitar sounds for Loop. Pete, incensed, began accusations of theft, and the relationship started to crumble to dust creating a rift that has lasted till this day. Pete was right: Loop were obviously too influenced by us. I mean, other bands were inspired by our sound, but retained their own sound and identity."

Meantime, according to Pat Fish, Gerald persisted with chasing The Jazz Butcher and Spacemen 3. The Corby businessman extended a dinner invitation to Pat, Sonic and Jason, all of whom politely accepted, as curious about Gerald's offer as they were about the free liquor. They all drove over to Gerald's sumptuous home on the border of Cambridgeshire and Northamptonshire. "We went to meet the family, and there was Sonic and Jason and there was me," summed up Pat. "And Gerald said, 'Well chaps, before we have dinner, would you like to have something to drink?' I told him I wanted a glass of beer. And this fellow, who'd spent about 10 days telling me how successful he was, came back out with a can of something called Royal Dutch. And, in them days, you could buy four cans of Royal Dutch for £1.20. It's the cheapest, weakest, wankiest, saddest beer. And when I see a millionaire, a self-confessed millionaire, hand me a can of fucking Royal Dutch, well, my bullshit detectors were going off."

Paul Adkins was beside himself, as Spacemen 3 took over VHF yet refused to complete the album. He'd occasionally pop over in the morning and find Sonic and Jason crashed out on a ratty mattress with the rotating light-machines still buzzing in the recording room. The band had now spent the better part of six months teasing and reworking the original demo-recordings with an expanded palette of FXs, overdubs, and dope-smoke. Many of the songs attained a whole new plateau of complexity. Jason often took time alone in the studio to record layer after layer of guitar onto available tracks, while Sonic continued working on new material and feeding it through the amps or the desk to produce strange harmonic effects.

Jason took his production obsessions to an extreme on other recordings of 'Walkin' With Jesus' and 'Transparent Radiation' where he overlaid multiple vocal and guitar parts on each other to create latticed weaves echoed and buzzing with textures. His recording of the former particularly recalled the studio-fied stratosphere of über-producers Brian Wilson or Phil Spector. "Jason and I had some arguments during *Perfect Prescription*, because he wanted to record with lots of overdubs of guitars," Sonic claimed. He took Jason aside during some of these early recordings with a brief admonition, "Jason, it sounds amazing. But, look, it sounds fucking great anyway. So we could either do live versions of what we've got, or we could do some amazing *Pet Sounds* things and then sound like weak versions of our records live." Of his tendency toward lush production, Jason admitted, "*Perfect Prescription* has a lot of horns; 'Transparent Radiation' has got a lot of strings. It's something we did work with in Spacemen."

GRAHAM WALKER: There was a lot of give and take between the two, as there was time to experiment with each other's ideas. As for the *Pet Sounds* question, I'm sure there is at least one track with a keyboard and guitar drone mixed so close together that it created a texture that is neither yet both. I think the concept album seeds came through discussions about *Pet Sounds* and that really famous concept album it influenced. Who decided what, Pete or Jason, I don't remember.

"*Perfect Prescription* was Jason and Pete's best collaboration, because Pete limited Jason's overdubbing, keeping a minimal feel throughout the record," mused Bassman. And, in fact, Jason agreed to skim down the extra guitar parts on these tracks, but held to a suggestion of bringing in a gospel choir to do some background singing on a few tracks. The two musicians walked to a local church a few streets from the studio one evening and surveyed their prospects. But they were not impressed, particularly Sonic who'd witnessed several amazing choral performances *à la* The Staple Singers, on a recent trip to the West Indies. He had hoped to find a traditional choir with a bluesy, almost dirty polyphony, but what they heard was thin and slick. They abandoned the idea and went back to tightening up the songs. For 'Walkin' With Jesus' Sonic and Jason finally hit upon a beautiful minimal tone with the aid of the Farfisa. The combinatory lilt of Jason's choir-boy vocals and the repetitive twinkle of the organ nearly reinvented the old favourite for an entirely new composition: the succulent fruits of collaboration.

After reworking some of Sonic's guitar parts on 'Take Me To The Other Side', both Jason and Sonic recorded the album version, which differed slightly from the demo. With some discussion and re-listening, Sonic agreed to excise the additional riff and some of the extraneous FXs. The lyrics were also altered from the original. With its new arrangement, 'TMTTOS' became a riff-heavy, one-chord, cymbal-crashing ode to the initial mind-fuck of a heroin-rush. As the album's opening track, it was vaguely reminiscent of Syd Barrett's lysergic-tinged 'Astronomy Domine', a rush of pounding Fender guitar and sinuous tremolo with a Stooges-style bass run. Increasingly, the mantra for all musicians involved was to tighten, minimise, and simplify.

'Ode To Street Hassle' was similarly modified from its original demo, as a number of experimental tremolo noises were eventually mixed out, evidently not solidifying from within the dry, nearly Teutonic atmosphere of the track. The band re-recorded 'Starship' with a thick almost gelatinous wash of interwoven fuzz-guitar, head-throbbing distortion, and wah with no audible percussive beat, bordering on the psychoto-ambience of The Velvets' first album but with the heavy axe riffing that was pure Wayne Kramer. "I certainly think it owes more to Sun Ra than MC5, but it does definitely owe a fair bit to the MC5,"

Sonic explained. "When we did that song live, we tended to do it more like the MC5 version. When we recorded, we decided to make it different, we decided to make it a guitar symphony – the drums are mixed out on that. They were very prominent live. I think about the songs as a stream. A lot of the songs on that record haven't got drums on them. I feel drums are a real anchor and when you're trying to take off, elevate the music, lift off as it were, the drums always anchor it down, tie it down."

'Feel So Good' was one of the few tracks not previously demoed during the sessions. When they got around to recording it, Jason, who like the rest had maintained a proper balance of inebriation and inspiration throughout the sessions, popped open a beer at the opening of his vocal track. The violent outburst of carbonation bled onto several other tracks of the song, thereby preserving a dipsomaniacal moment and indicating the atmosphere at VHF. 'Feel So Good' represented one of the "highest" moments on *Prescription*, the median of both the album and the heroin experience. A dark, deep-soul rich with reverb festoons the audible spectrum; call it splunkin'-jangle, it's electro-acoustic blues from a sepulchre. Jason's spent howl, simultaneously ecstatic and dumbfounded, can only repeat "Don't it feel so good/ Don't it feel just fine," as if tackling an asymptotic Revelation; an experience granted by the Covenant of Inexpression. Heroin becomes morphine in the brain. Words become sonic modulations. Signals become noise. But with the loss of articulation, the faint tingling of paranoia.

The closing track 'Call The Doctor' was a funereal slice of J. J. Cale and Lou Reed, a lamentable conclusion to the smack-addict clutched in the resignation of overdose. Sonic's interpretative stab at Cale's first album, the paced churning of blues-licks over distortion and fuzz creates a disorienting backdrop for his moonshine lullaby. He invokes the last thoughts of a dying addict, whose plaintive appeal, "You better throw away the spoons and all the other dirty things/ 'Cos when the law arrives this evening, I don't think they'll wait and ring," is less an assertion than a posthumous regret. The guitars clash and reverberate as Jason's lead licks build momentum, plunged forward by overdriven bass and the faint twinkle of a distant Farfisa, roughly simulating the gothic chime of a headstone bell. As the dying user reaches for his last shred of inspiration, he begs his lover, "Hey there's the door now pretty baby, see who's on the other side/ Tell them to back up with the wagon now I think I'm going for a ride," a macabre reversal of the first track's automotive rush for the approach of the hearse.

'Soul 1' was an astral invocation of a muggy Memphis dusk plunging into the haunted hours of a Midlands nocturne. The Stax line-up had already proven a major influence to Sonic and Jason via Otis Redding and The Staples Singers, the deepest displays of Afro-American soul, and through its most definitive British R&B homage, The Stones' *Sticky Fingers* ('Soul 1' bears a remarkable similarity to 'I've Got The Blues'). The Jazz Butcher's Alex Green added saxophone and Mick Manning contributed wailing trumpet over Jason's slide-guitar and a bluesy keyboard melody. 'Soul 1' evoked a morose and wordless lament, an "ambient" elegy penned for both Sam Cooke and Brian Jones as if they'd succumbed to some fictive double-murder plot. 'That's Just Fine' was yet another instrumental written more in the style of 'Ode To Street Hassle', with its slow ascendant guitar and thick bass, though this track proves a bit looser, more in the style of a jam. The original Northampton demo contained Sonic's vocal meanderings, which were cut during remixing at VHF with the intention of re-recording them at a later date. Other recordings included a dual-vocal version of The Spades' 'We Sell Soul' (located on *Epitaph For A Legend*) and a Velvets-style jam with Jason on "Lou Reed"-guitar and Sonic on feedback.

Gerald popped his head into VHF's cramped control-room during the *Prescription* sessions at the invitation of Sonic and Jason. Through the smoky window, he watched the two guitarists working feverishly on 'Transparent Radiation'. The differences between their shambling live performances and the intense concentration Gerald witnessed in the studio was as contradistinct as night and day. "When they recorded 'Transparent Radiation', there was a certain magic in that recording that wasn't around [the music scene]," he said. "'Transparent Radiation' really was crafted. It took quite a long time to record, and they took a long time to perfect it. It really was an act of love doing it. They loved the track, and it was meticulously recorded. There was definite chemistry when Jason and Pete worked together. They were in the studio for hours and hours and hours every night, but they were very patient with one another."

Another local musician, Owen John, brought in his violin to add a beautiful ascending overdub to a second version of 'Transparent Radiation (Flashback)' that added a lush, symphonic tone. For the original version of 'Transparent Radiation', Sonic laid down three different vocals, one in the centre and two adjusted to opposite sides of the spectrum. During mixing, he varied the vocal tracks randomly simulating a hazy psychedelia. For the 'Transparent Radiation' single, they segued the multi-vocal version with 'Flashback', inserting 'Ecstasy Symphony' as an interlude between them.

Work on 'Ecstasy Symphony' was the first complete example of Sonic's increasing reputation as a retro-electronics experimentalist, a label encompassing both his affection for vintage analogue technology (what would later be termed "lo-fi") and it's strange co-dependency on his narcotic/psychedelic investigations. Adkins recalled 'Ecstasy Symphony''s origins stemming from similar work he and Graham Walker had experimented with in the studio. "Paul and I had created some 'enchanted forest' tracks for a pantomime at the local theatre using guitar harmonics and the reverb unit maxed out on all its settings," Graham agreed. "Our intention was to create a self-oscillating texture taking as long as possible to repeat, shimmering almost imperceptively behind the track yet constantly changing. I always imagined the sound of whales, hundreds of miles away, but, mixed with a keyboard drone and a fiddle it became part of the 'ecstasy' sound." Paul and Graham were excited about using the desk as an instrument in itself, rather than simply a recording device. Sonic, who'd been tampering with similar methods during twilight exercises at the studio, assimilated some of the descriptions he heard from Graham and worked at manipulating drones at the mixing desk with a collected series of effects. "I was very pleased with the effect I'd managed to get from just eight stereo tones through different effects: the impact, and effect of the way they interwove and just the quality of it," Sonic concluded.

The full-length piece, nearly 10 minutes in duration (although it did sustain a number of truncated herations on various releases), consisted of an A note taped down on a Vox organ and recorded onto eight separate tracks. Each track was then treated by a series of different analogue effects, electronically modulating the timbre of each identical tone. One track was fed through a phaser, providing the swooshing, multi-channelled sensation; a second through a fast autopan which produced an enlarged sense of spatiality; through various tremolo speeds, creating the vibrational, glitchy sounds; and a backwards tone simulating the psychedelic phenomenon of temporal reversal. Sonic also discovered that if he played Jason's Colorsound wah-pedal by hand at a very slow rate, he could add beautiful, gauzed blurbs over the organ tone. The string sounds were lifted from 'Transparent Radiation' and superimposed on the final product. "The flanging and phasing and tremolo-ing and reverbed organ tones in 'Ecstasy Symphony' just seemed to encapsulate everything we were trying to do," Sonic mused. "It could fall under the heading of 'Taking Drugs to Make Music to Take Drugs To'. That was what 'Ecstasy Symphony' was all about."

Musically, 'Ecstasy Symphony' recalled the seemingly strange aberrations (though in retrospect they are anything but) of Eno's transition from *Another Green World* art-rock to the delay-loops of *Discrete Music* and his polytonal *Ambient* series, *Metal Machine Music*-era Lou Reed, or Steve Reich's phase experiments. In the case of The Spacemen, as with Eno or Reed, the presence of the "experimental" or an experimental philosophy was locatable even in their early popular works, however minutely. Sonic attempted to distil his influences and motives by comparing, "In 'OD Catastrophe', everything there is in E: the guitars are going E-E-E, power chords and the bass is doing E, everything is just ringing in E, and then it's got feedback over the top of it in E. I mean, it's not so far from 'Ecstasy Symphony'. We'd done one chord music and two-chord music, and even two-note music. And 'Ecstasy Symphony' is one-note music." Agreed long-time friend Pat Fish, "To me the development came very early. I think when you listen to stuff like 'Ecstasy Symphony'; he's been on that trip ever since. That's what he likes to explore." That the tradition of this pop-art concoction consistently challenged and enthralled, explained Spacemen 3's aesthetic and musical appeal. While much of the early-Eighties post-punk fringe imploded from the pressure of "sped-read" philosophy and anti-musical formats, works like 'Ecstasy Symphony' proceeded from a traditional rock/blues framework and probed its textural or "vertical" permutations.

While 'Ecstasy Symphony' had, in name, foreshadowed the imminent British E craze that would flood clubs from London to Manchester in the next two years, its arrhythmic, ambient tones did not suggest any of the drug/dance confluence. If anything, it represented Ecstasy's salad days, before the second Summer of Love or the Detroit/Chicago/Ibiza three-pronged invasion, when a select few Britons enjoyed it purely as a "head"-drug, an acid substitute, to trip and chill to. No four-to-the-floor beats or Roland 303 bass-line synthesisers were required. 'Ecstasy Symphony''s prescient atmosphere was rooted much more in the palimpsest of the past rather than the kitsch-bleep of the Phuture. Although, in an odd twist, 'Ecstasy Symphony' would gain larger popularity during the early Nineties with the inception of the ambient-house/ IDM craze. The extended electronic piece was sampled heavily and appeared in a number of different guises, including, most notably, *Flying High*'s 'Symphony In E' from The Irresistible Force, a.k.a. Mixmaster Morris.

In July the 'Transparent Radiation' 12″, consisting of the two versions of the title track intercut with 'Ecstasy Symphony', and backed with 'Things'll Never Be The Same' and 'Starship', was released on Glass. As before, reactions were positive but few and far between, although *Sounds* declared it Single of the Week and continued singing the praises of the band. "Spacemen 3 are great rock'n'roll," the weekly wrote. "Their music is as timeless as any you care to name. 'Transparent Radiation', in fact, ignores most standard notions of time, clocking in at a modest 38 minutes. It's an acid haze of a Mayo Thompson song which hovers like an ether extracted from some key Velvets out-take, spliced up by an ambient wedge of psychedelia called 'Ecstasy Symphony'. Flip it and you're dropped inside 'Funhouse' walls with The Spacemen's own gnarled plea for love 'Things'll Never Be The Same', which lopes (assisted by several battalions of wah-wah pedals) into a 10-minute, wordless howl through The MC5's 'Starship'. Side one is drifting, feathery clouds, side two an electric thunderstorm."

Nearly nine months after entering VHF, Sonic and Jason sat down to mix and order the final song list. The notion of combining and ordering the disparate tracks into a "concept" album took precedence, along with finalising an appropriate title. "So *Perfect Prescription* was kind of a concept album," Sonic explained. "It was about our better and worse experiences with drugs. It goes from being right out of it, to 'Call The Doctor' which was about an overdose. 'Things'll Never Be The Same' was about having your first hit and realising the change in consciousness and perception that comes about through it." Said Jason, "*Perfect Prescription* was only our second album, but we never went anywhere near it again." This final stage of completing the album would take both songwriters nearly a month of concentrated mixing and remixing, despite Barker's rapidly attenuating patience and Paul Adkins nearly throwing them out of his studio. Sonic delivered numerous DATs of preliminary mixes to Glass' headquarters, before scratching a number of "finished" tracks for newer versions. Dave Barker was very pleased with what he heard, despite waiting nearly a year for the results. "The second record was a huge step forward from the first, which is pretty derivative really in retrospect," Barker explained. "Some groups need time to develop their sound or ideas or whatever, but it was less than a year really between the two records." The feeling shared by both musicians/producers was to capture a gritty, minimal tone that would bring the guitar to the fore without erring too far to the high-end and sacrificing the low-end "chugging" that was so essential to their blues roots. They mixed the vocals low and the drums even lower. Contrary to the futurist science-fictive electro textures that had become excessively hip in the early and mid-Eighties, with the synth-pop trappings of "industrial" Martin Hannett-style pro-duction, Sonic and Jason eschewed the trebled instrumentation and "clean" drums for guttural drones. "The general sound tone was anti-Eighties," Graham recalled, having sat through the various mixes, mastering, and cutting. "As far removed from the plastic synthesised brass sounds as possible. A peasant's stew of root veg rather than a medley of individual sushi portions. In terms of production, it's akin to having full fat, gold top guitar sounds without being semi-skimmed by EQ." Simul-taneously they abandoned or, rather, exorcised their closet Hawkwind gleanings and replaced them with a cumulous religiosity, aided, in no small part, by the inclusion of the Farfisa and acoustic guitars. Throughout the recording and mixing process, Kember and Pierce regarded The Stones' *Sticky Fingers*, Laurie Anderson's *Big Science*, Panther Burns' *Sugar Ditch Revisited*, and Penguin Cafe Orchestra as instrumental and lyrical Rosetta Stones.

When Bassman and Rosco got hold of some of these earliest DATs, they were awestruck at Jason and Sonic's mixing. A number of Bassman's bass lines were noticeably different on tape than they had been in the studio, and Rosco's drums were almost inaudible. It was as if Spacemen 3's rhythm section had been wiped or, rather, phased out of the individual tracks. "*Perfect Prescription*, I mean, I like the album a lot more than *Sound Of Confusion*, but I just really didn't feel like I contributed much to it," Bassman explained. "Or Rosco, for that matter," he added. "I mean, Rosco will always be derided as an eccentric asshole. So maybe he got what he deserved. Because he basically got mixed out of the album." Much of the bassist and drummer's ire centred on Sonic.

> SONIC: Pete Bain was never someone who used to come to practise and say, "Hey, I've got this great riff! Let's jam on this and make a song!" Not once. Not ever. It would always be a matter of either me, or Jason, or both of us together in that role: telling him and Rosco what to play . . . Don't forget. It was my band. My band. Yeah.

> ROSCO (sarcastically): Yeah, it was Pete's band.

For the album's cover, Sonic proposed a glossy photo of a table littered with discarded drug paraphernalia. He collected a prince's ransom of morphine, methadone, and omnopon ampoules, as well as stolen pharmaceutical boxes. Bits of dope and other works. On the back sleeve, Sonic had written out the track listing on a prescription form from a chemist's script-pad. Dave Barker, who had a particular interest in cover designs, was less than enthused with Sonic's suggestion. "I'm not sure if Glass felt it was too controversial," Sonic said. "Maybe hassle from the drug companies themselves. So they decided to do it the way they did. I think they thought it would look more like a bootleg for some reason." In the end, the idea was scrapped for a more conventional cover.

The band brought in a friend and local photographer Craig Wagstaff, who shot a series of pictures of the band messing about in the studio and others of the two songwriters (minus Bassman and Rosco) brandishing their Fenders. *The Perfect Prescription*'s record sleeve featured the anaesthetised figures of Jason and Sonic glaring towards the imaginary fourth-wall with a mix of alacrity and innocence. Jason peered forward with the blank yawn of a time-traveller captured mid-flight, while Sonic posed, out-stretched guitar in hand, with a mock seriousness, one-part Tav Falco, two-parts William Webb Ellis. A Vox amp-stack rested beside them providing that perfect bit of retro-cool charm, as if invoking The Beatles' classicism or The Velvets' Gothicness. The opto-kinetic swirl of Monterey Pop microdots sweep across the background engulfing the eye in psychedelica. "I must admit I am not a great fan of this sleeve's artwork," said Sonic, upon inspecting the finished LP's cover art. Bassman concurred for very different reasons: "I hate that album cover. Everybody I know . . . I mean . . . anybody that knows them personally hates that album cover . . . hates the cover: that stupid mock pose. Jason looks natural. But Pete Kember's pose just makes me puke."

September's release of *The Perfect Prescription* garnered little in the way of critical attention and instead maintained the trend of anonymity. Few English papers picked up on what was easily one of the most profound albums of the year, if not the decade. Recalled Dave Barker, "I don't remember seeing any great reviews in the UK, except for *Sounds*. The European reviews and US fanzine reviews that I remember were generally good, sometimes great." In fact, it would require an American hardcore fanzine to pick up on The Spacemen, long before the British weeklies would be singing their praises and sucking their cocks. In *Forced Exposure*, Issue number 14, Byron Coley cooed with blood 'n guts vehemence: "Sweetly, simply put, Spacemen 3 are the only English band that I'd walk across the street to piss on. Meaning mostly that I wouldn't even bother to piss on any other English band that comes quickly to mind. . . . From the twee, sustained chirp of their 'ecstasy sound' to the stark naked, Eskimo-inspired string-beat of their most primally fish-trouncing duntage, Spacemen 3 are world class mindbenders and each of their records deserves a 'greasy' 'spot' on yr 'shelf'. Drop a pane on yr eyeball, get in the tub, and crank up *The Perfect Prescription*. If you don't end up singing the band's praises, yr a goddamn fatso."

In a strange twist, it was the American underground's rapturous reception to *The Perfect Prescription* that ensured the album's place in the canon, as well as establishing a positive buzz for the future of the band. From the pages of *Forced Exposure*, news of the album reached Seattle and fuzz-rockers Green River (soon to become Mudhoney) where Mark Arm became a huge fan of *The Perfect Prescription*. Word reached Red Rhino, distributors for Glass, that Sonic Youth's Thurston Moore hailed the album as a recent favourite, prompting the company to push more copies into the American indie market. The album also made a massive impression on Boston-area musicians, including Galaxie 500 guitarist and future Luna front man Dean Wareham. "I remember picking up *Perfect Prescription*, because I liked the cover; their album covers were very funny," Wareham explained. "When we started Galaxie 500 in 1987, I think we were doing something similar. I felt like the Spacemen 3 sound was more 'American' than their English contemporaries, and *Perfect Prescription* was strong from beginning to end. I loved the acoustic guitar groove on 'Walkin' With Jesus' and 'Ode To Street Hassle' and the way the drums were low in the mix, opening up space for other things. What really stands out is just the perfect mood that they created. That is not an easy thing to do; a nice mood is often spoiled by a singer, for example, or by lyrics that don't ring true. I can't really speak for all those involved, but it seems to me there was very little cross-influence between the American and English scenes of the time. I think most of us in indie American bands were suspicious of the English bands. And I think if you looked at US fanzines of the time you would find the same thing." (Interesting aside: Wareham recalled playing 'Ode To Street Hassle' to Lou Reed years later during the VU reunion tour with Luna in support, but Reed characteristically failed to comment on either the song or Spacemen 3. . . .)

To add insult to injury, although Dave Barker appeared to be doing little to push *The Perfect Prescription* off the shelves, Glass' own Josh Hampson and his upstart band Loop released the '16 Dreams' and 'Spinning' 12" singles on the Head label to rapturous critical acclaim. Recorded at Cherry Studio in Croydon during the summer, '16 Dreams' and 'Spinning' consisted of warbling soundscapes of echoed vocals, wah guitar, and drones that drew more than a smattering of interest from the London papers. An August '87 *NME* feature article proclaimed that Loop's music was, "Built from layer upon quivering layer of variously distorted guitars . . . A dozen blurred echoes – Suicide, prehistoric Floyd, cheapo sci fi, the Mary Chain and others – eddy and swirl before gelling into their optimum, uniquely Loopy, configuration . . . sometimes mesmeric, often brilliant, and always *deafening*." If the uncanny historical comparisons between Loop and Spacemen 3 were not patently apparent, then Hampson's own *raison d'être* seemed to have been pulled from an old Spacemen interview:

> "Basically," Josh recalls, "we got into this to try and kick out some of the shit. We were all despondent with the jingle jangle school and fed up with the way pop was going back to the mid-Seventies, everybody nice and safe . . . We wanna create an atmosphere where our music is *inescapable*. Whether you're at the front, the back, or wherever, we want the music to surround you. Most of the bands

133

that I love – the Stooges, the MC5, even some Heavy Metal – play really loud . . . [but] we're even more dependent on volume to help the music out, to help create the mindf**k."

Said Mark Refoy, "I remember there was all this press at the time in *Sounds* and *Melody Maker*: like all these live reviews saying how brilliant Loop were. And the writers were using all these phrases, that, if you substituted the word Spacemen 3 for Loop, it would describe Spacemen. I remember thinking at the time that if I was in Spacemen, I'd be a bit pissed off!" Even sardonic jabs at Loop's expense twisted the knife deeper, as when an *NME* reviewer wrote of the band, "Loop represent the 'A'-level version of the bogstandard Grebo/Acidhead night-out. Not content with merely being crap, they want to be challenging, pioneering crap. An over-long lecture on nihilism given by the surviving members of Lynyrd Skynyrd; and don't they realise that the only person allowed by law to still own a wah-wah pedal is Prince." "If any British band should have endured the title of 'Grebo/Acidhead pioneering crap' with wah-wah pedals *it should be us!*" screamed Sonic at the glut of Loop reviews.

Hampson exacerbated the situation when he pleaded ignorance of The Spacemen in a number of interviews that followed Loop's inflated reception. It was as if he'd only faintly heard of Spacemen 3, even though they'd played together throughout '86 and '87. He denied any sort of influence on their part upon Loop's development or sound. Sonic was incensed with the articles, and furious at Loop's sudden success at his band's expense. "I don't exactly know what happened but a falling out between Pete and Robert [Josh] occurred somewhere or somehow," said Barker. "They can both be stubborn and opinionated." Hampson's connection to Spacemen 3 was to become a sore contention for both himself and Sonic as the two guitarists' friendship disintegrated. Spacemen 3/Loop shows would not last beyond mid-year. Future Spacemen 3 acquaintance and archivist Mark Lascelles was a regular at many early Loop gigs, and recalled Josh's indignant attitude towards his former friends. "I saw Loop loads of times and even did a small interview with Josh once," Lascelles explained. "I remember one small exchange vividly word for word:

Mark: Do you know Spacemen 3?

Josh: Sort of.

Mark: Do you get on?

Josh: Sort of.

Mark: Would you play with them again?

Josh (without hesitation): No."

CHAPTER SIX

Take Me To The Other Side

1987–1988

At some undisclosed moment over the summer of 1987, Jason finally consummated his relationship with Kate Radley. Kate's fling with Craig Wagstaff had begun to disintegrate after the couple moved to London, where he worked as a bus driver between photography work. Craig and Kate often turned up at Spacemen 3 gigs between Rugby and Hammersmith, where she and Jason flirted, courted, and fucked without mentioning a word to either Craig or the rest of the band. It was difficult not to notice her when she floated into a room or a club, every inch of her body had the chiselled grace of a femme fatale. And Sonic and Bassman observed Kate's constant presence around the band beginning with the closing months of the year.

"Jason began to spend more time around the two of them until I realised Jason was moving in on Kate," remembered Bassman. There were some rumours about the nature of her relationship with Jason, possibly prompted by his seeming "overnight" friendship with Craig – in Sonic's words, they'd become "pal-ly, pal-ly" – although no one was sure if such rumours were merited. Bassman added, "When I broke the news to Sonic, he was incredulous and immediately bitter." Sonic finally put two and two together. "Jason started saying that he was going down to London to see his big mate Craig," he recalled. "What he was actually doing was shagging Craig's girlfriend while he was out driving buses all day." Jason had definitely begun to have a reputation as a hot-blooded, skirt-chasin', randy ol' bastard, but then again, Kate's reputation was equally well reported. "She was basically just a local girl that was into shagging all the musicians," said Goff Roderick. "I think she was just one of those heartbreaker types."

"I found her totally false as a person, like a flirt beyond hell," Sonic said. "I just thought it was unnecessary to overlap relationships like that. Two-timing. That's really like playing with fire – just really unnecessary – and she had a real history of that. And Jason became a part of it."

Kate eventually dumped Craig when she and Jason became exclusive, openly acknowledging their affair to both friends and gawkers. But Craig continued following her to Spacemen shows, a cuckold swollen with fury both at his friend's betrayal and for the dashing and attractive new couple. "Craig took it bad and drank himself into a stupor," Bassman claimed. "He went into a real self-destruct period." Sonic was displeased with Jason's involvement in this love triangle for nothing but the unpredictable element he'd suddenly brought into The Spacemen inner circle. The spectacle portended something insincere and, in the case of Kate, a potential cauldron of contention. "Sonic acted like he was betrayed by Jason," Bassman continued, "and he made Kate's life difficult from the start of their relationship."

Throughout the Summer and Fall, gigs became more numerous as a result of the 'Transparent Radiation' single and *Perfect Prescription*'s belated but positive word-of-mouth. The band played a number of Clarendon shows back in Hammersmith to promote their new releases, including a June date with Glass-label mates The Perfect Disaster, close friends and allies of The Spacemen. Through a connection at Club Mankind, Sonic and Jason were introduced to Genesis P. Orridge, whimsical czar of Throbbing Gristle and Psychic TV. Genesis was reasonably well acquainted with The Spacemen catalogue, and offered a support-slot for a Psychic TV-sponsored "Riot In The Eye" festival at The Electric Ballroom on September 24. PTV was suffering the nadir of its musical career steeped as Gen and Company were in cathode-tube "magick" and numerology (1987 was plagued by obsessions with the number "23"). But P. Orridge had a morbid cult-of-personality (perpetuated in no small part by his founding The Temple Ov Psychic Youth) that ensured only the strangest of the strange would typically venture to his gigs. The Spacemen had no idea what to expect of the show. They walked backstage to find peculiar accoutrements, like mounds of food dyed in psychedelic colours and oddballs gliding along the floor with piercings in the strangest places. "PTV's audience was very *different*," laughed Sonic. "Most of them had like pierced dicks. They were kind of a strange bunch, like professionally strange types. Genesis was obviously a very strong character and had a very strong personality. But Psychic TV's music at the time was dreadful: really funky and wishy-washy. I have to say I didn't have much taste for it."

Future Bowery Electric guitarist Lawrence Chandler popped into the club that evening to catch Psychic TV and witnessed his first and only Spacemen show. "I was in London at the time, and I walked into this club in Camden and Spacemen 3 just happened to be playing. And it really didn't sink in until after the fact. I just have this vague recollection of two guys sitting onstage. I couldn't tell you much about the show." About The Spacemen's musical impact on him, Chandler waxed philosophical: "Someone said it was just like an ego-less music. And that's the idea. That it's much more inward looking than an outpouring of ego. What I liked about the drones were the overtones. It's just like with the drones, the more you listen, and the more you focus in on it, you start to hear the various harmonics. And there were such complex melodies sort of dancing around in the harmonics. Really complex but really beautiful. It seemed more like channelling than working out a melody. Later, when I met Pete [Kember], I went out and bought all their records and really got into them . . . And I think Bowery Electric's music is just a continuation of that." Spacemen 3 were low on the bill and while their set mesmerised the mercurial P. Orridge, the audience was less impressed with the half-hour's worth of continual guitar feedback and tremolo drones. "I don't think their audience was particularly into what we were doing at the show," Sonic added. Despite the poor response, Genesis suggested the band consider switching to his own Temple label and invited them back to his PTV squat in Hackney. According to Sonic the band politely declined . . . the interior of the house was rumoured to be filled with occult members straddling sex-furniture.

In October and November, in between shows in London, the band rotated between The Black Lion and The Old Five Bells in Northampton. After an October 17 London show with Robert Calvert (formerly of Hawkwind) and The Starfighters, Sonic finagled a support billing with Hawkwind and Suicide. With all the inane and inaccurate press references to Hawkwind over the years, neither Jason nor Sonic cared much for playing with "the English Grateful Dead", but Rev and Vega's Suicide were still major musical heroes to the Rugby band who'd followed their progress for the previous 10 years.

The group drove to Leeds on December 12 for Acid Daze II, held at Queens Hall and featuring Hawkwind, Suicide, The Pink Fairies, Spacemen 3, and several other lesser bands. Queens Hall was less stately than its name might imply and was little more than a tram shed with a stage. It was an acoustical nightmare for Spacemen 3 but Suicide was electric, playing a short 20-minute set consisting of one extended synth piece. The Hawkwind fans were restless and lobbed numerous projectiles at Alan Vega including filled beer cans. For Suicide this was nothing new, and Vega reacted by singing louder, taunting and teasing the hippie audience, literally feeding off of their displeasure. Sonic was completely blown away and cornered Vega and Rev backstage, quizzing them about their gear and their knowledge of The Silver Apples. The next night, The Spacemen roared down to the London Town and Country for another support with Suicide and punk-band 999 before concluding December at The Roadmender in Northampton.

Meanwhile, European agent Gunter contacted Sonic at the end of the year with plans for a massive Continental tour starting mid-January that would run nearly six weeks and wind through Germany, Austria, Switzerland, Holland and Belgium. The details were worked out through another German booking agent called Dietmar Lupfer, who proposed calling the tour "Sonic Boom '88" unbeknownst to the band. The Sonic Boom tour would be the first major excursion for Spacemen 3 and offered them a litmus test for the all-important European market. Unfortunately, the tour would also breed the earliest irreconcilable differences between band members and especially Jason and Sonic's fragile collaboration, which had just enjoyed a nine-month "Indian summer".

The band played a warm-up to the European shows at Dingwall's in London at the beginning of January '88 with anonymous noise-makers The Wood Children. As The Spacemen took the stage, Gerald Palmer looked on eagerly from the back of the house, alongside a squadron of suits. Palmer had called in favours from every major booking-agent throughout London, assembling, among others, Jeff Kraft, Paul Boswell, and John McIver from Asgard. This was his newest prospect, explained Gerald, to the small crowd of dignified businessmen. Outwardly, he was beaming and confident. Inside, he was anything but. "I kept telling the band they really had to tighten up," Gerald explained. "They couldn't continue with the constant delays and gaps in their set. Forty-minute sets with 20 minutes of gaps wouldn't work. But they didn't listen to a word I said." According to Palmer, the set was absolutely appalling from the first note. Gerald literally buried his face in his hands with embarrassment. Before the band could even finish, nearly every agent patted Gerald on the back and exited with a soft chuckle.

Exacerbating the situation was the appearance of a raving and drunken Craig Wagstaff at Kate's side. "He turned up totally smashed that night," Bassman remembered. It seemed the surreptitious affair between Jason and Kate had finally boiled over onto the public stage. "Craig was nearly suicidal," added Sonic. "He was so drunk that he was just beyond it, just fucking wild." By the end of the band's short set, Craig had stumbled outside with drink in hand and collapsed near the club's entrance. A harsh January freeze glazed over his inert body. "Somebody came to get me and said Craig was pissed out of his brain and crashed out," laughed Sonic. "Fucking pathetic. We helped put him in the back of our van, where he slept off his two bottles of vodka."

Meanwhile, Gerald stormed out of Dingwall's in disgust, screaming, "Fuck this! Fuck them!" He drowned his sorrows in dinner and drinks at a local French restaurant before encountering Rosco outside the club hours later, where he unleashed "You're utter crap! I don't want anything to do with this band, if this is the way you're going to carry on!" Gerald screamed at him from across the Camden street. "After that, I didn't speak with any of them for a month or two," Gerald laughed. "I just lost interest. They were 'Hawkwind Hippie Shit'. They were crap. They had all the raw material, all the ingredients, but they weren't putting it together. And they were quite frankly appalling."

The Spacemen prepared throughout January for what would be their longest tour to date, the month-plus sojourn in Europe. Much had gone into the planning and networking, bolstered by the moderate success of the previous year's foray into Holland and Belgium. Practices and technical rehearsals were strenuous, sometimes fierce, all in preparation for making the best possible impression on the European market. With the added responsibility Sonic had taken upon himself came the requisite pressure, which he often redirected onto his fellow band members. If there were any prior doubts about who barked the orders, Sonic's determined and "autocratic" methods had now extinguished them.

ROSCO: Pete liked to boss people about and stuff. We were rehearsing to go on tour and we'd just play the same song over and over. And Pete would just go, "No! Stop! You didn't do it like that last time!" Fucking just going on and on and on at everyone in turn. But what's really happening is Pete's coming down off his hit of smack. He'd have a hit just before the practice session, and he'd be fucking brilliant for a bit, but then he'd start fucking losing it. By the end he'd lose his voice. And it'd come time for him to do his vocal, and, the same guy who'd been interrupting the whole time and bitching to everyone, would be singing completely out of key.

SONIC: Of course, they didn't like to be told they were doing it wrong, but Pete Bain and Rosco wouldn't practise enough, wouldn't be professional enough. They'd slip up the whole time. Pete didn't know his scales – he got off on these little fucking runs which would totally ruin the whole mood. Jason would usually leave me to do the dirty work. I would say he used to leave 90 per cent of that to me, and it's never a popular role.

While Jason, Bassman and Rosco departed for Germany to settle in before the first date, Sonic skipped over to Holland to load up on the cheap and plentiful hash that floated around Amsterdam. He'd decided to abstain from using heroin during the bulk of the tour for lack of connections and fear of border crossings, and instead supplemented his cravings with heavy amounts of hash and cannabis. Knowing it would be difficult to procure a sufficient amount of dope while on the road, Sonic had seen fit to stock up on provisions for the entirety of the month. He offered to buy supplies for the others, who only assented to a meagre quarter-ounce, to which Sonic forewarned them of his refusal to share. Everyone in the band was a chronic dope-smoker, and, as such, could not survive the trip with a paltry quarter between them. But money was tight, and estimations were short-sighted. Meantime, they'd taken on Goff and his loads of coke and dope, to drive them 'round the continent. Certainly, with all parties concerned, the drug supply would never fall short of abundant. Unfortunately, as Rosco explained, "It all went bad from the first day we went on tour. It was all fucked up, because we were forced into a situation where nobody really knew what was going on. And it was kind of new and exciting, but there wasn't really any money so to speak."

They all met up in Köln on January 11 for the opening gig at the Rose Club. It was in the club that they first spied the tour posters manufactured by the Boom agency: a black-and-white French nouveau shot of the band with the caption: SONIC BOOM TOUR '88. Jason was displeased and confronted Sonic about the name, to which Sonic claimed ignorance. Unsatisfied with what he saw as Sonic's clandestine attempt to hog the spotlight, Jason threw up his hands and prepared for the show. Still, the evening went well, with another bone-crunching set-list comprised of 'Come Together' (MC5/Troggs), 'Rollercoaster', 'Take Me To The Other Side', 'Things'll Never Be The Same', a newly rehearsed Sonic composition 'Revolution', 'Little Doll', and concluding with the cacophonous screech of 'OD Catastrophe'.

Only days into the tour, everyone came to understand the true meaning of European hospitality, as they discovered the venue riders waiting for them backstage. Liquor, wine, beer, it was all free flowing, and, with the exception of teetotaller Sonic, The Spacemen took advantage hand-over-fist. From the first drink onward, the divisions between them manifested themselves, as Jason, Bassman, Rosco and Goff partook of the plentiful spirits, only to incur Sonic's wrath. "It was so Spinal Tappy that it was unbelievable," Sonic recalled. "Pete Bain and Rosco were the worst offenders. It was just the most unprofessional shit. In Pete Bain's mind, he was in The Sex Pistols and smashing up hotel rooms, you know. And I was saying, 'Don't smash up the dressing room if you want to come back and play this venue next year.' I just wasn't interested in that sort of pathetic moronic attitude but he was."

"That particular tour was really the biggest source of quite a dark period from my point of view," said Bassman, blaming Sonic for the disharmony between the musicians. "There was absolutely everything disastrous going on and Sonic was absolutely abysmal to be with." Even from the earliest day-trips through Germany from venue to venue, Bassman claimed Sonic was attempting to foist his authority over his bandmates in the most quotidian of decisions. "In the van we all had one seat and no leg room," Bassman continued. "Sonic sat on two seats with ample leg room and continually smoked fat joints."

Over the next week, they played gig after gig, from Hanover to Hamburg to Oldenburg to Bremen – where a local paper reported, "The dirt is missing yet . . . It's a higher kind of rubbish. You cannot see it! . . . An evening of contrast awaits you" – and on to Berlin. All the while a slow schism was building between Sonic and the rest of the band over what he saw as the nocturnal bingeings, the missed soundchecks, and the below-quality performances. On the other hand, Jason et al. increasingly allied themselves against Sonic's controlling behaviour and patronising attitude. As the first week drew to a close, the quarter-ounce of dope trickled to nothing, causing a sudden rush of panic. Rosco and Bassman had already tapped their supply of hash. Every irritation was amplified, every long stretch of road another soul-sucking moment of boredom. Sonic puffed away from his huge brick of hash.

As promised, he refused to share his supply with anyone, thereby compounding the "us vs. them" paranoiac mood infusing the touring van. "And after a few days of this I was ready to kill him," admitted Bassman. "People offered hash or grass many times on the tour. Most times Sonic would take all the dope and smoke himself silly. One time a German guy gave me a small piece of hash, and Sonic insisted I show him how much he had given me, as if he had a decision whether I could keep it or not and he was the only one worthy to receive gifts."

SONIC: The other problem we had at the time was Goff. When he got to Europe he decided he was going to have the biggest piss-up he could. He was getting like Pete Bain, Rosco, and Jason – to some degree – pissed outta their heads every night. And this is our driver, who at the end of the night's gotta drive us to the hotel – often 10 miles away – and he's getting pissed out of his fucking head daily.

BASSMAN: As a driver Goff was invaluable. He loved driving and could eat up the miles whilst chopping out lines of coke for all and sundry. He was our equivalent of Neal Cassidy, a guy with an irrepressible personality.

GOFF RODERICK: I used to have a few Jack Daniel's with Jason and them. It was all highly amusing on the road, because, Jesus Christ, it was hard work. When you're doing a gig every night all over Europe for seven weeks . . . I mean after the gig you end up going on a mad one. Half the time you haven't even slept.

SONIC: Well, you can stay up partying all night for the first week of the tour, and then you're ill for the next three weeks. You might as well be dead. You're shit, you know, and that was what they were like. They would use and abuse the hospitality of everyone. Anywhere we went, they would just take stuff off the top shelf all day long.

PAT FISH: I heard extraordinary stories, and Sonic was just livid. There was one story about Pete Bain swigging from a bottle of Jack Daniel's onstage, but it turned out to be tea in a Jack bottle. Now the thing is I've known Pete Bain as long as I've known any of them, and I wouldn't have thought there was a fucking molecule of pretension or affectation in him. And why on earth he would indulge in that sort of behaviour is beyond me. So I don't really know if it's a true story or not.

Whether or not it was as a result of Goff whispering encouragement into their ears, or simply the combative effects of the alcohol, tempers nearly gave rise to body blows between Sonic and Bassman. With drugs in short supply, Bassman and Rosco took to drinking even more heavily from the generous tanks of German hospitality. Even Jason, who'd comported himself with enough discretion to please Sonic, jumped whole-heartedly into the drinking binges, slogging back to his random motel rooms well into the morning. Sonic was severely nonplussed by his partner. "I think Jason'd be very embarrassed to talk about this, because for a while he did lose it, definitely," he confided. "Because it was all new to him. He never had people fucking lavishing all this shit on him – giving him drugs, bottles of fucking liquor – to any of these guys, a bottle of bourbon and they'd fucking be creaming themselves."

GOFF RODERICK: Jason and Pete used to hardly ever speak to each other, because Jason didn't think Pete was taking it seriously because of his heroin problem. But it was the same with Pete: he didn't like drinking, and he hated people who drank.

For all the inebriated levity and hijinks Goff brought to the tour van, his decision to bring along his girlfriend as the T-shirt seller all but sent Sonic spare. If it was one thing Sonic and Bassman would agree on throughout the tour, it was that Goff's missus Kathy was the feminine anomaly in an atmosphere of sweat, booze, and coke-fuelled machismo. "They rowed like cat and fucking dog from beginning to end, with her storming off from the van and jumping on trains to get away," remembered Sonic. "You name it. It was the most pathetic shit. Of course, I was going fucking mad. I mean I was totally getting pissed off." Bassman concurred, "Goff and Kathy's domestic spats continued to a point where they even provided some distraction from the unpleasant atmosphere. Sometimes it was Kathy who decided to split. We would follow her in the van, as she dragged her suitcase along the road with Goff trying to coax her back in the van. Goff would do the same thing. Then it was both of them who would take off together in an attempt to get back to England, but they always returned." But Goff rejected their petulant groans as mere misogyny. "They were just shocked that I brought a woman on tour with us," he said. "They really didn't want a woman on tour with them. It was the absolute worse thing that could happen to them – having a woman on tour – but she did her job. She sold the T-shirts. She did everything she could. She was actually part of the crew. In them early days, when there was such a small crew, everybody was busting their asses with like matchsticks on their eyelids."

But Goff, who'd imbibed from one side of Germany to the other, and whose constant quarrelling with his girlfriend had rattled already taut nerves, was exacting a toll on the group. "One night we found a note from Kathy," Bassman said, frowning, "saying she had taken the T-shirt money and was leaving. Goff chased after her and they both ended up getting locked out of the hotel and spent a freezing night in the van." Shortly afterwards, Goff phoned back to Rugby to discover his sprawling mansion was being repossessed. He "threatened" to abandon the tour in order to retrieve his property in England, effectively leaving the band to hobble on without a driver. As one can imagine, Sonic was devoutly perturbed, while the rest of the band was just plain pissed. It was all coming to a head. "I told Goff, 'Look, we'll lend you the money that we earned on the tour, and you can send it back to England,'" Sonic explained. "'You won't need to go back. Just finish driving the tour and pay us back when we get back.' And he was like, 'Oh nice one man yeah.' We never saw a penny of that fucking money back. Not one penny of it. At the end of it, he was like, 'You owed me that for driving you on the tour.'"

The band decided to pull Goff from the driver's seat through the final stretch of Germany. His lunacy had gotten the better of him, as his brain receptors fizzled and popped on large quantities of liquor, frequent cocaine binges, and minimal sleep. In a matter of a few short weeks,

Goff's status reverted from absolute asset to total fucking liability. "He was crazy," recounted Sonic. "I liked the guy so much, but he was a total fucking nutcase, and he was the worst possible choice for anything you needed to rely on. He was just so unreliable." To Goff's credit, his automotive pranksterisms often provided a centrifugal energy to the road-weary band teetering on collapse. And, Goff claimed, he even saved their necks on occasion. He pointed out, "We were driving from Germany, going down this huge massive hill. And they'd insisted I take a rest. Suddenly I realised we were about to drive straight underneath a lorry. And I had to grab the steering wheel and whack the van over." The van veered to the side of the precipice and screeched to a stop. Everyone took a much needed smoke. "They actually knew that I saved their lives at that moment. And mine as well."

Another week of shows took them through Heidelberg, Ravensburg, Stuttgart, and Munich, and into Vienna, Austria, to perform at the V4 Club. If there was any hope that the fresh Alpine air might do much to reduce the tension, these feelings were quickly dashed by particularly horrendous shows. "The first major falling out was in Munich," recalled Bassman. "Goff had helped himself to something from the backstage rider. Sonic decided that this was not on and rounded on Goff, telling him that he was not entitled to take food as he was a crew member and was already having much too good a time. It went on until Goff exploded and retaliated with justifiable venom. Sonic was too scared to take it any further and backed off." Goff claimed his remonstration to be nothing more than blowing off steam. "Well, I always spoke my mind, but I don't remember anything specific," he said. "There may have been some problems at Wiesbaden, when I told Pete he needed to get a grip or something."

Sonic slouched in the rear of the van spewing venom at what he saw as his rapidly disintegrating band of dipsomaniacal wankers. More than likely, the grey situation was coloured bleaker for Sonic, who'd spent nearly a month with irregular shots of junk in his system despite four years of solid addiction. For their part Jason, Rosco and Bassman had suffered Sonic's housemaster attitude for long enough; they were a fucking rock'n'roll band, for fuck's sake. And who were they to take remonstration from a fuckin' smack addict! Jason continued imbibing at an inordinate rate, pillaging bottle after bottle of bourbon and beer, until he'd pass out on the bed or on the floor. Bassman found Jason sprawled out on his bed one evening, ravaged by booze having blacked out. The young drunk was lying on his back and began gurgling up large chunks of acrid vomit all over his clothes and the bed sheets. Bassman grabbed Jason and turned him over onto his side where Jason spewed the rest of the bile

Sonic Boom *in media drone*, 1986 *(Craig Wagstaff)*

Natty Brooker on drums in Banbury, 1986.
(Craig Wagstaff)

Bassman and his eponymous instrument, 1986.
(Craig Wagstaff)

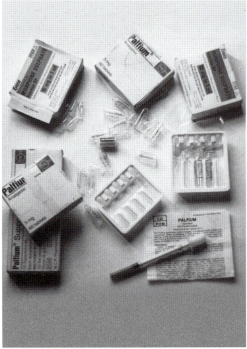

Jason's doodles circa *Sound of Confusion*.
(Reproduced by kind permission of Mark Lascelles)

SYRINGES AND AMPULES AND PILLS…:
Prospective cover for *Perfect Prescription*
later used for the *Taking Drugs…* demos.
(Sonic Boom Collection)

WALL OF SOUND: Spacemen 3 take a break during recording at VHF Studios to pose in front of their gear. From left to right: Bassman, Sonic, Jason and Rosco, 1987. *(Craig Wagstaff)*

Jason Pierce, axe-slinger, plays in the VHF parking lot during *Perfect Prescription* sessions. *(Craig Wagstaff)*

I FEEL VOXISH: *Perfect Prescription* cover photo with Sonic and Jason, Summer 1987. *(Craig Wagstaff)*

Bassman, Jason, Sonic and Rosco against the wall, February 1987. *(Mike Morton)*

EURO TOUR 1987: Amsterdam poster for 16 March gig. *(Mark Lascelles)*

Sonic and Jason backstage with members of Sirens of 7th Avenue, Camden, 1988. *(Andrew Jackson)*

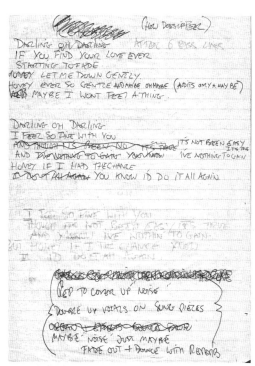

Sonic's original 'Let Me Down Gently' lyric
sheet with additional notes, 1988.
(Mark Lascelles, ©Sonic Boom)

Sonic and Jason play one of their last performances
together at the Town and Country Club, London,
1989. *(Colin Bell/SIN)*

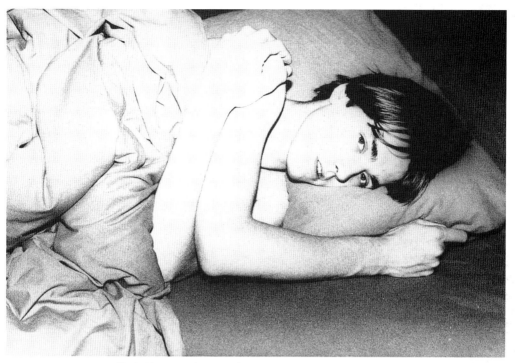

Sonic Boom, underground pin-up, 1989. *(Jayne Houghton)*

Still from the 1988 'Revolution' music-video.

PLAYING WITH FIRE: Will, Sonic, Jason and Jonny surrounded by flames in a
1988 photo session. *(Steve Double)*

down along the carpeted floor. "I waited until he was safely asleep," said Bassman with a smile. "But when Jason woke in the morning, he noticed he had vomit on him and was like, 'Who's fucking puked on me!' "

SONIC: I don't remember Jason getting into bed taking his boots off or his clothes. He'd just crash out on the bed night after night. Then, of course, all the next day he was miserable as fuck. If you think junkies are bad to be around when they're sick, fucking be around fucking hung-over people. I was just so sick of it! I didn't want to be around a bunch of hung-over fuckers.

PAT FISH: But I know from personal experience that this kind of drinking in the hothouse environment of a tour party can lead to first-class paranoia. Just plain, honest down-home paranoia, entirely lacking in any rational basis. Drink is a depressant, right? So if you're living it large and having a grand time on the road with all the funny foreigners and so on, the nasty effects of the liquor are not always apparent. Instead you tend to internalise all the depression and resentment until you go bad inside. Then, with the appropriate liquor-induced release trigger, all this festering crap will surface over something of no importance whatsoever.

When the van finally pulled into Innsbruck's Utopia Club on January 28, the whole touring clique was suffering from exhaustion and verging on homicide. Like the mythopoetic Donner party who'd attempted to cross the snowy peaks of the Rockies only to feast on the flesh of their own family and friends, nobody in The Spacemen line-up could ignore their emaciated frames and dwindling funds. This was especially true for Bassman and Sonic, whose only renewable sources of energy resulted from their mutual hatred of one another. "To get the point across I hated the sight of him," Bassman contended. "It got so I was feeling total repulsion at his odious presence. Sonic's sexual orientation explained a lot about his attitudes to us. He never quite had a conventional relationship. He was openly aggressive to female fans, throwing one Swiss girl down a flight of stairs."

"They just lost it, they lost the fucking plot," claimed Sonic. "They forgot what they were there to do. They just took the piss from end to end and it was really unpleasant." Neither denied cannibalism as an option. Not for nutrients, mind you, but simply to rid the van of their greatest irritant. Starving and withdrawn as they were, there remained in front of them nearly two more weeks of shows. "There was all this sort of conflict at the time," said Rosco. "But," he added, " I think they all reckoned that that's what made the band so good onstage. I think that's just a pile of shit. I think you can make a good sound on stage and still chill out with your mates and enjoy it."

From their tiny Alpine hostel, Bassman, Jason, Rosco, Goff and crew absconded to a nearby mountain retreat, skipping the afternoon sound-check and leaving Sonic to his own devices. Goff remembered Sonic was laid out in his bed, nodded out, and ignored the invitation to accompany them. Bassman, however, claimed he prompted the last-minute excursion as a way to ditch Sonic. "We just got in a van and took off. We all just said, 'Fuck you!' and left him," he said. Goff convinced everyone to pop onto a local cable-car and ride up to the mountain retreat. "We just went up this mountain and it was really nice you know," Bassman continued. "We went to a cafe. Unwound really. Nobody really talked about it. It was just like a feeling. And that was at the point that Sonic was so painful to be around that something had to break the kind of monopoly that he had on us."

Bassman and Jason walked along the cafe's twists of wood and rock, with the majestic vistas of the Austrian valley below. To break the eerie silence, Bassman poured out his feelings about the band, his concern for their future and his deep loathing for Sonic. "'How can you stand him?'" Bassman implored. "And Jason never quite knew. I said to Jason, 'This is terrible! Why can't we just form a band without Pete?'" Jason simply shrugged his shoulders and walked on. "If Jason was really such a good friend of Pete's, he would have told Pete what I said and Pete would have said, 'Hey what's this about you forming a band with Jason without me?!' And he would have kicked me out of the band. But he didn't. Jason never thought like that," Bassman claimed. The two musicians joined back up with the rest of the crew and enjoyed the afternoon smoking and drinking, thousands of feet up. "We had a fine time and headed back to the hotel," concluded Bassman, "but we were kind of expecting Sonic to be snarling like, 'Where the hell have you been?!' But instead he was sitting there and he was very morose." In fact, Sonic was swollen with loathing and regret. "I wasn't even talking to Pete Bain by the end of the tour; I wasn't talking to any of them," he claimed.

For whatever reasons the tension subsided during the final 10-day journey through Bern and Zürich, Switzerland. The van stopped over at the ski-resort town of Lausanne on the next evening and the tired caravan walked into an upper crust nightclub packed with superannuated jet-setters. A poor choice of venue (but a common experience for young bands in Switzerland), the band looked on at the unassuming patrons and cringed: the Swiss audience was decked out in Alpine resort fashion and sipping brandy. By the end of the performance, the entire audience had moved from their seats around the stage to the rear of the room (those who hadn't walked out) as Sonic and Jason roared into a ¾-hour version of 'Suicide', a new composition debuted during the tour. They skipped backstage after 20 minutes of the song to skin up before returning to the stage for a rousing 10-minute conclusion. As the Vox amps fizzled to a close, the club lurched into a deadening silence. No encore would be necessary.

Sonic was unusually silent as he sat in the back of the van, while Goff drove fast and furiously northward to the Netherlands. To add to their woes, The Spacemen had handed over the few thousand in earnings they'd made from weeks of blood, sweat, and tears, to their raging driver. No one believed Goff would ever make good on it. A concoction of apathy, antipathy, dope, and drink had rendered the entire band numb. Sonic would chain-smoke joints at a fervent rate, ignoring everyone in the van, while the others smiled quietly to themselves as they continued to drink through the rider, all the way to Holland. "Yeah, that's when Jason told me that that was it. He was going to leave the band," Goff beamed, proud to be in the young lad's confidence. "And I was probably the first person he ever told. It was while we were drinking a bottle of Jack Daniel's in the van if I remember. He knew he was going to leave the band then."

ROSCO: I remember when we finally got to Holland there was one gig when Pete was so out of it. He turned around and we're on this really tall stage some place. There were loads of people there. And he turned around from the microphone and accuses the other three members of the band of being out of time with him. Like he's one on his own and we're three, and it's obvious we're all tight.

GOFF RODERICK: Pete was normally off his trolley on that tour, do you know what I mean? Just on a different wavelength. Pete was like the spaced-out man in the corner.

SONIC: We were on the road. I didn't buy any heroin or anything stronger than hash for weeks. I was travelling everyday through borders and customs. It was just impossible to keep any sort of supply, and I made no attempts.

Once in Amsterdam, the band headed straight for the concert venue, the infamous Milkweg (Milkyway), which doubled as a cafe/bar/head shop where travelling bands could load up on a variety of cannabis, hash, and space sweets complete with mushrooms. The crowd of concert-goers and freaks that night were a testament to Amsterdam's progressive atmosphere. Even The Spacemen, England's own pharmaceutical cos-monauts, were weirded out by the hoary oddballs prostrate on the dirty rugs and the strange guy dressed in an alien outfit smoking at the bar.

The band stumbled onto the stage after nine o'clock, with Jason and Sonic taking to their stools in front of Bassman and Rosco. Everyone was severely stoned on the particularly strong hash that circulated at the bar. Sonic was rarely speaking to his mates, much less playing with them. They all looked quite dour as they stood looking down at the rickety stage, failing to acknowledge the audience or each other.

If the Milkyway concert was indicative of the consummation of a month's worth of Spacemen performances, then the disintegration of relations between members was not the only insufferable effect of weeks of debauchery. From the beginning of the evening's performance until its shambling conclusion, the guitar/bass/drum correlation sounded sluggish, un-tuned, and out of step. The instruments lumbered and lurched in an awkward delay, all a weary testament to the hazy, dyspeptic wash of maladroit inebriation. Jason and Sonic's guitars sizzled at random, while Bassman's bass-runs appeared and disappeared at strange intervals, and the drums were severely out of time. Attempts at 'Mary Anne' and 'Rollercoaster' meandered rather than chugged. Jason's work on 'Walkin' With Jesus' was one of the few positive glimmers in the morass of indiscernible riffing. The powerhouse-rush of 'Revolution' was reified into a drunkard staggering for the pisser. Admitted Sonic, "It wasn't the best show, but it was one of the better shows. There were mistakes that needn't be in there. There would always be one or two songs that would be good."

Only the set-closing 'Suicide' was an absolute gem, truly the zenith of an otherwise derelict evening. A charged, dense piece of electro-art, 'Suicide' was a one-chord exploration of everything textural, kinetic and radiophonic, a labyrinth of disorienting wah-wah pedal, waves of varying tremolo speed, and the primal scream of feedback. From up above at the mixing desk, the engineer added brilliant effects over the PA, wrapping the sprawl of noise into deep-echo and sending Jason's guitar swooping and panning around the stage. As the final song of the evening, it was a fitting ode to its namesake: both the band and the action. It was as if, for a brief 12-minute space, all bitterness and discontent simmering from the month-long ordeal, came rushing through the fibrous *bricolage* of arms, fingers, pedals, leads, amplifiers – suffusing in some pagan-science ritual where straw sprouts into gold. Someone in the band had slipped the sound engineer 25 gilders to pop a cassette into the mixing-board before the show, and afterwards Goff jumped up onto the balcony and grabbed the tape before anyone nicked it. He passed it over to Sonic later in the evening, who slipped it into his pocket, certain that a viable bootleg might eventually come in handy.

It was during their tedious journey back from the Netherlands to the Midlands that Sonic reached his limit with both Bassman and Rosco. Their behaviour over the course of the tour had been unconscionably boorish, he felt, and, more to the point, stereotypical of what promoters had come to expect from a "drug-band". Rosco's other major fault was his habitual attraction to and inclusion of certifiable girlfriends in the touring party. One particular harpie had aggravated Sonic and Jason during transit no end, leading them to agree to a "no chicks on the bus" policy. Goff's screeching bird cemented this policy following the European journey. Sonic assured his best mate that tours were for work, not schmoozing, and Jason wholeheartedly consented to keeping groupies and girlfriends away from business. Sonic felt certain that what was left of past tumult would be allayed when he and Jason did just that: got back to business. "It was tough touring Europe. I know when we went back the next year we had real trouble," Sonic said, frowning. "A lot of the promoters at the venues said, 'Oh people were really disappointed with it last year'. We had real trouble touring the next time we went back." Sonic felt part of his mission was to educate the arrogant and misguided masses that drug-users weren't deviants, and drug-bands weren't comprised solely of misguided punks. And in one fowl swoop, he saw his band become just that: a grizzled hunk of pissed buffoons.

"That's when they were splitting up," claimed Goff. "That's when they knew Spacemen 3 was going to be no more. But that was [also] the point when Spacemen 3 were ready to take over the world, and they knew that as well. In actual fact, at the end of that European tour when it was all dissolving, I actually exacted a promise out of each one of them that, if the band split, they would all do one last gig for me. And all of them, even Jason, agreed. So to this day, I'm probably the only person on the planet who has the power to make them do one final gig." Despite Goff's certainty of an imminent disintegration, Sonic's unwitting perspective believed the contrary. In his mind, Bassman and Rosco deserved the hook post-haste. They had already presented their resignation letters, albeit on the cragged stage-floors of Europe. Jason's status, however, was far from jeopardised. He was indispensable, and more to the point, they were best mates.

Sonic's fidelity to Jason might not have been fully reciprocated, as Jason had become more aware of the former's hell-bent and obsessive personality. The European journey taught Jason just how cruel and unwavering Sonic could be when the viability of his band . . . *his* band was challenged from the inside. Any dissention would be excised. But Jason also understood that there were few, if any, alternatives worthy of what Spacemen 3 had already become in his mind. It was no mere garage-punk fling – it was religion. "Jason always said about this band: 'You do it and you suffer because that's the price you pay for being Spacemen 3,'" Bassman insisted. Furthermore, Jason's ongoing relationship with Kate kept him pleasantly distracted from the laborious rancour of dealing with these internal conflicts. But, soon enough, it seemed, Jason would turn a corner in his future plans, to which Sonic remained blissfully oblivious.

'Too Much Synth On The Brain . . .'

The DREAMWEAPON: to produce again but as anew. For droning is like schizophrenia: a process and not a goal, a production and not an expression. Neither the product nor the intention, but rather the production. Neither the subjective nor the objective, but the movement alongside. It is this vectoral concurrentness which allows for the re-production again, a re-demonstration that mandates the DREAMWEAPON be not simply a repetition in time – time as a quantised measure of quality – but rather a regenerative innovation that invariably falls back upon the original through a folding-over, a patchwork of intensities. But not from an inherent lack, the basis of any correspondence theory of meaning; rather from the ecstasy that flows between the two, an indeterminate, an unthought, that floods over into the real with saccharine melody and desire. The original (the product) is an inscription, a burning, a cutting, a recording of the production (in fact a reproducing) linked, or rather feeding back along the interstitial patches of a synth-machine.

JUNE 29, 2002
M1 MOTORWAY EN ROUTE TO LONDON

Sonic drives at Autobahn speeds in his ramshackle red Mini hatchback, weaving between cars and lumbering lorries somewhere along the M1 between Rugby and London. He's playing a small club gig at Islington in the evening. I'm shifting in the passenger seat, chain-smoking cigarettes and gazing at rolling pasture and the occasional livestock dotting the landscape. The glove-compartment latch is broken and the strand of tape holding it closed fails miserably against the constant jostling of the car, causing the thick rubber door to crash down on my knees every few minutes. The radio doesn't work but the roar of wind and the clopping sounds of the motor make for excellent soundtrack. Sonic's girlfriend Anita – a short-haired pixie bearing an uncanny resemblance to Jean Seberg – sits in the back seat, holding on gingerly to a number of his fragile synths, careful not to touch or jostle the pre-set patches while balancing drinks and rolling joints.

In between lane changes, Sonic puffs heavily on the never-ending strings of dope and drops an occasional "fuck off" from his window at passing motorists, albeit with patent lethargy. His driving is nearly as infamous as his lifestyle.

EM: Tell me about all the synthesisers you've got in the back seat?

SONIC: Umm . . . well the main ones I use are the Serg synthesiser, which I custom-made, the Fenix – spelled FENIX – and once again, its another modular synthesiser. And then the other stuff I use is an EMS synth and then I usually use a Speak 'n Spell and a couple of other little bits. Like tonight I'm going to use the Air synth and that's probably about it.

EM: These are all analogue synths right? I mean, do you find working with analogue to be more enjoyable than digital?

SONIC: Well, using an analogue synth is like driving a car, where you get in and you can control the whole thing with your hands. Whereas digital is more like flying a plane or something, where it's all pre-programmed in and you're just sitting there. Just pushing buttons that are instigating pre-recorded sequences of sound or music. So analogue stuff is a lot more hands-on.

EM: Is working with analogue gear much more difficult?

SONIC: It's a lot easier to work on analogue synths once you know what you're doing. Like I said, it's a lot more hands-on, just literally feeding patches between one part and another. Whereas in the digital domain, it's all got to be done through a programming interface you know, it can be done with as little as five or six buttons.

EM: How do you decide to set up the patches?

SONIC: I usually set up stuff beforehand. Before each gig I see how I feel and what I want to try. Then I patch it up accordingly.

EM: Do you find that there's a lot of discipline that has to go into the learning of it, both the technical and theoretical aspects?

SONIC: There's certainly lots to learn technically. And then there's all these myriad ways you can interconnect them. It's very flexible. You really never stop learning on a Modular synth.

EM: Do you think people are generally more frightened of that kind of electro music than the more acoustic-based stuff like Spacemen 3? Is that kind of electronic/drone texture present in the Experimental Audio Research material still very much anathema?

SONIC: In general there's more demand for Spectrum/Spacemen stuff than EAR material. I get offered more EAR shows and festivals, but more people come out to see the Spacemen 3 and Spectrum material. I don't know about EAR being anathema. Could be . . .

could be. People generally perceive electronic-based music differently than they perceive acoustic-based music. I don't see why it should be that way.

(long pause . . .)

Sonic peers, disaffected and plaintive, at the stretch of buzzing concrete that vibrates beneath us. His eyes are glazed. The sweet smell of hash curls through the car's interior, making me slightly nauseous. He seems confused or perplexed but he shakes it off and takes another drag, flicking the roach out of the window.

SONIC: Sorry, I'm just really tired.

We leave the Motorway and drive into Islington. The 100-mile trip has taken only an hour. Sonic reverently points to the building where Joe Meek shot his landlady. An admonition: too many electronics on the brain . . .

CHAPTER SEVEN
Revolution Or Heroin

SPRING–SUMMER 1988

Shortly after returning from a miasmic voyage around the Continent, Rosco pulled up stakes and walked away from Spacemen 3. He'd had enough of being the unappreciated drummer; he'd had enough of fulfilling an obligation with absolutely no return; he'd had enough of Sonic's abuse and Jason's muted apathy. "I got back from that tour in Europe and I had no money for rent for the Oxford Street house," he recalled. "It was just total chaos down there. I owed several months back rent that I couldn't pay. Natty had trouble paying too. Jason had his money for rent but wouldn't help us out. He just told us to get fucked, so I told him the same thing and moved out." Rosco claimed he was reduced to selling off his drum kit to pay the landlord, only to find himself without a band or a home.

"When Sonic got back, he was really down on Rosco," Pat Fish recalled. "Rosco was certainly profoundly unwelcome. Pete had gone from being quite friendly towards him to being right rude. Virulently opposed to him." When Sonic would turn up in Northampton and crash out on Fish's couch, he'd often take a grape-scented, plastic octopus from Pat's bookshelf, plop it on his head, dance around the front room, and call it "Rosco The Octopus". Although Fish was never completely certain to what Sonic was referring, it was patently clear that he was taking a royal piss on his former drummer. "His attitude toward Rosco really changed after that tour," Fish continued. "I don't know what happened with Pete Bain. I assumed it was just collateral damage."

Sonic's derision toward the rhythm-section was exacerbated when he discovered that Rosco and Bassman were both planning to exit to join another local up-and-coming Rugby band called The Darkside. "Rosco wanted to leave anyway, so I gave up on him," he recalled. "Pete Bain actually had a pact with him where they were both going to leave the band together. And then, in typical bumbling fashion, Rosco fucked off and Pete Bain decided to stay."

The band had already signed up for a short UK tour through the North within a few weeks of returning to their native soil. Whether or not Rosco chose this brief hiatus to walk from the drum-seat of his own volition, or was nudged firmly by Sonic's dominating personality, his stint with the band concluded sometime in February, and he stumbled from one Rugby band to the next in the coming months. "Right before that tour, Pete Kember asked me not to leave," he insisted, "but by that time the bubble had burst for me. I didn't want to get involved with The Spacemen again." Bassman, however, had not determined his future in the band to be quite so clear-cut.

More difficulties arose when Kate's earliest encroachment into the tour van during the spring of '88 caused Sonic to lambaste Jason for reneging on their earlier agreement. The couple sat huddled together to and from the gig, while Sonic fumed from the back seat. Jason's head just seemed to slip out of the game, out of the band, and away from his mates. At least according to his spurned bandmate. With a week-long UK tour imminent, Sonic wanted to forestall Kate's appearance at the van door before she became the "fifth" Spaceman. He took Jason aside one evening prior to the band's departure and levelled with him: Kate was a distraction . . . she fucked with band morale . . . she wasn't welcome in the tour van any longer. It wasn't Sonic at his most tactful and Jason tried to shrug it off although it was a stinging invective at both himself and his girlfriend. He ran to Kate immediately, springing the news, only to have her instantly break down in sobs. She was sure Sonic hated her.

The band embarked for Manchester on March 18 before travelling on to Scotland. Sonic picked up a temp drummer, Dave Morgan from The Weather Prophets, to fill out the touring roster in Rosco's absence. The first evening's performance took place at The Boardwalk, a dank but spacious warehouse that befitted Manchester's detritus *chic*. The Spacemen took the stage tentatively as to the modest crowd's likely reaction, and eased into their set. Perhaps buoyed by the atmosphere of the city and his lack of rehearsal, new drummer Morgan contented himself by pounding away Jaki Leibezeit-infused beats *à la* Can throughout the set, radically altering the droning, repetitive thud of 'Rollercoaster' and 'Things'll Never Be The Same' into a groove-laden palette for dancing. Happy Mondays' singer Shaun Ryder appeared on the floor with an entourage of musicians and rogues, all of whom were drinking and gyrating to the electric dronage. Unsurprisingly, the Manchester audience dug the funkified noise in a big way, while Jason and Sonic – more keen on *White Light/White Heat* than on *Tago Mago* – merely scoffed at their guest drummer's reinterpretation. Despite their displeasure, the performance went well for The Spacemen who were thereafter welcome into the fold of The Hacienda Club – the Max's Kansas City of Madchester – and into the drug-fuelled fellowship of The Mondays. By year's end Sonic and Ryder would become hard and fast mates, colluding backstage after Mondays' shows to score dope and get high together.

Manchester was on its way to becoming the hip epicentre of British music culture in the spring of 1988. After a period of Smiths-style guitar revival in the middle portion of the decade, the city's ecstatic youth had reverted to the industrialised jazz-funk of Factory's earliest prospects – the subtle synth-grooves of The Durutti Column, A Certain Ratio's Northern Soul rhythms, and New Order's commanding indie disco – combining it with the beats of the Balearic house/techno synth-fetish amalgam that swept in from the South courtesy of the London club Shoom. As Simon Reynolds commented in his electro opus *Generation Ecstasy*, "With its combination of bohemia and demographic reach, Manchester was well placed to become the focus of a pop cultural explosion. House – which was played as early as 1986 on local Piccadilly Radio by DJ Stu Allen – chimed in with a long-standing regional prefer-ence for up-tempo dance music. . . . By 1989, the famously grey and overcast city had gone Day-Glo; Morrissey-style miserabilism was replaced by glad-all-over extroversion, nourished by a diet of 'disco biscuits'." Manchester's own rock groups were among the earliest con-verts. With their second single 'Elephant Stone', The Stone Roses made their first major rhythmic advance towards a fusion of sugary Sixties melody and groove, while The Happy Mondays slogged away in the studio completing their first rave 'n roll album *Bummed* complete with a hit single 'Wrote For Luck'. These subtle symptoms of a thorough "funkification" would envelope the city in the subsequent year's Mad-chester hysteria. It was difficult for The Spacemen, who were steeped in the traditions of Velvets' avant-head cool, to comprehend thoroughly the flared fashion and Scally attitudes as they explored the city's squalid interior. 'What the fuck are they smiling about?' was the general con-fusion, for Manchester was more bleak and desiccated than the Midlands. What was the big secret?

The band continued travelling to Glasgow and Edinburgh for back-to-back dates followed by a gig in Leeds. By then Morgan's anomalous drumming had alienated him from the band. When he split after the Leeds show, Sonic coaxed a friend from The Perfect Disaster to finish the tour on percussion. With yet another *ad hoc* line-up, they played two nights at Take Two, Sheffield's own funkified temple of groove worship. At the end of March, Sonic, Jason and Bassman returned to Dingwall's to showcase much of the new material they'd road tested throughout Europe. The set included the London debut of 'Revolution', 'Suicide', and 'Repeater', of which the latter augmented The Spacemen's heavily distorted sound with Neu!-inspired tones. In April they played North-ampton and wowed the few patrons that stayed for the entirety of their set. Alas, some things had not changed. "I went to see them at the Road-mender," recalled Mark Refoy, "and some other dodgy Goth band was supporting them. But they brought tons of people and the place emptied when they finished. So there was just me and about 30 others in the audi-ence. But The Spacemen had really changed from when I saw them before. They were doing this amazing track called 'Repeater' and it was fucking fantastic!"

At the invitation of Genesis P. Orridge, Jason, Sonic and Bassman (with another random pick-up drummer) reprised their Psychic TV per-formance at the conclusion of April at the London Astoria. Their opening set went off without incident though the lukewarm approbation from the PTV crowd was little improvement from their previous Electric Ballroom showing. Even the musical fringe that populated the "profes-sionally strange" followers of Psychic TV just didn't seem to get Space-men 3. With quintessential P. Orridge aplomb, Psychic TV enraptured the audience with a set of synth squelch and home-fried beats. The Spacemen stood at the side of the floor watching as a circuited collection of black-and-white televisions around P. Orridge featured an unedited surgical sex change. "At the end of their set, about three dozen of their friends got up onstage dancing with them," recalled Sonic. "And during the gleeful abandon of the moment decided they should all strip off and show their piercings or something. Which they all did. And, of course, the band finished and went offstage. And there were like 40 people left standing there looking for their socks, which they'd wildly thrown off."

The band returned to Rugby to find Gerald Palmer eager to develop his relationship with them. Bassman saw Palmer's encroachment as the *coup de grâs* to any notion of Spacemen 3 retaining its few democratic trap-pings. In his estimation Palmer was the ultimate businessman, an elder square in the Thatcherite tradition of greed and corruption, who under-stood little of the band's spirituality and saw only the cartoonish possibili-ties of a Sex Pistols-like marketing campaign. Unfortunately, Bassman's view represented the minority and his days in the band were, conse-quently, numbered. "Pete and Jason thought and think still that they should have a much larger percentage of the band's proceeds than me and Pete Bain," explained Rosco. "The royalty split at that time was 30/30/20/20 between us and them. Pete Bain and I didn't have any proper consultation or legal advice so we got shafted. Even though the band was a full-time thing, we had to go sign on at the Security Office to try and stay alive." Sonic refused to indulge such petty financial bickerings from his no-talent bandmates. "Jason and I always earned more than Rosco and Pete, because they never used to put any effort into it," he retorted. "We only earned 10 per cent more than them, but we did 80 per cent of the fucking work, so there was never any reason for them to get equal recompense. Pete Bain always wanted the band to be a four-way democracy, but he'd never put the work into it."

> BASSMAN: When Gerald Palmer got involved there was a period of time when we weren't really happy with the situation. And I don't think Jason was either, and Jason was certainly vocal about it . . . But at that particular point I think the relationship with Gerald Palmer and The Spacemen was very new. So what Pete did, he talked to Gerald and they schmoozed. They got very close to each other. Gerald was very manipulative. He knew that he was just taking the band's novelty to exploit. And this is behind everybody's backs, you know. We just didn't hear about it. It was just a meeting between them. And I think Jason, as soon as he showed any sign of dissent, he soon shut up when it was formulated that *they* were Spacemen 3. Just between Jason and Pete. They agreed that myself and Rosco would always be treated as disposable in some ways. We were never going to be on equal footing. We were never going to be included in any kind of business or anything like that. So Jason was just included on the business side of things. For now he had his cut and he was happy with it.

Bassman's indignation with these clandestine discussions was justified. For the proposed three-way partnership would effectively exclude the rhythm section from any legal ownership of the name Spacemen 3. It was a practice all too common to young rock'n'roll groups bonded by "pure" intentions, only to be transformed into business "outfits" with the aid of management. Similar "incorporations" had littered the history of those most rebellious of bands and their financial impresarios, from The Stones and Allen Klein to The Velvets' Steve Sesnick and The Sex Pistols' McLaren. But to Palmer's supreme credit, he instantly recognised that the financial and creative bonanza of Spacemen 3 lied solely in the writing partnership of Kember/Pierce. And who would disagree with his estimation? Spacemen 3 *was* Jason and Sonic. "I think I encouraged them not to sign Pete Bain and Rosco," admitted Gerald. "There was an instability in the band, and my relationship with the band was really just with two. They had a serious break in morale between them. Like the usual arguments: 'You're not putting enough into it,' or 'You're not committed.'"

"Pete Bain wanted to fuck off because he was so pissed off at Pete

Kember, Jason, and Gerald . . . the whole band," observed Goff, himself an inadvertent casualty of Palmer's entrance. Whatever unofficial status Roderick maintained, with his maniacal *élan* and charley visions, was co-opted by Gerald's sanctioned authority. "Gerald just came in because he saw fucking mega dollar signs, but he didn't see the fucking cracks. In my mind, he saw Spacemen 3 as a commercial venture worth managing. I think he saw Pink Floyd there. The only trouble was they were already in the process of splitting up." Sonic was more than happy to exchange a surly bassist and a cocaine dealer for a straight financial adviser. As he saw it, Bassman's modicum of talent did not make up for his uneven performances, grouchy attitude, and explosive temper. Bassman sat on the sidelines for much of the recording of *The Perfect Prescription*, pouting at his apparent exclusion from Sonic and Jason's writing bouts, and he'd drunk himself across Germany, slushing up to the stage at the last possible moment to flail away at his bass. More importantly, Bassman's presence always created an element of uncertainty within the band, from his first exit to join The Push, and through his second phase with the band, taking the piss out of Sonic at every possible opportunity and casting aspersions on Gerald Palmer's belated entrance. The month of May would be Bassman's last as a Spaceman.

The austere and acrimonious conditions of touring taught Sonic other lessons of survival, none more severe than the desperation provided by an absence of gear, especially junk. Recognising his addiction, Sonic decided to register himself as a heroin user in order to procure a supply of methadone. He drove to a clinic in Coventry where his name was put on the national registry – which had, by the late Eighties, ballooned to thousands upon thousands in Britain – and he was given a prescription for weekly dosages provided in an ampoule or linctus. Liquid methadone of approximately 30 millilitres equalled 1/8 gram of heroin, or one bag in potency, to be provided for the rehabilitation of heroin addiction. The doctor handling Sonic's "illness" nodded politely to his newest patient with a toothy grin, as if to assure him that he was well on his way to a monotonous, morphine-free existence. Sonic drove back into Rugby, having digested his first supply with a mild snort. Fifteen years later, he would make the same weekly trip to the local hospital for the same prescription for the same drug for the same monotonous, morphine-free existence.

By the summer of '88, the band had been crippled by the successive exits of their third regular drummer and on-again, off-again bass player. Although a modest buzz began to mount on the back of *The Perfect Prescription* and the six-week Euro tour, neither Sonic nor Jason felt Dave

Barker was sufficiently attempting to capitalise on their growing acclaim. Nearly nine months after their last album and single releases, only a few thousand pounds had trickled in and Glass Records was sinking deeper and deeper into insolvency.

The July release of The Spacemen's final single on Glass, 'Take Me To The Other Side', built on the positive vibe generated by *The Perfect Prescription* and made its way onto the pages of every major weekly. The *NME*'s Helen Mead declared it "Most Exalted Single of the Week" and wrote, "Following on from their cobalt crystal cover of 'Transparent Radiation' last year, the quartet from Rugby have again kicked the ball over the H posts. 'Take Me To The Other Side' coats your spine in shrink-wrap shivers, toasts your brain on afterburner rhythms, and invokes a dribbling LSD monster who devours your inner spirit and spits out a ghoul. Burn baby burn, and let your consciousness be damned." *Melody Maker* slobbered with lugubrious poetics, "'The Other Side' is infinite, has no towns called Pett Bottom, and we ectoplasm our way through on Spacemen 3's cyclic reverb that's simultaneously informed by birth and death via the heartbeat." Only *Sounds* retreated from such bandwagoning, resurrecting the stinging Loop connection, "Spacemen 3 have the talent to create a throbbing electric cathedral of sound, *à la* Loop, but 'TMTTOS' isn't it."

The two Spacemen guitarists could only look toward Josh Hampson's growing success with Loop and cringe. Although Hampson assisted Barker at Glass throughout '85–'86, the A&R man didn't take Robert's muso intentions much beyond the fantasies of an air-riffing punter. But Barker had evidently missed the boat and he missed out on signing Loop too, who went on to release a number of hugely successful singles in late '86 and '87 along with their sprawling debut LP *Heaven's End* on Head. Although the album did not exactly fulfil the enigmatic sonorities of the '16 Dreams' or 'Spinning' singles, *Heaven's End* provided enough atmospheric noise for the *NME* to rank it #58 in its Writers End Of Year Poll, concomitantly declaring Loop the new champions of drone-rock. In fact Loop's debut sounded more metal than minimal. But it was little wonder that the music press could hardly decipher the difference between the religious zeal of Spacemen 3's *Funhouse* homage and Loop's wank-for-wank's sake tribute to Blue Cheer's cheese-metal *Vincebus Eruptum*. Where were the immediate referents? They didn't exist in the ongoing pure-pop Fantasia of London, among the cloying twee of The Pastels or the jangle-thrash of The Jasmine Minks. In conjunction with Sonic's press offensive, whereby he took every interview opportunity to slag off Hampson as a charlatan and Loop as a Spacemen 3 covers band, the provincial Rugby band appeared as embittered and sore losers in the eyes of the London rock press. But Sonic and Jason weren't about to pack it in. Just the opposite. The change in band personnel allowed for possible revitalisation, as they were already on the hunt for a new bassist around Rugby, preferably someone with an equal fixation for The Stooges and a little less attitude. The problems with Barker also held the potential for moving on to a bigger label with more financial dependability and wider distribution.

At the time they had signed with Glass Records in 1986, Jason and Sonic negotiated their modest contract for two albums over three years, and they both signed on the dotted line. With such elementary trappings and no obvious alternatives, the Glass deal seemed the only choice to kick-start careers that they had been peddling aimlessly for four years. The Spacemen had responded in due fashion by turning over consecutive albums, but found that they still owed Barker another year. Neither Jason nor Sonic wanted to wait around for another year, biding their time on a label whose glory days had long since passed. The Glass roster, that had once boasted an interesting crossover with Creation, saw its short-list of potentials waning.

Dave Barker had met Alan McGee as early as '84 in Islington at The Living Room, and the two labels consistently fought for many of the same acts through the mid-Eighties. The Pastels promised much in their first days with McGee but Stephen Pastel never pushed his group beyond an adolescent aesthetic – ambition was anathema to anorak-pop – relegating the band to mere novelty by the time they landed at Glass. Likewise, The Jacobites apparently bungled the opportunities that Nikki Sudden had made the most of during his time with Swell Maps. Pat Fish, who had been hesitant to suggest Glass to Spacemen 3 back in 1985, had taken his band to Creation in the meantime. Phil Parfitt's Perfect Disaster, a Coventry noise-band who'd recently returned from a two-year hiatus to France and signed with Barker, would make the move from Glass to Fire round about the same time as Spacemen 3. Barker's label was on its last legs. "Dave Barker became such a pain in the ass to deal with," Sonic lamented. "We weren't getting our royalties, or we got them extremely late." The Spacemen wanted out from under the aegis of Glass. But Barker stood firm and pointed to the contract and two-year-old signatures. He wasn't about to let them walk. "They had built a following by playing live and the records seemed to sell consistently by the time of *Perfect Prescription*," said Barker. Spacemen 3 was the most promising band on his roster and he wagered that if he could thwart their defection, he'd stave off Glass' demise.

When the Glass discussions reached a stalemate, Sonic finally agreed to enlist the assistance of Gerald Palmer. As he explained, "We realised that we needed someone to deal with the business side of things, so we could concentrate on playing and writing the music. I didn't start Spacemen 3 for money or business." For Gerald it was quite the opposite, and he made his fiduciary presence apparent to Barker almost immediately. "Gerald was and is a businessman, but he also genuinely loved The Spacemen," Barker sighed. "I liked him, and still do, although there was a period when I could definitely have lived without him." In fact, as Palmer's first act of business, he hit up Barker for all the unpaid royalties and threatened legal action for strategic leverage, while simultaneously attempting to convince him to release The Spacemen from their contract. By way of compromise, Gerald negotiated turning over the live recordings from the spring's Amsterdam concert as incentive for Barker to walk away. "There were royalties that he hadn't paid," claimed Palmer, "and he had more than adequate opportunities to pay. But the reason he didn't pay was because he didn't have the money. Glass was a tiny operation and his distributor was going out of business. There was hardly anything left."

When Barker released a portion of the Amsterdam gig as *Performance* in mid-July, critics and punters finally took feverish notice. Spacemen proponent at the *NME*, Helen Mead, described *Performance* as ". . . all swirling sub-Sixties rock riffs and trance beats, meshed with understated passion starved vocals. That resolve into a hypnotic mind dance. . . . No other movement is possible. This explains why for a live album *Performance* has the lowest applause level I've ever heard." *Sounds'* Jon Orsman finally acknowledged the Spacemen/Loop connection, a minor accomplishment in itself, when he professed, "Live, Spacemen 3 are better than any band wearing the same badges. They play the same style of music as Loop, only better, a garage/Stooges/MC5 hybrid to be taken with a pinch of stimulant . . ." Even John Peel belatedly jumped upon The Spacemen bandwagon, spinning the band's 17-minute 'Rollercoaster' on his late-night Radio 1 programme, only to play several other records over its prolix entirety with the flippant remark, "It's still going!" Sadly, the critical "plaudits" and growing sales yielded little money for Barker, who insisted most of the profits for the album were lost when distributor Red Rhino declared insolvency. "I owed them money," confessed Barker, "but I didn't have it. It was always a continual struggle chasing funds in from distributors and exporters. I think that was the main trouble. When my distributor Red Rhino went bust, it owed me a fair amount, and I couldn't pay them." At his wit's end with Palmer and an ungrateful rock-band, Barker waved goodbye to Spacemen 3. Barker's label did, in fact, dissolve the same year, after Glass' distribution collapsed and Robert Hampson walked for a full-time gig with Loop. In a strange twist, Barker would follow soon after The Spacemen when he agreed to bring his roster to Fire Records in exchange for a new subsidiary label, Paperhouse, which he ran for a number of years.

Upon release from the inwardly spiralling Glass Records, The Spacemen found themselves in the surprisingly unfavourable predicament of free agency. Once again Sonic suggested Gerald consider coming on-board in an official capacity as manager; in fact, he was already serving as an *ad hoc* representative of the band, campaigning for other record labels and laying out cash for singles sessions and one-off shows. But by the late summer of '88 Spacemen 3 had failed to ascend the fiscal or public relations ladder, dwelling in an obscurity nearly as dense as their Reverberation days. Both the band and their business Svengali came to an impasse. Palmer had gone on an aggressive campaign on behalf of the band, posting numerous records and demos to Chapter 22 in Birmingham, and Rough Trade and Mute in London. When Gerald eventually got Geoff Travis on the phone, the indie label guru complimented the music but balked at the prospect of signing Spacemen 3. "At the point of being free from Glass, nobody was interested in The Spacemen," said Gerald. "We couldn't get any deal or any money."

When Alan McGee heard *The Perfect Prescription* for the first time, he knew that this was a band that could travel far in the indie-world. Pat Fish had played McGee the album shortly after it's release in late 1987, effectively hooking the Creation magus on the band's composite blend of psychedelia and gospel. "What I loved about them was *Perfect Prescription* and all the really gospelly music songs," remembered McGee. "I could always spot quality and when I heard 'Walkin' With Jesus' I decided I wanted to sign them. Really because of that song alone." Dave Barker concurred. "Alan really loved them; in fact, Alan and Dick Green managed Peter for a while after The Spacemen split." With his patented Glaswegian ardour, an abrasive blend of fiery idealism and business aplomb, McGee pursued the two Rugby musicians at numerous London shows. When the Creation chief got wind of the fact that The Spacemen were shopping for new labels he began informal negotiations – as was Creation's practice: no contracts – through Palmer.

"The Spacemen were essentially 'adopted' by the Creation scene in '88," Pat Fish explained. "They used to play a lot at Speed, a club run by Douglas Hart from The Mary Chain, and the Monday night club at Dingwall's. Most of the Creation scene of the day were usually there at those nights: Primal Scream, The Weather Prophets, Felt, Kevin Shields, and Alan McGee." With his love of dope, Sonic often spent these London outings sharing joints with characters like Pete Astor, Guy Chadwick, Bobby Gillespie – The Primal's singer was particularly keen on the fabled Rugby drug clinic that was known to prescribe methamphetamine to patients at the time – and McGee, until everyone was properly stoned. "I had kinda become friends with Sonic," recalled McGee of his earliest encounters with the band in 1988. "And him and Jason would kinda like vie for my attention, and it became apparent you couldn't be Sonic's friend and Jason's friend at the same time. So I ended up being Sonic's friend." McGee's first impressions of Jason and Sonic were that their narcotic lyrics were not hyperbole. "There was so much drug-use going on in the band that it was hard to keep up with it all," McGee cited, himself a heavy cocaine user at the time. "Sonic was just off his nuts and then later on Jason was completely off his nuts. They were kinda on that death-race to oblivion." The Creation boss recollected being offered a linctus of liquid while driving with Sonic during an excursion around London. When McGee inquired as to its contents, Sonic deadpanned, "Methadone, you want a glug?" He shook his head. "If I had glugged it, I probably could have killed myself," added McGee. "The Spacemen were definitely one of the most infamous drug bands. I think the only band that took more drugs than Spacemen 3 were The Happy Mondays."

Gerald travelled to Creation's 83 Clerkenwell Road headquarters to mull over a prospective deal, only to find a scruffy and feral McGee scurrying inside his shoebox-sized office. The Creation boss had been negotiating his heavy coke addiction along with his earliest explorations into ecstasy, all of which left Gerald with the impression he was completely strung-out and unpredictable. McGee was desperate for money. He looked up at Gerald with a simple response, "I like the band. I like the music. I don't have the money." According to Sonic, McGee consented to do an album but could offer nothing in the way of an advance. "We needed an advance of £2,000 for us to live on," he explained. "But Alan said, 'I can't do that.' But to be fair he'd just signed My Bloody Valentine."

In fact, the money situation at Creation was much more dire. McGee and Dick Green had ridden the first-wave of Creation's success by 1987, using the success of The Mary Chain and the C86 scene as leverage to negotiate a second-tier label, Elevation, distributed by WEA. Elevation set a precedent that would, throughout the Eighties and Nineties, conflate the differences between indie labels and majors. But Creation and McGee were perpetually in the red, always playing catch-up to defray costs and avoid insolvency. The label had amassed an impressive roster of "hopefuls", few of which had actually shown any profit. Primal Scream acted like rock stars but failed to deliver anything moderately successful apart from their earliest jangle-hit 'Velocity Girl', the persistent request of which caused Bobby Gillespie to react by pulling a Nikki Sudden, dressing and drugging like The Stones. My Bloody Valentine only hinted at their history-making transformation in the early days of '88, and generally just irritated the folks at Creation with all the racket. When the first backlash happened, McGee was left depending on groups like The Weather Prophets and Felt to stay above water. According to Palmer, "Alan was waiting for a £50,000 pay-off from Warner Brothers, which would have got him out of insolvency. But he'd gone over-budget with Elevation and Warner Brothers wanted to cut the ties. The whole thing was a fiasco."

With absolutely nothing to show for themselves, neither money nor prospects, band and "management" were defeated. There were only two alternatives left for Sonic and Jason: one was packing it in and the other was getting into bed with Gerald Palmer. "That's when I suggested they just carry on recording," recalled Palmer. "But I was about to pay for these recordings, so I wanted a production deal." Gerald's insistence on a production/management agreement resulted from his poor impression of managers: their financial responsibilities and legal impotence in the face of fickle and often "two-faced" clients (i.e. "artists"). Years of concert promotion had revealed to him an assembly line of young managers used and then dismissed when the first hint of fame and money appeared. Gerald recalled a particular entrepreneur who'd emptied his bank accounts and mortgaged his home in service of a up-and-coming punk band, only to be fired upon the entrance of a major label. The manager was left holding a tremendous debt without recourse. Palmer swore he'd never let the same thing happen to him.

The agreement that Gerald presented to Sonic and Jason consolidated record company and management into one relationship. Explained Palmer, "They essentially signed a recording agreement with me, and, as a consequence, I became their manager as well." Thus Gerald consented to finance the recordings, touring, and personal expenses for the band, in return for ownership of the recordings and a 50/50 profit-split, not uncommon to indie labels. He also owned a healthy portion of merchandising sales, which included the highly coveted gig T-shirts (thought to have sold more than the studio albums prior to *Playing With Fire*). In return Sonic and Jason would receive a small advance, 50 per cent of the profits (to be split amongst the band proper) as well as a share of the ownership rights. The albums would then be licensed to outside record companies/distributors for a fee, allowing Palmer to retain all rights to the master-tapes.

GERALD PALMER: The three of us signed the agreement down at Pat Fish's house. Pat and his wife Barbara witnessed it. I'd agreed to give Pete and Jason a thousand apiece as an advance, but when I got there I'd forgot my checkbook and so the check was drawn from a different company altogether. When they looked down at their checks, it said 'Albright Cleaners Limited', which caused Jason a good laugh.

Will Carruthers was hanging out at the Oxford Street house quite often by the summer of '88. He'd extracted himself from the sketchier vibe of amphetamine and joined up with The Cogs of Tyme after Gavin persuaded him to take up the bass. Will gravitated to his new instrument with a studious flair, learning the rudiments within weeks, and then practising continuously until he'd mastered the rumbling vibrations of Dave Alexander-style bass lines. He had an ambition for his bass that easily marked him as a frustrated guitarist. He played a couple of gigs with The Cogs of Tyme, at which point his skills already outshone the rest of the band. Sonic had heard good things about Will, but he also knew him to be a fucked-up kid who'd spent much of his time banging speed and drinking himself into black-outs. "I used to really hate him," recalled Sonic. "He was always getting drunk and being a pain in the ass. He'd been hanging around with his speed crowd and doing some crazy shit. Like waking up one morning with a blue dot tattooed on his face. I mean Will used to be the craziest motherfucker." Since the Reverberation days, there'd been a strange divide between A-heads and smack-users in Rugby. Each group remained suspicious of the other: A-heads were babbling idiots cranked up on bathtub concoctions, while smack users were hopelessly blissed-out junkies.

"One time Will came down to Oxford Street, and he started playing some head games with me, like taking the piss, and I told him to fuck off," Sonic said. "I wasn't going to talk to him. Then he kinda broke down, and I had a real conversation with him and since realised that often when people try to play head games with you they're trying to relate to you." As the two sat and talked it became apparent to Sonic that Will was a perfect candidate to play in the band. Not only did he seem completely genuine and sort of endearing in a way, but also he spoke like someone who considered music a vocation. The Spacemen guitarist understood completely what he meant, because such recognition was scarce in Rugby. Will also expressed his doubts about continuing in The Cogs of Tyme and his aspirations to move up the ladder. It wasn't a careerist thing, just the hunger that drove any musician out of his bedroom and onto a stage. Such things were music to Sonic's ears.

Sonic had already begun demo-ing prospective compositions for an upcoming album on his portable four-track. He decided to pursue the idea, using his Vox Starstream guitar, which he'd already experimented with on 'Repeater', so-called for the odd double-percussive effect. The FX-junkie had purchased the unique axe at the end of the previous year in a vintage shop in Earl's Court after coming across a photo of it in *Making Music* magazine. Goff Roderick accompanied him on the trek, shouldering a large bag of cocaine, which they snorted off their fingers as they browsed for gear. Brain receptors buzzing on a C high, and noses caked with white powder, they'd encountered the oddly shaped teardrop guitar, which Sonic immediately recognised and bought. It was an unusual guitar, even among teardrops, and the shopkeeper had actually been renting it out for use in videos because of its alien appearance. The Vox Starstream was a semi built by Eko in the late Sixties and had myriad installed effects, including treble and bass boost, a hand-operated wah-wah, built-in tuner, and the aforementioned repeater. For Sonic, he'd come face-to-face with his dream guitar.

Like The Beatles, The Stones, The Velvets, and numerous garage-punk noiseniks before them, Spacemen 3 endorsed an expanding palette of Vox gear and the retro-analogue. Vox was the dominant artillery for England's first major sonic assault on the expanding terrain of pop music, ergo The British Invasion, crackling through nearly every R&B, freak-beat, and psychedelic band's AC30 amplifier (and wah-wah pedal). But in the 25 years since The Animals proudly hocked Vox Continentals on the radio and Brian Jones straddled custom-made Vox teardrops, the first hip gear outfit had tumbled in rank to an ever-growing industry of circuit builders and soundscape wizards. Their trademark fetishism developing slowly through the first two albums, both Sonic and Jason had amassed a small arsenal of Vox gear by 1988, including organs – unique for their inverted white-on-black keyboards – and amps with their buzzing and crispy sound, complete with its antiquated control-panel of effects. "The Spacemen always seemed to be about using what was around," remarked Will. "They'd pick up something that'd been forgotten and give it a bit of a dust-off, like all the colour wheels and the old gear nobody wanted." Like the serialist images of Warhol, Lichtenstein, or Oldenburg, The Spacemen "sound" gradually became littered with obsolescent gear that was re-used, reformatted, and re-contextualised into completely novel objets d'art.

By early summer, Sonic had laid down a vastly different sound schematic with the aid of his Starstream, producing demos called 'Honey', 'I Believe It', and 'Let Me Down Gently', in addition to previous tracks, 'Repeater', 'Suicide', and 'Revolution'. "I was really going out of my way to write different sorts of songs, unusual stuff," insisted Sonic. He was eager to plunk down in a studio again and commence work on a future album though he found his writing partner less enthused. For his part, Jason recorded a few new demos, including a beautiful gospel-blues tune 'Lord Can You Hear Me?' But he'd been spending more and more of his days and nights away from the "band" (i.e. Sonic) and with Kate. On a number of occasions, Sonic popped down to Oxford Street to visit only to find Jason's upstairs door locked. He needn't be told what was going on. Sonic became concerned and more than a bit pissed off at what he saw as a major distraction to Jason and the band. For Sonic, Spacemen 3 was the love of his life. He expected Jason to be equally devoted. He'd given Jason bits of songs to work through in hopes of sparking some creative jag but Jason failed to respond with product. During one exchange, Sonic finally laid out an ultimatum: write more songs or no split credit. "I wasn't prepared for him not to write songs and still get half the credit," Sonic said. "He was just hanging out with Kate the whole time, larking around with her while I was working away. And when he did write songs, they sounded just like my songs. Like Jason was copying the same effects and style but diluting it."

Gerald contacted ARK Studios, a tiny operation in Cornwall, and arranged for a month of recording time beginning in June. He'd only detected the slightest vapours of discontent between his two clients and he assured himself that packing them off to record was the best route to success. ARK seemed as good a place as any to Palmer: managed (or rather inhabited) by hippie miscreants and Cornish musicians Webcore, the eight-track studio had been suggested to Sonic by a sound engineer referred to simply as Pat – his hippie ethos seemed to preclude the use of a surname – during the European tour. The session time cost next to nothing, which meant another long studio hibernation and more dosh for food and dope.

Although Bassman had all but left the band months before, his vacillations and those of his bandmates delayed an official dismissal until the closing days of May. It was during his final gig at The University of London that Bassman, enervated by his diminishing status within the group, literally witnessed his own gear turn against him. The lead on his amp blew moments before walking onstage, leaving him to chew through the wires in a last iconic gesture. "I can hardly remember the performance," he shrugged, "but by this time our set had been so well played, we were on automatic pilot. It was a bit like being a rabbit in the headlights." He rigged up his bass and played through the set, but the symbolism of the moment was not lost on him.

Like many London club-goers that evening, Mark Lascelles wandered in off the street to catch the lead act Gaye Bykers on Acid. Standing among the throng of indie-kids, acidheads, and odd ravers that packed the floor of the ULU stage, he recalls his first Spacemen 3 experience as a testament to the religiosity of noise. "There was a large section of the audience that laid flat on the floor for the whole gig," observed Lascelles. "I later learnt that this was fairly normal and all these prone people were on acid." Sonic and Jason sat motionless on stage bent over their vibrating arsenal of guitars, pedals and amplifiers, fashioning an unbelievable racket that bore itself against the crowd and resembled, for a moment, an anthropomorphic hulk of contracting tissue. Lascelles found it at once fantastic and terrifying. The near hour-long set concluded with a fuzzed freak-out sending whooshs and crackles reverberating against the walls. "The end of the set will always remain with me," he said. "Sonic and Pete Bain left the stage with feedback and fuzz screeching away. Then Jason picked his wah-wah pedal up and, with his hands, sent a roaring wowowowowowowowo across the room before trudging off the stage." The crowd heaved and writhed in sonic meltdown from these unknown garrisons who, for all intents and purposes, had just invaded London.

And Exit Bassman . . . following the ULU gig and with no hint of a change in The Spacemen camp, the band's indecisive bass-player refused the trip to Cornwall. Jason and Sonic were obviously closing ranks, and, in response to these machinations, paranoia crept in. Because neither Gerald Palmer nor Sonic had yet arranged van transport for the 250-mile journey Bassman realised he would remain idle in Rugby or stranded in Cornwall. Living on the last few pence he had stowed in his pocket, and entirely dependent on the dole, he also knew a month-long sojourn at ARK equated to complete insolvency and potential homelessness. Bassman confronted Jason with his concerns at Oxford Street shortly before the sessions began but his mate just shrugged his shoulders and advised him to hitchhike. Bassman couldn't believe his ears. Now he was absolutely certain that he was being edged from what remained of his membership. With news of his resignation from The Spacemen imminent, Sonic met Bassman at the Oxford Street house to discuss the future of the band. It was with relief and sanguine pleasure that Sonic finally dismissed his old friend (and recent foe) for the last time. He took equal gratification in divulging the former bassist's replacement: a much younger, more naive, and less accomplished Will Carruthers.

> BASSMAN: I saw Sonic as a tyrant, a bully, and a dysfunctional person, who gained pleasure from manipulating and controlling other people. To be around him for so long finally took its toll. Jason was the only person I could confide in. We talked about the band, and his response was, "It's not exactly spiritually fulfilling is it Pete?" But Jason was going to tough it out the whole way. He was

definitely going to see something out of it. And he definitely deserved what he got, because Sonic wouldn't have ever been a musician if it wasn't for Jason. But Jason Pierce would have always been a musician. Always. He was a musician when I met him, and he's a musician now.

WILL CARRUTHERS: When Pete Kember asked me to join, the first thing I did was go down to Pete Bain's house. I told him if he wasn't into it, I wouldn't do it. But he told me to go for it.

Will made the trek down to Gavin's house to break the news of his exit from The Cogs of Tyme. Gavin wasn't exactly pleased with the announcement. The almost incestuous relationship between The Spacemen and Gavin's various groups had, over the past several years, led to numerous personnel trade-offs and personal conflicts. Gav and Sonic had rarely spoken following the collapse of the Reverberation Club, and in the ensuing two years, Spacemen 3's career continued to blossom while The Cogs of Tyme's potential rarely strayed far from the local pubs of Rugby, where they performed a shambling garage-punk to the same drunken crowd of yobs. But Gavin was also pissed because he knew Will was a competent musician, and The Cogs had already gone through every other guitarist in town. "If you join them, Pete Kember's going to drive you crazy, and you're going to hate it," Gavin warned him before he left. Will shrugged his prophecy off as the embittered words of a betrayed guitarist. "I know that if I was Will's age, that I would have done exactly what he did, because The Spacemen were fucking brilliant," snickered Gavin. "But it was like a little over a year later and Will turned up at my door and said, 'I should have listened to you,' but by then it was just too late."

The reformatted Spacemen 3 – minus drummer and plus Will Carruthers – packed for Cornwall to begin recording backing tracks for what would become *Playing With Fire*. Gerald secured van transport for the various bits and bobs of guitar, amps and keyboards, sending Jason along with the driver, while Sonic followed in his silver Metro. Will followed several days later tagging a ride with Kate whose abrupt appearance at ARK proved to make escalating tensions evermore uptight. Sonic was severely displeased with his first impressions of the spare Cornish village. What was promised to be a professional, fully equipped facility was little more than a secluded country-house surrounded by tin mines and hosted by a rouged network of Travellers. These elusive bohemians often ambled through the front room and into the bantam studio during mid-take. The only thing worse than the setting was the macrobiotic diet of lentils and tofu they were expected to survive on.

With Will and Kate's arrival on the scene, Jason and Sonic parted company and concentrated on their own compositions, leaving Will in the odd position of bassist-cum-diplomat. He would work out his individual bass lines in an adjacent garden with each songwriter while the other disappeared off into the studio to record. "It was a really pleasant time, just sitting in the garden working on songs," Will said, smiling. "I was having lots of fun messing around in the back, smoking a lot of hash and drinking some beer. It all seemed pretty chilled really." Will was none the wiser to his bandmates' estrangement and took the challenge of recording with a resin-coated gusto. The Three plunked down on the studio floor stoned out of their gourds during twilight work sessions before passing out in the living room.

After a solid week of skinning up and putting down track-by-track bits, Sonic and Will drove back to Rugby for a weekend's refreshment, leaving Jason to continue working on his own. Over the course of the month-long encampment at ARK, Jason rarely left the studio despite Sonic's bi-weekly excursions back home. Will recalls Jason's occasional departures resulting from weekend trips with Kate. Whether Jason declined Sonic's invitation or was refused transportation in his silver two-seater was never made clear. In the absence of his best mate's companionship, Sonic developed a closer fraternity with Will during marathon trips between Cornwall and Rugby in the former's Metro, resulting in a tight professional and personal relationship. Often the guitarist and bassist whiled away the eight-hour round trip smoking hash and swapping cassettes of The Beach Boys' *Smile* and *Smiley Smile* with Suicide bootlegs *Half Alive* and *Ghost Rider* in the car's tape-deck. The sundry melodious slipstreams of 'With Me Tonight' and 'Wonderful''s baroque psychedelia hovering over 'Rocket USA''s click-clack rhythms proved the defining inspiration for *Playing With Fire*.

"When it came down to working, nobody, including myself, practised as much as Will," lauded Sonic. "He was a fucking professional." But other, more sinister things ballooned from the new collaboration. "That was around the first time I tried heroin," Will claimed. "I was begging for it basically. I had been wanting to try it for ages, you know, like 'Yeah, yeah let's get into it!'" At first Sonic hesitated about turning Will on to his gear. "Will had no way of accessing it, so the only way he could get it was through me," replied Sonic. "But he'd been a serious speed freak and drinker, and it certainly wasn't my idea to turn him on. Will wanted it and he persevered. He started using very rarely and very occasionally."

WILL CARRUTHERS: The first time I used, I banged it, and I just remember this *whoooosssshhh* where I just sort of melted. Then I went back to my flat and I copped a nod, you know what I mean? I copped a nod, my first nod and I had dreams. And I can see them now you know. I can see those two dreams now: I dreamt of a fridge and I opened the fridge, right, and cockroaches fucking poured out of this fridge. Absolutely thousands of them. But I was kind of, it wasn't a horrifying thing, because of the way you feel. But I was aware of it even though I wasn't like "ahhhh!" screaming like maybe you would be otherwise. But by this time I was pretty used to weird visions. And then I had a dream, like immediately afterwards, of a really gnarled old crone's face. An old woman, a very witchy, very gnarled crone's face just laughing at me. . . . And the crone is like in charge of decay and the turning over of things. I don't know if it's relevant but that's the one bit of symbology I've been able to fit that into. And it does fit, do you know what I mean? But those two images are like fucking burned into my mind. And it was the first time I ever did it.

Back at ARK, it was with added displeasure at the studio's limited 8-track desk and dubious sound engineer, that the three generated crude versions of 'Honey' and 'Lord Can You Hear Me?'. Exacerbating the already poor environment, ARK engineer Pat rescinded his original "pro bono" offer and demanded payment to cover studio expenses. Sitting in the multi-functional "control booth" neither Sonic nor Jason liked most of the playbacks they heard. Weeks into recording and the situation appeared more and more hopeless. Everyone tossed in the towel the following weekend and escaped Cornwall for several days of rest, relaxation, and dope. "The engineer Pat decided to get out the tapes after we took off," said Sonic. "And he mistakenly wiped several tracks that had been done weeks before." Upon returning the following week and discovering the omissions, Sonic confronted Pat about the missing tracks. The engineer only threw up his hands in a "shit happens"-gesture. "That's when things started to get a little bit fractious," Will added. Pat declared his intentions to play a larger role in recording and remixing in the band's absence with an eye toward a production credit. Sonic's mouth literally dropped to the floor. "There was a big fallout," Will continued. "One of many. I should have seen the signs back then really. It was just a big ugly scene. Pat told Sonic and Jason what he wanted to do and they told him to get fucked." There was a limp screaming match inside the studio: "Bollocks to you!" "Fuck you then!" The ARK sessions came to a lacklustre conclusion.

"We wasted a lot of money really because the results weren't that great," claimed Gerald, having gone over the slim results of three weeks' work. At the conclusion of the month, the band moved out of ARK and brought the master-tapes back to Rugby and VHF. "We did most of the album back in Rugby, re-recording a lot of the songs," Sonic insisted. "Jason and I found that we couldn't really experiment to the level we wanted with just eight tracks, because we wanted to add lots of textural overdubs."

Problems in Cornwall had actually just punctuated a tenuous relationship that had begun disintegrating toward the end of recording. From Sonic's recollection, most of Jason's tracks were composed quickly and on the spot in the studio and relied mainly on Will's solid bass playing for their formation. On Will's part, he saw something odd going on between Jason and Sonic although he wasn't completely aware of what it was. Paul Adkins, who reunited with The Spacemen nearly a year after the *Prescription* sessions, pointed to a possible source for their seeming estrangement in the studio. According to Adkins, "Pete and Jason were getting used to the studio at that point. Instead of going for a live feel they wanted a more polished and produced sound. So they started by putting down tracks individually as opposed to playing as a band." What the three guitarists created in the Rugby studio was an electronic concoction of love and dope, the seamlessness of which belied a collaboration's nascent corrosion.

A paean to Brian Wilson's twilight lyricism, 'Honey' invoked an autumnal sadness peculiar to The Beach Boys *Smile*-period and through the overcast grey of *Surf's Up*; likewise, 'Honey''s ping 'n blurb textures recalled Neu! instrumentalist Michael Rother's "singing" guitar. Barely sustaining itself with the twinkle of Vox organ and the scattered hum of a repeater effect, 'Honey' envisages a lonely acoustic troubadour pledging love and lust to his muse: "Honey . . . Won't you take me home tonight/ Honey . . . Won't you take me home tonight/ Feels so right/ Feels so right . . ." The addition of a flutter multi-tap reverb effect to Sonic's near spoken Teutonic voice – a grizzled Germanic thickness reminiscent of Nico blended with Lou Reed's druggy insouciance – bathes the vocal in an echo chamber. The Continental organ rises and falls through flange and tremolo to almost religious effect. The lyrics repeat in a drunken mantra, the plangent plea stumbling in its inebriated simplicity. As the song closes, and awash in a spangled resonance, the vocals become indecipherable, embracing a forlorn drunkenness and phasing out to a tactile hum. Likewise, 'Come Down Softly To My Soul' is an astral piece of guitar cantering on a simple two-chord riff, with Jason's dulcet croon hovering above and steeped in reverb. The jangle of a Rickenbacker

6-string adds a sweetness vaguely reminiscent of *Queen is Dead*-era Marr but without the requisite ostentation. The guitar is lean and minimal, adding only the sparest bit of lead over Will's catchy bass riff. Though Jason and Sonic's future interests are differentiated here for the first time, their inspirations and methods remain closely tied. Jason's keen sense of melody is restrained by a fierce simplicity (and likewise Sonic's obsessive droning is expanded by Jason's intuitive ear for pop) making each song equally engaging.

'How Does It Feel?', a spoken-word piece grafted on top of the 'Repeater' instrumental, begins with another Brian Wilson-style plea, "When I saw you, you looked so surprised/ And the oceans flowed through your blue-grey eyes/ And I stood and gazed through hot summer days/ So tell me: How do you feel? . . . ." whereupon the tremulous pulse of Vox Starstream guitar blazes from the foreground, phasing ever so gently between channels, and then recedes into a flicker. The Starstream repeats and repeats, building a crackled swath of analogue warmth, random shards of sinewy bleeps. Nearly eight minutes long, the track constructs its own unique pace of swirling guitar and echoed vocals. Jason's guitar enters with a melodic riff skipping over the glitch of Sonic's repeater, thickened with the fuzzy swell of Will's bass. It is only then that a drum-machine pumps an elastic filling between the stringed consistency, the first percussive beat on the album. Sonic's vocal morphs into electro-glitch menace, the bass and guitar building upwards in deliberate fashion. The eponymous question takes on haunting tones, from lovesick innocence to retributive ire, and disintegrates into the fuzz drone.

A hymnal companion to 'How Does It Feel?', 'I Believe It' radiates from the chime of a Vox organ played over a rotating drone.

Hovering in a vacuum as a lethargic vocal croons of excursions into narcosis ("From Friday night to Sunday morning/. . . Oh Lord take me higher"), the repeater effect slices through the fetid atmosphere and quickens the tempo. The track develops into an organ-inspired rave-up blending the elegy of traditional blues with the fiery sacrilege of a Beat rap. In a lyric reminiscent of Patti Smith's religious vitriol or 'Heroin'-era Velvets, Sonic rants: "Jesus died for my sins/ Lord look at the state I'm in/ Look all right but I'm fucked within/ Can't go through it all again . . ." Jason pulls rhythmic licks from his Fender, which plop against the sizzle of the Starstream guitar and chugging organ.

The first side's icy repose makes the muscular singe of 'Revolution' all the more unsettling. The track opens with a flame of clattering feedback and barrels forward with a droning two-note riff, both moronic and pulverising, *à la* The MC5's 'Black To Comm'. From its quasi-political lyric "I'm sick. . . . I'm so sick", 'Revolution' is a 1988 British revamp of John Sinclair's militant '68 White-Panther "rock'n'roll, dope, and fucking in the streets" mantra. But 'Revolution' addresses a post-hippie, post-modern, post-AIDS globe precipitated by the retreat of sex back into the body, where Thatcher replaced Lyndon Johnson, ecstasy and heroin replaced acid, and tribal wars replaced Vietnam. The decade of privatisation had turned completely into itself and the personal had become the political. Subculture proliferated into complicated networks of identity based on exclusivity rather than union. When Sonic references *Kick Out The Jam*'s rousing intro, "It takes just five seconds . . ./ Of decision/ To start thinkin' about a little revolution . . .", his bid is to a revolution of consciousness, a thoroughly post-Sixties turn toward individual "self-improvement". Although The Spacemen's particular method of altering consciousness may have been skewed predominantly towards psychedelics and opiates, the message in 'Revolution' is wholly universal: "You change now!" At Sonic's command, guitars and bass assault with heavy distortion as the riff builds faster and faster, until the overdriven amps burst into a shambling whine of feedback and careen into silence.

'Let Me Down Gently' – a soft, pliant reworking of 'Honey' – centred around Will's swelling bass line, humming with organ and pedal effects (including more languorous hand-modulated wah) and sonar bleeps. A slightly more drifting comedown with the sacrosanct organicity of a hymn, it provides lilting counterpoint to the rush of 'Revolution' and dissipates into the ether as quickly as it appears. Jason's atmospheric 'So Hot (Wash Away All Of My Tears)' is the most lush and scintillating song on the album. Paced by Will's bass line, Jason's guitar/organ work, and dolloped with the bells-and-whistles sounds of the Vox organ, 'So Hot' is a whispered and slowly unveiling hymn that presages *Lazer Guided Melodies*-era Spiritualized. Of his contributions to the album, Jason remarked, "All the songs are written in an ambiguous way. People can relate them to their own circumstances."

After consolidating and honing earlier jams and live performances, The Three laid down a near 10-minute version of 'Suicide' culled from a series of shows and in-studio performances. A monstrous songscape, 'Suicide', is a riveting one-chord ode to Stooges' chug and Suicide bleep. The extended instrumental piece developed as a result of a number of jams between Sonic and Jason where the former would tape down the keys on his organ and rapidly modulate the tremolo speeds through the amplifier, while the latter would match these alterations with the warbling undulations of a wah-wah. The opening sequence of 'Suicide' builds on an ascendant organ riff barely audible over the hum of the tremolo drone as Jason's Fender skitters along the slipstream. The middle portion of the track rides the crest of the bright organ riff, borrowed as much from Suicide's 'Ghost Rider' as The Stooges' '1969', repeating *ad nauseam* with a concrete bass line tucked underneath to provide a propulsive rhythm. Jason's guitar screeches and warps through myriad drone-colours, as he chokes every available modulation out of his wah pedal at ultra-slow speeds. "Then the song goes into a long drone where I tape all the keys down on the Vox and manipulate the tremolo speed," explained Sonic. "Jason would follow with the guitar he was playing and he'd build it up, then we'd all slow down the drone to a slow sort of pulsing until the song died away."

As final homage or possibly a bid for paternal approbation (The Spacemen were, after all, a result of "record-collection" rock) Sonic and Jason sought out Suicide front man Alan Vega for his trademark vocal contribution to the erstwhile instrumental. By a stroke of sheer luck a gruelling autumn tour schedule brought the electro-duo from across the pond to play a series of dates with Siouxsie and The Banshees throughout the South. In the 10 years since their record debut, New York's original electro-punks had undergone less of a mainstream dilution than a subcultural canonisation. Various and sundry new-wave, synth-pop, and industrial acts from the vicious throb of the Sheffield scene to the syrupy pop-over-Alesis croon of Soft Cell to post-punk compatriots The Cars scored hit singles and popular acceptance by revisiting the Suicide formula. Punk ideology, with its emphasis on the guitar/bass/drums triad and its concomitant loathing for synthesisers, relegated the Rev/Vega collaboration to a footnote. However, throughout the expansive indie-spheres of the Eighties, Suicide attained a near mythic status, and fodder for any number of up-and-comers eager to cover their most obscure tracks. Vega often auditioned Suicide covers as they sprang up randomly over the years: R.E.M., Henry Rollins, Loop, et cetera, with insouciant regard. But this Spacemen 3 tribute song was altogether different.

"I really loved Spacemen 3," said Vega, "one of the few bands at the time that I actually did like." Upon hearing the clattering, squealing cascade of sound slated to be the backdrop for his vocal, Vega consented heartily to scribble down some lyrics and accompany the band to a studio outside of London to lay down his track. Gerald shelled out the cash for a late-evening session coinciding with Suicide's London appearance. Sonic recalls Vega mentioning his working title of 'Till The End Of Time' over a phone conversation during late autumn though Vega failed to produce any written lyrics at the time, content in his ability to blend a *bricolage* of rough "sketches" and improvisation into his final studio performance.

As it turned out Suicide's much-anticipated contribution failed to materialise. Jason, Will and Sonic turned up at the Siouxsie/Suicide concert in Brixton only to be refused entrance by a meat-headed bouncer, their names omitted from the guest list. It took hours to blag their way past the entrance ("None of us considered paying to see Siouxsie and the fucking Banshees," recalled Sonic) from which they sheepishly waited for their vacillating guest star.

SONIC: Eventually we got in, and we were supposed to wait in this sort of balcony area for him. We waited for fucking ages. And then he sort of turned up and said he had other plans basically. Too tired and whatever . . .

WILL CARRUTHERS: We went backstage and we're like, "Nice show, do you wanna go?" We've got the studio all booked and he says, "No man I'm really tired. I don't think I can be bothered," and we're like, "What the fuck?!"

ALAN VEGA: They came down – we were doing a show in London – and they came back after the show. And I was like, "Sorry I can't." It was already like one or two in the morning. It was impossible. And they got pissed because we had been talking about it for months. And I really wanted to do it.

SONIC: We booked a fucking studio, so it cost us even not to do it. We went really out of our way to work with him, and he was a real shithead. I never thought of him the same since really.

Worked out largely prior to the Cornwall sessions, 'Lord Can You Hear Me?' was a solo recording in all but name. The song follows the motif of suicide with an aching petition for salvation. One of Jason's two-chord classics in the 'Walkin' With Jesus' lineage, the song builds on a simple blues rhythm with euphoric Floydian slide-guitar and crescendos with a heavy dose of sustain and reverb as the vocal fades deeper into the slipstream behind Pat Fish's wailing saxophone. "There were about seven tenor sax takes all mixed up together," recalled Pat. "The saxophone itself was a long-dead heap of tin, basically, and I was annoyed not to get a better sound. Still, Jason seemed happy with his huge pile of wheezing horns." As a masterful blend of lyrical diligence and rotating soundscape, 'Honey' and 'Lord Can You Hear Me?' bookend each songwriter's attendant muses and exclusive styles, the former an almost winsome and minimal ambience while the latter sounded equally evanescent but with roots in gospel and blues. The aforementioned songs also birthed emergent resentments in the studio by pronouncing a delinquency on the part of either guitarist to include the other in any stage of their respective recordings.

SONIC: (about Jason's songs) I thought they sounded great, but I didn't know what I was meant to do on them. I'd always write stuff with a part for Jason; there was always something for him to play on guitar. But he didn't return the favour.

PAUL ADKINS: By the end of those sessions Pete and Jason were working apart much more than working together or as a band. It was almost a night-and-day difference from *Perfect Prescription*.

The *Playing With Fire* sessions also included work on several covers arranged and performed separately by Jason and Sonic. Respective versions of the traditional 'May The Circle Be Unbroken' and Suicide's 'Che' further highlighted the divergent paths each songwriter chose for future inspiration. Jason's rendition of the former, with its roots in both Carter Family country-blues and Staples Singers gospel, introduced an airy blend of atmospheric vocal and "cotton-patch" tremolo guitar that would redefine not only his Spacemen 3 sound but his early Spiritualized work as well (although this aforementioned arrangement differs little from Roebuck Staples' original production barring a slight change in pitch and the absence of the third chord). Sonic's 'Che' testifies equally to an obsession with atmosphere and vocal effects, but more to the electronic mantra-like qualities of classic Suicide. His rendition, much as Jason's, showed little obvious differences from previous versions, although the addition of an extended feedback-guitar/bass intro and Sonic's patented Teutonic vocal elevates and thickens Martin Rev's original composition. Backing tracks were also recorded for a prospective cover of The Troggs' 'Anyway That You Want Me', which Bassman presented to Sonic during a record binge shortly before his exit from the band. Sonic dug The Troggs' single out and worked through the catchy riff before presenting the song to Jason and recording a vocal overdub. Jason loved the song and suggested he try the vocal. Sonic hesitated at the request but eventually acquiesced and was blown away by Jason's rendition. Faced with what was a much better version in the eyes of everyone, Sonic reluctantly handed the song over to Jason. Along with an instrumental Perfect Disaster cover 'Girl On Fire', both songs were eventually scrapped at VHF due to time constraints.

At the end of June, the boys headed back to Dingwall's for another headlining show with My Bloody Valentine in support. The Valentines were in the process of recording *Isn't Anything* in a Wales studio for Creation, an album that would map out the band as the next acolytes of Velvets-inspired noise, ("This was everything 1988 was half-consciously leading up to" wrote Chris Roberts in *Melody Maker*) and up-end all their previous efforts at sonic alchemy. The Spacemen and The Valentines had met each other the previous year in Northampton when Sonic and Jason caught Kevin Shields and company opening for The Primitives at the Roadmender. MBV had recently completed the *Ecstasy* and *Strawberry Wine* EPs – a blend of their earliest Birthday Party-style goth-jangle with the buzz-saw noise-craft of The Mary Chain – and Shields and Sonic shared an instant rapport, checking out each other's collection of guitars, amps, and pedals.

The Valentines had, in all, skipped between four different labels since their formation in '84, and even resorted to the high-modernist approach of expatriating to the Continent for a year before reformatting and returning to Britain. Having reconfigured their jangly/goth sounds, MBV had met up with Alan McGee and signed for their first Creation single 'You Made Me Realise', sealing their fate as arbiters of the 'shoegazing' generation. What part Spacemen 3's trem-heavy noise played in Shield's whammy-bar revelation remains speculative, but it certainly seems feasible to state that The Valentines would not have been able to blaze such a trail unless The Spacemen (along with Sonic Youth and Swans) had already cleared the path for them. "I don't say they're following us as much as Loop but I know My Bloody Valentine did change massively after playing with us, after seeing us," said Sonic. "I used to use a Guyatone distortion pedal which I painted black, because every fucking band we used to play with would come up to me and go 'So what distortion pedal are you using?' And the next time we'd play with them, they'd have the same fucking pedal, like The Shamen and My Bloody Valentine. It's only ever really had one sound as a distortion, but it was a good one in combination with the Vox amp. It used to sound really good. Alan McGee always used to be blown away by the distortion sound I used to get live."

Shields openly attributed The Valentines' watershed transformation – and raison d'etre – to its inclusion in Spacemen 3's vein of sonic design. "Bands like Spacemen 3 [shared the same attitudes as us] . . . ," he agreed. "They were more prepared to go in other directions besides the heavy guitar or the weird guitar. They'll go soft and play melodies but they're also a bit more freaked." Of the MBV/Spacemen 3 connection, Alan McGee openly postulated, "Kevin Shields might possibly have ripped off some of his sounds – Pete Kember's – that's completely possible."

Following The Valentines' short set, Sonic and Jason took to their stools. As David Cavanagh mordantly remarked in *Sounds*: "When seats are provided for musicians at a rock venue it means one of two things – either Hank B. Marvin and Mark Knopfler are about to convene for a spirited precis of Rodrigo's 'Concierto De Aranjuez' or those weird Spacemen 3 chaps are in town." Will's first proper gig since joining the band, he literally held the vomit in his mouth as he played.

The band ran through quick versions of 'Rollercoaster' and 'Walkin' With Jesus' but delivered with ferocious takes of 'Revolution' and 'Take Me To The Other Side' and ended the evening with another extended 'Suicide' blaring through dry ice and strobes. The drone-drone of a Farfisa whined on for nearly a quarter of an hour after they'd left the stage, but the audience, whether from the expectation of encore or physical paralysis, were transfixed and refused to move.

The show proved solid and afterwards they hung out with The Valentines briefly before hopping into the van. Far from the reputation they would soon gain, Will remembers everyone from MBV being friendly and quite ordinary. However, upon leaving, Will discovered his Ratt Distortion pedal to have gone missing from the stage floor and someone jokingly accused Kevin Shields of the infraction. A prescient allegation and certainly a portent of things to come from The Valentines. "They were still kind of doing that indie–jangle stuff, do you know what I mean?" Will recalled. "They changed, you know. I think a lot of bands changed. No other band sounded like Spacemen 3 for a few years. It was like 'Fucking Hell!' Do you know what I mean? Nobody!"

Like so many other gigs dating to the beginning of that year, Kate stood in the audience watching Jason and the band play to rapturous applause. Things had changed drastically by autumn however; in addition to spending much, if not most, of his free time with Kate, Jason initiated Kate's presence backstage at gigs and travelling in the tour van. When the two attempted to board after the Dingwall's show, Sonic refused her entrance, and a heated argument ensued. Sonic had had enough of Kate's omnipresence, and Jason had had enough of Sonic's bitching. Sonic slammed the van door shut on them, leaving Jason and Kate to find another way back to Rugby.

PAT FISH: Kate was still fairly new on the scene. My wife and I, on the other hand, were old hands on the bus. It seems that, as a guest, I was allowed to bring my girl on the bus, but the band followed the not uncommon No Girlfriends On The Bus Rule. It appears that in the confusion of blagging rides home after this gig, this rule was suddenly enforced. Of course, the wife and I had no idea at the time. We just piled onto the bus, as instructed, and rode home. I think we thought that Jason was staying in London with Kate or something. We really didn't know much about her at this stage, as she and Jason would kinda huddle together for most of the time. So truth to tell, I was fairly oblivious at the time. I can't recall Jason or Kate ever having a go at me about it, though.

MARK REFOY: I remember going to see Spacemen 3 at Ding-wall's. It was a great gig actually, but I remember, at the end, I got the train back to Northampton from London, and I saw Jason and Kate on the train. I asked them what the fuck they were doing?! And Jason said him and Pete had an argument – something to do with not letting Kate on the bus – and Jason was saying a few things like, 'You don't know the half of it, what goes on.' And I didn't pry but I knew then that things weren't alright in Spacemen 3-land.

"But they were still growing as players and as a unit," added Fish, "until they reached the point where they caught on fire and their gigs would get incendiary." By mid-summer, the band (along with drummer Thierry) appeared at the Mean Fiddler for a concert that proved pivotal. Gerald turned up at the rear of the club, brandishing a crew of London agents he'd cajoled back into his fold, including Asgard co-owner Paul Charles and booking agent John McIver. "I invited them to come back," Gerald explained. "I told them to forget about Dingwall's; that this was a completely different band. It was water under the bridge. Time had elapsed. The Spacemen had done more gigs and rehearsed more. They really were a different band." Pat Fish stood near the front of the swelling crowd of punters, listening intently to a band he'd witnessed over a dozen times before. But this night something was different. As Sonic and Jason battled through extra long takes of 'Rollercoaster', 'Things'll Never Be The Same', and 'Starship', the guitars hit a preternatural mix of drone and lock groove.

"There was this massive response from the audience," Fish recalled. "People were just wandering in off the street to see them and they were in awe of the sounds. And by the end of this song, I'd thought they'd done enough, hit the limit. Then without stopping it just kinda mutated into 'Revolution'." All the suits standing around Gerald froze with drinks in mid-gulp, looking vaguely like designer deer caught in the headlights. "They were going into this thing that I'd never seen them do before," Fish added. "And, at some point, I wasn't just watching my mates having a good night. It was something totally different. I started having mad ideas that I was watching The MC5. I had this feeling that I was witness-ing something completely classic." As the set closing 'Suicide' roared to a blinding conclusion, Gerald looked over at his coterie. Everyone was gobsmacked. When one of the suits finally caught his breath, he jokingly accused Gerald of hiring ringers for everyone in the band. "Are you sure it's the same Spacemen 3 I've seen before?" he asked. Palmer assured him it was. They all grabbed another beer at the bar, and Gerald leaned over to the Asgard boss. "Paul, what's the action?" he slyly inquired. Paul

Charles looked up at Gerald with a simple response: "I think this band could be huge." And The Spacemen got a new agent on the spot.

In addition to Creation's interest in the band, which had failed to work out, Fire Records had also put in their bid for The Spacemen. The tiny Highbury label was the brainchild of Groovy Cellar's Clive Solomon, who'd turned his love of Sixties psychedelic pop toward musical A&R, providing competition for Creation and Glass. "Along with Creation, Glass was probably my other favourite and rival label," Clive said of his early days at Fire. "Creation was more jangly, Glass was more psychedelic and Fire was maybe more art-school. Out of all of us, I think I had the widest taste in music! I coveted a few of the bands Dave and Alan had, but I don't think there was mutual envy there!" Clive had first encountered Spacemen 3 at roughly the same moment as McGee. Journalist Robin Gibson had raved about the Rugby group to the Fire chief for ages, and finally popped in a tape of *The Perfect Prescription* for Solomon to hear in late '87. Clive was equally mesmerised by their sound. "At the time, they were so unfashionable in terms of the current trends," Solomon continued. "But I loved the music. Spacemen 3 were the best psychedelic band around. By '88, the time we were actively courting them, I think things had changed, and the press were picking up on them."

Solomon began his bid for the Rugby band during their sessions at ARK in an attempt to hammer out an agreement with new management Gerald Palmer. Solomon was more than keen to recruit Glass' psychedelic expatriates but Palmer's insistence on a short-term, two album licensing deal left little possibility for Fire to profit if The Spacemen suddenly exploded from the indie market to a mainstream sphere. Solomon wanted to sign them outright, or, at the very least, agree to a longer licensing period. Palmer refused both offers. The licensing agreement stalled numerous times over the summer months. The two businessmen argued, prodded, and offered/counter offered throughout the month of July while Gerald held out for any last-chance alternatives from Creation, Rough Trade, or 4AD. None came.

"When our negotiations were quite advanced, Gerald did let it be known that Creation were interested," recalled Solomon, "but I think more to help him negotiate the deal he wanted. I always felt that Gerald preferred to sign to us than Creation, as we wanted and needed them more. They might have been just another band at Creation, whereas they were an enormous priority for us. Also, I think I was probably more businesslike in my approach than Alan, which I think Gerald related to." And, in fact, the Creation deal had long been dead on arrival. McGee was so ensconced in the worlds of Guy Chadwick, Kevin Shields, and ecstasy, he had little extra time to donate. Agreed Ride manager and McGee conquest Dave Newton, "I think that if Spacemen 3 had signed to Creation then it's possible that they would have achieved greater success than they did. But by the late Eighties, Creation would have been much too focused on House Of Love and My Bloody Valentine to really have done justice to Spacemen 3. But, then again, bands seemed to swap labels much more then." Ironically, Fire and Creation would spar to sign both The Spacemen and Ride; while McGee would go on to have massive success with the Oxford "shoegazers", Solomon would be left with the remains of Spacemen 3. "Gerald decided to go with Fire over Creation," McGee lamented. "And in retrospect that was a bad move for the band, because we went on to make five or six classic albums after that and Fire didn't."

It was with resignation that Palmer drove Sonic and Jason down to London to meet Solomon at the Fire offices and seal the licensing contract. As Palmer put it, "I didn't want to do a deal with Fire. Fire wasn't our first choice. It was more than a difficult label to deal with."

As was the style of indie labels at the time, Solomon's private domicile and workspace were one and the same. His tiny desk and office space were shoved into the front room and kitchen of his Highbury flat. Staring at the lanky and patrician guitarist huddled near his soft-spoken and equally striking partner, Solomon considered great possibilities. Future stardom for Fire. Future stardom for Spacemen 3. Staring at the cramped quarters of their new record company, it must have occurred to Fire's newest prospects that there was little difference in moving from one micro-label to the next.

'The Mathematics Of Rock'n'Roll Fission . . .'

The DREAMWEAPON occurs alongside . . . it is the amplified constriction of a mechanical propulsion. Which is to say that it is generative as well as limiting, a radiophonic tide. It is the deterritorialising flow reverberating from inside . . . in consumption, digestion, excretion. "The retained elements do not enter into the new use of SYNTHESIS that imposes such a profound change on them without causing the whole triangle to REVERBERATE," quoth Deleuze. The dreaded Oedipal triangle: guitar/bass/drums, but underneath it lies the salvation of fuzz. Robert Moog's entire family sleeps on the soft bedding of stereo mesh. The patching of a tone from an analogue synth. It begins with the oscillators, which produce waves fed into a labyrinth of tonal modulators. It ends with magnetic tape or digital codices.

NOVEMBER 2002
WEST VILLAGE NY WALKUP

Dean Wareham, Sonic Boom, and I lounge in Victor Bockris' Perry Street apartment on a Sunday evening, eating and drinking to the sounds of Dylan's *Basement Tapes*. I'm the odd man out, having abstained from substances, while Sonic and Victor exchange fat spliffs and polish off a bottle of cheap vodka. For his part, Dean has politely declined the circling joints and instead swallows some discreet pills. The conversation turns toward the parallel histories of Spacemen 3 and Wareham's own Galaxie 500: the trials, tribulations, and credits.

DEAN WAREHAM (about songwriting credits): Even if I'd written the whole song, I'd give 10 per cent of the credit to each person, because it keeps everyone happy and keeps the band together.

SONIC: The only thing is, though, I've been in that situation, where me and Jason write all the stuff and the rest of the band – the bass and drums – only did so much, and then at the end I'd sorta say, "Okay, we'll split it 30-30-20-20." And then, at the end, there's a big argument, because they didn't get equal split on it. I mean you give some people an inch and they'll take a mile.

DEAN WAREHAM: Yeah, I understand. I mean if you're staying up all night working on lyrics, going over them again and again . . .

SONIC: Yeah, but then again, there's this whole mentality that says, "Bass players don't write music, only the guitar players write it."

DEAN WAREHAM: In Galaxie 500, I wrote probably 80 per cent of the material, and we split the publishing equally three ways. And it kinda pissed me off, you know. And their [co-members Damon Krukowski and Naomi Yang] attitude was, "Well, it's all being done collaboratively!" and I said, "Yeah but come on . . ."

SONIC: It does certainly start to cause resentments.

DEAN WAREHAM: It's something you should sit down and figure out ahead of time. But you never do, because you're starting a band with your best friends and, "Everything's going to be great!", you know.

VICTOR BOCKRIS: The thing is collaboration is a very difficult thing on any level.

SONIC: But it always turns out good stuff, and the more antagonism there is the better the material.

DEAN WAREHAM: The thing about being in a band is – I mean if you're in a play with other actors and you collaborate, it's three months maybe and by the end you're at each other's throats – but if you're in a band you do it for like five years.

SONIC: Yeah, you're spending like six weeks at a time solidly with the same people. And they may be great musicians, but they're probably nutty as fuckin' fruitcakes.

CHAPTER EIGHT
Playing With Fire

SUMMER 1988–1989

Following weeks of recording delays, including last minute mixings, debates on graphics, and mastering, the band delivered the final cut of *Playing With Fire* to the Fire offices in Highbury. A substantial departure from the Fender slinging squall of *The Perfect Prescription*, the first 10 seconds of 'Honey''s Wurlitzer-hum and Vox guitar pronounced *Playing With Fire*'s incongruent features of minimalism and the pastoral reconciled. Whatever new lysergic or morphine-induced whim skirted through their heads and led to these evocative sonic overtures was completely novel and yet instantly recognisable: mid-Seventies Krautrock and electro-punk spilled over the album like the emerald wash of absinthe down the gullet. The duo of Kember/Pierce had become schizoid-artisans crafting involuted landscapes of ice and steel or corpuscular passageways of blood and bone. Rather than filling the audible spectrum with every available gutter noise, *Playing With Fire* relied almost exclusively on absence. These recurring lacunae, far from an omission, achieved startling effects by magnifying its very expanse: silent stereoscopic rivulets swelling into cavernous spaces of third-dimensional depth, bathed in textures of cobalt blue organ and the saffron sparks of dying amplifiers.

The choice of title for The Spacemen's third album, however prescient or psychic it appeared in light of future events, was a titular allusion to a '65 Stones B-side. Likewise, the single-word archetypes that surrounded the front-cover – REVOLUTION: PURITY: LOVE: SUICIDE: ACCURACY – referred to a John Sinclair-penned slogan for The Motor City Five management company Trans-Love Energies Unlimited. Or, as Sonic told Chris Roberts in a *Melody Maker* interview, "Well, the key words are Purity, Revolution, Accuracy, Love, Suicide. Most of the feeling we try to sum up are attained through cannabis or amphetamines or whatever. Or that really intense feeling of being close to someone you're totally in love with and who's totally in love with you. That intense oneness is very drug-like." The front cover of *Playing With Fire* was scorched in a flaming red background with *Mystery Science*

Theatre 3000-meets-French New Wave-style photographs of the band on the flip side. The album art was nearly as hip and marketable as the grooved record inside.

That was the projected excitement, at least, as Sonic, Jason and Will drove to Highbury to supervise the artwork and song credits at Solomon's office. The Three sat down in Fire's close quarters with Solomon and Fire's public-relations multi-tasker Dave Bedford to organise both the work at hand and the budgeted commercial campaign for the album's late winter release. For all its appearances, Solomon and Bedford were quite certain they'd finally found a potential goldmine for their relatively anonymous label. That is until the nasty business of songwriting credit went from routine to violent. Will shrugged, "The time it first became apparent to me that there was a split between Pete and Jason would be in the Fire offices – the first time I ever went down to a record company office – and Pete and Jason were fighting. They were screaming about songwriting credits."

Sonic was convinced that his previous warning to Jason over songwriting had been taken to heart, but, in fact, it was quite the opposite. Jason was certain his guitar-lines in 'Revolution' and 'Repeater' and his wah guitar in 'Suicide' mandated split-credit for those three tracks and objected when Sonic volunteered his name alone. To Jason's credit, he'd tackled this songwriting debacle with his partner before in the privacy of the studio. But Sonic was shocked at what he saw as Jason forcing the issue in the Fire offices as a last-ditch effort to win the argument. He objected immediately to Jason's contention, shouting that he'd composed and played 'Suicide' for Bassman and Rosco long before he'd even mentioned it to Jason. But Pierce persisted, contending that Kember's finished composition was a reworking of a song that *he'd* written even earlier. Enraged, Sonic swung at Jason, sending chairs toppling to the ground and mouths around the office to drop. "Well it wasn't much of a hit," Will chuckled. "It was more like hair-pulling, slapping sort of shit."

Dave Bedford looked on in horror at Fire's newest acquisition. "I don't think anyone will be able to explain it properly," Bedford philosophised. "They were very close friends – they started the band together, but musically and socially they drifted apart. There was never a specific incident – like in a lot of talented bands – there's just a lot of friction between them." Sonic stood up, looking away from Jason and over to the silent Bedford and Solomon. "I actually think Bedford was fucking gobsmacked," he recalled. "But me and Jason – oh yeah – I swiped him a couple of times, two or maybe three occasions, but I never connected with him. I don't know anyone who has. Will's tried to hit him a couple of times, but he never managed to connect really. He's a ducker, ya know. A little fucker. He knows what he's doing you see, so he's ready for it all the time."

When Gerald received news of the melee, he set to work on the phones for damage control. He placated Solomon on one line and on the other persuaded Sonic to meet Jason and himself in Corby to work out a compromise. To complicate the situation, Jason warned that he would pull his songs from *Playing With Fire*, effectively shelving the album, unless his demands were resolved. Sonic's frustrations reached much beyond the slap fight in Highbury. He was certain that Jason's motives resulted from a prophecy both men knew had come true: the inequality in compositions for *Playing With Fire* – roughly seven to four in Sonic's favour – proved Jason's primary concern was not Spacemen 3. Once again the argument reverted to Kate Radley.

Back in Rugby, Sonic sought out Bassman to corroborate his claim against Jason. But Bassman was the last person who wanted anything to do with Spacemen 3 or Sonic Boom. He wasn't about to stick up for a guy who'd taken the piss out of him from day one and welcomed his departure from the band with glee. Unfortunately, whether or not Sonic was in the right, he'd alienated everyone around him who could prove it.

> BASSMAN: Sonic had the idea to do the song. He may have played it to me but what difference would it make. Jason's guitar work took it beyond a simple tribute song and I believe he deserved as much as Sonic.
>
> But Sonic was raging with indignation that Jason wanted his share. He enlisted my support and reported back to Jason that I was in agreement, which was not true. Whatever the situation, I was out of the band when this went down and cared very little. I do not want to undermine Sonic's efforts as a songwriter – he certainly wrote some great stuff – but on the other hand, he was too much of a plagiarist, often borrowing large elements of other's music.

Jason and Sonic arrived at Gerald's office separately during an afternoon row that would take until evening to resolve. In the four-hour screaming-match that could be heard throughout the Corby office floor, Gerald attempted to resolve the barrage of accusations and epithets hurled from opposite sides of the room. He was particularly shocked to witness Jason, the paragon of introversion, responding to Sonic's acid tongue with equal vehemence. The businessman's initial exposure to his talents' fickle passions, with all its necessary dissonance, was a thinly veiled omen, and he observed the hint of a deeply rooted fissure welling between his clients. Gerald attributed much of the disharmony to what he saw as Sonic's irrational behaviour prompted by a heavier dependence on drugs, especially heroin. Not that Gerald often popped over to Rugby to check in on his boys' gear supply – quite the opposite – but he saw a glazed look and failing judgement in Sonic that could only be the result of addiction.

"It was a lengthy, lengthy meeting and very tense with lots of recriminations," Gerald claimed. "And Pete had a very, very bad habit, where he tended to drag up the past every time you'd had a dispute. He had difficulty moving forward or forgetting the past every time there's a contemporary dispute. And Pete caused more problems by dragging up the past." The possibility of negotiation appeared remote: Sonic absolutely refused to cede ownership of 'Revolution' or 'Repeater' to Jason, who renewed his threat to delay the album unless he was credited. Gerald bore no false pretensions of unearthing the true author of the songs; he simply wanted to resolve the argument and move *Playing With Fire* further along the conveyor belt and onto the shelves. He didn't have a clue who composed what and, frankly, he didn't give a fuck. It was only during a particularly Biblical moment that Gerald finally suggested 'Suicide' be split down the middle. Surprisingly Sonic consented to donating half-credit to Jason on this track alone and the feud ended. But the damage was already done.

> JASON: Spacemen 3, from my personal view of it, had mainly to do with songwriting. I'd had an agreement from the start of the band that I'd share songwriting credit. When we got to the third album, *Playing With Fire*, Pete started writing songs on his own, and it was the first time he'd tried to write songs and claim the credit for them. That's why the credits on that album are kind of weird. I wasn't even that bothered about mine or anything, but at the end of the day it did seem kind of weird to me. So we tried to carry on, but it seemed weird having spent all of my life doing that band and making it what it was and then have to fold over that.

> SONIC: Originally we split the money and the work, but Jason evidently took that to mean he didn't have to work. He could just cash the cheques. I always wanted to split the credits with Jason, but I found it impossible to lie in the face of his absence of songwriting. I was devastated to lose such a genius songwriter.

During the songwriting feud between Jason, Sonic, and Fire Records, Gerald enlisted the aid of London booking-agent John McIver. Palmer sincerely believed the only way to mend his clients' estrangement and prepare for the album release was to put the band on a non-stop schedule.

Of course, the very first stop landed at Hammersmith's Waterman's Art Centre for the Dreamweapon folly, a seemingly irrelevant appearance more comparable to busking or bar mitzvah than Royal Albert Hall. McIver regularly provided musical acts for Waterman's, and when a listing appeared for "Indian"-influenced musicians to provide Eastern-style background music, he contacted Palmer with the booking. "Can Pete or Jason play the sitar?" inquired McIver, to which Palmer, with his typical business acumen and aplomb, responded "I haven't got a clue. But they can soon learn" Unfortunately the sitar and saz Jason and Sonic used during the X-Parties and "Indian Summer" events of '87 were long since gone. Sonic's electric saz was pinched during a forgettable gig in Long Lawford (though many eyes pointed to Rosco as the culprit). Similarly Jason's sitar actually belonged to Rosco who refused to lend it to his former band- and room-mate when he parted from The Spacemen and Oxford Street.

Along with Pat Fish and another local musician Steve Evans, the drummer-less group set off to play the infamous Evening Of Contemporary Sitar show at The Waterman's Art Centre in Hammersmith, where their combination of Vox Starstream and Fender met with much hostility from film-goers and venue alike. Though the material itself suffered little from the absence of a drummer, the band continued to face the inevitable question of replacement when they booked more gigs in the autumn. Thierry had walked after only a few gigs, any hopes of drumming for his favourite band dashed after an increasingly hostile campaign instituted by Sonic. Will and Jason had taken up razzing the French fanatic, until they'd settled on a regular rotation of insults. Everybody took to calling Thierry *Theory*, at which point any comments directed at him took on the intro "*In Theory*". The poor guy hardly knew if he was coming or going by the end.

At the conclusion of August a suitable replacement was finally located. Word came through Mark Refoy of a potential drummer in Northampton called Jonny Mattock who'd played a few gigs on the same bill as Refoy's Telltale Hearts. The Hearts had disbanded by late '87 leaving Refoy to take a nursing job at a local psychiatric hospital where he recognised Jonny ambling the halls in a custodial uniform. Mattock was slogging away with local Northampton band The Apple Creation, another garage-inspired clan that had fallen well short of a record deal. When Jonny heard The Spacemen were looking for a new drummer, he jumped at the chance.

"I had two extremely weird and contrasting phone calls from Pete and Jase inviting me for a rehearsal at YP in Rugby," said Jonny. "First I got a call from Pete or Sonic as he called himself. He sounded like he was on a spaceship, as he was trying to have a conversation with me with The Red Krayola or something blaring from his stereo in the background. The general gist of his conversation was, 'Did I know Mo Tucker and Keith Moon?' . . . to which I replied, 'Yes.' About half an hour after I put the phone down with Pete, Jason rang, sounding totally like the other end of the spectrum . . . no music, very faint voice, but asking the same questions. I already thought this band was a bit funny." Jonny drove out from Northampton the following week and made his way into the rustic, two-storey Youth Projects building on Lower Hillmorton Road, dragging his drum kit into the rehearsal room. Ambivalent as to what he might find, Jonny popped through the door of the upstairs loft and began assembling his kit. Sonic, Jason and Will stood silently skinning up. Ever the diplomat, Sonic shook Jonny's hand and observed, "We don't use hi-hats." Jonny smiled to himself and replied, "Okay. No problem."

JONNY: Then, for the next three hours, I was blasted by three chords. Pete was the only one that said anything. Jason just sang. One of my mates met me later and asked me what they were like, as they had just got a front cover of the *Melody Maker*. And I couldn't give him a straight answer, apart from they were different and I liked them. Pete had given me a copy of *Perfect Prescription* to listen to, so I had all this beauty on record and slabs of noise live!

SONIC: Straight away it was obvious that he could do it. He was good conceptually and stylistically. Natty had this Mo Tucker interest and tribal thing about him and Rosco had this sort of Keith Moon thing. Jonny was a more straight-ahead type drummer. Good drummer, inventive, solid. And he worked brilliantly with Will. Those two just clicked as people in a second, you know, they were best mates, still are. Yeah, they were both just brilliant to play with. Tight on the spot.

With Jonny in tow for his debut performance, The Spacemen travelled down to Hammersmith's Riverside Studios for a 24 August gig alongside grooving Love And Rockets alter-egos The Bubblemen. As both bands stood smoking before showtime, Jonny convulsed like a frayed bundle of nerves. Everyone passed their half-used spliffs to him before walking onstage to tune up, leaving the much addelpated drummer stoned-out with four curled-up Rizzlas protruding from his lips. As the set began, Jonny attempted to make his way to the drum kit but was so smashed he could hardly see in front of his face. He finally plopped down on his seat and the new foursome lit into a stellar set. A few fanatical punters rushed the stage and began gyrating near the amplifiers before being escorted off by security. Neither Jason nor Sonic even noticed, lost as they were in the soundtrack. When the strobes and dry ice finally kicked in during the rousing set-closer 'Suicide', Jonny was in heaven. "Pete would just come up with, ya know, playing two notes on a keyboard," he explained, "but I think it was important like that. Ya know, it worked well together with Jason sitting down over his guitar. And he had me and Willie just stood in solid backbeat and it was cool, ya know. As far as I could see, that worked well." It was evident that Jonny had found his new band.

The 'Revolution' 12″, b/w 'Che' and 'May The Circle Be Unbroken', appeared in November courtesy of Fire and debuted to near rapturous applause by the music press. However, much dispute had gone into the choice for a single from the long list of possible tracks. Gerald, now with production control, had the ability to cast a vote along with Sonic and Jason. Sonic was quite clear on his desire to have 'Revolution' released, as he believed it a short and effective précis of The Spacemen's raucous lifestyle and sound. Although *Playing With Fire* was to have a decidedly softer sound, no one thought choosing something as minimal as 'Honey' or 'So Hot (Wash Away All Of My Tears)' would be wise. But Sonic also believed 'Revolution' to be his baby, with full credit going to him alone. Jason was angered by this decision, and Gerald actually suggested 'Suicide', the lengthy instrumental credited to both Spacemen. " 'Revolution' was a track that Jason didn't necessarily want as the single," confessed Gerald, "but we agreed on it. I admit I had my doubts about it. It wasn't my first choice either. At that time, I felt that 'Suicide' might have been a stronger track for radio play." Sonic once again refused, claiming 'Revolution' to be the only obvious choice. " 'Revolution' was Pete's choice," Gerald continued, "and Pete was ultimately proved right."

> PAT FISH: All the dispute over *Playing With Fire*'s single appeared to be more of a directional thing to me. Sonic was profoundly not taken with 'Lord Can You Hear Me?', which was difficult for me because I played all those saxophone solos over it. From the outside looking in, I thought that Pete found himself frustrated inasmuch as it seemed that Gerald was often taking Jason's side in these discussions. And Pete was being quite hard-minded about it, and I dare say Jase was as well. Of course, Gerald was simply seeing it in terms of how much product he could sell to kids with fucking anoraks.

"There was a lot of press starting to come in as soon as that single came out," Will explained. "Lots of press. *Perfect Prescription* and *Sound Of Confusion* had gotten buttons – no big deal – but suddenly all of the journalists were interested, there was a new record company, and things moved up a gear." In truth, it was the buzz of 'Revolution' that suddenly made the band brilliant music-press fodder. With its release at the tail end of '88, all of the London papers languished in "Rebirth of The Spacemen" head-lines and overzealous rationalisations of hitherto dismissive attitudes toward the "pissy Loop rejects". *Melody Maker* declared the band's latest entry "Single Of The Week" and pontificated, "'Revolution', with a blur of guitars and a lazy drawl, kicks you lovingly off the sonic diving-board and plunges you headfirst into the pleasure-pool, sweeps you upwards and downwards and you believe it all because it feels . . . ecstatic. They should be the movement, the global fix." Sarah Champion of *NME* lauded, "A beautiful flame of feedback, that formerly only US bands could achieve, sets you on fire. Not noise for noise's sake, but noise to bring power to the people. . . . 'Revolution' brings the message that there is hope for indie music yet!" The complete turnaround was uncanny. 'Revolution' entered the indie charts instantly and peaked in the Top 10, the highest showing yet for a Spacemen 3 release. By year's end, 'Revolution' would also mark Spacemen 3's first entry into John Peel's Festive 50, ranking number 41 among Radio 1 listeners as one of the best singles of 1988.

With the one-two punch of 'Revolution''s radio esprit, The Spacemen became the indie phenomenon of late 1988, hovering just between The House of Love's brief flirtations with success and My Bloody Valentine's drone/dance synthesis. All ears turned eagerly for the release of *Playing With Fire* at the beginning of '89. For the moment Spacemen 3 repre-sented and punctuated the fervour of the new British underground and the exciting potential lying therein.

STEPHEN LAWRIE (THE TELESCOPES): Spacemen 3, The Jesus and Mary Chain, Loop, The Telescopes, and Sonic Youth were about the best live bands you were ever likely to see in your life.

NEIL HALSTEAD (SLOWDIVE/MOJAVE 3): I really got into music when I was 14 or 15. The first bands I was really into were bands like The Jesus and Mary Chain and The Smiths. Then I sort of got into a lot of American bands like Mudhoney, Dinosaur Jr., and Sonic Youth. Also My Bloody Valentine and Cocteau Twins. Around 16 and 17, that was the music I was really into . . . The common factor was really loud guitars, just noisy fucked-up guitars. Stuff like Loop and Spacemen 3 were around at the same time and I was into them. I grew up in Reading and it's close enough to London to have a lot of bands come through and play gigs. For a period of two years, we just seemed to have really good bands come through all the time.

DAVE NEWTON: I remember watching Debbie Gibson on *Top Of The Pops* with the volume down while I played 'Revolution' on the record player. I think Spacemen 3 fitted into the transition from Echo & The Bunnymen through The JAMC and then finally onto My Bloody Valentine and Ride but I don't feel that they were directly influenced by any of their contemporaries. I always felt that they were existing in their own world. I think that they influenced what was going on around them but they weren't taking direct influences themselves. I even think that a lot of what Spacemen 3 were doing was influential on something like *Screamadelica*. The many gigs that I saw between '85 and '90 were some of the most exciting that I've seen.

MARK CLIFFORD (SEEFEEL): Spacemen 3, Loop, and others definitely helped pioneer a new direction at the time, but I can even hear predecessors to them in some Sixties and Seventies music. Regardless, I think they certainly shook a few people up at the time.

DAVE PEARCE (FLYING SAUCER ATTACK): I remember what it was like in 1988 over here: there were kids like me and Richard Amp [guitarist for Amp], and we were sick of that jangly indie crap like the June Brides and stuff on Subway Records that had taken over after a blast of early Mary Chain had livened things up again. . . . Anyway the *Melody Maker*, especially Simon Reynolds, started really pushing that idea too, and by 1988 were giving a lot of space to some people who really had got into some fresh ideas and had started pushing the use of the guitar onwards again (amongst other things). And we got the records and made our assessments. And our faves were A. R. Kane (as I say I still think that 'Up Home' was the last great leap forwards), then MBV and Loop about equally, and the runts of the litter were Spacemen 3! Also there was Dinosaur Jr, American Music Club, Talk Talk's *Spirit of Eden*, all good times. But y'know we'd play the 'Revolution' 12″ by Spacemen 3, and, compared to the expanse of ideas on 'Up Home', it just sounded so bloody lame. Still does to me.

DEAN WAREHAM (GALAXIE 500/LUNA): I don't know if 1988 was an important year for indie music, but it was important for me. It was the year that we made the first Galaxie 500 album. The Spacemen were probably the only English group of the time that I was excited about. I was also listening to a lot of older stuff: The Velvets, Love, The Thirteenth Floor Elevators, Big Star, and lots of Jonathan Richman. The contemporary bands I really liked were Sonic Youth, Beat Happening, Yo La Tengo, Bongwater, B.A.L.L., Opal, and The Feelies. I would say that The Feelies and Spacemen 3 were my favourite bands of the Eighties.

MARK ARM (GREEN RIVER/MUDHONEY): I would say that Spacemen 3 were definitely one of my favourite bands of the Eighties.

But while 'Revolution' may have piqued the attention, much of the coverage remained for the controversy. The first major cover story released on November 19, 1988 was a helluva scoop for all the wrong reasons. Chris Roberts from *Melody Maker* reported very candidly on his time spent with Sonic Boom, who had by this time conducted many of the interviews without Jason's presence. Roberts dutifully reported much of the conversation with Sonic concerning life in Rugby, The Spacemen philosophy, and rumours of heavy drug use. But Sonic did the writer one better driving them both over to Boots pharmacy to pick up his methadone prescription. When the front-page story came out, the descriptions of the Boots incident, along with the cropped photos of Sonic minus the band left Jason severely displeased. What for Sonic was an honest confession of his drug use became a feeding frenzy for the tabloids.

SONIC: When we were first doing interviews we were getting half a page here and half a page there. The journalists, you could see the look of glee on their face, when I'd say something about us using drugs. Like I'd be so stupid as to openly admit to taking drugs and, you know, even associating with people who did because it was taboo. And you'd see them practically fucking hopping up and down, sitting on their hands with glee at the prospect of seeing this in print. Headlines and stuff. Like anybody fucking cared. It was hardly fucking Keith Richards or something.

JASON: It seemed weird to have somebody who was, at the time, believing the press. He's [Sonic] good at press, good at talking, that whole side of it. He was great at it.

The controversial publicity opened a torrent of media exposure, as staff writers from the *NME*, *Sounds*, and *Melody Maker* flooded the backwater. Articles would have large quotations attributed to Sonic confessing things like, "You couldn't tell what drugs I've had today. You'd be amazed if I told you . . . you would expect me to be crawling around in the gutter." In an interview with *Melody Maker* journalist Paul Oldfield, Sonic took the opportunity to offer a tirade: "There is a revolution, a drug revolution, happening in this country, I'm convinced. When we first heard about Ecstasy last year, it wasn't even known around these parts. Now it's everywhere and is a socially acceptable drug. . . . But as soon as something useful is discovered, it's suppressed. MDMA was a drug developed for research psychologists, just as LSD was, but now it's been made illegal. The difference with this drug is that it's so manageable that many more people will use it and have their minds altered." Or in a contemporaneous Q&A with *Sounds'* Ron Rom, Sonic took to his soapbox when he challenged, "It's not about machine guns and bullets it's erm, about a revolution in people's minds, and thinking about how they can change the world in their own small way."

More insidiously, the music press' staff writers began referring to Sonic as sole leader of the band, enlarging his photo over the others or removing Jason, Will and Jonny altogether. "Pete Kember was seen as the head man, because the press always wanted to focus on one person," Will explained. "They wanted a leader when there were two major creative forces within the band, and Jason was always the more passive." The PR fumble unintentionally shifted the power from within the songwriting duo when Jason discovered his more popular partner was edging him out. "Pete never considered himself leader of anything until some bastard wrote 'Sonic Boom, leader of Spacemen 3'," said Jason. "At the time I didn't give a shit, but in a way I think Pete's got a bigger safety net than most people as far as drugs are concerned. So saying in the press that heroin's cool, that you can eat three square meals a day and still be an addict – it isn't the same situation for other people. Most people think, 'Do I buy three square meals or do I get my next hit together?' "

Sonic approved of his new status, when, in a *Melody Maker* interview, he confessed, "I've always been the one to drive this band on really. I assume that's from the competitive schooling. The band is my design and the rest are totally into it."

At the time, Sonic was unaware of how much his publicity stunts were alienating Jason, who continued shacking up with Kate and saw less and less of his bandmates. "By that time, there were things involved a lot more pernicious than drugs: fame, money, jealousy, and paranoia; you know, all that good shit," concluded Will.

While 'Revolution''s plaudits and Sonic Boom's scandalous comments headlined the British music papers, new interest in Spacemen 3 originated from the most unexpected of places: Los Angeles. Greg Shaw's

LA-based Bomp Records, legendary for its wealth of sixties psych/garage re-releases and seventies proto-punk, was in the market to acquire and distribute English talent for the American indie market. Bomp's 25 year history as an alternative music publication and label verily exemplified the definition of "independent" long before the term was dropped and swapped like cheap currency. Shaw's long career on the fringe of the music business, dotted with near misses and incredible "what-ifs?", read like a catalogue of post-'65 (counter-)cultural events and a cast list of the famous and infamous. From his earliest fanzine experiments with *Mojo* and a young journalist called Jann Wenner – who would later use Shaw's example to found a little enterprise called *Rolling Stone* – to run-ins with musical heroes like Syd Barrett and The Grateful Dead, to collaborations with Lester Bangs and John Sinclair, Shaw had not only archived and reported rock history, he'd been a part of it. Shaw founded *Bomp* USA as a magazine and mail order service in 1970 when he was employed at United Artists as a public-relations assistant. Bomp expanded with the addition of its own record label, releasing The Flamin' Groovies 'You Tore Me Down' in 1974, before Shaw travelled to England in '75 to witness the birth of The Sex Pistols and punk-rock.

Throughout the Eighties, Shaw built Bomp Records into one of the largest archive labels anywhere. Most of the entrepreneur and vinyl fetishist's re-releases were said to come from his own record collection, which had a near-mythic status of its own, said to number in the hundreds of thousands (he had also spearheaded the *Pebbles* reissues project in conjunction with Lenny Kaye). Suffice it to say that Greg Shaw had been around the block many times over and seen just about everything. To paraphrase L. Bangs, "If he hadn't seen it, it's probably 'cause it wasn't no good anyway". Shaw had heard many glowing comments about Spacemen 3 from friends and business contacts in England, and during a trip to London in '87 he stopped in at The Marquee to catch them live. It was another near-miss: The Spacemen had cancelled their appearance for the night's show, but Shaw grabbed a handful of their albums and singles before returning to the USA.

"I was in love with the records immediately," recalled Shaw, "so I got in touch with Glass through mutual friend Erik Lindgren from Mission of Burma. From there I was put in touch with Clive Solomon – an old acquaintance from the Groovy Cellar days – where I learned that Bomp was on the short list of US labels the band wanted to work with." Kember and Pierce received word from Shaw of his interest in bringing Spacemen 3 to a US audience. "Greg just thought we were the best thing that he'd ever heard since like 1968 or something," recalled Sonic with a laugh. But Palmer and Fire Records were looking less at Shaw's résumé than the pay cheque. "Bomp obviously wasn't the right label from a commercial point of view," Gerald asserted, "and in terms of financial muscle. But Greg obviously believed in the band and was very committed to making it work." So committed, in fact, that when Clive Solomon sprang a $10,000 price tag for the rights to *Playing With Fire*, Shaw suppressed a choking groan. "I'd never spent that much money in my life," he gulped, "so I borrowed it from my mother! Because we were seen as an archive label, having the hottest record in England would create a completely new image for our label and show we could promote a new artist." As part of the contract, Bomp had a sub-licence to the upcoming album, as well as investments in future music videos and touring revenue when Spacemen 3 finally hit American soil.

Sonic continued to work on new material throughout the holidays and into the beginning of the year, until he had a glut of new bits demoed with no platform on which to release them. *Playing With Fire* was not scheduled for release until February, which meant there would be heavy touring and press with little time scheduled for another Spacemen session. Jason continued spending much of his time with Kate, and unbeknownst to Sonic, was increasingly seeing his musical counterpart negatively, and with some degree of justification. Sonic had taken over Spacemen 3 not only from the administrative side (which had always been the case to some degree) but was now becoming the public-relations voice for the whole band. When Sonic announced his intentions to begin work on a solo album, Jason realised that his grip on the band was dwindling and its immediate future was sorely compromised. In a move that further estranged the songwriting duo, Sonic took to demoing any new material on his small four-track before sharing his ideas with Jason. He was uptight and on his guard. But then who could blame him for his persecution complex after the 'Suicide' debacle? Still, the resulting paranoia essentially asphyxiated what remained of their writing collaboration.

The original intention behind the solo album, eventually christened *Spectrum* (whether a pseudo-scientific or Ecstasy reference is unclear), was to provide a separate outlet for Sonic's more experimental meanderings, *à la* 'Ecstasy Symphony'. It was during the *Spectrum* studio sessions at VHF over the holidays that Sonic first recorded variations of what would become 'Octaves' and 'Tremoloes'. Essentially, a short collection of buzzes and clicks fed through the desk at different intervals over drones, both tracks were sparse, lyric-less, and contained a harmonic evanescence that surpassed Eno's ambience and recalled LaMonte Young's sine-wave studies. 'Octaves' and 'Tremeloes' embodied Sonic's search for hypnomonotony and presaged his later work as Experimental Audio

Research. More songscape than song. More atmosphere than architecture. At its best, a pleasant distraction; at its worst, a study into disappearance.

Andrew Lauder, head of A&R at Silvertone Records, had boasted a long and productive past in the music business. Best known for his acquisition of The Stone Roses in the late Eighties, he'd also run the Radar label, hip indie paragon Stiff, and worked for Demon Records. While at United Artists during the Seventies, he'd scouted and signed Hawkwind, Kraftwerk, The Buzzcocks and The Stranglers. By the late Eighties, Lauder's newest brainchild Silvertone was one of the coolest new labels in England with an eye for breakout talent. After hearing 'Revolution' in November of '88, Lauder was certain that Spacemen 3 was just the band he and Silvertone had been waiting for. Sonic's obscurantist and "gourmet" tastes for vinyl had led him to Radar and Stiff long before Lauder came knocking with a proposition. By the inception of the *Spectrum* recordings, Sonic Boom proved to be as eager to work with Silvertone as Silvertone was to work with Spacemen 3.

"The main reason Pete got the solo deal was Andrew Lauder," Gerald recollected. "Andrew was so in love and infatuated with Spacemen 3. It was a process of courting Pete hoping that this would influence the decision of where he would sign Spacemen 3. And I think it was worth doing. Silvertone sold like 30 or 40,000 copies. But the main motive for doing this was to persuade Pete – who was perceived as the leader – that he would influence me and Jason in terms of signing the band to Silvertone." Lauder offered a reasonable contract for Sonic and Gerald's consideration: a one-off deal for Sonic Boom solo material with an option for future albums, along with a £10,000 advance that included the publishing rights. Also included in the deal was an unlimited budget for the record sleeve and art, of which Lauder was adamant Sonic take advantage. It was a "no lose" deal for the musician. In Silvertone's charitable zeal for The Spacemen franchise, Sonic was given almost complete artistic freedom for his *Spectrum* project.

"Silvertone were just so gung-ho about everything," said Sonic of Lauder's intentions. "And they were going to throw so much money into the packaging, and do all this crazy stuff that I just thought it was crazy to waste it with an album like that [of experimental works]. Because I think I would be right in saying that people would have hated it big-style. They wanted it to be like a Spacemen 3 album, so it had to be somewhat song-based." Convinced that his 'Octaves' and 'Tremoloes'-inspired material would certainly now be tabled for a later date, Sonic turned from his ambient compositions and back toward the traditional material he'd been writing since *Playing With Fire*. He had long since concluded that his expanding songbook had recurring thematic elements, bent slightly toward the sombre and introspective. Since working on material for *Playing With Fire*, much of his compositional work relied heavily on sonorous texture, abstract lyrics, and spare rhythm. His goal for this new solo album would be to exorcise this obsession and release something akin to Lou Reed's cathartic *Berlin* in hopes of returning to more uplifting work on future Spacemen records.

In fact, *Spectrum* became a dark slab of minimal soul, a weary testament to the ravages of lost love, junk sickness, and escapism. Sonic's originals 'Help Me Please' and 'If I Should Die' bookended an inchoate collection of songs and songscapes that border on the collapse of an electro-confessional and contain chilling covers of Doc Pomus' 'Lonely Avenue' and Suicide's 'Rock'n'roll Is Killing My Life'. *Spectrum* quickly shaped up to be a sullen and brooding opus that elided the ferocity of fuzz and feedback implicit to Spacemen 3 and left, instead, a bleary croon *à la* Nick Cave, Leonard Cohen, or Tav Falco. Sonic's previous titular reference to suicide in *Playing With Fire* expanded into *Spectrum*'s dominant motif, albeit a tranquil and mellifluous wrist slitting.

Sonic was grateful to have Will pitching in ideas and opinions for *Spectrum* throughout the recording sessions. In addition to contributing bass to most of the prospective compositions, Will huddled up with his mate to discuss edits, overdubs and mixing. "When Will appeared he certainly did seem to team up with Sonic," said Pat Fish, who turned up on several occasions to the *Spectrum* sessions. "Hardly surprising, really. At a time when drummers tended to be a bit impermanent (or even French), and when Jason would have been spending increasing amounts of time with Kate, it's no great shock to find Sonic and Will hanging out. I think Sonic was happy to have Will around, I think that Will's freshness and enthusiasm were a support to Pete." The two would often sit together at VHF Studios through the night listening to playbacks much as Sonic had done with Jason the previous year. Their fraternity had strengthened, largely due to Jason's perceived apathy towards the future of the band. And the nagging pleasures of heroin use that had recently seduced Will into recreational splurges alongside his bandmate.

It was at an *ad hoc* gig in November at small London club Drummonds, that Will and Sonic teamed up for the latter's first solo show. Although the last-minute performance was billed as 'Sonic Boom and Jason of Spacemen 3', Jason stood at the bar most of the evening drinking with Kate. Will popped up onstage to accompany Sonic as he worked through some of his earliest *Spectrum* material, as well as a few of his tracks from *Playing With Fire*. The short set was characterised as the quieter side of Spacemen 3, with the electronic cascades of 'Honey' and 'Angel'. "It was just me doing a solo show and Will playing bass," said Sonic. "That's all it was. I don't remember it being a particularly good show. It was very patchy. But, at that point, I probably wasn't on the best terms with Jason."

At Will's behest, Jason sat in on the recording sessions briefly to contribute bits of wah-guitar onto a rave-up track called 'You're The One'. Will was well aware of the unspoken bitterness between his two mates, and his hope was that Jason's appearance at VHF would ingratiate him back into Sonic's graces and vice versa. But Jason remained professional and stoic with little word to anyone, and departed immediately when his work was complete, presumably into the arms of Kate. Jonny appeared at VHF to provide spare bits of live drumming, though much of the album relied heavily on click-tracks, drum-machines, and sequencers. "During that time, Sonic was beavering away at *Spectrum* constantly, and his interest in sequencers was really brewing up around then," confirmed Fish. Mark Refoy and members of The Perfect Disaster also turned up for session contributions.

When Refoy walked into the studio with Jonny one afternoon after the holiday, he couldn't help but notice Jason's absence. He briefly recalled his encounter with Jason on the train nine months earlier, and the contentious comments he'd made. But his concerns melted away as soon as he plonked down with his guitar. Mark was thrilled to be sitting in with one of his favourite bands, especially after receiving a personal invite from Sonic to contribute to *Spectrum*. Over the afternoon and evening, Mark added a chugging riff to 'Rock'n'Roll Is Killing My Life' and a slide-solo onto the album opener 'Help Me Please'. He had a blast hanging out with Jonny and Will between takes, and by day's end, Refoy was hooked on The Spacemen. He couldn't wait for another call.

Gerald Palmer, on the other hand, was not thrilled with the progression of Sonic's *Spectrum*. His mind was set on getting the band together in the studio to record a new Spacemen single before sending them out on the road for an arduous *Playing With Fire* support tour. "I have to say musically I didn't feel the *Spectrum* album was the direction Spacemen 3 should have gone in at all," Gerald confessed. "I think it would have had a detrimental effect on Spacemen 3 if *Spectrum* had been a Spacemen 3 album. It may not have been if Jason had contributed to the songs with his sort of input because it would have changed the feel of them . . . [But] to be honest Jason never really complained." *Spectrum* was taking up precious time and space that could be dedicated elsewhere. Palmer was less than taken with the little snippets of *Spectrum* he'd heard by way of VHF. He found that tracks like 'Help Me Please' and 'If I Should Die' had little to no pop-sensibility or commercial appeal, and the album's potential cross marketing with Spacemen 3 could be disastrous.

SONIC: In retrospect I wouldn't have done that solo album, ya know. It was more hassle than it was worth. I mean I did it because I had more songs than I could . . . I was writing more songs than I could put out in Spacemen 3 by a long way. Someone gave me the opportunity to do it. So I did it. I never thought for a moment that it would cause resentments in the way that it did. But, ya know, for Jason it did. I don't think Jason ever said anything, but I think I did get a whiff of it maybe at some point. I reassured him that this was just a side-thing. But there had already been these arguments over him not writing enough stuff. So the fact that I had excessive stuff might not have gone down well with him.

JASON: It [*Spectrum*] sounds unfinished, unresolved. It sounds like he really lost heart. I mean, he has got some really good tracks on it [though].

JONNY: Pete just had his own bunch of songs with Willie and Jason on them. So it was perceived as just Pete's own stuff, and it didn't bug Jason or anyone. Everyone liked *Spectrum* and we played it in the van as we were touring Europe in '89. Whether Pete was planning to branch out, who knows what was going on in his head?! Spacemen 3 was still very much happening at that time.

PAT FISH: Pete would phone up round about this time and say, "Pat, I'm coming over." And what he'd actually mean was him and Willie are coming over. 'Cause in them days Willie wasn't the swaggering warlord that we know and love today. He was quite young and inexperienced. The Doug Yule to Sonic's Lou, you know? And, yeah, they'd be over here quite regularly. And you did realise after a bit that you hadn't seen Jason for the longest time. I mean, Jonny, Willie and Pete were all sorta like regulars around here, you know? And you realised you hadn't seen very much of Jase. But then again, you see, he got the girlfriend thing happening. And it was fairly clear that they hadn't really got more than about 90 seconds a day for anyone else apart from each other. Didn't think much of it but yeah, it was obviously coming apart.

The Spacemen greeted the new year performing at Dingwall's on January 2, 1989. Nearly a thousand punters packed into the tiny confines of the Camden club to catch a set by the hottest indie band in England. A guest list that included the 'Who's Who' of the Acid and Ecstasy culture, mixing with A&R scouts and muso journalists, pushed toward the front of the stage and squirmed against the walls. Suits from Warner's and RCA dodged the bodies of stoned-out kids aiming for floor space to crash out. Alan McGee, with media darlings My Bloody Valentine and The Mary Chain's Douglas Hart in tow, sauntered through the crowd. Rumours that The Happy Mondays were down from Manchester sent a buzz through the audience like a toaster dropped in a bubbling wash-basin. Even psychedelic-relic-turned-Metal-Messiah Lemmy Kilmister appeared at the bar to catch the band so often criticised as "Hawkwind Hippieshit". The raw power pumping from the floor overwhelmed the band as they ascended the stage. The guitarists took to their stools and stared shoeward. The opening riff of 'Rollercoaster', with its electric flow of reverbed guitar and distortion, promptly drowned out anything but a droning E chord.

PAT FISH: That was an epic show. The place was heaving. And Dingwall's was a long thin room, and unless you're in the first 150 people, it's pretty hard to know what's going onstage. I guess they got 600 or 700 people packed in. And they're really going for it. Jonny on drums by now, Willie's on bass I guess. And I think they were doing 'Suicide', that was the last number. And they just go into it, and they just layered and layered it. Jason's fucking on fire. And they've got a smoke machine and it just spins like God knows what, out of control. And this fucking 'Suicide', it was ridiculous, the smoke machine got going, they had two mad halogen lamps, or maybe three, that would just like flash at the back of the stage, and the smoke filled up and the thing got madder and madder and madder and madder. We were right down in front so we could see this through all the smoke. Both Sonic and Jase just like blacked the guitars to feedback, or were just playing the feedback, the effects, and shit. And yeah, Jase's guitar was just leaning up, and he was just playing with the speeds on his delay and shit. And Jonny and Willie were still thudding away. And eventually Sonic and Jase arrived at a moment where they decided that they've got things just so and they could stay like that for a while. And they left it. They were gone. But in the smoke, nobody saw them go except the very few at the front. And Willie and Jonny carried on for a bit. And then Jonny stopped, just took it down to this little shaky bit. And then Will was gone. And then Jonny was gone. And they were all gone, but nobody knew. The stage was thick with smoke. And, with the exception of about nine of us, the entire nightclub thought they were still on stage playing. I took off to their dressing room and we had a joint and a glass of beer and a bit of a chat. It was still going on outside, and it was awesome, it was fucking wonderful. But you're in there and you realise there was going to be no applause tonight.

You'd foregone the applause 'cause like, ya know, this shit is still going on. Yeah, that's what we thought at the time. About 10, 15 minutes later arrangements are made and everything is just gently brought to a close and it stops. And all the fucking punters broke into applause! Twenty minutes after they've left the stage and the punters all go, "WHOOAAA!" They didn't know the band'd gone.

After the set, Jonny stumbled over to the bar, head bent downward in a narcotic stupor. He blinked at a pair of white leather boots and squinted his eyes. Jonny looked up to see Lemmy staring down at him with a drink in his hand. The drummer stood stone-faced, admiring the bulbous warts and wrinkled contours of Lemmy's face. After an awkward pause, Lemmy reached down and took Jonny's hand, shaking it gingerly with a gruff, "Wicked gig, mate!"

At the end of February the band prepared for a month-long tour of the UK to promote the release of *Playing With Fire*. Gerald secured one of his cronies to tour-manage and drive the rental van. Everyone piled into the rear seats with joints in their hands, and the hash smoke curled through the cabin before the van hit the M1 out of Rugby. This was Spacemen 3's first extended hitch with Will and Jonny on rhythm. And as they headed up to Glasgow for the tour's first show, this shot of new blood appeared to wash away much of the ill feeling brewing between Jason and Sonic. Will and Jonny brought a certain amount of light-spirited, hash-induced levity to the group that had previously been absent. Sonic purchased an arsenal of water pistols for the day-long drive, and the four bandmates took on Yippie-inspired hijinks, spending much of the trek smoking joints and soaking the poor driver.

The Glasgow show went off without a hitch, a positive indication of things to come. As always, Sonic and Jason remained stool-bound and refused to acknowledge the audience, but the hour-long set proved as powerful as ever, ending on the 20-minute whine of 'Suicide'. The next evening they landed at Edinburgh where they spent the evening pranking their support-band Birdland, an allegedly promising young goth/jangle group that inspired a particular hatred from The Spacemen. After trashing all their gear at the end of a shambled set, Birdland swaggered offstage to find Jason, Sonic, Jonny, and Will lying in wait with their water pistols. The hip, mascara-clad youths cowered in the corner as The Spacemen showered them en masse. To add insult to injury, the club owner cited 2000 quid in equipment damage and kicked them out. The Spacemen couldn't help smiling at their support's incompetent posings as they began their own set.

On February 27, the *Playing With Fire* LP was finally released on Fire, and the band celebrated the evening by performing at The Newcastle Riverside. The next evening it was over to Leeds where Richard Formby and Mike Stout (who would both play a part in Sonic's future Spectrum line-ups) stopped by to catch the show. The band made a swing across the north Midlands, through the college circuit, stopping at Keele University and Nottingham Trent Polytechnic, where they played a particularly shitty student watering hole. The student turnout was bolstered by the regular rotation of 'Revolution' at college discos, solidifying The Spacemen's popularity with teenyboppers and young record scroungers alike. A reporter for *Melody Maker* said of the show, ". . . ambient music for airports on fire, a multiform maelstrom so enormous you could surrender to its swirl for weeks."

The following evening's Chester gig proved to be more psychedelic than even the band would have hoped. A last minute venue switch moved the night's performance from nightclub Oliver's to an area health club and resort called Knights. Sonic and Will took an odd Ecstasy variant called Spectrum as they sat 'backstage' in the weight room and sauna tripping to the strange vibe and drunken sprawl of their surroundings. A gnarly gang of smoothies converged stage-side and started physically ripping up the joint. Nobody backstage knew if they'd turned up for The Spacemen or to catch support-act The Venus Flytrap. "We'd never seen those kind of people at our gigs before," Will remembered. "There was never a group of people that were into us, do you know what I mean? It was always like a weird mixture of like old hippies and bikers and young indie kids and ravers. But we'd never seen those football types at gigs and then all of a sudden they turned up. Me, Jason, and Pete just looked at each other, knowing we were all going to be beaten down." Sonic watched from the weight room, tripping, as the health club was systematically destroyed. The band passed joints between them as they waited to take what was left of the makeshift stage. Suddenly a thick, muscled bouncer decked out in full black tie sprang up beside the band and glared down at them. He walked straight towards them, before Will and Sonic panicked and tried to cover, hide, swallow their joints. With comic timing, the stern bouncer paused, removed a long hash-pipe, and filled it up with his own stash. After hitting it several times, he turned to the band and squeaked, "I ain't going out there. They're all fighting."

They took to the stage late in the evening, dodging random rivulets of vomit and empty Newcastle Brown bottles hurled this way and that. The band played a wonderfully playful and trippy set buttressed by the wiggling pleasures of Ecstasy. The joints were plentiful that evening between audience and performers, and the revolving circuit of sweet smelling smokes transformed the entire health spa into a Victorian fumiere. Joint rubbish littered every flat surface and broken glass shards bent the overhead lights into beautiful prismatic shapes. Will and Sonic were beyond smashed, and by set's end, they sat in front of the collapsing walls of the weight room grinning like fools in a chthonic Bosch landscape. "By the end of the night, they'd just wrecked the place completely," Sonic chuckled. "The room we'd been given as a dressing room was a weight room with mirrors all around it, and they'd chucked the weights into the mirrors and smashed all those up. The other room had a sauna in it, which was piss-yellow with beer cans spinning around in it. The pay phone was just gone . . . I don't even know what happened to it. They ripped all this electrical shit out of the wall. They just trashed the place in the most crazy way."

The Spacemen stopped off for a gig at Warwick University, where Sonic's family made a surprise visit to catch the show. And then up to Manchester for their first and only appearance at the famed Hacienda on a drizzling Monday evening. Unlike the previous year, when The Spacemen played a crowd-pleasing set at The Boardwalk, the new Madchester scene had little patience for the drone-based, trad-rock rhythms of 'Revolution', 'Suicide', or 'Take Me To The Other Side'. The monolithic club filled to no more than a quarter of its capacity, mostly pale gothic-rockers and snobbish indie kids. The few Ecstasy-fuelled partygoers darted quickly when they realised there would be little soundtrack for dance. Spacemen 3 was a lot of things but it wasn't disco. The Hacienda's poor acoustics did not flatter the whirring "drone-drone-drone" emanating from The Spacemen's transistor amplifiers. Despite music journalist John Robb's review which noted, "Spacemen 3 are better at this carbon monoxide garage trip than a thousand overrated US geetah schmucks," the more pointed question would be if anyone in Manchester cared. In the space of only a year, the city had completely changed, and the new youth culture passed up The Spacemen, electing instead to support the rave 'n roll of The Happy Mondays or the slick pop of The Stone Roses. The infamous coke-heads still haunting the club's bathroom stalls and the lagered smoothies at the bar were increasingly being converted or replaced by a throng of baggy kids sailing on E and ready to groove. In an emerging post-Morrissey "cyber-hippiedom" that gripped the second-city of pop, the guitar was proclaimed more obsolescent than incendiary.

When the van headed to Rugby for an evening's respite, Sonic invariably found Kate huddled next to Jason upon the next morning's departure. Kate rarely acknowledged Sonic for fear of his retributive snarl though she chatted with Jonny and Will as the van pulled back onto the

M1. From the front seat, the two lovebirds cuddled quietly and laughed to themselves. A rancid and ashen cloud drifted from the rear, where Sonic sucked heavily on his hash and glared at his best mate. Jason refused to glance backwards. The atmosphere was fetid and heavy: everyone waited for the deluge. For a band that originated with all the fucked-up children, Sonic thought, when had it been reduced to the most hackneyed rock'n'roll cliché?

GERALD PALMER: I really understand where Pete was coming from, but I didn't have a great deal of sympathy, because I couldn't really see how it affected the band. Because all they would do is sit slumped in the van smoking dope the whole way down. They weren't engaged in intellectual conversation. So it seemed trivial. Irrelevant. But progressively it did start to cause tension and a bit of a wedge.

PAT FISH: Kate was one of those people that got really attached to whoever she was with. And with Jason she was in there all the time. Pete found it a bit hard to deal with. Plus, Pete'd been around other groups and they were mostly male dominated cultures. And most of those groups would decree "No birds on the bus!" In truth, Pete probably picked that one up from hanging around with us. And even in the dressing room, 10 minutes before going onstage, it was hard for Pete to get head to head with Jason, 'cause Kate's got him huddled up. Whether Kate was messing with Jason's head or not, there's no way for me to say, but just by being constantly present I think it was preventing Sonic from getting in there and continuing the arrangement. So it was pure and simple: no birds on the bus!

The next night's schedule led back to Birmingham and Burberries Club, where the interior remixed an arboretum with a disco-hall and the audience seemed lacklustre, as was the style of Birmingham natives. Then over to Oxford Poly for a thin reception with local support Wild Poppies. The gig at Liverpool University was a memorable one if only for its 'pay-no-attention-to-the-man-behind-the-curtain' histrionics. The student-sponsored supper club set the band up behind a partition wall and introduced special-guests Spacemen 3 by whipping up the curtain and cueing the lights at the first note of 'Rollercoaster'. The stage had a refreshingly nostalgic feel that resurrected the mythos of classic British pop. Posed before the backlighting with guitars in hand, Sonic and Jason portrayed a classic likeness to the brothers Davies or Barrett-era Floyd beaming from *Top Of The Pops*.

To Portsmouth with support-band The Telescopes where a punter/

reviewer missed the point, when he observed Spacemen 3 were "like a post hard-core, more sane Hawkwind" but got it right when he added, "The band showed up A. R. Kane as amateurs in comparison and they ran circles round Loop . . ." Dates followed at Essex University in Colchester, a nightclub in Cardiff, and then a long van trek to Brighton's Escape Club, stomping ground for recent London ex-pats Primal Scream. Bobby Gillespie and Throb skulked near the bar in full Keith Richards regalia, soaking up the massive Spacemen drones. "I was speeding," recalled Gillespie of the evening. "Their audience always used to sit on the floor, smoking and tripping and I couldn't get to the fucking bar because of all these hippies. I had to kick a couple of people to get them out of my way." The Spacemen pummelled the audience into prostrate submission with the pacific sounds of 'Mary Anne' into the fierce feedback of 'Starship' and the ravaging shreds of 'Revolution' and 'Take Me To The Other Side'.

SONIC: That was kind of a myth. Because some reporter said the thing to do at Spacemen 3 concerts was to lie down. But it wasn't really until people said that's what you should do, that people started doing that.

The van chugged northward back along the M1 and slid into Rugby for a three-day layover before the final leg of the tour. Everyone scattered for home to relax, including Jason who headed to a newly acquired walk-up flat he shared with Kate on Hunter Street. The news was broken to the rest of the band, and Sonic treated the announcement as anti-climactic, or rather a *fait accompli*. On the morning of their departure from Rugby to Morecambe in the North, the van pulled up against the kerb on Hunter. Jason and Kate skipped out from the stairwell and down to the open door, where Sonic stood blocking their entrance to the van. Jonny and Will sat silently inside.

JONNY: When Jason and Kate came to the van to get in, Pete told Jason she couldn't come. Pete just went, "No. No girlfriends." It was really weird behaviour.

WILL CARRUTHERS: Yeah, he didn't want her in the van for sure. I think there was a point on one of the tours – I couldn't tell you which one, because that whole year was just a blur of tours for me – but I do remember a point where Pete was like, "Right, no partners in the van".

SONIC: I blame Jason, you know. I discussed it with him without Kate there, so as not to upset her. To try and work out something.

ברוך הבא בשם ה'

5681

WELCOME TO THE ONE WHO COMES IN THE NAME OF GOD:
The band stands in front of a synagogue, 1989. *(Phil Nicholls)*

SPACEMEN 3 HALVES: Photo taken at Kember's parents' Dunchurch mansion of Sonic with Will, Jonny and Jason peering from behind iron bars. *(Jayne Houghton)*

EURO TOUR 1989: Gent poster for 23 April gig. *(Mark Lascelles)*

'...LAY DOWN UPON THE CARPET': Sonic Boom takes a break during hectic touring, Ravensburg, 1989. *(Sonic Boom Collection)*

Inset: Dog Boy's doodled passport photo from 1989. *(Sonic Boom Collection)*

EURO TOUR 1989: Arnhem poster for 21 April gig.
(Mark Lascelles)

THE TOUR THAT NEVER WAS: Bomp poster
for the cancelled American '89 expedition.
(Charlie Pritchard)

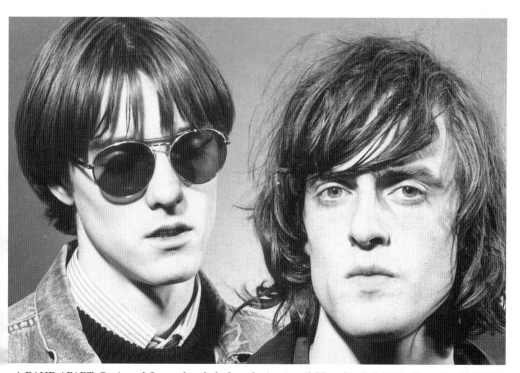

A BAND APART: Sonic and Jason shortly before the irreconcilable split, Fall 1989. *(Steve Double/SIN)*

Sonic Boom, studio necromancer, 1989.

'Sweet Tooth' by Mr Ugly AKA Natty Brooker
used for *Recurring*, 1991.

Sonic at Dunchurch, 1991.
(Martyn Goodacre/SIN)

Jason at Hunter Street, 1991.
(Martyn Goodacre/SIN)

Spiritualized Phase 1 (from left to right): Jonny, Kate, Jason, Will and Mark, 1991. *(Joe Dilworth/SIN)*

Spectrum Phase 1 (from left to right): Richard Formby, Sonic Boom and Mike Stout, 1991.

Spiritualized performs an early gig in Brighton, 1992.
(Piers Allardyce/SIN)

Spectrum at Subterrania, London, 1993.
(Sonic Boom Collection)

Jason and Kate. *(Mike Diver/LFI)*

Sonic Boom, cult figure and post-rock icon, New York, 1994. *(Alex Kramer)*

Jason Pierce, *NME* centrefold and indie-rock High Priest, London. *(Antony Medley/SIN)*

And he storms off . . . She must have hated my guts for thinking that I hated her guts. Like I must hate her guts just because I didn't want her on tour and I didn't want her around.

Following the Morecambe show and a drive to Sheffield they returned to London to play Notre Dame Hall. Rarely utilised by rock bands since a Sex Pistols' gig in the late Seventies, the space was an underground and domed stage-in-a-round, and an acoustic nightmare. Throughout the show, odd harmonics produced by the self-contained echo chamber made the set barely audible. Having thwarted Kate's attempts at riding along in the tour van once again, Sonic also did much to push away Jason from accompanying the band on this final round of gigs. On a number of the final dates, Jason rode along with Kate to the venues, appearing at the soundcheck and at gig time and then immediately disappearing with Kate back onto the road. Sonic was not amused. And Jason didn't care.

No one at the *Melody Maker* or *Sounds* HQs sniffed the sulphur burning somewhere between Rugby's town centre and the village of Dunchurch. And the London weeklies and glossies (fashionable Q Magazine even ventured a review) volleyed plaudit after unctuous plaudit northward to Warwickshire following *Playing With Fire*'s frenzied February release. The Spacemen's third LP (and the first to chart) climbed to the number one spot on both the *NME* and *Melody Maker* independent charts within weeks. With a cocktail of irony and self-deprecation endemic to British rock critics, the ever-loquacious Chris Roberts gushed, "Spacemen 3 are perverse. They can no longer deny it. *Playing With Fire*, an extraordinary record, is the last thing we expected and very probably a work of warped genius. . . . Spacemen 3 have taken a courageous gamble in giving us this hymnal hologram instead of rocking out. They've done guitars before. Their earlier records are great. But this one is a vortex of vacuums, a mirage, a (it had to come) hallucinatory hypnosis, and as such is wilfully indulgent, defiantly grandiose. . . . *Playing With Fire* achieves its objectives in a magic roundabout way. It is, I have decided at long last, a major coup."

Danny Kelly concurred in his *NME* review that, "The Spacemen 3, the band that had painted themselves into rock's most inescapable-looking corner, have done the full Houdini . . . And they've done it by the simple expedient of avoiding the Loophole altogether, and digging up the courage, from God only knows where, to radically alter the face of their own noise. From the very first note of 'Honey' you hear the new Spacemen 3 . . . *Playing With Fire* has proved me wildly wrong. It is a curious, brave, intriguing record, quite unlike anything that you're likely to hear elsewhere." But *Sounds*' David Cavanagh drafted the superlative "high-concept" critique when he announced, "The vastness of the project is overwhelming. . . . They can do it all – turn you on, threaten you, make it all seem worthwhile. Spacemen 3 have kicked out the aimless jams, opted for colour, space and sensuality, and come up with the last word in English psychedelia." The Rugby iconoclasts, heretofore ignored, were canonised at last.

Gerald Palmer and Sonic officially signed over *Spectrum* to Silvertone at the conclusion of March. The bulk of Sonic's debut was already completed when Gerald licensed the project to Andrew Lauder. In a production agreement identical to Spacemen 3, Palmer bank-rolled and owned the masters of Sonic's solo work (as Kamikazi Music) and inked distribution-rights to Silvertone/Zomba Music with a multi-album option. Despite his growing disappointment with *Spectrum*'s content and logistic implications, Gerald was more than satisfied controlling the diversified interests of his clients with an eye toward cornering a bourgeoning Spacemen monopoly. Jason had yet to broach the subject of producing solo work of his own to Gerald.

But that would shortly change.

'Dreamweapon In Brooklyn, Episode 2 (Drone Off . . .)'

The DREAMWEAPON will index rather than represent, vocalise rather than speak – to quote Deleuze, it goes about its own business – inducing mere appearances alongside a world in-itself.

SPIRITUALIZED
October 2003
North Six Club, Williamsburg, New York

The cirrus streams of a phased and flanged Farfisa wheeze and slurp with the undulations of a cybernetic space opera. A rapturous overture for Spiritualized. Seven shadowed creatures climb onto the platform to the crackled applause of 300 plus. Jason slumps to the side of the stage and plumps down on a wooden stool. He straps a Fender to his side much like a six-shooter, then perches his foot precariously over a series of tremolo and wah pedals. The guitarists standing nearby riff on a series of cracked and distorted drones that combust on impact and burn away. The five-minute "white-noise" intro verges on stringent Robert Fripp guitar ambience, looping and fizzing like incinerated jumbo jets careening toward the Earth. The glissando of chimes shimmer around the surface of six-stringed debris, as do the cumulous swathes of Vox organ drones. The stage lamps warm to a sun-kissed yellow, fragmenting into prismatic glints through a heavy smoke. Smog billows up from the rear of the dais and envelops the band in chthonic mystique. Cymbal crashes swell and splinter with the headaching rattle of a thunderclap. Everything from beyond the arsenal of digital amplifiers has a phantasmal sense of floating. Floating on fire.

His pursed lips to the microphone, Jason exhales briefly, and the brief injection of a human voice wraps the audience in a downy glow. There is an implosion. Limbs and torsos thrust forward.

The overhead beams crank to a blinding, saffron intensity and sear away the eyes of the audience in a mushroomed flash.

Hours later, I crawl out from under the charred wreckage and through the thick, reinforced door that leads backstage. I make my way through a subterranean labyrinth toward the source of cackling voices and whiskey-saturated guffaws. The cramped quarters, rigidly

211

square and painted in sooty shades, resemble a black box or a bunker. Jason, pallid and irradiant, reclines silently on a leather sofa, surrounded by a cadre of well-wishers and survivors. There is a slight fluorescence to his skin.

He looks toward me in silence, satisfied by my sudden encroachment on the scene. With a nod of his head, one of Jason's cronies rises from his chair and closes the great iron door shut behind us. . . .

CHAPTER NINE

Spacemen Are Go!

EARLY 1989

The year 1989 suggested possibilities for a meteoric rise. *Playing With Fire*'s overwhelming response had already assured its status as one of the breakout records of the year. The weeklies included issue-by-issue coverage of The Spacemen's tour calendar, gig reviews, PR gossip (mostly "leaked" by Fire's Dave Bedford), fan commentary, blurbs, and best-of lists. Queried for his favourite films by *Offbeat*, Sonic listed *Shade Tree Mechanic* at number one and *Gimme Shelter* at number 10. Likewise *Melody Maker* included him on their "Best of '88" survey, for which he cited My Bloody Valentine's 'You Made Me Realise' as his favourite single, Tav Falco his Man of the Year, and 'We Are The World' the Non-Event of 1988.*

America beckoned as well: Greg Shaw delivered the $10,000 lump sum to Fire to begin pushing *Playing With Fire* across the country. Shaw had essentially rendered Bomp Records (and himself) broke in the process of earning a meagre piece of his favourite English band. Even with a career considered superannuated in the "live fast, die young" world of rock'n'roll, Shaw was riddled with concerns for the future: what if Spacemen 3 sink like a stone in the US? what if album sales don't recoup the advance? what if the band doesn't stick together? His tensions were not eased when he flew to London to attend a promotional party for the band, only to hear that Jason refused to meet anyone. Apparently the brilliant guitarist, in whom Shaw had sunk a large portion of his assets, was hiding in the bathroom for the evening. Shaw attempted to shrug it off as artistic temperament, with which he was only too familiar.

More evidence of American interest came from expanding Seattle-based label Sub Pop, whose 1988 roster included Soundgarden, TAD, The Fluids, and the little-known Nirvana. Then there were the avowed Spacemen enthusiasts Mudhoney. Mark Arm and Steve Turner's newest band, following the demise of Green River, was one of Jonathan Poneman's first acquisitions on Sub Pop. Having released an EP filled

---

* 'We Are The World' was number 1 three years earlier in 1985!

with grunge, fake-blues, and punk-pop, Mudhoney embarked on a massive European tour with Sonic Youth throughout the winter and spring with only a 12-song back-catalogue. It wasn't long before they encountered the blistering MC5-inflected sizzle of 'Revolution' and decided to add it to their set-list. "One day we got into the Rose Club in Köln early, and so I thought I could use my college DJ-ing skills and make a mix-tape for the road," recalled lead-singer Arm. "And one of the songs I put on there was 'Revolution' and another one was 'You Make Me Die,' a Mighty Caesars song. And the more we listened to this tape the more we were like, 'Hey we could pull off these two songs.' They're both two chords essentially. And they're great songs. And so we started doing them to kind of pad out the set." Mudhoney introduced 'Revolution' into their regular rotation throughout Europe, the UK, and then back to the US, where Sub Pop took notice of the cover's staggering popularity. "It had to do with that guitar sound," Mark continued. "The repetition of it. And the lyrics too. Like when it comes up to the 'REEEVVVolution . . .' part. It's that whole late Sixties fire-in-the-gut, Black Panthers to The Weathermen kinda thing."

In the three weeks between completing their last UK hitch and embarking on yet another gruelling six-week tour of Europe, Gerald plopped The Spacemen down at VHF Studios to record material for a prospective summer single. Gerald was adamant that the band move more product while the residual momentum from *Playing With Fire* kept Sonic and company on the front pages of the music press. Fire also packaged and released the promotional *Threebie 3* in conjunction with *Playing With Fire,* a collection of the band's catalytic live performances. The album included versions of 'Starship', 'Revolution', 'Suicide', and 'Repeater' all culled from the Milkweg '88 show though withheld from Glass' *Performance* LP. The closing track 'Live Intro Theme (Xtacy)' was a full-length variant of 'Ecstasy Symphony' that often prefaced Spacemen gigs, and was provided for those who had not previously purchased the 'Transparent Radiation' 12″.

To kick off recording Jason brought Will and Jonny to VHF to begin working on an expansive and lush song tentatively entitled 'Hypnotized', which Jason had been tooling with since the end of *Playing With Fire* on his own recently purchased four-track recorder. Sonic traded off with the rhythm-section to record his own 'Just To See You Smile (Honey Part 2)'. Following from Sonic's *Spectrum*, which he also continued polishing and honing simultaneously, neither guitarist contributed more than a brief day's session adding work to the other's song. Sonic did not even appear on the final version of 'Hypnotized' though the track hardly suffered for it. "We [all] went in for the session, but Jason presented the recording of 'Hypnotized' as a sort of *fait accompli*: like parts that I would have played on it had already been done," the spurned Sonic explained. "Jason had a lot less need of my talents than I had of his."

"Pete claimed that Jason wasn't working hard, but I think Jason just worked in a different way," clarified Gerald. "They weren't collaborating in the same fashion from before. Jason tended to be very slow when he does things. He just does things in a different way. Pete is much more 'get up and go!', 'Do things!' Kinda the opposite of Jason. I'm not sure if anybody is a perfectionist, but some people really come close in their attention to detail. And Jason certainly is that kind of creature. He listens and listens and tapes so many versions [of his songs]."

"Pete and myself used to work as some kind of partnership – we complemented each other," agreed Jason in a 1991 interview. "No song was ever one person's, whereas both of us now have a lot more in our heads as to how they should sound, so it's hard for either to take input from the other. Or from anybody for that matter." But if anything symbolised the corrosion of their former partnership, and Jason's insinuations concerning the future, it was this first recording of 1989. 'Hypnotized' was the start of the Spiritualized sound," he admitted. "In hindsight, when it was recorded I thought, 'Yeah, here's something I want to explore more.'" As if through awestruck divination, Jason channelled and deposited the chilling, cerulean beauty of 'Hypnotized'. Conceptually and harmonically similar to much of what he'd composed earlier, 'Hypnotized' boasted a melodic and textural playfulness unlike anything in The Spacemen oeuvre. Beginning with a dulcet and chiming organ intro that leaps across the spectrum, 'Hypnotized' revisited the hallowed motif of 'Walkin' With Jesus' with a swirling two-chord keyboard glissando. But where the latter droned with a nocturnal plea for absolution and death, the former buzzed and radiated with a luminescent abandon. Fusing the vocal drifts and cascading guitars of '69-era Velvets over the rotary warmth of early Kraftwerk, Jason intoned, "Her sweet kiss it elevates my soul/ Honey I ain't blind/ It's lit up all around my soul/ Left me hypnotized". In propulsive, bluesy layers of overdub, guitars and organ ricochet through hermetic spaces all swathed in cumulate echo and reverb. A wheezing horn section enters as Jason's multi-tracked vocals build through spires bouncing toward the belfry. The vocals pause in hymnal cadence, then swell into the refrain: "Well baby turn on/ Well baby turn it on . . ."

"They were definitely recording independently," said Gerald of Sonic and Jason at that point, "[but] there was no announcement that this is what they were going to do. It sort of evolved this way. Around the 'Hypnotized' period is when it became evident that they were recording separately . . . Pete was in the studio recording pretty consistently.

Recording all the time. I think he was still recording *Spectrum* tracks at that time. And Jason was doing the same thing, which became the single 'Hypnotized'." If Gerald desperately coveted a star-making vehicle to launch his investment from obtuse, droning indie-rockers to mainstream phenoms, then Jason delivered the goods with 'Hypnotized'. The increasingly cloistered guitarist failed to share his early demoed ideas for the track with Sonic, leaving the latter stupefied when the song suddenly coalesced in the studio.

"There were elements of 'Hypnotized' where I felt like I was being impersonated a bit," impugned Sonic. The two songwriters once again feuded over the origins of their compositions, prompting Sonic to confront Jason with a cold admonition, "Look!" he yelled. "We need to have two lots of influences coming into this band. Not just one." His accusations were merited. While the chiming instruments and inviolable lyricism was pure Pierce, the lush and ebullient atmospherics – the mesmerising mix of phased, flanged and reverbed "tones" – was absolute Kember. In fact, 'Hypnotized' boasted the same flutter multi-tap reverb effect that appeared on 'Honey' and 'Let Me Down Gently'. "My input was more noticeable on earlier stuff," confessed Jason. "We must have soaked up some of each other's input because we didn't need each other to produce the music anymore."

In the face of such a revelation as 'Hypnotized', Gerald had very little desire to indulge Sonic's whingeing. "You work one way and he works another," Gerald exclaimed and left the slighted guitarist to his own devices.

Recorded during the same session, Sonic's lilting 'Just To See You Smile' was a figurative and literal flip-side to 'Hypnotized': obverse sides of the same coin though inextricably linked. A titular wink to The Beach Boys, 'Just To See You Smile' was a vaporous piece of ambient-pop hovering the stratosphere of Brian Wilson and Phil Spector. Verging on mere whispers of melody and exotic shimmers of strings, Sonic's reconfigured sequel to 'Honey' threatens to float skyward if not for the repetitive tom-tom percussion. Sizzles of Vox guitar snake through the ebb and flow before dying into a gentle bass-run. Snippets of drunken meanderings like "I love you/ To the moon and back . . ." buoy up in Sonic's heavily echoed falsetto. A lush pop-soundscape extending the most heartfelt moments of *Playing With Fire*, 'Just To See You Smile' also prefaced the ephemeral melodies of Spectrum's *Soul Kiss (Glide Divine)*.

In mid-April Gerald loaded his Rugby boys back into the tour van for their second massive European excursion. The band was still recovering from their month-long UK dash and constant recording sessions, but morale remained high. And despite the in-studio bickering between Sonic and Jason, the long, miasmic ride between the Midlands and the Netherlands saw everyone in a playful mood. In the driver's seat was a mild-mannered tour manager called Rod, an associate of Gerald's, who was a squatty, raven-haired square peg from Scotland. Rod was told to keep the van moving quickly, the money rationed, and the lads in the back seats legal. Of course, from the moment Rod turned the clattering auto out of Rugby, out came the dope and water pistols. Poor Rod would not make the return trip in one piece.

The band packed away their caches of dope as the van idled at checkpoints through France and Holland. Unlike the previous year's disasters in the Netherlands, the gigs were disciplined and explosive affairs, drawing larger and larger audiences along the way. Sonic and Jason agreed to keep the set-lists more or less identical, emphasising the raucous and garage-y drones of *The Perfect Prescription* with earlier rockers 'Rollercoaster' and 'Mary Anne', and concluding with show-stoppers 'Revolution' and 'Suicide'. "I mean *Playing With Fire*, we'd never get away with the quiet stuff on that," Will surmised. "We were just trying to blow people's heads off. I think it was so successful live, you know. It went over so well at the time and it was nice to play that real high octane, like, powerful stuff. It was so direct that it instantly connected with people." Agreed Jonny, "It was harder to do the quieter stuff. It didn't really come across. Pete had a Farfisa keyboard he brought on tour. But it really didn't convey live. So we did a lot of the stuff off *Perfect Prescription* and *Sound Of Confusion*: 'Mary Anne', 'Rollercoaster', 'Take Me To The Other Side', yeah, all those. We did do a slow one, occasionally, like 'Transparent Radiation' or 'Lord Can You Hear Me?'."

The band took advantage of their stop-off in Amsterdam to score cheap smack before departing. Sonic and Jason paid a hundred quid to a dealer who'd wandered backstage after a show looking to pawn a few grams on the cheap. When he returned with the goods several hours later, he included a copy of Aleister Crowley's infamous *Diary Of A Drug Fiend*. With its permissive dictum "Do what thou wilt is the whole of the law", Crowley's manual of drug euphoria and addiction became required reading for everyone in the van over the next four weeks. As for the large cache of smack, it disappeared within days; Sonic, Will and Jason smoked it down, relaxing to the sounds streaming from their own skulls. The smoke hazed over half-forgotten dates in Arnhem, followed by a detour to Paris for a performance at The Rex Club. On their departure from France, it was Jonny who swallowed a large clump of hash and spent the day doubled over with sickness. After disappearing into a bathroom for hours, Will sought out and discovered his close mate passed out and nearly submerged in a lapping tide of vomit. Jonny's bandmates hoisted him out of the stall, threw him into the back of the van, and headed toward the next border crossing.

Rod turned the van northwards into Belgium. Jason stretched out in the second row of seats, sleeping until well past noon, when he'd pop up and reach for the crate of beer or bottle of whiskey. Will and Jonny sat near each other in the middle laughing and cracking jokes. Sonic lounged behind them, chain-smoking joints for the entire day's journey. "It wasn't full-on fucking arguments all the time," Will insisted. "We had some good times on that tour. We had our fucking water pistols tormenting the road managers. It wasn't like we were all lying around in the back of the van, like, fucking Keith Richards in the Seventies, do you know what I mean? Most of the time we were just twatting about. But Spacemen 3 were pretty good on the road. We weren't like hotel wreckers or nothing. We were pretty well behaved."

"In Belgium I remember we got a good-size crowd, because I suppose we started to get a bit of press by then," Jonny recalled. "While we were in Gent, Jason broke a string and didn't have a spare guitar. So everyone left the stage except me. I was mousing around the stage squeaking like a mouse. I suppose you had to be there . . . but it was hilarious! Then, later on, Jason broke another string and up came the shout, 'Bring back zee mouse!' A light interlude in the life of a seriously uptight drone band."

Will agreed: "Jonny went backstage and then rabbit-hopped onto the stage with these mouse-ears and then rabbit-hopped off it. We were laughing so hard, because it was like . . . you get to that point that you've done so many gigs and your emotions are so frayed." The evening's show in Gent complete, the band headed back to a local dive to sleep it off. Everybody that is but Rod. He was hardly sleeping at all. He'd been popping pro-plus pills – Speed that was disguised as a male potency tonic – from the moment they hit the Continent and his grip on reality was beginning to slip. Comparable to 20 cups of stout, black coffee, each tiny pill allowed Rod to helm the long rides alert and refreshed and zonked. As he wobbled between hypertension and exhaustion, he jerked and gesticulated like a fool. He was irritable and sloppy around the band and Sonic wanted to give him hell. When Sonic discovered Rod had misplaced a tuner following the Gent show, he demanded the tour manager pay to replace it. Rod was drunk off his tits and whizzing off the pro-plus, stammering a slurred series of expletives with inarticulate bravado. Sonic persisted and Rod lunged from his seat and out into the street where he disappeared for a night's bender.

The drive from Belgium to Denmark was dreadful for Rod. He was hung-over and speeding out of his head as he steered toward Copenhagen.

Errant squirts of a water pistol streamed against his cheek. The boys in the back laughed out loud. Everyone was waiting for Rod to blow his top. "Those pills were doing his head in," laughed Jonny. "So Pete was just giving Rod hell, just saying, 'Oh no, we're not going to make it in time.' That sort of thing. 'Oh we're never gonna make it to the gig.' And this guy, Rod, he just snapped."

By the time the tour pulled into Copenhagen, Rod was mentally and physically exhausted. He'd had it with driving and he'd had it with Spacemen 3. But more troubles were yet to come. Rod had been so wasted in Belgium that he'd forgotten to book the hotel rooms. And Sonic was livid. The van stopped at hotel after hotel in the city, but a week-long business convention had booked up every available vacancy. Rod finally had to settle on a small houseboat outside of the city. By the time they drove over to the Barbue Club for the soundcheck, Sonic was screaming at Rod. Between the driver's seat and the rear of the van, there was an exchange of "fuck off's" and "fuck you's". Rod cracked. He jumped out of the van with his suitcase and briefcase and yelled back: "Fuck you! You can drive yourselves!" Someone inside hollered that Rod's briefcase had all of the passports and cash. Sonic jumped out after him and grabbed him in the middle of the street.

> SONIC: I jumped after him and said, "Fine if you want to go, great. See ya later. But you ain't taking the bag with you." And I grabbed it. So we're both standing there, we're fucking holding this bag. And Rod went to swing at me. So I was like, well I just couldn't stand there and let him swing at me, so I head-butted him. And he sort of looked at me and I head-butted him again. And one of his teeth came out. He let go of the bag and stormed off grunting and whingeing. And I was screaming after him, "Hey, you can have your money and your passport."

> WILL CARRUTHERS: So Pete ran after him and fucking head-butted him, and he got the money and the passports back. So we drove off and left Rod with no money and no passport . . . and no teeth! Well a couple.

> GERALD PALMER: Rod was destitute without his passport . . . without anything actually. And he rang me first and was really upset, and I said, "Well there's nothing I can do Rod. It was your job to take care of business. Get back yourself. It's not my problem." And then Pete called a bit later and explained, and I went ballistic as you can imagine. So I don't know how Rod got back. I think he went to the British Consulate.

Left to their own devices, Jonny and Sonic took turns at the wheel. They veered from Sweden into Denmark heading back to Germany with a modicum of currency and limited sense of direction. The band noshed on cheap sweets and hash. Jason ended up leaving the caravan and catching a train down south to Hamburg. Back in his Corby offices, Gerald frantically called up his black book of cronies, associates, contemporaries, and casuals, in desperate need of a tour manager *pro tempore*. Less than two weeks into the tour, and The Spacemen had deposed the only ruling authority aboard. Gerald could hardly bring himself to imagine the Merry Prankster-inspired anarchy that overtook his rental van. "It was sorta like a mad bus from fucking Stockholm to Germany!" Jonny laughed.

"They were in this very, very precarious situation with a tight budget," recalled Gerald. "They had a gig a bit further north, and I think Pete had to drive all the way around the Baltics into northern Germany. And, in the meantime, I was able to recruit another tour manager, whom I was flying out to meet them." Between tours with The Jazz Butcher, Pat Fish was settling down to a salubrious Northampton evening, when he received the frenzied call from Gerald. "Pat! Pat! I'm your best mate, right?! Look Pat, mate, about tour managers . . . I need a tour manager. And I heard you had a good one," Gerald enthused. His sycophantic meanderings fell on deaf ears. Pat wasn't about to give up The Jazz Butcher's best tour manager. But Gerald was unrelenting. "Yeah, but you've got another one, haven't you? A spare one, an emergency tour manager," he demanded. Pat laughed over the phone. "You mean Dog Boy?! You don't want fuckin' Dog Boy." Gerald didn't care, he just needed a warm body. "Look Gerald," Pat continued, "don't even consider Dog Boy, all right?!" The Jazz Butcher's comedic liaisons with the tour-manager affectionately crowned Dog Boy – no one can recall his Christian name – had left him somewhat of a caricature. "He was a sweet boy, ol' Dog Boy, really, but he did inspire some classic abuse," laughed Pat Fish. "I've got a drawing somewhere of how my band sees him: it's just a picture of a huge wallet with a little fat stickman attached to it." And, in fact, Dog Boy was a short and bulbous creature – mordantly described by The Jazz Butcher as a "chunky porkfuck moaner" – who believed in a Spartan approach to chauffeuring young bands from here to there. His bellowing corpulence aside, Dog Boy's sanctimonious attitude and cartoonish lack of direction led him to suffer scathing monkeyshines from any and every band he encountered. One of Dog Boy's consummate performances came during a two-month European tour with California Paisley-band Green on Red, during which time he was reputed to have lost nearly a dozen tour vans throughout the continent.

Gerald recruited Dog Boy, nonetheless, shuttling him down to

Heathrow where he caught the first plane into Hamburg. Dog Boy had strict instructions: keep the reins on the Rugby boys and maintain the tour. Sonic, Will and Jonny had navigated down to Hamburg by this time, where they met up with Jason (who was still on edge from the Rod incident) to play a gig at the Markthalle. Word came from England that a new tour manager was arriving imminently to helm the van. When they met up at the crowded Hamburg terminal, Sonic christened their new driving milquetoast. "He chucked his bag in the van and got in," Sonic observed, "and I saw him and I went, 'Dogboy!' And, of course, from that moment on it was over. He just dug his own grave."

Dog Boy's gravest mistake was trying to exercise Draconian rule over a retinue of pranksters. Phrases like "Ten clicks to the border" were met with four confused faces. The closest The Spacemen came to adhering to Dog Boy's military standards was to reach for the water pistols and soak the tour manager between joints. It was altogether less Admiral Wellington and more Sergeant Bilko. SQUIRT. SQUIRT. "We took the piss mercilessly out of him," Will recalled. "It was just . . . that was like our sport, you know what I mean? Really we were just bored. When you've got four fairly energetic people in a van bored out of their fucking minds, it's like, 'What should we do today?' You know, like the list of constructive things you could do rapidly recedes, and then it's like, 'Let's go prank this fucker!' "

The tour continued through Western Germany, headlining at Dortmund, Enger, Heidelberg, and Bremen before arriving at Berlin's Loft Club, where the warm reception guaranteed an electrifying show. The song lists for the evenings expanded for multiple encores, with rare inclusions of 'I Believe It' and 'Lord Can You Hear Me?' alongside the usual teeth grinders. 'Walkin' With Jesus' also experienced subtle reconfigurations when, alongside the bubbling Farfisa and guitar, Jason took to singing the original "heroin" verses that were not used on *The Perfect Prescription*. Sonic and Jason also performed a bluesy improv dubbed 'Bo Diddley Jam' that they'd worked out during previous rehearsals and debuted along the tour. A titular nod to one of their most formative influences, 'Bo Diddley Jam' was an inchoate din of Jason's wah-guitar and Sonic's quaking tremolo that whizzed, popped, and skronked like an electrical transformer.

While the gigs continued to satisfy, things in the tour bus were less than stellar. Despite sell-out shows and solid T-shirt sells, the band's meagre living conditions were beginning to tear at their wallets and their stomachs. The £10 a day stipend ordered by Gerald and dispensed by Dog Boy was barely enough to buy a few sweets and a tiny bit of weed. So food was scarce and drugs were scarcer still. Booze and dinner became a luxury, a responsibility for club promoters to provide before and after shows. The rider was sacred. But Dog Boy's eccentric customs extended to an appalling rudeness at the promoter's expense, which did not bode well for a group of hungry musicians waiting to eat. Relations with promoters were exacerbated when The Spacemen discovered they were following just a few days behind The Happy Mondays on the same gig circuit. "No more English," replied club owners in Teutonic groans. Dressing rooms were trashed and gear was broken all along the way. Sonic phoned Gerald at every opportunity to complain about money, food, and Dog Boy, who'd follow up with his own berating phone calls.

"He'd [Dog Boy] ring me every two or three days to let me know everything's okay, and he only had a few weeks left on the tour," said Gerald. "So I assumed that it was a piece of cake and it should be. But he pleaded with me several times to let him come home." Taking the piss out of Dog Boy intensified by the second week of his tenure. When the van stopped outside an Eastern Bloc checkpoint, Jason slid an extra identification photo of Dog Boy, complete with doodled ears and snout, into his passport before passing it along to the frowning MP at the gate. The border guard flipped through all of the IDs before coming to the graffiti'd image of Dog Boy. The musicians sitting in the van couldn't contain their laughter when the guard did a double take at the passport and shook his head at Dog Boy, before passing them back through the window.

SONIC: He was one of these people who only ever said like eight phrases. He was speaking this, like, dumb-downed English to everyone: "We go now, yes?" "We eat now, yes?" "All is good, yes?" Ya know, these people can speak like 18 fucking languages and he's talking to them like an idiot. So after about two weeks of this, I wrote down on the wall in the dressing room all eight of the phrases he used. He only used to use eight. "We get in the van now, yes?" "You're 10 clicks to the border." That's how pathetic he was.

PAT FISH: Years later I'm in the dressing room in a venue in Germany, and I'm sitting in an arm chair. And on the wall beside me is recognisably Pete's Spacemen graffiti – he uses a certain kind of sharpie – and it just says: "Oh my God! Dogboy!"

The tour made its way further East through Nuremberg, Linz, and into Austria and the desolate craters of Communist Hungary. For a lark, Gerald had scheduled a gig in an off-the-wall club deep inside Budapest, and no one was sure what awaited them. The city itself had a paradoxical mystique, of a country and culture imbued with an exotic history tempered by Communist grey. It was at once an intriguing and depressing equation of Kafka and thrift-store fashion. It was by pure good fortune that Dog Boy was able to locate the dilapidated club called Fekete Luk. A strange creature wearing a shell suit and resembling, for all of the tattoos on his arms, hand, and face, something of a human inkpad greeted him at the door. The venue's interior was a testament to the skid-row eclecticism of the East: the pungent aroma of piss and shit wafting from the non-flush toilets, and a screeching PA jerry-rigged from bits of hi-fis and gutted speakers.

The spare floor filled with bodies by show time. Shadowed arms and legs contorted to the waves of a stereo blasting everything from Abba's greatest hits to Sonic Youth's *Daydream Nation*. The glare of an overhead light revealed a grizzled Hungarian wrapped in a nun's habit and covered with swastikas. "Just strangeness. Strangeness," Will surveyed from the stage as The Spacemen fired off with 'Rollercoaster'. The club owner sauntered through the crowd sporting a Kaiser-style helmet embossed with an Iron Cross and painted in psychedelic colours. "Very strange," concurred Sonic.

GERALD PALMER: Very few bands ever went to these countries – I didn't know any other band at the time – unless you were The Rolling Stones. Small independent bands that were going to play these venues were unheard of. But my policy was, as long as they're out there, let's do more gigs. We gotta pay the bills. We gotta travel.

The band returned West to a gig in Innsbruck, and further south into Germany and Switzerland for shows in Saarbrücken, Mainz, and Geneva. In the small alpine village of Thun, adjacent to the champagne majesties of Lake Geneva, the band appeared at the tiny Cafe Mokka. A two-storey wooden chalet of sorts, the rustic arrangements and cramped quarters was an unusual Swiss take on the house party. A crowd of locals appeared from nowhere that evening, milling about the floor and drinking at the bar. The band's set extended well beyond the two-hour mark, with multiple versions of 'Revolution' and a half-hour 'Suicide' that transfixed the sombre Swiss villagers. Sonic took obvious pleasure in the strange atmosphere and broke his typical stage (un)performance to groove and dance. After the show, Jonny got properly out of it and discovered a flammable passion for van surfing along the brisk mountain expressways. Dog Boy was certain none of them would make it back to Rugby alive.

JONNY: We were like *wooohooo!* Just high out of our heads, ya know. Just totally smokadelic. [But] in some places we were booked into the wrong venues, ya know. We'd be booked in these supper-clubs in fucking Switzerland. And people were sort of like sitting down to eat dinner, ya know. And there's us going GRRRRRR! Ya know like making a fucking holy racket, ya know.

Between phone calls back and forth to Europe and organising upcoming appearances throughout Britain as well as a slot in August's Reading Festival, Gerald busied himself preparing a new Spacemen single for release. He sent DATs of 'Hypnotized' and 'Just To See You Smile' to Clive Solomon and Dave Bedford in Highbury, as well as a few of his associates in London and several friends in his Corby offices. Of the dozen copies distributed, Gerald received a unanimous reaction: to push Jason's track. Gerald needn't be told twice – he adored 'Hypnotized' for its commercial appeal – and without a second thought he agreed to promote it as the A-side.

With the requisite three-month lead time for a single release, and given Sonic and Jason's absence, Gerald decided to pursue all of the necessary mastering, cutting, promotion, and artwork for 'Hypnotized' himself. "So that was the decision I made in their absence," said Gerald. "I told Pete that I was going to do it when they were away on tour. And, of course, he was enraged." From a hotel telephone somewhere beyond the Alps, Sonic berated Gerald late into the evening. Sonic insisted that he and Jason always had the final say in creative matters. Gerald countered that as both production company and *de facto* manager, he had a legal right to the material. Sonic claimed he and Jason were agreed that the single would have to be suspended until their return. But Gerald didn't hear a word from Jason that evening. He was sure it was all a matter of sour grapes on Sonic's part.

GERALD PALMER: Pete was absolutely incandescent on the phone. He just wouldn't hang up. [He] kept ringing me back and screaming and shouting, "How dare you dismiss 'Just To See You Smile'!".

SONIC: We were away on tour when that was put together, and there were some problems with it. Gerald put the whole thing together. He was just doing his job, following up, telling us we needed to get another single out there. He was really pumping it. Unfortunately when you bring someone in like that, sometimes they overstep their authority.

GERALD PALMER: Pete had arrogantly assumed that automatically 'Just To See You Smile' was going to be the A-side, that it was going to be the track that was going to be promoted. But I didn't have any instructions to that effect.

SONIC: I always knew 'Hypnotized' was the catchier of the two. But, you see, I thought a song like 'Just To See You Smile' should be able to be a single. But no one else seemed to see it like that – as a single. They didn't see any song that has dead air in it, or any song that stops and starts – any song without an obvious chorus.

GERALD PALMER: It's not that I didn't like 'Just To See You Smile'. I think it's a great track. I listened to it a lot. But, as a single, it's not anywhere in the same league as 'Hypnotized'.

By the close of May the band ended up in Italy, performing in Milan and Rimini before making the long transcontinental drive home. The Italian shows were bathetic experiences after the more unexpected triumphs in Germany, Hungary, and Switzerland. The turnout was quite low and the Italian audiences didn't quite 'get' Spacemen 3's trademark distorted/tremoloed/wah-ed geyser of sound. The anticlimax of the shows mirrored relations between Sonic and Jason. While Sonic's frustrations from the 'Hypnotized' fiasco reflected itself in an increasing isolation from his cohorts, it also directed itself toward Jason and his apparent approval for the single. But even more so, Jason's head was above the clouds with drink and thoughts of Kate. They'd been separated nearly a month and much of his free time was spent nestled in phone boxes cooing to his lover. "I seem to remember spending long periods of time sitting in a service station keeping the van waiting for him, because he was on the phone to Kate," Sonic said. They were doing all the lovey-dovey stuff which gets pretty boring when you're all sitting in the van waiting to get to the next gig. The last thing you want to do is sit in a van for another half an hour because he wanted to use the phone." Jonny and Will were only as good a buffer as their own situations allowed. Everybody was hungry and spent. Everybody was ready to come home. Everybody but Gerald. Palmer insisted on extending the tour to Greece and possibly over to Spain before coming back to the UK. No one on the Italian side took this news well – not Sonic, not Jason, certainly not Dog Boy – skint as they were and burnt out on travelling and each other. It was only an 11th-hour reprieve that came in the form of serious political unrest in Greece that pre-empted Gerald's directive. Similarly, Spain experienced its own social chaos with a wave of insurgent terrorist attacks by the Basque ETA. Certainly, the band must have had a laugh at Gerald's expense on their way home: "The only thing'd stop Gerald Palmer from conducting business was a complete national revolution . . .," one of them sniped. Agreed another, "The only notes Gerald cared about were the green kind!"

"We came back from the tour in May," Jonny recalled, "and things became really strained between Jason and Pete, but I don't know why." From Gerald's perspective it was Sonic's garbled whingeing and marathon harangues towards his bandmates that had finally opened the floodgates. "Pete came back complaining about every other member of the band: Willie, Jonny Mattock, and Jason," Palmer insisted. "But it was a very tiring tour and there were grievances all around, so I thought it was probably just factors of touring. I never recognised Pete's isolation and assumption of being the leader, until he became this megalomaniacal figure."

> PAT FISH: I remember when The Jazz Butcher did an '88 tour around Europe – 50 dates including the UK by the time we came back. And the band didn't know each other very well when we started, and when we'd come back we got tightly bonded. We were 10 times the group we were. That's usually the story, too. And Sonic was sitting next to me on the sofa, and I was telling him about it. And I was going, "Oh yeah, he laughed, and he slapped him, and he tripped him up and he went crunch across the hotel room." And Sonic was going, "Sounds like hell." And, sure enough, when Spacemen 3 came back from Europe everyone had these seething resentments. Sometimes it's better to just be a little bit Iggy Pop and get it out of your system.

> GERALD PALMER: But, even with all the problems, when Spacemen 3 came back from Europe, they really were the hottest band on the planet. They were so good live. They were unbelievable. They were so tight.

Soon after the van exited off the M1 and back into Rugby, Dog Boy made a final visit to Gerald's office. He turned over gig receipts, expense forms, and cash returns, before announcing his official resignation from the tour management profession. Dog Boy had spent years driving all manner of rock outfits from one corner of Europe to the other. But it only took four weeks with The Spacemen to convince him to get out. He looked up at Gerald and smiled, "I'm finished with the music industry. Spacemen 3 have done it for me for good." Years later, another member of Pat Fish's Jazz Butcher spied Dog Boy sitting in the bar of a Hong Kong airport. He didn't recognise the former van-driver at first for all of his formal attire and various iron-on patches. It was only after a long discussion over drinks that the ugly truth became evident: this pilot was, in fact, Captain Dog Boy.

"Through that entire tour we only got 10 quid a day – 10 quid a day – that's all we were paid!" Will recalled. "I remember, after the tour, we'd be in the papers, and there would be these interviews where Pete would be spewing about drugs. And my landlord came out one day and I was behind in my rent – I'd spent my rent cheque on food – and he came up behind me and said, 'I read that! I read that article in the paper! You've got your money for your drugs, haven't you?! But you don't want to pay me?! Get out!' And he chucked me out of the fucking flat." Will had come to his wit's end with the bullshit: all hype and no money, Gerald's omnipotent control, Sonic and Jason's bickering, and tour exhaustion. Now he was practically homeless. Will was naive, but he wasn't a fool. A cloud of suspicion converged upon him, a creepy-crawly paranoia that had lingered in his bones since his bandmates' brawl at Fire. Will didn't quite know how to articulate the lump in his gut until long after. "If it hadn't been for the band being on the verge of success, I think they [Sonic and Jason] would have just gone their separate ways," he claimed. "Maybe before *Playing With Fire*, or at least during. I think that's what kept them together: the idea that they were both onto a good thing and they were about to hit pay-dirt which is always pretty important if you're a junkie."

The Spacemen bassist flipped through the copious weekly coverage of the band, bingeing on Sonic's philosophical gaffs: "Escape and getting out of your head and all this has got its time and its place, fine. But ideally everyone should be trying to change what it is they're escaping from. So they can stay there without worrying about it." Will choked back his laughter at the indigestible irony of his situation. "I was living with my mum . . ." he shrugged.

'Chocolate Crunch Alchemy . . .'

The DREAMWEAPON is a luminescence, if such sensual disparities bear the uncanny glint of an alchemist crouched over his mutation enchanted by golden slumbers, or the evanescent revelations of an acidhead gyrating to a particle accelerator.

June 20, 2002
Anonymous Terraced Home in Rugby

I'm crashed on Sonic's sofa drinking a weird concoction of beer and lemonade, and glancing at a recent episode of *Big Brother* on ITV. It's a fairly unreasonable hour, but his living room has a certain timeless quality as all the curtains are permanently drawn. Toy gizmos and cereal-box trinkets cover shelves, tables, any and all flat surfaces, along with an expansive collection of CD jewel-cases, record sleeves, and dog-eared books. A number of old synthesisers and guitars rest pell-mell throughout the room. The walls are lined with cartoonish opti-kinetic paintings saturated in phosphorescent hues.

Sonic sits across the coffee table, eyes narrowed into linear slits, svelte face motionless, legs akimbo on the floor. He rolls a rather fat joint from a hefty stash, laughing momentarily at the telly. The conversation drifts for a while, as he skins up, and plays with a plastic ray-gun sitting nearby. I try to get some questions down on tape but things seem a bit directionless at the moment. He chews on an assortment of pre-packaged sweets as I light up another cigarette.

We talk over the irradiated tones of the television in stunted sentences and half-completed thoughts. Sonic excuses himself with a polite start, and then jumps from the floor, disappearing up the stairs.

He returns, some 20 minutes later. His expression, when he plops back to the floor, is one of complete sedation and bemusement. His eyes stare frequently towards the ceiling as he sucks on a nearby roach. . . .

. . . I make my way out of the door with Sonic and we load into his red hatchback. He zooms me up Clifton Road across the roundabouts of Rugby, with a short detour up towards Dunchurch, before landing me at my Hillmorton Road destination. I climb up to my room and sit by the mobile waiting impatiently for the ring. More than a month

228

stuck in Rugby and still no word from Jason, despite his management's assurance of an imminent call. I stay up till past two a.m. and doze off with *Lazer Guided Melodies* on my portable and the faint odour of toffee on my breath.

CHAPTER TEN

Hypnotized

SUMMER–AUTUMN 1989

After a month-long sojourn in Europe, Spacemen 3 returned to the UK and played a second one-off at Waterman's Art Centre in Hammersmith on May 30. Mark Refoy took the train from Northampton and appeared at the Hammersmith theatre hours before the scheduled set. Jonny had called him up days before, filling him in on all the events of the European tour and inviting him to the London gig. Mark found Jonny hanging out in front of the stage and they puttered about while Jason strolled by quietly from backstage. Jason and Mark exchanged brief greetings before the former disappeared again, and Sonic appeared on the stage area. Sonic smiled broadly at Mark and shook his hand with gingery enthusiasm. "Come here. I want to have a word . . .", Sonic said, beaming at Mark. He and Jonny sauntered over to Sonic for what appeared to be a pep talk of sorts. Mark couldn't help wondering what was going on. Sonic continued, "We're thinking of getting another guitarist in the band to fill out the sound, and we wanted to know if you'd be interested." Jonny smiled at Mark's complete shock.

Sonic explained that while the four-piece was scheduled to tour the UK throughout the next month, he wanted to ease Mark into the recording of the new album, and then rehearse him for later gigs. For Mark, the offer couldn't have come at a better time. Burned out at having toiled away with his post-Telltale Hearts group, a poppy band called Wild (though Mark remembers the name belied the sheer boredom of the band) since '87, he'd decided to pull up stakes in Northampton and make a permanent move to London to look for work. When Sonic offered the job of third guitarist, Mark had very little to consider. Although a shudder of suspicion twinged his skull, followed by the faint query "Why are they asking me?", Mark shrugged the thought from his mind quickly and agreed.

"It's still a mystery today why they asked me," Refoy ruminated. "Maybe they got me in because I was a fan, because I think I knew a few more chords than they liked." If Mark was looking for any evidence to corroborate his vague uneasiness, he only had to wait through the evening's multi-hour soundcheck. The band walked onto the stage area to tune-up and run the usual 20-minute test for mikes, amps, PA levels, etc., but Sonic continued to tinker away. Johnny, Will and Jason were baffled though not surprised with Sonic's sudden obsessions onstage. What was to be a quick soundcheck turned into a marathon of playbacks.

> SONIC: I'm sure you could find, like, two hundred soundmen who would say I annoyed them by spending too long trying to get my vocals sounding right. The other thing is that I used echo in the monitors – I think it's crucial – and it was always a problem with the monitors. The engineers never wanted to do it.

"Pete was being really fussy at that gig for some reason," Jonny said, shrugging. "He was doing this soundcheck and it went on for about three hours where he was going on and on with 'Transparent Radiation'. And the whole band had to be fucking drawn out on the stage watching this thing." Unlike their previous excursion to Hammersmith the year before, the band performed in a theatre rather than the lobby, and played a regular set with individual songs rather than a 45-minute drone dream. But a year on, and with unmatched success at their backs, the reception was much the same. According to Ian Gittins, who reviewed the evening's show for *Melody Maker*, "People in sharp white shirts leave in droves, constantly. The lank kids in black that are left jerk to the front and, in turns, mosh, fight and lie down. Moshers fall in people's laps. Sonic is heckled. He may talk about drugs, but all that's at work *here* is alcohol and testosterone."

After convoking the audience with the problematic 'Transparent Radiation', the band ran through their usual back-catalogue blitz: the MC5 wallop of 'Revolution', the skittering and nocturnal 'Rollercoaster', the supremacy of 'Walkin' With Jesus', interspliced with the softness of 'I Believe It'. A number of drunken suits razzed Sonic and Jason between songs, including indignant shouts of "Rebels!" and "Suicide!" (although to their credit they might have just been requesting said song). The show ended without incident, and there was a smattering of applause. From the side of the stage, Mark Refoy looked on with glee. Buoyed up on the sounds of the show, he contemplated his future: "third string" guitarist for his favourite band. It was tantamount to being escorted from fan club toadying to backstage "all access" or being plucked from the audience mid-concert to sling axes with the best. It was every guitarist's wet dream. Of course, this was a drone band and there was to be no axe slinging.

The Spacemen departed for a tour of the UK on June 10. The van's stifling atmosphere proved to be quite different from the levity that permeated most of the European trip, although the band's arsenal of water cannons did make regular encore appearances. Jason was conspicuously absent from the tour van during the first week's travels to Tonbridge, Leicester, Bristol, and Exeter. He turned up at soundcheck with little to say to Sonic, while Kate would hang around the stage before and after the show, and accompany Jason back to Rugby in her car.

The live shows remained stellar, as if tension between the two guitarists was feeding back through their transistor amps and showering the audience with a deafening crunch of tremolo, distortion, and wah-wah. An expanding retinue of Spacemen fanatics eagerly swallowed this feedback. Despite maintaining their solid set-list and generally wowing their fans with multiple renditions of 'Revolution' and mantric 'Suicide' marathons, there were some complications. The first date at Tonbridge ended in disaster when technical troubles with the PA system ground the show to a near halt. Nothing seemed right that evening. The show turned into a shambles rather quickly and the promoter threatened to withhold pay.

The next week's shows produced a marked improvement, although a non-stop week of shows from Hull to Carlisle created more concern when Jason joined his mates in the van. "It wasn't just like all-out war all the way, [but] there were some fights and the atmosphere was occasionally thick," recalls Will. Although Kate (and Jason) granted Sonic's fondest wish by making herself scarce from van travel, the rest of the band wondered at what cost. In yet another glum affair, Sonic discovered that their battery of water pistols were lifted during a gig at Aberdeen. The final show at Carlisle's Twisted Wheel on June 26 was a lacklustre conclusion, with the band playing to a rapidly thinning, disinterested crowd.

The escalating tension between Sonic and Gerald perpetuated by the proposed 'Hypnotized' single reignited shortly after the band returned from touring. Just weeks before the record's scheduled release, as Gerald recalled, Sonic phoned him at his Corby offices, enraged and abusive, repeating his demand that 'Hypnotized' be either cancelled or shelved until he and Jason could agree on its track-listing and artwork. Gerald refused to concede his authority and refuted the claim that Jason was equally displeased. In fact, Gerald had spoken with Jason in the interim and he reassured Gerald that 'Hypnotized' was absolutely perfect for release. When Sonic persisted with his claim that Gerald had overstepped his bounds as management, Gerald calmly replied, "I'm not going to change it, Pete. That's the single. End of story," and hung up the phone.

SONIC: We never even got to see the 'Hypnotized' cover until it came out. I suspect it was all about money. That was the way Gerald wanted to deal with things.

GERALD PALMER: I had an answer-phone tape with 180 minutes of Pete berating me on the phone. Just berating me, offending me, accusing me of ripping them off. On and on and on, just because he couldn't get his own way. And Jason was very happy with the single. Ask Willie. Ask Jonny. I'm sure they were very happy for it being the single. I think the only person who wasn't was Pete. The 'Hypnotized' record terminally damaged our relationship. But I stand by the decision, and I would do it again. I'm just sorry that it ended up causing about two weeks of abuse I received at the hands of Pete.

By the beginning of July, the feud over the single came to a stalemate. According to Gerald, Sonic acquiesced to the 'Hypnotized' record only when he understood it to be a *fait accompli*. The belligerent phone calls between Rugby and Corby tapered off, and Sonic quietly resigned himself to Gerald's managerial whims. Unfortunately, for The Spacemen and for Gerald, Sonic refused to forgive Gerald for his A&R blunder and was determined to punish The Spacemen impresario for his audacity. The 'Hypnotized' 7″ single appeared in stores on July 3 to instant commercial and critical approbation. The most anticipated release yet by Spacemen 3, 'Hypnotized' proved immensely popular for its fusion, or rather consummation, of the traditional "Spacemen" sound – pulsing rhythms, droning guitars, soporific keyboards – with a wide-reaching and radio-friendly appeal. Gone were the buzzing amplifiers, distorted (mis)treatments, and experimental gleanings, for a shimmering piece of pop confection as airy and melodious as The Velvets' 'Candy Says' or The Beach Boys' 'I Know There's An Answer'. The Brothers Reid would have been humbled by such an original tribute. 'Hypnotized' rocketed onto the *NME* and *Melody Maker's* Independent Top 10's the first week of release, edging past The Stone Roses and The Happy Mondays. "We got more radio play, more press, more plaudits than any single we ever did before or after. It charted, it got played, you name it, it did it," Gerald remembers.

Sounds declared 'Hypnotized' Single of the Week, adding, "The Spaceys' latest is positively ethereal, a Velvet Underground-sounding blend of rotating guitar and organ, a shimmering hazy love song from Rugby's finest. 'Hypnotized' sees the Spaceys transcend even their superb *Playing With Fire* LP, their use of horns and violin accentuating the obvious differences between them and contemporary guitar reprobrates Loop and Walkingseeds." *Music Week* concurred, "Aptly titled single for the alien trio, as they whip up a hazy, atmospherically swelling sound that envelops all in an unforgettably mesmerising way." After a mere two weeks, 'Hypnotized' reached the number one spot on the *Melody Maker* indie singles chart and was only held off the *NME* number one by The Stone Roses' 'She Bangs The Drum'. 'Hypnotized' would also reach the number 33 slot in John Peel's year-end Festive 50.

With all of the electricity surrounding their hottest single in the UK, word came from Greg Shaw in Los Angeles that a proposed North American tour was reaching critical mass. Gerald had put up nearly $15,000 to Shaw's $5,000 for tour support, promotions, and advertisements. Shaw had also taken a very rough music video of 'Revolution' filmed by Sonic and Jason in early '88 and edited it to submit to MTV. The video, a jumble of jump cuts and awkward zooms of the band lip-syncing to the song, was crude and rudimentary but intriguing nonetheless. After some logistic delays, producers at the music network decided to air 'Revolution' on their "experimental" late night show *120 Minutes*. "I can't tell you what a thrill it was to see that intense overload of sound and colour on my TV!" recalled Shaw. "The video was all set to coincide with the tour and the press was all excited." The American tour was scheduled to commence in September, with a dozen cities in the Northeast, South, and West already booked. The venues were mid-sized arenas and ballrooms, taking in between 2,000 and 3,000 fans nightly, much larger than anything the band had ever played before. "Greg had helped and we got a US agent who booked about 10 or 12 dates," estimated Palmer. "But the intention was for it to be 40 or 50 or 100 dates. The idea was once they got out there we'd tack on more and more dates, and they were going to be there until the end of the year."

Mudhoney's successful plunder of 'Revolution' had convinced Sub Pop impresario Jonathan Poneman to contact Gerald with the idea of a split-single between bands. Likewise, word of the band's live stabs at The Spacemen's most notorious song had reached Rugby, where Sonic and Jason were quite flattered with the tribute. When Poneman posted DATs of Mudhoney's debut album to them, Sonic immediately fingered 'When Tomorrow Hits' as his choice for a cover. The song's mantric and fuzzy electric-blues was perfect for a Spacemen retreatment. In fact, Mark Arm and Steve Turner had written the track in reverence to Sonic Boom's cacophonous style complete with droning guitar and narcotic argot. Sub Pop was thrilled with The Spacemen connection, offering to release, as an added bonus, a string of singles on their label for American promotion.

Simultaneously, interest from major US labels began stirring with the overseas promotion of 'Revolution'. Atlantic Records, RCA/BMG, Warner Brothers, and Elektra began making regular phone inquiries to Gerald's Corby office. There were already veiled hints of six-figure advances and multi-album commitments, though none of the A&R scouts from any of the labels had actually seen Spacemen 3 perform live. Gerald maintained his business façade despite the inordinate offers pushed into his lap. He knew that the American tour would not only spotlight The Spacemen, but drive up the prices between warring labels eager to sign them. Gerald conferred with Shaw on the topic and they agreed. "Once they [the labels] saw them live at the appropriate show in New York or wherever, they would have been blown away and we would have picked up even more money," Gerald projected.

In addition, former Chrysalis managing director Doug D'Arcy was shopping potential bands for his new offshoot label when he landed on Spacemen 3. D'Arcy had ascended the corporate ladder during his twenties, when he had helped sign Huey Lewis, Pat Benatar, and Billy Idol during new-wave's incorporation of punk. Following Chrysalis' descent into insolvency and repossession by EMI in the mid-Eighties, D'Arcy lost his position and sought funding for his own label. He found it through a former friend who was president of American-based RCA/BMG. The major label bankrolled D'Arcy's London based company, providing DD (the label's provisional name before it became Dedicated) with substantial moneys while allowing it an indie-label facia. And Doug D'Arcy wanted to christen his new 'indie' label with the hottest 'indie' band of the year.

From his first phone conversations with D'Arcy, Gerald enjoyed the music executive's mix of élan and business ethos. Both men were roughly the same age and had spent equal time plumbing the depths of the music business. Gerald admired D'Arcy's persistence despite the adversity he faced at Chrysalis. But he also recognised in D'Arcy a naiveté precipitated by years of primping and schmoozing in his ivory tower. Gerald recalls, "He wasn't in any way a fan of the band. He didn't understand the band in any way, shape, or form. You can't believe how naive he was; a babe in the woods really. Out of his depth." Gerald realised almost instantly that D'Arcy was a mark just waiting to be grifted. "We all thought he was a really false record-company exec," Sonic recalled of the band's first impressions of D'Arcy. "Just a slime bag from Chrysalis."

During the latter days of July, The Spacemen along with Mark Refoy took the stage together at The Imperial Pub in Rugby for what would be a stellar "hometown" finale. The show was partially organised as a warm-up to the large Town and Country Club gig scheduled for the coming week. But it was also a live "rehearsal" for Mark who was taking the stage for the first time as a Spaceman. During the soundcheck, Sonic cornered Mark and asked him what seemed at the time a rather odd question about the chord progression of 'Lord Can You Hear Me?'. Mark responded that it was only D and A, only to discover that Sonic couldn't recall the basic fingerings for the chords. For Mark, who prided himself on excellent chord-playing skills, he couldn't quite fathom Sonic's inability to grasp the most basic elements of guitar playing. He took Sonic around behind The Imp and demonstrated on his guitar until Sonic nodded his approval.

> MARK REFOY: And then during 'Lord Can You Hear Me?', Pete did these really good sort of feedback and loud power-chords. So even though he had a problem playing on the song, when he did play it it was really . . . what he did was great, you know? I think Pete and Jason just learned how to play what they needed to express themselves – which is the same for everybody – it's just they needed less to express themselves.

> PAT FISH: If Sonic had any sorta musical limitations you can be perfectly sure that Mister Mark Refoy will more than make up for them. If there's another guitar part on the record that needs reproducing, you know that Refoy can do it. Yeah, I think that was the last gig I saw, and it was back, ya know, back in the pub in Rugby. It's one of those lovely stories. And it all looked great from where I was standing. They looked like they really were ready for just one more gear change into the fast lane . . . and it never came.

On July 23, the new five-member Spacemen travelled to London to play in front of a sweltering crowd of hundreds whose bodies were pressed against the walls of The Town and Country Club. Recorded as the hottest day in '89, temperatures in London reached near 90 degrees that evening, and the atmosphere inside the club was something much more akin to smothering. The largest gig the band had ever headlined, it appeared that Spacemen 3 had finally arrived. The audience was mesmerised by the cobalt/electro sounds of 'Ecstasy Symphony' which reverberated with a Kraftwerk-like iridescence and throbbed from side to side. According to Ron Rom who reviewed the show for *Sounds*, "It started almost magically. A cosmic intro of beautiful lush sounds and a blitz of white spotlights had everybody dazzled, and when a big black riff emerged out of the silence we knew this was going to be a *heavy* night." Sonic segued into the ping-ping-ping repeater effect on his Vox Starstream and stood off his stool, an unusual display of onstage emotion. Jason sat across stage, thoroughly unfazed, as the masses upfront shot up and down to the skittering rhythms, and the bouncers fought back to overwhelm the rowdy bunch. "This is like The Night Spacemen 3 Filled Carnegie Hall! And it's glorious. That so many people will stand riveted in this heat to hear these marvellously monotonous monolithic mantras and watch these awkward lazy anti-heroes is some kind of mind-boggling statement," observed Chris Roberts who stood admiring the scene.

Enlivened by the kinetic atmosphere, Sonic called the band to play 'Revolution' twice throughout the set, which they dutifully performed, building a number of false endings before erecting a skyscraper of fuzz and feedback, which collapsed into a 15-minute 'Suicide' meltdown. "Someone said to me that the last Spacemen gigs always seemed to be building up to the point where we did 'Revolution', and everyone would stage dive," Jason remembered. "I think that was the beginning of the end, when we started to do that song twice a night. We had four albums worth of material and we were doing that song twice."

As if to underscore their almost diametrically opposed views, Sonic said, "I'm not sure if it was going in any good direction at that point. But some things were still fine . . . I mean live it was still great." In what was one of their final proper gigs, The Spacemen had proved beyond any reasonable doubt why they'd earned the moniker of "hottest" underground act of the year, and why nobody outside the band's inner circle ever imagined that The Town and Country was their swan song rather than a new beginning.

The five-piece Spacemen 3 re-entered VHF Studios to begin recording new material in the first days of August. Sonic, Jason, Will and Jonny worked out bits of material live, jamming here and there on songs before splitting to begin recording individual tracks. In contradistinction to both Sonic and Jason's original compositions on *Playing With Fire*, which were based entirely on a sparse and shimmering minimalism, their newest demos pointed to a more lush sound, chiming and spangled with heavy, rich layers of guitar, multi-tracked vocals, and thick keyboard effects.

Early work proceeded on backing tracks for new versions of 'Just To See You Smile', 'I Love You', and 'Set Me Free'. Sonic worked closely with Will on the bass rhythms and Jonny hung around near the drum kit for his cue. Mark appeared at the studio to watch the preliminary work and sort out where he might contribute some guitar-parts to the roughly hewn recordings. Mark was quite surprised to find, after several visits to VHF, that the band's two songwriters rarely appeared at the same time. "I think Pete and Jase would get on with their own bits and pieces," Mark said. "I remember them being together in the studio once or twice. But by this time, they'd done three albums or something, so they had their own way of working. But it was quite a tense atmosphere as well."

Once again Paul Adkins appeared behind the desk on various occasions to help with early track recordings. Paul was equally perplexed at Jason and Sonic's estrangement, but he attributed much of their odd behaviour to more sophisticated recording habits. "It started off with them playing as a band and recording together," Paul remembered. "There was interaction between them. Whereas when they started recording bits one at a time you can hear the difference . . ." Despite his rationalisations, Paul noticed Kate's constant presence in the studio, and wondered to himself if the problem lay there. On days when Paul would walk into the studio to find Jason recording, Kate would often sit quietly in the control room. Between takes, the two would cuddle close together, talking quietly and listening to playbacks. With his infrequent trips to the studio during Jason's recordings, Sonic noted Kate with much chagrin. "Kate would have been hanging around the whole time. And there was this bad sort of, you know [thing between us]. She thought I was Satan for a period. Probably still does," Sonic laughed. Kate and Sonic exchanged few glances and still fewer words, before he'd duck out of the studio for the afternoon.

> JONNY: She was around a lot. They were in love ya know. So it's, like, obviously he wanted her to be around. I didn't see her as a problem. It was just Kate was nice to talk to, ya know. And uh . . . a bit of a welcome relief, ya know, for me. Playing drums – I'd do my drums and then Kate would be around and we'd have a laugh. And I think, yeah, Pete found that a strain. Definitely. So I think that might have been something to do with their [Sonic and Jason's] arguments all the time.

> MARK REFOY: I can see why Pete thought Kate was a divisive element, because he was jealous of the attention he wasn't getting from Jason. I don't remember Kate causing problems. There's no way she'd cause problems! No way! Maybe her presence would upset Pete, because he saw her as a threat of some kind. I mean I've heard all those comparisons before, you know: I mean Kate being the Yoko, but I think that's unfair. I think, at the time, they were in love, and I think they wanted to be together. There's no way she had an agenda to interfere. I think she wanted to be Pete's friend, too.

On August 22, The Spacemen played a Reading warm-up gig at Subterranea in London. The house was packed as the band took the stage to the sounds of The Byrds' 'Mr. Spaceman', a kitsch-folk diversion from their usual 'Ecstasy Symphony' walk-on. They launched into a monstrous version of 'Rollercoaster', followed by 'Things'll Never Be The Same', with extra wah-wah provided by Mark Refoy; 'Take Me To The Other Side' followed, and they concluded with their usual ear-splitting triptych of 'Starship', 'Revolution', and a 20-minute 'Suicide'. Will and Jonny pounded away in a perfect rhythmic "lock groove" and Mark added a extra layer of texture with his solid rhythm guitar.

Sitting backstage after the show, amidst the crowd of press, scouts, and hangers-on that evening, were The Butthole Surfers and members of Galaxie 500. The interest of these US groups was testament to the band's ever-widening international appeal. Galaxie's Dean Wareham was particularly transfixed to see one of his favourite groups live and leapt on to the stage following the frazzled end of 'Suicide': "I was fortunate to see Spacemen 3 once," Wareham said. "Actually it would be more accurate to say that I heard them, it wasn't really possible to see them because they were sitting down onstage and it was kind of crowded." Equally smitten were Buttholes Gibby Haynes, Paul Leary and King Coffey who slumped into the dressing-room couch and skinned up with Will, Jason and Sonic. "I know that The Butthole Surfers were suggesting around that point, 'Why don't you come over and tour with us?'" Sonic recalled. And, in fact, upon the insistence of the Texas-based psychdelicians, Greg Shaw organised a large Halloween show in Boston with The Spacemen opening for The Butthole Surfers.

On August 25, over the Bank Holiday weekend, The Spacemen played the Reading Festival. The annual three-day outdoor event was given a sorely needed renovation in '89, when a new promoting team came onboard to draw larger crowds and book bigger acts. The pastoral fields of Reading were soaked with showers over the long weekend, adding a sinister gloom to the proceedings. The weather did not prevent the crowds from slopping from stage to stage. And despite one of the largest crowds in Reading history, The Spacemen's debut to the festival circuit was witnessed by only a few. The band was placed low on the bill due to scheduling difficulties and performed after Gaye Bykers On Acid, though given their enormous popularity, they should have very well played closer to the headliners New Order. Though the energy from the crowd could not compare to the hysterics of The Town and Country gig, the band played a respectable though uneventful half-hour set including 'Rollercoaster', 'Things'll Never Be The Same', 'Take Me To The Other Side', and concluding with 'Starship' and 'Revolution' before walking off to muted applause. Except for an errant boot that flew into Mark's face during the set, the performance seemed fairly routine. "Reading was great," Jonny insisted. "We should have done more big gigs." Mark agreed: "I still thought that it was going to carry on somehow. I wasn't thinking 'Oh . . . this is the end!' I didn't think that at all."

The bleak spectre of the rain-spattered grounds lent a silent and foreboding air as the band lounged backstage. Roadies cleared what was left of the band's equipment off the platform, hauling it through the drizzle. Will stood watching smoothies and squares alike guzzling lager from endless brown bottles. He was whirling from the palpable atmosphere of anti-climax that surrounded his bandmates. "And we just went and sat in the food tent and smoked joints all afternoon. We were watching people eat their dinner, I seem to remember," Will said. My Bloody Valentine climbed to the stage as afternoon stretched into early evening, wowing the growing throng with overdriven guitar and supple cooing. In the dying glow of twilight, bled colourless by the ashen downpour, The Valentines performed fuzzy dirges with funereal delight. Will gazed up towards the stage from the tent, closely watching The Valentines' eerie blend of tremolo, reverb, and drones washing over the stage. Live it was altogether too reminiscent of The Spacemen to be ignored. Alan McGee stood offstage watching his blessed cadre of "shoegazers" with wrapped delight. Sonic found McGee after the set and cornered him with an offer: "Come manage us . . ." After a long and laborious discussion with McGee, Sonic offered his idea up to the rest of the band. Mark recalled Jason objected immediately and an argument ensued. "Pete wanted to get McGee to manage us but Jason was saying, 'No . . . no . . . I don't want Alan . . . !'" Sonic was intent on dismissing Gerald Palmer once and for all from The Spacemen ranks. "Alan wanted us, he loved Spacemen 3," Sonic insisted, "but Jason wasn't into it at all. He knew Alan was too much on my side. In retrospect, he was still hooked up with Gerald and looking toward Spiritualized."

"We didn't have any management agreement between us," Gerald said. "Jason and Pete could have appointed other management if they wanted, but there was a large amount of outstanding money due to me so any deal would still have to go through me." In his official and unofficial capacity as record company and management, Palmer was flirting with the US labels to seal a major deal for a band eager to cut all ties. The executives at RCA/BMG had invited Gerald to their New York headquarters at the conclusion of August to discuss the future of Spacemen 3. Gerald was no stranger to the more posh affectations wealth afforded him, but even he was pleasantly surprised by the excesses of hospitality that the majors were willing to lavish upon him. He left his Corby offices for Heathrow Airport in a cavernous limousine, before he was deposited into the first-class cabin of a British Airways 747 *en route* to JFK. Upon his arrival in New York, Gerald was once again shuttled from the airport via stretch limo uptown to a towering hotel nestled off Central Park's opulent Westside. The suite reserved for Gerald was a voluminous pad commonly used by record execs and their guests for business, but the expense and affectation reminded him of something more akin to a seraglio. It was all a lovely formality. Gerald's meetings with the majors were all business; he wasn't easily swayed by the New York suit'n'tie pretension. RCA/BMG, Warner's, and Atlantic were all major contenders in his estimation, and the next move was to create a bidding war that would drive the price for contracting his band skyward. Preliminary offers from the labels rose well into six digits with a hearty advance and multiple album options. But Gerald wasn't ready to blow his wad just yet; with news of the American tour imminent, the collective tongues of every major label exec in New York would be wagging onto their immaculate office floors.

It was upon his return to Cambridgeshire that Gerald received the wonderful news for which he'd been waiting. The band's applications for US visas had finally come through. Problems with acquiring them had prevented Gerald from finalising the tour schedule. Both Sonic and Jason's drug arrests, in addition to Sonic's inclusion on the national drug registry, red-flagged the band in the US immigration offices. "And I got all that together, with much difficulty, and with lying and subterfuge. But I managed to get them visas despite their drug problems," Gerald confessed. "It was all in place: posters were done by Greg for the venues, and I think the idea was presented to do more recording over there as well." In addition, CMJ invited Spacemen 3 for an appearance at an annual New Music Awards ceremony to be broadcast on national television in November. *The College Media Journal*, to give the influential trade publication its full name, had lauded the group with the title "most interesting new band of the year", which, in addition to the MTV spots, would guarantee them wide airplay in the States. Excited about finally turning a profit in his business investment, Greg Shaw was also thrilled at having 'introduced' Spacemen 3 to the American market. As he had done so many times previously, Shaw was linking yet another group into a puzzular rock'n'roll genealogy, weaving a massive tapestry from garage/esoterica to Iggy to The Flamin' Groovies to The Spacemen. "I had no inkling of the turmoil," conceded Shaw. "I think all involved were hoping it would blow over."

Returned to the confines of the studio, Sonic and Jason's working relationship had only worsened into the Fall, where they recorded completely separate from one another. Will jumped back and forth from what was becoming two recording sessions as a desperate envoy trying to avoid complete collapse. "Yeah, it really fell apart during the making of *Recurring*," he recalled. "All the cracks were showing. I mean there were differences that weren't being sorted out and there were all these pressures." He attempted to smooth whatever rough edges he observed between his two closest friends, but neither Jason nor Sonic heeded his advice for reconciliation. Sonic did however pop in a few of Jason's demos that were lying scattered around the studio and was quite awe-struck to find more of his effects and tones littering the recordings. Sonic had always credited Jason's talent for mimicry, but he considered this downright plagiarism.

Kate's omnipresence in the studio continued to spark grief and animosity. But when Sonic heard from Gerald that Jason wanted Kate along for the duration of the US tour, he was absolutely outraged. "The issue came up of Kate coming out on the tour," Sonic recalled, "but I didn't want her around for a fuckin' month! I've seen it happen in a million bands where one of them has their girlfriend along as a tour manager or as the T-shirt girl. And it's just always the source of rifts and hassle and shit stirring, ya know. But Jason was trying to argue that he should be able to have Kate on tour, 'cause I might be just getting off with anyone any-where on the tour. So he should be able to have Kate along." As sure as Jason believed Sonic was tearing apart the band by trying to keep him and Kate apart, Sonic wondered if Jason was only pushing Kate further into the centre to sabotage their collaboration. "It was not a good atmo-sphere," Mark confessed. "I don't want to paint anyone in the wrong light, but Pete was very hard to be in a band with. Around that time, I remember Jason saying, 'I'm not getting on the plane to go to America for the tour.' And half of me was sort of relieved."

There was, in addition to the deepening chasm between Jason and Sonic, another rift between Gerald and his band. Despite all of the positive reviews, excellent PR, and constant touring, little to no money appeared in the musicians' coffers. This was especially true for Will and Jonny, who were not legitimate "members" of Spacemen 3 from a financial perspec-tive. So when royalty checks came in from Gerald's Kamikazi Music, Will and Jonny were given mere peanuts and they didn't understand why. "Will and Gerald did not get on," said Sonic. "They hated each other. And I think Will sort of felt tied to Gerald by default – which he was – because he wasn't managed by him. And Gerald was always like, 'I don't want to manage you Will.'" Their touring allowances alone had already sent Will packing back to his parents' house to live. "I was completely ignorant of the workings of the music business really at that point,'" Will said. "I was just quite happy to trust everybody's better nature."

Neither Sonic nor Jason had attempted to explain the business side of their various deals to the rhythm section, for they hardly understood it themselves. What remained was a tingling sense of paranoia that gripped everyone – including newest recruit Mark – surviving, as they did, on a meagre pittance tantamount to session pay. "None of us were sure of our status, really, especially me," Refoy said, "because Pete wanted me to join, but towards the end I got the impression I wasn't a real member and Gerald wasn't too happy with my inclusion." Moreover, while the band continued to sell their T-shirts in bulk along every tour stop and venue, no one saw any of the money at the end of the day. Suspicions pointed toward their management. "Gerald was no angel," said Sonic. "He was meant to be taking 20 per cent [of the T-shirt sells]. But, because he put up 100 quid for the first 100 shirts, he took 50 per cent, because he said he put down the money. But we were selling thousands of shirts. So the argument was, 'You should have taken your money back after the first 100 shirts and used our money to pay for them from then on. And just take your 20 per cent.' So he kept it funded by his initial £100, even though he was bringing in thousands and thousands of pounds."

Gerald was summoned to a meeting at VHF near the beginning of September at the request of Sonic and Jason to answer these charges. It was shortly after his return from New York and Gerald had an ebullient air about him, content that tour and signing were within his grasp. As he walked into the control-room, following an afternoon session, he noticed everyone present save Sonic. Will and Jason glared up at their manager with an equal amount of antipathy and apathy. Though it's somewhat unclear what followed from these proceedings, Jason, Will, and Sonic by proxy – he was out scoring – aired a long list of grievances with Gerald, whose irascible nature precipitated an intense argument. Someone pressed RECORD on a nearby tape deck to document all the accusations and Gerald's vague responses.

> SONIC: Will gave Gerald a particularly hard time because that was his speciality. And Jason also gave him a hard time about the way the T-shirt money was dealt with. Will said, "Why, when you're meant to take 20 per cent of the T-shirts, did you take 50 per cent?!" And Gerald'd throw something back in Will's face, like that he wasn't really even a signed member of the band, anyway. It was all that sort of crap really. So Gerald would never even answer the charges that were put to him.

When the harsh incriminations subsided, none of the grievances were resolved. Gerald ducked out of the studio and shrugged the argument off to artistic temperaments; or possibly as a manipulative move by Sonic to dismiss him from The Spacemen. He remained unaware that the conversation had been taped, and the band considered much of his duckings and non-sequitors to be admissions of guilt. At least Sonic and Will conceded as much. Jason was typically quiet about his position.

The band was eroding with steady momentum, and Gerald's best strategy was to delay the inevitable. But to do that he faced the fragile tightrope that hung between his two clients. And despite the precarious plunge that awaited him below, Gerald gambled the pay-off was more than worth the risk. He could literally smell the cash-in perched just beyond the US tour. Sonic was equally uncertain of his manager's ulterior motives. "I think Gerald knew that, at that point, in the band, with things as ropey as they were, that a tour was . . . I've always given him credit, at the very least, for thinking what would be the best thing for the band," Sonic opined. "But sending us on tour when things weren't going well [between me and Jason], ya know . . . I don't know." Within days of this first encounter at VHF, Jason and Sonic united at the former's Hunter Street apartment, where they waited patiently for Gerald to appear for a business meeting. When the lame-duck manager plopped down onto Jason's couch, he was all business enthusiasm. Little of the previous arguments shown on his thick, animated face. The two musicians stared uneasily at one another throughout Gerald's lecture: he was thrilled at the prospects of the US tour, which was totally finalised and literally days away. Gerald discussed more recording dates for the new album, this, that, and the other, while Jason stared away and Sonic seemingly ignored him.

"After I opened telling them what we had planned, making a fool of myself really, Sonic said, 'Well that's great Gerald but we don't want you as our manager. As far as we're concerned you're finished,'" Palmer growled. "Both of them were there, though Jason didn't say a word. Pete did. My emotions were – not in any particular order – astonishment, fury, ingratitude, rage, and disappointment." Jason sat stoic while Sonic waited on tenterhooks for Palmer's response. "He started to argue and Jason and I threatened to play him this tape from VHF," Sonic said, "which had lots of incriminating stuff on it. And, at that point, he said, 'All right, I accept it.'" Gerald's apparent concession to Sonic (and Jason's) decision was not as simple as personal estrangement. In fact, Gerald was quick to point out to his clients the details of their signed contract to Kamikazi Music. Having foreseen such an event years in advance, Gerald had protected himself from arbitrary dismissal by linking himself as the record company rather than the manager. Whether or not the two musicians who signed their souls to him had ever fully understood the contract was irrelevant now. After the afternoon's caustic argument cooled, Gerald took some glee in reminding Sonic that he couldn't be fired. As the production-agreement gave Gerald all rights to the recordings and the money therein, he was – on paper – as much Spacemen 3 as either guitarist. If The Spacemen flagship was going to drift on a pyre of flames, then all three men would perish together.

> GERALD PALMER: And at that point I said, "I'm not going to support this US tour! You better find the money for it. I'm not going to do this!" And that's when it all kind of fell apart. And Jason rang me afterwards, and I was just in a rage, saying, "How could you just fucking sit there?!"

> SONIC: I think Gerald always blamed me for the sacking. And I think he sort of approached Jason. And Gerald sort of put together the plan of, "Look you can do without this guy. He's just a pain in the ass."

> GERALD PALMER: The American tour was finished, but if you think I was going to blow the £10,000 or £15,000 I'd spent and not finish [the album] . . . I'd lost a lot of money that was just the recording budget to date. So it was agreed that we'd finish the album. Get everything sorted out and we'd deliver the single.

After the first driblets of rumour and innuendo reached Greg Shaw in Los Angeles, the Bomp impresario was despondent. Despite the moderate sum of money he collected from the American distribution of *Playing With Fire*, it was nothing compared to the sum he had invested in bringing the band over. Now with the tour cancelled, the loss of co-op advertising and ticket sales, and the PR vacuum, Bomp was once again in a hole and Shaw was once again on the dark side of cashing in. When he finally reached someone in Rugby to explain, Shaw was belatedly apprised of all the internal conflicts brewing between musicians. "They put up a good front right up until the last minute," Shaw observed.

When the dust had settled on this, their latest rupture, Sonic pushed on with recording work, while Jason withdrew from his partner's presence almost completely. As sure as Sonic believed Gerald to be out of their hair forever, Jason regretted taking part in the ambush, and coveted Palmer's continued advice. For Gerald, however, nothing had changed. He was intent on signing Spacemen 3 to a major before there was nothing left. Gerald went on a PR offensive – in conjunction with Fire's Dave Bedford – to blame the work permits for the band's 11th-hour cancellation. The story appeared in *NME*, *Melody Maker*, and *Sounds* as evidence of the band's continued solidarity despite American politics. "The story was that legally we couldn't get work permits easily, because we all had drug convictions," said Sonic. "Actually we did all get the work permits eventually. They cost a lot, but we did eventually get them. That wasn't the reason we didn't go on tour."

The US tour may have affected the "gazumping" between the New York labels, but Doug D'Arcy's newly christened Dedicated continued raising the stakes. Dedicated was not privy to any of the scandal triangulated between Gerald's offices, Jason's tiny Rugby flat, and Sonic's commodious Dunchurch mansion: the angry phone calls, the letters, the long-winded answer-phone messages. One of the few things Sonic, Jason and Gerald agreed on was maintaining the masquerade for Dedicated. "They were the one label we all knew we were going to go with," said Sonic. "So we had to keep it quiet to what extent the band was falling apart." Doug D'Arcy knew nothing and, consequently, Dedicated's purse strings knew no limit. "I don't know whether Doug even liked the band," said Gerald. "But he was swept away with the euphoria. He had a couple of A&R people that were excited and watched the band. He had a label and money. And it cost him certainly."

The new album, which was now pushed to the top of the agenda in the absence of a US tour, was taking shape at a determinedly slower pace than *Playing With Fire*. Recordings proceeded with half-hearted effort, stunted largely by Sonic and Jason's seeming refusal to work together. Their estrangement made the budding album's song list all the more surprising for its subtle and muted similarities. Jason's early demos included all new compositions entitled 'Feel So Sad' with an intro called 'Drive', 'Feelin' Just Fine', 'Sometimes', 'These Blues', and 'Billy Whizz' with an outro 'Blue 1'. For his part, Sonic continued his preliminary work on a new version of 'Just To See You Smile', 'I Love You', and 'Set Me Free/ I've Got The Key', along with a reprise of the latter, plus 'Why Couldn't I See?', and a gargantuan Krautrock paean called 'Big City (Everybody I Know Can Be Found Here)'.

Each set of demos made comparable strides toward expanding the palette of sounds engendered on *Playing With Fire* with more emphasis on soft textures, synths, and warm bubbling lacunae. As per the subtle shifts of sound saturating 'Hypnotized', songs such as 'Sometimes', 'Feelin' Just Fine', 'I Love You', and 'Set Me Free' had a lilting breeziness that whispered rather than crunched. A number of Sonic's compositions even had a lighter, almost playful tone shifting in and out of all the murky haziness. The acoustic 'Set Me Free' reprise had a open-mike, live-studio vocal track mumbling through the background, adding a goofily stoned innocence reminiscent of The Beach Boys' '65 *Party* LP. 'I Love You' was a bass-heavy, hook-laden love-letter grooving and pumping with a reggae-inspired riff from Bob Marley's 'Mr. Brown', while 'Big City' narrated the pleasures of ecstasy culture with the phased and sequenced bliss of Kraftwerk's 'Autobahn' and early ambient-house.

"If you just look at the track lists, you can see there is a distinct difference between Jason's songs and Pete's songs," Paul Adkins explained. "I think there was a slight difference in their approach. I think Jason's very much worried he's not going to do as well as he did on the last album. He's always trying to get a bit better and putting more in. Whereas Pete tends to just throw things down and not want to understand it. I think he's a bit worried about knowing too much about music. He's trying to keep it minimalist, so he doesn't really want to know. He doesn't even want to know the chords he's playing half the time. He'd rather just do it and make it sound like he wants." While Sonic's compositions concentrated on a 'Suicide'-like throb, all lateral pulsations and horizontal rhythms, Jason's songs were, by contrast, vertical spires with spacious echo and buzzing reverb. The medicinal balm of 'Feel So Sad' and 'Sometimes' belied its desperate lyricism, brooding and fatalist when compared to some of Jason's more romantic verses. The first recordings of 'These Blues' (eventually re-recorded and released as a very different version on Spiritualized's *Pure Phase*) at VHF was the pinnacle of Jason's moribund melodicism. Chiming with equal parts 'Come Down Softly To My Soul' and 'Lord Can You Hear Me?', 'These Blues' buzzed with a textured quietness that echoed from the rafters. Buried deep within the swirl, Jason's plaintive vocal sailed heavenward as if locked away in the bowels of an Episcopal chapel.

For all of the compositional differences between their tracks, Sonic renewed his claims of Jason's plagiarism to Gerald and his bandmates. Sonic claimed that his former writing-partner had ripped off a number of effects to a T on several of his demos, including the very same flutter multi-tap reverb that appeared throughout *Playing With Fire*. In addition, Sonic was livid at Jason when he discovered the latter's 'Billy Whizz' – a slang reference to amphetamine – demo, which he claimed to have penned years earlier during the *Sound Of Confusion* sessions. When Sonic confronted Jason about the accused theft, he only turned away in disgust from Sonic with a flippant response: "Prove it!"

Mark walked into the studio with guitar in hand, doubtful of what lay ahead for the day's recordings. He remembered, "I'd get a call one day from Pete saying, 'Oh, do you fancy coming over?' I'd say, 'Yeah' and come over, and then I'd get a call from Jase saying, 'Come on over,' and I would. I thought, 'Wow! This must be what it was like with The Beatles on the White Album, when Paul was doing his tracks and John was doing his, and you'd get a call from one or the other." On the odd day, he walked in to VHF to find Sonic working closely with Will and Jonny on backing tracks, and Mark sat waiting for instruction on what his guitar part would be for the song. He recalls playing various guitar overdubs on

'Set Me Free/I've Got The Key', 'Why Couldn't I See?', 'I Love You', and the Mudhoney cover 'When Tomorrow Hits'. On other days Mark entered the studio to find Jason talking with Will and Jonny, and they'd begin recording tracks and overdubs with a comparable working method. Throughout the sessions, Mark added guitar to 'Drive/Feel So Sad', 'Feelin' Just Fine (Head Full Of Shit)', and 'Billy Whizz/Blue 1'.

Eager to push his songs forward in Jason's absence, Sonic called on Mark to begin collaborating on compositions. Mark was quite keen to take up the role left vacant by Jason, and he attempted to co-compose with Sonic on a number of occasions, working through original material or flushing out incomplete snippets. "I wasn't thinking at the time that I wanted to be assigned a songwriter – I knew I was just a guitarist – but I was really keen to try to contribute and write songs together," Mark said. "I even went over to Pete's house one night. He invited me over and we played loads of records and we tried but it didn't really work out." Although nothing flowered from the Sonic/Refoy co-venture, the symbolism was not lost on anyone, including Mark. "I felt like a bit of a spare part, really," he continued, "because I couldn't really see how I was fitting in with the band or Pete. I heard all these subsequent rumours that Pete just wanted to get Jason out and get another guitarist in." Sonic's first attempt at a working collaboration with someone other than Jason was a sure sign that the damaged relationship was almost certainly irreparable. The divisions were obvious and the two camps were working to recruit the remaining members of the band.

Sonic was becoming increasingly frustrated as his work in the studio began to stall in the face of a splintered rhythm section. He became more demanding, more obsessive toward the instrumentals he seemed to be chasing around in his head. This difficulty translated into an erratic behaviour Sonic aimed towards everyone involved in his side of recording, including the drummer, bassist and guitarist he hoped to convert to his side. As if feeding off Sonic's confusion, Jason plunged head-first into his collection of songs, inviting Mark, Jonny and Will away from Sonic's tyrannical abuses. "I suppose I gravitated towards the Jason camp because Pete was – I hate using the word difficult, because he wasn't if you got on his level – he wasn't difficult, but he could be extraordinarily demanding," Mark said, shrugging. "And if he thought you'd done something right and really well, he'd still say, 'No, you've done it wrong. Do it again.'" Jonny agreed, "I think Pete was really down actually at that point. But he was, ya know, he was being nasty to Mark as well by then. And it's like he was just in a bad frame of mind. He was so messed up he didn't really know what he wanted." Sonic's obsessive behaviour during the sessions would manifest itself in the strangest ways, including odd demands on his rhythm section. Mark recalled Sonic's timing on recordings to be awkward and patently 'off', although he'd insist everyone watch his feet throughout a song to keep time.

Whether or not Sonic's fractious sense of reality was the central impetus for the band's steady demise or simply an effect, everyone in the studio noticed his thinning body and waning concentration. No one confronted Sonic with their suspicions, but it was apparent that his heavy dependence on heroin was contributing to his desperation. Jonny observed the high quantities of drugs floating through 1989 with muted distance. "Pete used to do that sort of thing [heroin] obviously away from me," he said. "I mean I saw Pete roll spliffs and Jason roll some spliffs. Jason would drink more than anything in them days. Did a little bit of smack now and again, ya know. And Pete as well. Pete obviously more than Jason." In actuality, Jason was almost completely drug-free at the time, bingeing on heavy amounts of whiskey and beer but staying clear of anything stronger than innocuous bricks of weed. The differences in their sources of inebriation only furthered the intrinsic distance of their relationship. "I don't know if I would blame it on the drugs. It was more complicated, a growing apart of ideas . . ." Jason ceded. "I guess we were writing about the things that were happening to us," he continued. "But even if you're doing quantities of drugs, that isn't necessarily the most all-encompassing important thing in your life."

Sonic became increasingly private with his usage, after he found he was the last remaining member of the band to flirt with disaster. Jason's descent into the early stages of adolescent alcoholism afforded little sympathy for drug addicts, and Will was mining his own climb from the opium den and into temporary sobriety. Sonic would often excuse himself with kit in hand to VHF's cramped toilet where he would shoot up before, during, or after long afternoons of recording. He was never disingenuous nor did he flaunt his habits among his bandmates, but the burnt caramel aromas wafting from the bathroom was a telltale sign of Sonic's unspoken pleasures. "I mean everybody smoked dope, but Class A's . . . were pretty much kept to themselves," Mark said.

Gerald also contended with Sonic's capriciousness despite being ousted from the inner circle of recording. Paul Adkins phoned Gerald one afternoon in Corby to let him know Sonic was failing to show at the studio at his appointed time. Apparently his absences had become habitual. Gerald was severely non-plussed with the news considering he was footing the studio costs. Sonic and Gerald were hardly on speaking terms. But their volatile relationship peaked during an incident at VHF when Gerald sent down his newest musical acquisition Chapterhouse to begin recording demos for their debut album. When Sonic turned up late in the evening to continue his own recording, he was outraged to find Gerald had filled his slot with these young upstarts from Reading.

> GERALD PALMER: Pete was so completely out of it. Chapterhouse was down there, and they were absolutely in awe of Spacemen 3 and Pete Kember. And Pete turned up and was abusive to them. And they were terrified. Pete was upset because he didn't want them there. And he went into the toilet at VHF, and he shot up and filled the syringe with blood. Then he handed this to Andy Sheriff from Chapterhouse and said, "Give this to Gerald. This is what he wants." I drove over [to the studio], because they were so bloody terrified they didn't want to go back into the studio again.

> SONIC: It was an argument with Gerald. And I said, "If he wants blood, then here it is." That was it. I never had any argument with Chapterhouse at all. I'm sure Gerald thought it was totally nuts. But it was typical of my frustration at the end. It was all just so fucked up I think.

In all, Jason contributed guitar throughout Sonic's list of potential tracks, including lead bits on 'I Love You', 'Set Me Free/I've Got The Key', and 'Why Couldn't I See?', as well as a thundering wah guitar on 'When Tomorrow Hits' and some unfinished work on a 'Repeater'-like track called 'Zoink' (for which the melody-line of Spiritualized's 'Sway' first appeared). Problems worsened when Sonic discovered that Jason was recording most of his tracks without any guitar parts written for him. Although Sonic made a point of including parts for Jason in all his songs, he was livid at what he saw as Jason's attempt to push him out of his recordings. Sonic confronted Jason during a particularly tense day of recording with an idle threat. "Well, we might as well have a side with my songs and a side with your songs," he fumed. Jason responded with surprising vehemence. "Yes, let's do it," he agreed with a half-smile. Suddenly Sonic felt as if he'd unknowingly stepped into a baited trap. He couldn't help wondering when his friend would finally pop the latch and bring the gate crashing down behind him.

"We weren't working as a band, in the studio, together or separately," Jason responded. "The tracks were pretty much recorded separately anyway so it seemed okay to do it on the album," he continued. "I think we got used to hearing it that way." The split was now reified into the whirring spindles of magnetic tape.

Sonic remained flustered with Gerald's continued influence as well, the spectre of which haunted the sessions from Fire Records on down. Sonic claimed there was bone-crunching pressure from Clive Solomon,

Dave Bedford and Paul Adkins to push the recordings into overdrive. He was certain that the hand on the compressor belonged solely to Gerald Palmer. 'Big City' was a repeated source of indecision and re-recording for which he blamed Gerald. The 10-minute electronic track originated in the early part of '89 using a simple four-track recorder. It was one of Sonic's first attempts at melding sequencers and samplers to the "feel" of Ecstasy, an 'un'acid-house composite of *motorik* and The Happy Mondays. But his passion for 'Big City''s experimentation changed when word came down that the heady "dance" track had single potential and radio air-play written all over it. "There was constant pressure from people like Gerald and record companies for something like that," Sonic said. "That's what it ['Big City'] sounded like to me. Like I was just trying to do what people wanted us to do at the record company – sounding more commercial and stuff like that."

"He's quite right," replied Gerald. "There was an element of pressure." Such pressure came in the form of a 'rave 'n roll' craze expanding beyond the confines of London's club scene and the Manchester gig-circuit which had already proselytised staunch guitar-rockers like The Shamen, The Soup Dragons, The Farm, and Primal Scream to the bliss of the dance floor. When promo copies of Andrew Weatherall's 'Loaded' remix – a dub-heavy take on The Scream's 'I'm Losing More Than I'll Ever Have' – began circulating in late '89, the indie bandwagoning officially kicked-off. "There was persuasion there, but ultimately I think Pete did what he wanted," Palmer continued. "The objective of 'Big City' was obviously to sell the new album on the back of its success. And I think Pete would probably freely admit that he didn't co-operate in our objectives."

After several months of recording, Sonic had logged twice or thrice the session time of Jason, but it appeared to those around him that his concentration and product was frustrated and disparate. Tracks like 'Zoink', early demos of 'Touch The Stars' – eventually appearing on Sonic's *Soul Kiss (Glide Divine)* – and a studio version of 'Bo Diddley Jam' were attempted and abandoned. Was Sonic just stumped or intentionally dragging his heels? "Pete was delaying things," according to Gerald. "He probably wasn't aware of what he was doing. But he was constantly ringing me for money. Constantly saying he wasn't able to finish the album. Just the usual drug induced sort of thing really." Jason focused little attention away from his own compositions – demos like 'Feel So Sad' and 'Feelin' Just Fine' had become increasingly spacious pieces with their laminal series of overdubs and edits – but remained very aware of his partner's splintered recordings. "A lot that went down with Spacemen didn't make it to the final mixes, kind of got lost in the production,"

Jason admitted. But in Sonic's defence, much of the confusion stemmed from a rhythm section that had migrated closer and closer to Jason in the interim.

> SONIC: Jason started seeing me as a pain in the ass, and I think he saw the whole feud as a good way to get rid of me. Because I didn't want Kate around on tour, and because I wasn't just gonna split all my songwriting credits with him. He didn't like it that he wasn't getting as many photo sessions. All these things just grated with him, and when he saw the opportunity to get rid of me, he did it.

> MARK REFOY: After getting to know them for a couple of months, I just thought it didn't look as if it was going to last. Not purely because of Pete. Not at all. We were all to blame for not being responsive enough. Pete was desperately eager for it to carry on but only on his terms. Jason would get more out of you by being less dictatorial. I think that's about as diplomatic as I can put it really.

"I wanted to see the band stay together," Will insisted. "I didn't want it to break up, but it's like, you know, if something's spinning really fast it takes one little crack for it to fucking fall apart." Will's last moment of grace came after he received his late '89 royalty cheque from Gerald's office, the amount of which he described as "buttons". After slaving away in Spacemen 3 for more than a year, travelling for months at a time, earning and kicking a small heroin habit, and composing one beautiful bass line after another over two albums, Will was ready to call it quits. "I think the final straw was my royalty cheque. I was living on nothing," he claimed. Will turned up at The Imperial one evening in September to catch Sonic opening solo for the visiting Telescopes. "That was Sonic's first show on his own," recalled the Telescopes' Stephen Lawrie. "We had Jason's front room as our backstage area. Everyone in Rugby turned out for it: The Darkside, Spacemen 3, Willie Carruthers, everybody." The Spacemen bassist stood at the bar after the gig downing one drink after the next in a fit of desperation. Pat Fish swung by to catch the show and was shocked to see Will in such hysterics. "He just wigged right out," Fish claimed. "It's just extreme pressure. But I remember at the end of The Spacemen he had one of those nights. Really just yelling and being unapproachable. There were just so many fault lines by then." Will ran into the toilet and rammed his head through the stall door, before someone from behind the bar grabbed him and hurled him out onto the street. "It was out of frustration with Pete, who was generally being a prat at this stage," said Jonny.

Will trudged back into the studio to complete work on 'When

Tomorrow Hits', his last memory of the band recording in its entirety. Jason and Sonic agreed to enter the studio together to work the song out live. But even with a temporary truce between his two best mates, Will left VHF for the last time and did not deign to look back. The atmosphere was such a shambles, hardly anybody noticed that he'd gone. By the time the real axe fell on Spacemen 3, Will was scrounging to pay off his debts by lugging bricks at a construction site.

By the time of Will's departure, the excitement revolving around the 'When Tomorrow Hits' cover had also become moot, as the Sub Pop connection rapidly unfurled. The trouble began when Sub Pop posted a copy of Mudhoney's cover of 'Revolution' to The Spacemen for their approval. Although the guitar/bass/drums remained faithful to the original version with subtle grunge variation, and Mark Arm's vocal possessed an interesting composite of Sonic's British drawl and a laconic J. Mascis style, the problem arose with the change in lyrics. As Mark Arm explained, "When we were going into the studio to record that song we stumbled upon some *Melody Maker* article where it sounded like Pete was advocating some junkie revolution in the streets. And the whole idea of an army of junkies getting off the nod and rising up and walking through the streets just seemed so absurd and funny."

As a last-minute tongue-in-cheek stab at Sonic, Arm altered the verses from a Detroit '69 rallying cry into a parodist slap at heroin addiction. Arm mused with a half-hearted, "I'm tired/ So tired/ Of getting up in the morning/ For that long uphill walk/ To the methadone clinic/ There's gotta be an easier way . . ." to the swell of swampy distortion. "Now hold on a second/ This burnin'/ There's a change comin'/ My blackened spoon/ I suggest to you,/ That it takes five seconds/ Just five seconds/ To put a morphine suppository/ All the way inside . . ." was a particularly gruesome image of an addict's literal anal retention.

Far from reacting with knee-slapping laughter to Mudhoney's razz, Sonic found their version of 'Revolution' churlish and offensive. Even Jason reacted with disdain at Mark Arm's poor jocularity. Finally something the two could agree on. When Arm received word through Jonathan Poneman at Sub Pop of their disgusted reaction, he was miffed and embarrassed. "I mean, at the time, I wasn't even thinking how it would affect those guys," Mark admitted. "I was just a young dumb kid. And I thought it was funny – I mean, like me and my group of friends – and these guys were probably gonna get the joke." Guitarist Steve Turner was furious with Sonic and Jason's reactions, dismissing the whole lot of the band as dour, humourless sods. He wanted nothing to do with them.

After the split-single melee, and despite the residual feelings of hostility between The Spacemen and Mudhoney, Sub Pop proceeded with plans to release a series of "non single club" releases of new Spacemen 3 material. Offers flowed back and forth over the terms and numbers of releases, until both sides stalemated on what was acceptable. "They wanted us to provide them with four exclusive tracks – for no fee I must add. And upon my assertion that we could give them one exclusive track and two different versions, they suggested we go in the studio and trot out a few MC5 rip-offs," Sonic said, similarly unimpressed with both the Sub Pop execs and the Sub Pop bands. "I'm pleased to say we kept our honour and went our separate ways," he continued.

Sonic's cover arrangement of 'When Tomorrow Hits' was already in the recording stages when the Mudhoney DAT appeared at VHF. The decision was made to retain the cover for the upcoming album in spite of the falling out, although Sonic's purposes for doing so were more for spite than tribute. Mark Arm was perplexed when he received a promotional flexi of the cover months later, only to be astounded with what Sonic had done with his track. "I remember reading an interview where Pete was just like really pissed off at us and said like, 'We'll show them. We're going to do a better version of their song than they did.' And they might have. I think their version is absolutely brilliant," admitted Arm.

At the conclusion of October, Silvertone released Sonic Boom's first solo single 'Angel' b/w 'Help Me Please' to muted plaudits from both the press and Spacemen 3 followers. No one was singularly emphatic about the song choice or the cold response, least of all Sonic himself. The Dedicated contract had now been on the table in various forms for months, and Jason spoke just enough to Sonic to inform him he wasn't going to sign it. Sonic threw up his hands in disgust. He needed money, and the advance from the signing would have afforded him and Jason well over 50 grand apiece. No one mentioned the money to Jonny or Mark. It was all to be split between Sonic, Jason, and Gerald. But if Jason refused to sign, there was no major-label deal and no money.

While Sonic remained in the frazzled stages of overdubbing and sequencing, Jason neared completion of his side of the album with rough mixes already in the can. "I used more time than Jason, but only because I had more work to do and more songs to complete," defended Sonic. "Jason was having his own problems being indecisive, because he knew he had a very 'samey' sounding group of songs." In fact, Jason's dissatisfaction with his mixes led him to pull his DATs from Rugby and remix them at London's Battery Studios. Ironically, free use of the professional Brent studio had been offered by Andrew Lauder as a gratuity to Sonic after his *Spectrum* recordings. But when the closeted musician, who was hibernating at VHF, passed on a migration down to Battery, Jason took advantage by enlisting its "house" engineer Anjali Dutt to tighten up his original mixes. Dutt – who was embroiled in My Bloody Valentine's *Loveless* tragicomedy at Falconer's Kentish Town studio and would go on to engineer sessions with The Jesus and Mary Chain, Swervedriver, and The Boo Radleys – was to render a pearlescent ambience to Jason's recordings, exaggerating his use of ultra-deep echo, heavily reverbed fuzz and phased tones, all of which bore uncanny similarities to Sonic's own work at VHF.

As Anjali and Jason beavered away at remixing what would be side two of *Recurring*, side one was far from complete. Sonic's obsessive personality and ambitious production had made him a constant presence at the Arches Lane unit. He was beside himself with indecision, having spent long nights alone in the studio trying to complete one recording after another. VHF became the laboratory of a mad alchemist whose experiments were popping and fizzing from the mixing board along the surface of his own viscera. "I think in some ways maybe it was better that the band split up, because I'm not sure it was going in any good direction at that point," Sonic confessed. His closest mate Will had said little before exiting the band, and Jonny and Mark were as good as gone. "I can remember once being in a record store with Pete, and Jonny Mattock jumped up from the other side of a record shelf and said 'hello'," said Pat Fish. "And Sonic had a pop at him. And he who has a pop at Jonny Mattock is having a pop against life." Jonny was as fed up with Sonic's erratic behaviour as everyone else. "Who wants to be in a band with somebody like that?" he mused.

'Radiological Shock, Or . . . Rock'n'Roll Is Killing My Life'

The DREAMWEAPON wants only what it wants.

The DREAMWEAPON is the oscillation of desire . . .

SPIRITUALIZED
March 2002
Numbers Club, Houston, Texas

Spiritualized opened a two-hour set with an effecting "white noise" intro/'Shine A Light'/'Electric Mainline' triptych to a perspiring crowd of collegiates crammed into the rickety nucleus of a Houston club. Ever the pedestrian, Jason shoegazes to the side of his rhythm section, his body limp against a guitar and greased locks flowing down over his arched brow. While the night's rendition of 'Shine A Light' exudes the most lazy and sun-stroked warmth of The Beach Boys, Pink Floyd, and J. J. Cale, the echolalic tones of 'Electric Mainline' invoke an alien chill precipitated by the spiralling intensity of buzzing strobes.

Standing near the rear entrance of the club, and with bursts of muscular apoplexy and indigestion bubbling into my throat, I shut my eyes tightly against the fizzing halogen lamps. Enduring the psychotropy that threatened to microwave my brain – like old family snapshots that burn bright and dissolve in a puff of silver nitrate – what remained was a foggy notion of absolute terror and paralysis that hovered somewhere onstage. Something, an apparition most likely, sauntered up from behind and tickled my spine, travelling with "sonic-boom" rapidity up the hollow passageways and to the blinking arcade housed in my skull. My eyes popped open with a start, pupils engorged as if to swallow the iris alive. Everything was moist with fear. From the din of Jason's treated guitar and the threadbare organ drones, a radiophonic phantom had reached out from the cartilaginous circuit of amplifiers and burned a great hole through the crowd. I had sweated through the same holocaust dozens, if not hundreds of times, since ingesting a violent mix of hallucinogens some years before. I was, in fact, a casualty of a new kind of lightning war.

256

I hobbled to the rear-exit just as Jason cranked his six-string into a blinding version of Spacemen 3's 'Take Me To The Other Side' and the irony was not lost on me. The Earth spun itself out onto the footpath where I bent down to vomit – dry-heaving of little consolation – before pushing out into the traffic. My destination was the infirmary.

I remain a devout Spacemen 3 fan.

CHAPTER ELEVEN
Phase Me Out Gently

WINTER 1989–1991

"I remember the date, it was the 14th of November," recalled Jonny. "There was a meeting round at Jason's flat on Hunter Street to discuss doing some more live dates and finishing the new album."

"Gerald Palmer phoned me up and told me to get over to this meeting at Jason's flat," recalled Mark Refoy. "Pete was late as usual, so I think we were all round Jason's flat waiting for him. Pete arrived and he started telling us, 'We've got a lot more work to do. This is just the start of Spacemen 3.' Then there was just silence – people were very afraid of speaking to Pete, like telling him they didn't agree with him – and it might have been Jonny who started the subject of Pete being difficult to work with."

Jonny continued, "I just got up and said, 'What's happening with this band, ya know?' – I remember that phrase – 'What's going on?!' Pete and Jason weren't talking to each other at the meeting. . . . It was just kinda bizarre. We kind of arranged to get together to just say nothing and disband. It was very odd, very strange, like breaking up with your girl-friend except you had nothing to say. Pete hardly said anything at the meeting. He didn't say, 'Let's keep the band together.' It's like he didn't want it to happen either. He was waiting for somebody to say something, but nobody said anything."

"Pete really upset Jonny and Jonny just walked out," Mark continued. "Then he looked toward me and said something about me being a 'true fan'. I said, 'I am a true fan, Pete, but I agree with Jonny because you are difficult. What can we do?' Then he said, 'I didn't realise you had an opinion about it as well.' So I got up and said, 'Well, I don't think I'm really needed anymore, am I?' I turned around to Jason and said, 'I'll see you then,' and Pete thought I was talking to him, so he said, 'Eh, doubt it.' Jason waved goodbye and me and Jonny left and went back to Northampton."

"So me and Mark went back on the train to Northampton," Jonny said. "The band was broke up as far as we were concerned because nobody said anything. There were no good vibes."

"We both realised that we'd either been kicked out of the band or Spacemen 3 was going to split up for good," surmised Mark. "It was all in Pete and Jason's court. They were left together to talk things out."

"They said I had too much say and *blah blah blah*," contended Sonic. "They said I had to accept Mark's songs, that if he was into the song, then we had to do it. I told them, 'I'm sorry. I've been doing this fucking 10 years, and you guys just walked in. And just because it's successful, you want to take it over as your own thing.' Mark's thing was that he was gonna write songs and I had to accept it and I refused."

"I heard later that Pete believed that I split up the band, but I think that's stretching it a bit," responded Mark. "But maybe I should have stepped out of the way to let them sort it out – not that it had anything to do with me – but I think they just needed to sit back and stop doing things for a while. They'd been working together constantly since 1982 and I think Jase – with Kate – might have been pulled in different directions than Pete."

"Mark was the spokesman that day," acknowledged Sonic, "and I very much felt he was responsible for a lot of it."

"Pete really got in above his depth is what I would say at this stage," explained Gerald. "I think Pete realised he was the one being frozen out and isolated by everybody else – including me. He was out on a limb. The king had been deposed. I managed to keep everything together for a while. I persuaded them to keep it together to a point where it was impossible for Jason to be with Pete anymore."

During the last days of the year – when the Christmas season and the dawn of the new decade had shone most brightly in the tiny gulch of Rugby – Gerald prepared to leave his Corby offices to take a holiday when he received a frantic phone call from Sonic. According to Palmer, The Spacemen guitarist was livid with his bandmates' evident resignations and defections to what he saw as an increasingly Machiavellian Jason Pierce. In a complete reversal-of-fortune, Spacemen 3's estranged impresario was now the only hand Sonic had left to play. "Pete rang me with all sorts of threats," Gerald explained. "He said, 'I want you to sack the other members: Mark, Jonny and Jason. I'm going to be Spacemen 3, and I'm going to recruit whoever I want.' It would have been easy to get new members. There would have been a queue of people we could have taken on. And Spacemen 3 would have been Pete with three or four other people hanging on his coat-tails. That was Pete's intention. That's what Pete wanted."

Palmer scrunched his forehead slightly and rubbed the beads of sweat from his brow as he listened intently to his "former" client. Sonic spelled out his exact plan for the future of The Spacemen. "I want to sack the band," Sonic reiterated. "I want to be Spacemen 3. And you're back on board. You can manage me." When he'd finished spilling his sizzling innards, Palmer lit in with his own version of the perceived tirade. "Over my dead body Pete. You're not Spacemen 3," Gerald repeated condescendingly into the receiver. "Absolutely not! You're not going to be Spacemen 3, and I'm not going to be back on board. It'll only work if you and Jason want it. Otherwise, you're not going to be Spacemen 3."

"I never asked Gerald to do any sacking of anybody," exhorted Sonic of Gerald's claim. "For him to say that I phoned him up to sack Jonny and Mark is absolute rubbish. That wasn't the way I worked at all. I always dealt with everyone myself. The only people who signed any contract with Gerald were me and Jason. Anyone else was totally peripheral. Gerald always made that absolutely clear to all of them: Jonny, Mark and Will. Blatantly. His whole claim is absolute bullshit!"

Although Jason or Sonic would emphatically declare the contrary, Gerald was shocked at the celerity of the band's complete disintegration. The disputed conversation between himself and Sonic proved a clarion call for Palmer that Spacemen 3 was approaching its final days. "Until Pete rang me that day, I did not realise how serious it had become – that they had totally broken down forever," he claimed. For the first time since his unofficial dismissal from Sonic and Jason's trust, Gerald reasserted his position as financial confidant.

His first act was a vain attempt to bring his two clients back to some mutual understanding; an endeavour that proved impossible as Jason refused any contact with his former mate. Serving as a messenger and diplomat between them, Gerald made afternoon visits to Sonic's estate in Dunchurch before moonlighting at Jason's cramped one-bedroom flat in Rugby.

"There were several meetings between Jason and me with Gerald in the middle," confirmed Sonic. "He tried to mediate between us . . . the whole thing was quite funny, because the band was already fucked by then." Sonic's seeming capriciousness had alienated not only Jason, Will, Jonny and Mark, but continued to irk Gerald despite his financial dedication to Spacemen 3's best interests.

What resulted in the meetings during 1989's closing days was the final devastation of Palmer and Kember's relationship. Gerald couldn't help but be drawn to Jason's whingeings and frustrations as he exorcised seven years of living under Sonic's rather cold shadow. While his ambassadorship continued in name, Gerald found himself looking toward Jason with the preferential care of a client and friend. Conversely, Jason saw in Gerald the vaguest glints of a paternal figure.

Negotiations between BMG/Dedicated and Spacemen 3 had dawdled for months when the contract finally appeared to be in the offing. "Spacemen 3 were the coolest band around at the end of '89," explained Gerald. "And it was a period when labels were spending far too much money. The advances were too big, the recording budgets were too big, it was ridiculous. And it was in that environment that we were able to manipulate the situation to get a great deal from Dedicated." The band's tattered relationship, following the resignations of Will Carruthers, Jonny Mattock and Mark Refoy, continued to be kept private, when Gerald requested a final change to D'Arcy's five album, multi-million dollar offer, including an advance cheque of £60,000 on signing. Working the lines between Sonic, Jason, and Dedicated, Gerald and his lawyers amended the conventional Leaving Members Clause from the record company's offer. "The Leaving Member Clause said quite clearly that, in the event that the band folds, the label can opt to choose from whoever signed the agreement – in this case it was only two – to become the band," explained Palmer. A standard inclusion in most prolix record contracts, allowing labels to hold on to a band's most talented members, the Leaving Members Clause also provided Dedicated with the power to recoup their investment should Spacemen 3 break up. "I went over that contract with a fine tooth comb," Palmer stated. "I had my lawyers work on it to the tune of over £15,000 making sure there was no possible loopholes.

"Essentially, they both could have their independent parallel careers," Gerald explained. "So there would be Spacemen 3 and then Pete Kember a.k.a Spectrum and Jason Pierce who would eventually be Spiritualized. It was conceivable that there would be three entities operating in parallel." Denying any insinuation that he was already aware of Jason's intentions for the future, Gerald insisted the provision was only amended to allow Pierce the same solo opportunities that Kember had with Silvertone. "Because Pete had got a solo career going, Jason wanted to be treated exactly the same," Gerald insisted. But while Jason remained aware of Palmer's tactical decisions toward Spacemen 3, Sonic was once again oblivious to his shenanigans. Was it a financial conspiracy or the guitarist's ill-timed narcotism?

All the fogged suspicions and ineluctable innuendo were revealed during a final three-way meeting when Gerald and Jason finally presented Sonic with an ultimatum for closing the Dedicated deal. "The whole thing became that Jason refused to sign the contract with RCA – we were going to stiff them for £60,000 – until I signed a partnership agreement," Sonic detailed. The partnership agreement was drafted by Gerald and Jason to work in conjunction with the Dedicated contract to cement the future of Spacemen 3 permanently. "The agreement said Jason owned half the name Spacemen 3," Sonic continued. "Even though this was the name I fucking came up with. So Jason and Gerald foisted it on me, blackmailing me with the Dedicated advance money to get me to sign it." It was with crafty resolve that Gerald literally dangled the agreement in one hand and a £25,000 cheque in the other, while a slobbering Sonic looked at his dwindling drug coffers and suddenly saw them replenished in a flash. "In the end, when I decided to sign it, I told Gerald and Jason to get fucked," said Sonic. "I signed it because the band was finished anyway. But I told them at that moment there was no looking back." With the sagacity of Solomon, Gerald had split the carcass of The Spacemen in half.

"The partnership agreement was to protect both parties," Gerald claimed. "I don't really remember any desire on Jason's part to take the name Spacemen 3. This was to protect them against each other. They both agreed to sign. And they both signed independently. They were both given independent advice. I can't think of any reason that Pete wouldn't want to sign it except to shaft me and Jason. Because, by signing it, it protected both of their interests. It meant that they were joined as a business as Spacemen 3."

"It got really silly," Sonic continued. "Everything had to be 50/50 everywhere. Didn't matter who did what. Everything had to be half and half."

Tensions reached the breaking point between Jason and Sonic, boiling over into physical desperation. Following a night spent drinking heavily with Jason at his flat, Jonny awoke the next morning to find Sonic screaming at Jason out on the street. Jason had risen early and popped down to the garage for a pint of milk, when Sonic swerved his mini onto the pavement and lunged at Jason. "I heard this screech of brakes and looked out the window, and there's fucking Pete shouting abuse at Jason on the street," Jonny claimed. "It was like Pete was just in a rage, cruising round looking for Jason." Sonic's logorrheic bitterness over the partnership agreement failed to phase a stoic Jason who stared at his former partner in stunned silence. Infuriated at his muted apathy, Sonic swung at Jason, before grabbing a large chunk of his slimy, matted hair between his fingers and ripping it from the roots. Sonic sped off, leaving Jason to stare at the fibrous clump littering the pavement. Jonny stood in rapt attention when Jason walked back inside. "Look what happened," Jason said, holding up the greasy brown clump. "What the fuck is going on?!"

"I tried my best to patch things up after that," said Palmer. "And Jason was adamant that it was over. Finished. Completely over." In one last desperate attempt to rein in the band, Gerald claims that Sonic broke down soon after his assault on Jason, imploring Palmer to mend what had occurred. In tears, Sonic demanded his former management not be the cause of the band's demise. Gerald looked towards his client with an unsympathetic retort: "I'm not, Pete. You're the one that destroyed it." Tales of aggression proliferated from Rugby via the small town rumour mill. A particularly savage fable had Sonic attacking Jason one evening and hurling him down a flight of stairs. But Sonic claims on the night in question he and Jason were not even together. As he understood the story, Jason had spent the night at former Protest drummer Robbie Smith's house drinking heavily until he tripped over himself and down the stairs, cracking a rib.

Pete Kember and Jason Pierce appeared separately at the Dedicated offices in London to ink their first contract with a major. A sacred moment for any struggling group of musicians who've finally arrived, Kember and Pierce were unusually solemn under the beaming eyes of Doug D'Arcy. Pete wandered into the offices early in the afternoon, sporting gargantuan, "fly-boy" shades that covered his sallow face and seemed to hide any recognisable expression. He disappeared quickly into the city's bustling traffic before Jason, with Kate and Gerald in tow, drifted in for the same bathetic ritual.

A few evenings afterwards, Doug D'Arcy and his entourage of personal assistants and close associates met his newest clients for a celebratory dinner in the small village of Lutterworth, just on the outskirts of Rugby. "I suppose the evening was a bit of a charade in some respects," Gerald confessed. "Because Pete was kind of *persona non grata* for the rest of us, excluding Doug who wasn't aware of the events that had happened." Palmer met the Dedicated crew at a formal Chinese restaurant near the M1 at eight o'clock on the dot, bantering and toadying as everyone stared towards the foyer for Jason and Sonic's belated appearance. Gerald openly exhaled with deep relief when Jason and Kate popped through the door and made their way around the large clothed table. Another half-hour passed before Sonic finally sauntered in, crouching down opposite Jason and without so much as a glance. With everyone in place, Gerald wiped his brow and smiled at his two recruits.

"I don't remember much that night," Sonic admitted. "I was fairly out of my head at the time, but I don't think Jason or I even ate." Instead, D'Arcy and Palmer discussed future plans for The Spacemen, while Sonic chain-smoked cigarettes and charmingly razzed the Dedicated boss. Jason refused to look toward Sonic, but answered D'Arcy with muffled, staccato replies. "We were there for two or three hours – Pete and Jason were sitting on opposite sides," continued Gerald. "I don't think they talked to each other, but they didn't say anything bad about each other. Pete was very entertaining and very articulate, while Jason was very taciturn. So the combination of that was just more of the same."

"They went their separate ways after dinner," Gerald added. "Doug went back to London and I went home. It was the last formal gathering." The final hoax behind them, Palmer received Dedicated's cheque, which he divided between himself and his two clients. Sonic and Jason absconded with £24,000 each, leaving Palmer with his 20 per cent cut, £12,000. Like a den of thieves, they each packed up their loot and parted company. Will Carruthers, Jonny Mattock and Mark Refoy were not offered a penny.

"I would have split it with all of them," said Sonic, "but after they fucked off from Spacemen 3, I told Jason he could split his half with them. Of course, he never did."

With the success of the recording deal behind him, Gerald convinced D'Arcy to purchase additional U.S. licensing rights for the upcoming album – tentatively entitled *Recurring* – to be distributed through RCA. Certain that *Recurring* would be Spacemen 3's breakthrough LP, and would prologue their successful tenure with BMG/Dedicated, D'Arcy once again proved unaware of the upcoming album's steady decline into detritus. By February of 1990, while Jason had exited Battery Studies with final mixes of his songs in the can, Sonic slaved away aimlessly without any sign of completion. Having been abandoned by Will, Jonny and Mark, the guitarist logged many solitary evenings in the stoned vapours of recording and remixing. "Pete was dragging his heels," Gerald asserted, "after he was given a ridiculous amount of time. I gave one ultimatum after another to finish, and he wouldn't."

"It was around that time Jason got me, Jonny and Will in to VHF to record 'Anyway That You Want Me'," Mark claimed. "I think this was even before we officially started Spiritualized and I know that we were meant to keep it hush-hush." Jason and his new cadre of best mates had entered the studio surreptitiously in the last days of winter to begin "jamming" on ideas for a new group. The seeds of Spiritualized had actually been conceived following Mark and Jonny's exit from Hunter Street the previous November. Convinced that their roles in Spacemen 3 had ended, Mark moved to London, and Jonny began looking for other gigs in Northamptonshire while maintaining contact with Jason. For his part, Will had moved from the "glamour" of gigging to the mind-numbing world of manual labour.

"We all figured it was over at the end of that November meeting," Mark continued, "and I didn't really expect to hear anything after." Jason approached Will during the first month of the new year in hopes of recruiting his talents, but the bassist was completely uninterested in re-entering the world from which he had just absconded. "Is it going to be a real band or are we just going to be your fucking stooges?" Will demanded of the guitarist. Jason responded with an emphatic reply, "It's going to be totally democratic." After much scepticism, Will assented, and Jason phoned Jonny and Mark in London. "I want to carry on with another band, and it won't be Spacemen 3," Jason explained to Mark. Refoy and Mattock agreed on the spot and Spiritualized began to take shape even as Sonic still struggled with the death-throes of Spacemen 3.

Within a week of Jason's recruitment everyone congregated at a small church hall in Rugby for the first rehearsals before moving over to Hunter Street. "It was a beautiful time," Jonny remembered. "The band still wasn't definite. It was just a jam. We were practising in Jason's spare room, and we had to keep it quiet because of the neighbours so I put T-shirts over the drums. We were just experimenting. We wanted to do a new sort of thing." The familiar arrangements between musicians made the inclusion of 'Anyway That You Want Me' appear less insidious than might have been Jason's intention. Left unused during the *Playing With Fire* sessions, Jason revisited his version with the intention of re-recording it. "We were also listening to The Troggs' version when we were rehearsing and I was trying to get a grip on the drum track," Jonny continued. 'Anyway That You Want Me' served as Spacemen 3's crowning epitaph and a final musical bond between Jason and Sonic yet to be severed.

"In Spacemen 3 we were all playing the same minimal riff, but with Spiritualized we played five different riffs – it's further forward, higher," Jason explained of Spiritualized's earliest philosophy. "We just didn't want to tread water and remain where we were, which would have been easy to do, because people would have bought into it. There's always people out there that don't accept progress."

"After we'd been rehearsing for a while, Jason said he was thinking of calling our new band Synesthesia," Mark claimed. "We turned up to rehearse later on and he had decided on Spiritualized instead and everyone thought it was a good name. Everyone just thought the name befit him."

"Mark's recollection is right," Jonny responded. "There was also a bottle of Pernod that we were drinking and on the label was something like 'Spiriteuse' that might have given Jason the idea."

"Jason telephoned me again around February and told me that he'd decided to start a new band called Spiritualized," Gerald recalled. "He was ready and I was on-board."

Sonic frantically phoned Richard Formby in hopes of recruiting his help to finish what he was unable to complete alone. Formby had just returned to the UK from a month-long US tour playing guitar for The Jazz Butcher when he got the call. Between producing The Telescopes, proto-shoegazers Pale Saints, and Cud at his Leeds studio, Formby was on the lookout for work and was thrilled with Sonic's invitation. "Pete came up to Leeds for the day and we jammed about on a few ideas," Formby remembered. "He asked me to help him finish his side of *Recurring* as the rest of The Spacemen had deserted him. I didn't know the exact details of the split between Pete and Jason. All I knew is that Pete was halfway through the album and he was having nothing to do with Jason.

"The sessions for *Recurring* and the start of the sessions for Spectrum's *Soul Kiss (Glide Divine)* were a bit blurred," Richard continued. "In fact, Pete had one or two pieces – 'Touch The Stars' was one – that may have been included on *Recurring* if they had been completed in time." The January 1990 release of Sonic Boom's *Spectrum*, following on the heels of the 'Angel' 12″, was met with muted approbation from record buyers and critics. With the LP's collectible opto-kinetic sleeve and Silvertone's own indie cache, *Spectrum* remained little more than a blip between the fervour surrounding Silvertone's hottest act, The Stone Roses, and the forthcoming Spacemen 3 album. Despite *Spectrum*'s lukewarm reception, Lauder agreed to pick up the option for a second Sonic Boom solo LP. "Instead of it being another solo record, he wanted to form a new band and have this second Silvertone release as the band's debut," Formby explained. "So he gave me half the advance he had been given, and I was on-board."

When Richard walked into VHF Studios days later, he was shocked at the amount of incomplete tracks and rehearsal tapes that littered the soundboard. Sonic and Richard embarked on a marathon, week-long recording session. They began by completing recording of the prolix 'Big City', upon which the former added some final keyboard overdubs and the latter bits of guitar. Formby also contributed guitar to 'I Love You' and a lengthy nine-minute version of 'Set Me Free/I've Got The Key' (much of which was faded during mastering). "Pete and I literally started 'Why Couldn't I See?' and 'Set Me Free (Reprise)' all over from scratch," Formby claimed. Overflowing with both melody and melancholia, Sonic strained to add his vocal overdubs with tongue firmly planted in cheek. 'Why Couldn't I See?' and 'Set Me Free (Reprise)' contained the songwriter's most castigating love letters to his estranged bandmate and friend. "You took my heart/ And you tore it to pieces/ You gave me love/ And then quickly retreated . . ." Sonic bleats over mantric guitar and sundry throbbing effects before implicating himself with equal vehemence, "Why couldn't I see?/ Oh why?/ Oh why couldn't I see?/ Oh why? Oh why?" Likewise, the bloated swell of catharsis and *rigor mortis* pervades the acoustic 'Set Me Free (Reprise)' as Sonic concludes with a prescient chuckle, "I think it's gonna end pretty soon . . ."

Pat Fish came from Northampton to add some flute overdubs to 'I Love You' but found the situation tense and Sonic's countenance wracked with a mix of confusion and ire. What was to be a simple flute solo took hours, as Fish withstood Sonic's barbed invectives and befuddled demands. "I had a very unpleasant time," Fish confessed. "Sonic would get insanely specific about what he wanted me to play, without ever actually revealing what that might be. It's like he had it down in his head, but the only way he could tell me if I was getting it or not was if it was off and he'd tell me that it was wrong." Fish literally blistered his lips and rubbed his cheek raw on the aperture before Sonic announced he'd gotten the take correct.

With Sonic still holed up at VHF in the midst of mixing and remixing his songs for *Recurring*, Gerald booked vacant time with Paul Adkins to smuggle Spiritualized into the studio. "I did not see Jason once during the *Recurring* sessions," confirmed Richard Formby. When Mark Refoy re-entered the studio to begin recording with Jason, he was surprised to see bits of Sonic and Richard Formby's gear lying around the control room as if they exited only minutes before. "Jason went in before The Spacemen album was finished," confirmed Adkins, "to record 'Anyway That You Want Me' but it was definitely booked as Spiritualized. It was itemised separately by Gerald." Adkins was hard-pressed to work scheduling magic to prevent Sonic and Jason from inadvertently crossing paths in the studio. "They had to be scheduled at separate times," Adkins added, "because there was one occasion when they did show up at the same time and ended up nearly scrapping in reception." The reality was a bit more insidious: while Sonic was aware Jason was recording separately with his ex-bandmates, he had only the vaguest knowledge of a new band appearing on the horizon. "When Jason booked time at VHF to do 'Anyway That You Want Me', he never said, 'Oh don't tell Pete!'" explained Mark. "But after we'd been in a couple of times and Pete wasn't around, it was just sort of understood. I think Jason didn't want Pete to know because it was something that was extra-curricular. I don't know if it was premeditated on Jason's behalf."

"We were at VHF laying the track down and the recording session was very laid-back with lots of friends hanging out and playing along," said Jonny of 'Anyway That You Want Me''s recording. In fact, the pacific calm inside VHF only resulted from Adkins' decision to cancel all of Sonic's booking times in order to please Jason and Gerald. When he phoned Adkins for more studio time at VHF, Sonic received word that the studio had been sold for lack of funds. "Of course, it was a lie," Sonic pointed out. "It turned out to be Jason recording 'Anyway That You Want Me'." The guitarist had been effectively excommunicated from VHF. "At a certain point, Jason and Pete both wanted to block book the studio so the other one couldn't get in," Adkins admitted. "And it just got to a silly point where neither of them would give the other one any sort of let-up, and I was playing piggy in the middle."

"Pete's recordings had already dragged on interminably," defended Gerald. "He obviously had demands of his own and he needed to fuel those needs. But I wanted to get the album done as soon as possible." As one deadline after the next came and went without response, Gerald finally placed a call to Sonic with one last ultimatum: "Either finish mixing the tracks yourself, or I'll do it for you," he demanded. Unfazed by Palmer's officious threat, Sonic continued work at VHF, until Gerald appeared at the studio one afternoon and collected all of the recordings. "Pete had numerous mixes, like 20 or 30 mixes of some songs – certainly double figures anyway – and he just refused to pick his final mixes," said Palmer incredulously. "So I chose for him." In fact, the various edits, versions, mixes and remixes of 'Big City', 'Just To See You Smile' and 'Set Me Free' had become so numerous and subtle only Sonic could detect the negligible differences. Such excessive detailing lent the increasing technophile the schizophrenic aura of a necromancer haunted by dead voices.

"I finally chose the mixes of Pete's tracks," contested Gerald, "and, of course, when it was finished, he said they were the wrong ones. When I asked him which mixes were right, he couldn't answer me."

"I wanted the laughter in 'Set Me Free/I've Got The Key' between all the tracks, which is a point of contention," said Sonic in a 1991 *Catalogue* interview. "I've always sequenced them and put the right gaps between songs but they [Gerald and Fire Records] cut the album behind my back. It's been done badly and it was seamed together wrong."

"As for Gerald Palmer, we've lost count of the number of times he was sacked, or whether he ever was sacked," responded Fire's Dave Bedford in a 1991 interview. "But we did the deal through his management company, so we're responsible to him. If Gerald didn't deliver the masters or administer the cut, it wouldn't get done."

It was well past February when Gerald Palmer phoned the Dedicated offices to verify the rumours that had since reached Doug D'Arcy. "Gerald really strung them along for ages," confirmed Sonic. "We were all sworn to secrecy not to announce anything up until the very end." A delegation of the Dedicated staff, including D'Arcy, assistant Karen Brown, and BMG lawyer Steve Firney appeared at the door of Palmer's Northamptonshire home within days of the announcement. Any illusory trace of British restraint evaporated when Gerald dryly stated all of the sad facts before them. "I had to tell them the painful truth, which was not very palatable," laughed Palmer. "And, in addition, because there was no Leaving Members Clause in the contract, if they wanted Jason as a solo artist that would have to pay again." With aid from BMG's corporate panoply, the entirety of Dedicated's legal team spent days scanning for loopholes amid their own contract's legalese. "They did everything they could to look through all the small print," added Gerald, "but it was over."

Despite working in the same studio throughout the beginning of 1990, the first official word of Spiritualized's existence did not reach Sonic until the release of the 'Anyway That You Want Me' 12" from Dedicated in June. "Spiritualized weren't signed to Dedicated at the time," said Jason, "but I finished 'Anyway That You Want Me' and told them they could put it out. Spacemen hasn't been on tour for a year, and didn't look likely to, so Spiritualized needed some product to go out on tour." It was after much cajoling that Gerald was able to renegotiate Spacemen 3's collapse in Spiritualized's favour. Jason had already instructed Palmer to begin shopping for another label deal, and with his usual acumen, Palmer delivered a line of A&R men to the guitarist's door. After the litigious threats subsided from Dedicated and BMG, Doug D'Arcy was resolved to score something from the Spacemen 3 fiasco even if he had to pay through the nose. With other major labels like Elektra throwing large coffers of cash towards Spiritualized, RCA/Dedicated ultimately proposed to "re-sign" their previous client to yet another six-figure contract. "We had several other offers, but Jason was very generous and gracious to Dedicated," Gerald explained. "He was under no compulsion to, but Jason liked Dedicated and Doug at that time so he decided to stay." As for the exact amounts, in total that Dedicated poured into both the Spacemen 3 and Spiritualized agreements, Palmer would only admit, "They spent a small fortune."

The sense of mutual admiration and fidelity between label and act ended with Jason. Spiritualized's supporting cast was more suspicious of Dedicated's managing director, prompted in part by Jason's decision to put the band on retainer. D'Arcy's patronising attitude failed to bring the rest of Spiritualized into his fold. Lounging behind his large mahogany desk in a finely pressed Versace suit, Will found his new boss to be particularly despicable. When the bassist and Jason brought a copy of 'Anyway That You Want Me' to the Dedicated offices in London, D'Arcy's first response was, "I like it, but could you put some more guitars on it or something?" Slighted by a "suit", Will shot back, "Who the fuck is this dick?! Look, man, why don't you get a band together and do it yourself!" For Will, Mark and Jonny the pleasure of music making continued to far outweigh the nuts and bolts of marketing and finance.

"Everything had really started to change by then," Will explained. "Major labels like RCA started to see that indie-rock was starting to sell more and becoming more mainstream, so they moved in en masse and started setting up these little indie satellites. Just more corporate crap really."

It was little surprise that Spiritualized's debut single also infuriated Sonic. When a gleeful journalist informed Sonic of Spiritualized's first official release, he stammered, "Conniving fucking sewer rat!" before walking out of the interview. "It's a funny thing about Spiritualized," he said, "because Jason said I was too domineering and he and Mark and Will wanted to express their own ideas. All this sort of crap. And the first thing Spiritualized did is a cover of a song that I suggested during *Playing With Fire*." The single's cover produced an equal degree of controversy, as it bore a large, transparent sticker over the Spiritualized sobriquet reading SPACEMEN 3. In addition, Jason dedicated the single to Kate Radley. Reviews at the time compared the lush production and song craft to everyone from Van Morrison to The Waterboys. Opinions were mixed at best, one weekly declaring it Single of the Week, while another stated its deference to Sonic Boom's upcoming releases. In a final twist of the sabre, the PR announcements in *Melody Maker* and *NME* for the new single came from none other than Dave Bedford, Fire's press officer who'd also worked with Silvertone to publicise Sonic's solo work. "The first thing I heard about Spiritualized was in the papers, because everyone had been sworn to secrecy by Jason," said Sonic. "Around Rugby, Jason had this big policy of 'You're friends with me or you're friends with Pete.' According to him, you couldn't be both, and a lot of people were dumb enough to go in for that."

"Spiritualized was on the road pretty much straight away after The Troggs' cover," said Will. With long-standing local mate and musician Steve Evans brought on as keyboardist, Jason, Mark, Will and Jonny covered the length of the country several times over during the latter end of 1990. Reaction from the tiny crowds was divided at best. "Those early gigs were fucking tough," Will continued. "I mean we did some real shit shows. After being in Spacemen 3 – when we were selling out The Town and Country Club – we were suddenly playing to 20 people again,

because everybody just thought Spiritualized was Pete's back-up band."
Indeed, Spiritualized's first live performance at Glasgow's King Tut's
Wah-Wah Hut in June was so uncharacteristically quiet from both stage
and audience that between the drones of soda machines and guitars a
surly Glaswegian could be heard remarking, "I shoulda brought my
grandmother!"

With sets comprised of the tranquil and lilting songscapes of *Recurring* –
including extended renditions of 'Feel So Sad', 'Sometimes', 'Hypnotized',
'Feelin' Just Fine' and the unreleased 'These Blues' – as well as Spiritualized compositions 'Step Into The Breeze', 'Girl' a.k.a. 'Harmony', and 'If
I Were With Her Now', any attendant punters convinced of a Spacemen
3 assault were surely nonplussed. "All the sets on that first tour were so
quiet and serene, and I think people just didn't get it," Mark observed.
The band toured Liverpool, Birmingham, Bedford, and London, before
hitting Paris for a one-off at La Locomotive. "We were up and down
the country loads of times doing gigs everywhere we could," added
Mark.

Because of constant rehearsing and touring, during which the band
would jam out lots of material, the set-lists had ballooned to include
many new songs by September. "We set up the band to be a live band,
and everything else comes second to that," Jason explained. And indeed,
gigs throughout the autumn and early winter included the effervescent 'I
Want You' and 'You Know It's True', as well as the J. J. Cale-inspired
'Run', Buffy Sainte-Marie's 'Cod'ine', and the Reed/Cale gem 'Why
Don't You Smile Now?', many of which would find their way onto
Spiritualized's first album, *Lazer Guided Melodies*.

By the beginning of 1991, and with excruciating tour schedules ahead
of them, much of *Lazer Guided Melodies*, along with the accompanying
singles, had been recorded. Sessions for the debut album had extended
from November through January between Rugby and London. In addition, singles 'Feel So Sad' – released in June – was laid down at Comfort's
Place in Surrey, 'Run' b/w 'I Want You' – released in August – at VHF
and Bath-Moles, and November's 'Why Don't You Smile Now' b/w
'Sway' completed in the village of Strixton.

"Those first experiences were a real change from the uptightness of
The Spacemen," Jonny asserted. "There was a lot of development going
on. Willie was coming out with his amazing bass lines. And there was a
lot of good guitar work going on between Jason and Mark that would
never have happened with Pete present. Mark was a melody man so they
really combined well. Mark helped Jason to bring out those melodies he
had in his head."

"Working in Spiritualized was much easier, it was much more of an ensemble thing where ideas were worked out as a band, as a democracy," Will agreed. "Jason was never as sure as Pete of what he wanted. But he guided everyone, because he had the melody in his head and we'd try to jam it out."

As a posthumous finale to the icy demise of Spacemen 3, *Recurring* – delayed until February 1991 – ironically consummated what long-standing hero worship both songwriters had preached for *Smile*. A mythic schizoid opus composed of melody and confusion, Brian Wilson's con-voluted pastiche of Americana found a correlate in *Recurring*'s use of lush orchestration, split-tracks and reprise, puzzling order, and a "summery" album cover. Similarly, the final results proved a truncated mess of possi-bilities. A cryptogram used to assemble myth and apocrypha, or carrion left for the vultures. In fact, as its release, *Recurring* served as little more than a nagging "what if" for mourning punters and brief distraction for music critics previously absorbed in the scintillating wasteland of acid-house. The accompanying single, 'Big City' b/w 'Drive' – released as a double A-side – failed to capitalise on the pervading synthesiser/dance trend and dropped imperceptibly from the indie charts. Although Sonic had hardly spoken face-to-face with Jason in over six months, he was not surprised to find his ex-bandmate absent from the single's final cut. In a jocular "fuck you", Sonic cut his eight-minute version of 'Big City' before gleefully fading several minutes off Jason's extended track. "It just kept going and kept going . . . kept going, kept going . . .," he amusingly commented. "I asked the engineer . . . for his opinion, and he said he thought it should be faded. Normally I'd consider that desecration but in this instance it was a blessing."

The *NME*'s John Mulvey opined of *Recurring* in a February 1991 review, "Total separation was a smart move – there are no recrimina-tions, no artistically debilitating presences. Instead we're left with two satisfying sides unhappily joined, as our heroes shoot out on tangential paths from the same template." Mulvey's critique openly favoured Jason's effort over Sonic's, having concluded, "Whilst still largely muted and introverted, there's a far more focused air about Jason's side. Where Sonic shakes with nerves, he shimmers with confidence . . . The next step for two fairly loopy, determinedly separate careers. 1989's 'Hypnotized' may have marked the end of the band as a creative unit, but these are striking death throes."

"Most of *Recurring* dates back to 1989 and, not surprisingly given the absence of Sonic and Jason from each other's material, there's a slight schizophrenia about it," wrote Chris Marlowe in *Select* Magazine's April issue. "But followers of Rugby's psychedelic contingent can rest assured that Spacemen 3 still manage to redefine rock music's relationship to time and structure the way Kraftwerk might if only they had a heart. And several guitars. With effects pedals. Perhaps the unique clash of thoroughly opiated visions was too good to last; if so, *Recurring* is a fitting epitaph."

"The first thing that strikes you about *Recurring* is that The Spacemen are fanatical musical magpies," agreed *Vox*'s Steve Malins. "Laurie Anderson, Blondie, The Rolling Stones, The Velvet Underground, Kraftwerk and The Beach Boys have all been enthusiastically raided for ideas. The second feature is that drugs may have inspired the mood, but the instinctive, sensual final product is more poignantly universal . . . Aiming high, they often fail. But the real gem on this album, 'Feel So Sad (Reprise)' is pure blues in its spine-tingling honesty . . . Pierce's sound is more lyrical and dramatic, building songs into climaxes. It's interesting, however, to hear the differences between them. Together, or rather separately, they have produced a strangely moving album, blissfully free from self-consciousness or blind sophistication."

Recurring's release revisited much of the slanderous name-calling and rumour-mongering that had settled over Rugby since the close of '89. The *NME, Melody Maker*, and *Sounds* assigned staff writers to "cover" The Spacemen debacle with long-winded features and slap-dash interviews. "The *Melody Maker* interviewer asked very loaded questions," charged Jason. "And later on, she said Pete bad-mouthed me, so I knew what to expect from then on. I could match him bitch for bitch but to air it in the press is pretty messy." In the same interview Sonic contested, "Jason hasn't spoken to me in over six months, even when I've said hello, until the other day. I told a journalist we didn't speak, and then Jason shouted at me for saying it. I didn't even know these were separate interviews until the first one for this album!"

A February interview for *The Catalogue* trade-paper exemplified how the inflated conflict became perpetuated by scandal and paranoia. Freelance writer Martin Aston travelled to Rugby for a Q&A with Sonic at his Dunchurch home before dropping by Jason's apartment. Sonic drove Aston over to the Hunter Street flat where the reporter rang the bell for ages without reply. Days later in London, Jason phoned up Aston, claiming he was in all afternoon waiting to be interviewed. According to Aston, Fire Records accused Sonic of intentionally taking the writer to the wrong building. "Fire were really good to us until they knew this was the last album," retorted Sonic to Aston. "They told my first interviewer that I was going to be really difficult, hard to deal with, a real pain-in-the-arse."

"I thought Fire were all right," Jason responded. "I was always consulted over record company concerns. So no complaints that I can think of. It's all history if there was."

"It's been rewarding and difficult at times," Dave Bedford concurred. "Pulling my hair out and screaming . . . Even at the beginning, they had two very strong, opposing personalities and opinions. When they were both adamant about something, that was tiring. I got used to it. But Spacemen were more difficult than most because of having two people not really working together or speaking. But that's more than made up for by the fact they're a great band and they sell records. It's a great shame because they could have been potentially huge. But that won't happen now."

"I find it loathsome that the press are making more of our personal relationship than they are of our music," answered Jason of Spacemen 3's fall-out. "Pete and I were best friends . . . to use his words . . . I don't want to be drawn into a public slanging match with him."

"Jason just always came across as being nice and sweet," Gavin Wissen said, "but, in retrospect, I really think Jason was probably egging Pete to open his mouth and piss people off. Pete and Jason were really close, but I think it was Jason that was a bit more sly."

"I really did think of Jason as my best friend," said Sonic, "but I guess he was and he wasn't." In the halcyon days of their friendship, when the youthful zest of Spacemen had yet to decline into juvenile bickering, Sonic pointed to an instance where he lent Jason £50 that he failed to repay. When confronted with the outstanding debt, Jason was heard to say, "You were stupid for lending it to me . . ." According to the "hoodwinked" musician, some things had just never changed. Of course, in the inimical aura of divorce, who is one to believe?

"In retrospect, I thought I was better friends with Jason than he probably thought," Sonic insisted. "Jason was much more scheming and manipulative than I ever gave him credit for. I also think that most people were looking to take the course of least resistance the whole time, and that wasn't a course I was interested in taking. I was interested in doing what I felt needed to be done and getting that across. I guess that upset people."

Gerald is quick to contest this narrowed invective, claiming the two musicians' friendship only ended when Sonic failed to recognise Jason's growth. "They were collaborators, almost like a married couple, and Jason proved to be the passive and subservient wife who was taken for granted," he eulogised. "Until, all of the sudden, Jason turned from an ugly duckling into a swan, realising he could do more. And it was very unpalatable for Pete to accept this maturity and confidence."

"Some people will miss Spacemen 3, but only as some kind of

corporate image label to market," concluded Jason in a fitting elegy. "I don't see that it should be a full stop for Pete or myself."

Rugby's diminutive size and population made its streets, rehearsal rooms and social gatherings primary locations for an inevitable post-breakup encounter. And there were several for Sonic and Jason following the final Spacemen dirge so sadly enumerated by *Recurring* and resurrected in Spiritualized. One particularly overcast Midlands afternoon found Jason and Kate staring eyeball to eyeball with Sonic in the bustling market of Rugby's town centre amidst a straight crowd of oblivious locals. The latter's once pallid anger warmed to an unusual and effusive charm as he leapt toward his former bandmate with a polite "hello". Jason's svelte face contorted before resting fitfully into an expression of passive abjection and smirk. After the screaming, the tours, the fistfights, the music, the heroin, the money and the fame, he found there was little to say. "Jason was like a stone: he was very evasive," recalled Sonic. "It was obvious any friendship was gone. It was like looking straight through someone who once had substance and colour." Kate cut a similarly marbleised pose. The couple walked on stoically muttering to themselves. Sonic stopped momentarily and, glancing back at his estranged friend, shook his head. Then he bobbed forward and disappeared into the crowd.

A perverse curiosity compelled Sonic to attend a Spiritualized show in Nottingham and catch up on his bandmates' new activities some months later. The guitarist's lithe 74-inch frame only reaffirmed his enormous presence as he stood watching from three rows back, his eyes locked onto Jason's, before circling the perimeter at Will, Jonny, and Mark. Somewhat reminiscent of Syd Barrett's frigid gaze at successor David Gilmore's initial gigs with Pink Floyd, the musicians onstage maintained the paralytic fear of deer caught in headlights. "I tell you the whole lot of them were just terrified that I was there," Sonic added. After watching for 15 minutes, he turned his back and left with a mix of disgust and resignation.

Within a year, Jason's newly discovered resilience led him away from the detritus of Warwickshire to the gilded streets of London. Handing over the key to their flat to resolute friend Craig Wagstaff, Jason and Kate packed their bags for the last time and sped off down the A428 toward the motorway without regret or elegy. His final moments with Sonic and the *grand guignol* of Spacemen 3 had grayed any remaining idyll of withstanding Rugby's days of future passed. Now, with the love of his life and his new band to hand, he couldn't plunge down on the accelerator fast enough.

In a further confrontation at the Phoenix Festival some years later, Jason was mortified at Sonic's sudden appearance backstage alongside befuddled co-conspirator Bassman. The Spiritualized guitarist managed a greeting to his former bassist but turned away from Sonic. When Kate happened on the scene she shot a venomous glare at both men. They were not welcome. During the evening's performance in front of thousands of cheering punters, Sonic and Bassman were thunderstruck at Jason's success. Song after song elicited fervent screams and mystified awe from within the massive tented grounds. Nearly half way into the hour-long set, the two Rugbians recognised the opening electric-acoustic groove of 'Walkin' With Jesus'. "Yeah," Sonic thought, "Jason's doing the real stuff now. The crowds going to love this!" The song's powerful build and climatic freakout came to a rousing end to only a smattering of applause. To Sonic's horror, there was a hushed sense of boredom. "They didn't know it, they'd never heard of it," he lamented. "The audience went almost completely silent. It was like death."

'Junk Mail'

JULY 1991
MASS MAILOUT

Dear Spacemen 3 followers,

Apologies for the delay in responding to your Spacemail – caused by the personal turmoil within the band – which I'm sure you are aware of. I suppose it's only to be expected with two such committed and idealistic individuals as Sonic and Jason, who have worked together for seven years in a close and intense relationship – the future of Spacemen 3 "Art of Music" is uncertain!!! But in the meantime Jason and Sonic are pursuing their individual dreams.

Love Spacemen 3

AFTERWORD: SMILE

It is now fifteen years since the inimical breach of Spacemen 3, providing us more than a decade to enjoy the progressions made by Jason Pierce and Pete Kember in experimental-rock's "millennial aura". As recently as September 2003, *New York Times* critic Neil Strauss resurrected the underground mythos behind Rugby's infamous narconauts, declaring "[Spacemen 3's] music filtered garage rock through the long lens of minimalism. With whispered vocals and droning guitars, Spacemen 3 turned songs into textures and albums into moods long before Radiohead . . . Since splitting up, both Mr Kember and Mr Pierce have released high quality albums on their own . . . But as good as their post-Spacemen efforts have been, none have matched the breathless beauty, sonic intensity, and musical prescience of their work together." What Strauss failed to grasp in his short revisionist account was how the bifurcation of Spacemen 3 at the conclusion of the Eighties shaped much of the "post-rock" succeeding it. A term invented by Simon Reynolds for a series of disparate bands – predominantly as a reaction to the monomania of grunge – it had been applied to drone acolytes Bowery Electric, Bardo Pond, Low, Flying Saucer Attack and Jessamine, to multi-instrumentalists Tortoise and Stereolab, to indie/ambient crossovers Labradford, Seefeel and Christian Fennesz. The frantic suiciding of Spacemen 3 served as spectre for these underground collectives founded in – or at – the band's wake.

Comprising sonic avatars as diverse as Martin Rev's Casio-mantras, Brian Wilson's glides and chimes, the electro drones of LaMonte Young, and the underground traditions of free jazz, Boom's Spectrum and Pierce's Spiritualized recontextualised the minimal psychedelia of Spacemen 3 into the Nineties with a *bricolage* of non-rock influences: "hyper"-analogue synthesis, musique concrete, orchestration, white-noise, and space-aged pop. Along with periodic collaborators Kevin Martin, Tim Gane, Thurston Moore, Dean Wareham, John McEntire, Evan Parker, and Aphex Twin, Sonic Boom and Jason Pierce remain arch-influences in the post-indie, post-noisenik, post-Eighties, post (post-modern) tapestry of post-rock.

Spectrum's transmutation from album to band yielded 1992's *Soul Kiss (Glide Divine)*, a 70-minute collection of fuzzy-wuzzy pop and solar ambience pressed and enclosed in a viscous exoskeleton. A near perfect concoction of Apollonian dreams and Dionysian infatuation, *Soul Kiss* contained the sun-streaked and aquatic drift of 'Waves Wash Over Me' and 'Sweet Running Water', a sizzle of feedback snaking like the ionic burn of a hairdryer dropped into the washbasin. The evanescent glide of 'Touch The Stars' teleported via brittle keyboards from the sea to the sky and lounges briefly in somnambulance before plunging back down to Earth. The final two tracks echo and flange from a crypt or subterranean cabaret, 'The Drunk Suite' with a cinematic sluggishness that fades into 'Phase Me Out (Gently)', the wordless croon of a schizoid descending. Following the album's completion and release, Richard Formby exited Spectrum's ranks, leaving the band a solo project in all but name.

As the new decade progressed, Spiritualized continued to grow in popularity, mixing bone-shaking drone-rock with hummable melodies while turning more and more listeners on to an enriching sonic narcotic. 1992's *Lazer Guided Melodies* – along with My Bloody Valentine's *Loveless*, arguably one of the most profound albums of the decade – nearly defined the heights of dream-pop's soporific grandeur, combining the lulling guitar waves of Spacemen 3, Galaxie 500, and the shoegazers, with the synthesised phase-tones, strings, and tremolos of the emerging IDM scene. From the gilded edges of 'You Know It's True' to the Teutonic blues of 'Take Your Time' and the blissful gospel of 'Shine A Light', *Lazer Guided Melodies* boasted some of the most haunting and lush compositions in the Spiritualized oeveure. The following year saw a series of the band's most seminal releases, including the *petit*-symphony 'Medication' and the ambient/drone opus 'Electric Mainline', as well as the summery and narcotic *Let It Flow* EP with its shimmered choral arrangements. Following tours with The Verve and an appearance at Glastonbury, Spiritualized made major inroads into America on The Mary Chain's Rollercoaster Festival, finally fulfilling the possibilities of Spacemen 3's pre-empted '89 tour.

Spectrum followed the modest success of *Soul Kiss* with the *Indian Summer* EP, a five-song collection of covers that reconfirmed Sonic Boom's consummate taste in obscurantism and exotica, and further exhibited a growing obsession with the Apollonian and Dionysian in pop music. Sonic weaved new versions of Daniel Johnston's 'True Love Will Find You In The End', a nocturnal narcotic lament sprinkled with confection and dusted with a faint hint of calliope, complete with a dulcet-and-phased voice pleading ". . . just step into the light . . ." 'Baby Don't You Worry (California Lullaby)' is a sun-baked invitation for innocent frolic, as incandescent and airy as the citrus waters of the Pacific. 'Indian Summer' is another juvenile chant with the syncopation of a campfire sing-along and humming with drones, a momentary respite from the first frigid grasp of winter.

Spectrum's final album on Silvertone Records appeared as 1994's *Highs, Lows, And Heavenly Blows*, a winsome mist of songs dedicated to the drift of youth and time. 'Undo the Taboo' begins with a pulsing keyboard and transforms into a spoken-word chant before the fuzzy slice of overdriven guitar bleeds the track dry. 'Feedback' is a frightening sound-sculpture of standing waves that lingers long after the guitars and synths have disappeared. Songs such as 'All Night Long' blur faint textural pulses with an emaciated plea for intimacy, adoration, death (or collectively: transfiguration). 'Then I Just Drifted Away' and 'Take Your Time' are ephemeral-pop, sugared and wafer-thin gossamer. Similarly 'I Know They Say' and 'Take Me Away' chime and hum as twilight visions projected upon heavy eyelids: songs of prepubescent phantasm tempered by age and regret. A seamless tapestry of texture and melody, *Highs, Lows, And Heavenly Blows* extended the narcotic modalities of *Playing With Fire* and delivered the final word in the genre of ambient-pop.

As the original line-up of Spiritualized – Will, Jonny and Mark – withered away by 1994, Jason Pierce ascended to the role of *de facto* solo artist/producer with a larger and larger repertoire of session characters which would expand to include The Balanescu Quartet, The London Community Gospel Choir, Angel Corpus Christi, and Dr John. The *Pure Phase* LP recast Jason in the tradition of *über*-producers Joe Meek and Phil Spector with the album's sprawling collection of floating ballads, experimental instrumentals – including a cover of Laurie Anderson's 'Born Never Asked' – recurring themes and symphonic rock. In a final act of studiofied grandiosity, Pierce released *Pure Phase* with separate mixes for each stereo channel.

Pierce's increasing reputation for mixing wizardry was galvanised by the two-and-a-half year delay preceding 1997's *Ladies and Gentlemen We Are Floating in Space*. Rumoured to have been recorded in a marathon two-week session, *Ladies And Gentlemen . . .* endured more than a year of mixing, remixing, and re(remixing) before its belated arrival. Pierce's obsessions with the mixing-board belied the "swampy" ambience and voodoo-blues that littered the album, as the polished tones and minimal drones were eschewed for the bizarro jazz-rock of Captain Beefheart, Professor Longhair, and Gong. Buttressed by Spiritualized's U.S. tour with Radiohead, *Ladies And Gentlemen . . .* appeared on numerous "Best-of-97" lists and confirmed the band's identity as post-Britpop innovators. By the time of 2001's *Let It Come Down*, Pierce's most accessible and "maximal" work, Spiritualized had nearly made the famed crossover from indie-rock favourites to pop-music left-fielders. Almost but not quite.

Sonic Boom jettisoned himself from Silvertone Records via airlocked capsule (pharmaceutical and/or rocket-propelled) to the nebulae of deep-space with his late-Nineties releases, including a Spectrum/Jessamine collaboration *A Pox On You*, and the *Songs For Owsley* EP, as well as the formation and release of Experimental Audio Research albums – *Phenomena 256, Beyond The Pale*, and *The Koner Experiment* – all of which displayed a more variegated use of tape experimentation (samples and found sounds, including the more outlandish "insect and animal noises"), analogue synthesis (EMS VCS3, Synthi A, Serge Modular System, OSCar), and hyper-analogue exotica (Theremin, vocoder). The Spectrum LP *Forever Alien* endeavoured to merge the electronic alchemy of Clara Rockmore, Louis and Bebe Barron, Richard Maxfield, and Delia Derbyshire, with a traditional pop-song structure. *Forever Alien* records the bleeps and blurbs of a vintage synth-machine as it wandered the cerulean recesses of the galaxy, leaping with itinerant speed between post-War Europe and the pre-millennial frontier.

While Spiritualized appears to only ripen with age, Spectrum peaked early according to many pundits. *Soul Kiss* and *Highs, Lows . . .* endeared Sonic Boom to many avant- and ambient-rock critics intent on tracing the potential future of Spacemen 3, but Spectrum's uneven progress through the Nineties spurred a general consensus that Sonic's drone-rock had become too obscure and too (nostalgically) synthesised to inhabit the pop-music continuum. In the world of popular music, obscure is typically a euphemism for esoteric, and esoteric is irrevocably anathema. Equally, while Jason Pierce's success in the pop/rock format has prescribed Spiritualized the dubious honour of being Pink Floyd's heir apparent into the new millennium, Sonic Boom's narcotic cult-of-personality and seclusion from the "industry" has left the former Spaceman with the madcap aura of a Syd Barrett figure. Composing alongside other post-rock aficionados – including collaborations with AMM's Eddie Prevost, Jessamine, MBV's Kevin Shields, isolationist Thomas Koner, and the elusive (and infamous) Silver Apples – Sonic Boom's compositions continue to teeter between rock obscurity and musical legend. Much like AMM, whose musical improvs inspired many of the up-and-coming British-psych bands of the late Sixties (Pink Floyd, The Soft Machine, and Tomorrow), will Sonic Boom be pigeon-holed into obscurity while his minimalist-rock continues to inspire the plaintive and stroked synths of Radiohead, The White Stripes' rediscovery of garage, or the metallic drones of Black Rebel Motorcycle Club?

Regardless for those hipsters, indie-rockers, philosophers, schizoids, and addicts locked precipitously into the DREAMWEAPON's insular hum, Spacemen 3 remain mythic creatures. Toiling against a laborious decade, from within space but from time without. Possessed by a seemingly infinite digression of anomic impulses: drawn to silence, they inevitably beget a nascent noise. Transcending drones and transmitting boredom. Tapping into an electric mainline. Having embarked, submerged, and de-realised, these 20th-century alchemists returned with a precious radiation contained in their Vox amps and once again unleashed it upon a post-nuclear world.

AS TO THE WHO, WHAT, WHERE, WHEN . . .?

Pete "Bassman" Bain entered Rugby band The Darkside, along with Rosco Roswell, Goff Roderick, and Craig Wagstaff, following his departure from Spacemen 3. The Darkside maintained a solid following for several years before signing onto a lucrative Beggars' Banquet contract, recording two great albums, and promptly folding. Blame falls on several shoulders for the collapse. Wagstaff punched Bassman's lights out. Bassman attempted to kill Rosco on many occasions. Goff fuelled the entire band with enough coke to finance a small South American country. Bassman founded "space-pop" group Alpha Stone in the mid-Nineties and continued guesting on Sonic Boom's Experimental Audio Research albums. He maintains residence in Rugby and runs YP Studios on Lower Hillmorton Road.

Upon leaving Spiritualized in '92, Will Carruthers busied himself with various odd-jobs around the Midlands and the North, including but not limited to ditch-digging, slaughterhouse detail, sand-blasting, roadie for Oasis and Rod Stewart, waiter, wanderer, poet extraordinaire. He joined Sonic Boom on Spectrum's '97 *Forever Alien* tour and '01s *Songs The Spacemen Taught Us* (lovingly dubbed Spacemen 2/3 by a New York newspaper). In 2001, under the freelovebabies moniker, Carruthers released a collection of pastoral gems called *Written In Sand*, an LP that rivalled any post-Spacemen album. Though Will's reputation as a rambling man precedes him, he's chosen to settle down in Rugby to tend his garden, read folklore, and groom his Van Dyke. He is currently working on several projects.

After leaving Spiritualized in '94, Jonny Mattock returned to University, later reascending the drum stool for a stint with The Breeders. Mattock now resides between Northampton and Bristol, where he plays drums alongside best mates Sean Cook, Damon Reece and Mike Mooney for Spiritualized off-shot Lupine Howl, who have released two albums and collaborated with Massive Attack, Portishead, and Gorky's Zygotic Mynki.

Mark Refoy has released numerous albums under the name Slipstream and remains close mates with Northampton local Pat Fish. Refoy recently toured the States with The Pet Shop Boys and played with Johnny Marr. The most recent Slipstream album, *Transcendental*, appeared in 2003.

Stewart "Rosco" Roswell emigrated from Rugby and the UK after The Darkside broke up. After wandering the Continent, and most notably starring in an Italian soap opera, he returned to his ancestral and musical roots, recording a handful of dancey space-pop singles through Jungle Records and DJing in several North London clubs. He currently lives and works in Camden.

Along with Alan Moore and Rockingham Castle, Pat Fish remains a Northamptonshire institution. Boozer, intellectual, and troubadour, Fish has released an entire cannon of Jazz Butcher albums since the early Eighties and has intermittently reformed The JBC to critical plaudits. Fish, Carruthers, Refoy and Mattock still often indulge in inebriated orgies of music making and bloodshed. One recent twilight lapse into drunkenness resulted in Will smashing a guitar to bits in his front room *à la* Pete Townshend while Pat abetted him in inebriated ecstasy. Fish had no comment.

Gerald Palmer managed Jason Pierce/Spiritualized until the mid-Nineties, when the two separated amicably. Palmer retains control of Spacemen 3's back catalogue as well as the trademark. From his Northamptonshire offices he runs Third Stone Records which, in conjunction with Pete Kember, continues to re-release and re-package Spacemen 3 material, including most recently *Forged Prescriptions*, the long awaited reissue. Plans are in the works to complete a similar two-disc re-release of *Recurring*, currently out of print. In addition, Third Stone intends to repackage rare material from Chapterhouse, Bark Psychosis, and Spectrum/EAR.

Tim Morris, Gavin Wissen, and Natty Brooker continue to reside in and around the Rugby area. Wissen has played in several local garage-bands in addition to collaborating with poet/icon/shambler Billy Childish, and currently works within the local Arts community. His most recent release was under the moniker The Guaranteed Ugly.

Kate Radley parted company with Jason shortly before *Ladies And Gentlemen . . .* and is now married to The Verve's Richard Ashcroft.

SOURCE NOTES

BOOKS:

Artaud, Antonin. *Selected Writings.* edited by Susan Sontag. Berkeley: University of California Press, 1988.

Bangs, Lester. *Psychotic Reactions And Carburetor Dung.* edited by Greil Marcus. New York: Vintage Books, 1988.

Baudrillard, Jean. *The Illusion Of The End.* Stanford: Stanford University Press, 1994.

Bockris, Victor. *Uptight: The Velvet Underground Story.* London: Omnibus Press, 1983.

Bockris, Victor. *Keith Richards: The Unauthorised Biography.* London: Omnibus Press, 1992.

Cavanagh, David. *The Creation Records Story: My Magpie Eyes Are Hungry For The Prize.* London: Virgin Books, 2000.

Deleuze, Gilles and Felix Guattari. *Anti-Oedipus: Capitalism and Schizophrenia.* Minneapolis: University of Minnesota, 1983.

Fish, Mick. *Industrial Evolution: Through The Eighties With Cabaret Voltaire.* London: SAF Publishing, 2002.

Looking Back On The End of The World. edited by Dietmar Kamper and Christoph Wulf. New York: Semiotext(e), 1989.

Neal, Charles. *Tape Delay: Confessions From The Eighties Underground.* London: SAF Publishing, 1987.

Palacios, Julian. *Lost In The Woods: Syd Barrett And The Pink Floyd.* London: Boxtree Publishing, 2000.

Pynchon, Thomas. *Slow Learner: Early Stories.* New York: Back Bay Books, 1984.

Reynolds, Simon. *Blissed Out: The Raptures of Rock.* London: Serpent's Tail, 1991.

Reynolds, Simon. *Generation Ecstasy: Into The World Of Techno And Rave Culture.* New York: Routledge, 1998.

Robb, John. *The Nineties: What The Fuck Was That All About?* London: Ebury Press, 1999.

Rogan, Johnny. *Morrissey & Marr: The Severed Alliance.* London: Omnibus Press, 1992.

Toop, David. *Ocean Of Sound: Aether Talk, Ambient Sound And Imaginary Worlds.* London: Serpent's Tail, 1995.

Weiss, Allen S. *Phantasmic Radio.* Durham and London: Duke University Press, 1995.

Young, LaMonte. *Notes on The Well Tuned Piano.* New York: Gramavision Records, 1981.

ARTICLES

Gary Boldie, November 1984, Spacemen 3 live review.

Ear To The Ground, August 1985, Spacemen 3 live review. Sean Cook.

Zigzag, January 1986, 'Sooner Or Crater'. Pat Fish.

Forced Exposure, Summer 1986, *Sound Of Confusion* review. Byron Colely.

Bucketful Of Brains, August 1986, *Sound Of Confusion* review. Jon Storey.

Andy Hurt review, Autumn 1986, *Sound Of Confusion* review.

Music Week, July 19, 1986, *Sound Of Confusion* review.

Sounds, August 16, 1986, Concert review. Ricky Kildare.

New Musical Express, August 16, 1986, Concert review. The Legend!

Next Big Thing, September 21, 1986, Issue 21, *Sound Of Confusion* review.

Buscadero, September 1986, *Sound Of Confusion* review. Giovanni Strumia.

New Musical Express, November 22, 1986, 'Walkin' With Jesus' review. Dessa Fox.

Sounds, November 22, 1986, "Sounds Confusing". Ricky Kildare.

Forced Exposure, Autumn 1986, 'Walkin' With Jesus' review. Byron Colely.

Northampton Mercury And Herald, July 1986, "Spacemen in orbit". Compiled by Dave Freak.

Bucketful Of Brains, February 1987, Issue 19, 'Walkin' With Jesus' review. Jon Storey.

Vera Buzz, March 1987, Holland.

De Morgen, March 12, 1987, "Spacemen 3, De Verveling Vanuit De Ruimte". Lieven van de Woestijne.

De Gentenaar, March 12, 1987, "Spacemen 3 Op Zoek Naar Hypnotische Minimale Punk".

Frissons, 1987, Issue 2, Doktor Kriptik. (Boretown, Fevrier.)

Push, Buzz, Spring 1987, Issue 5, "More Science Fiction".

Cut, January 1987, Volume 2, Issue 1.

Sounds, February 21, 1987, "Crimes of Passion". Ron Rom.

Melody Maker, March 7, 1987, "Weird Out".

Melody Maker, February 28, 1987, Spacemen 3 concert review.

Sounds, 1987, "Needles and Pins".

Rugby Advertiser, Summer 1987, "They have lift-off!". Steve Williams.

New Musical Express, August 1, 1987, "Throbbery With Violence?". Danny Kelly.

New Musical Express, Autumn 1987, *Perfect Prescription* review. Jack Barron.

New Musical Express, Autumn 1987, "Most Exalted Singles Of The Week", 'Take Me To The Other Side' review. Helen Mead.

Articles

Melody Maker, Autumn 1987, "Pick Of The Pops!", 'Take Me To The Other Side' review.

Sounds, Autumn 1987, "Single Of The Week", 'Transparent Radiation' review.

New Musical Express, May 28, 1988, "The Unbearable Being Of Lightness". Helen Mead.

Forced Exposure, Spring 1988, Issue 14, "Spacemen 3: Urine Salesman Of The Apocalypse". Nigel Cross and Byron Colely.

Conflict, Summer 1988, Issue 48, "Spacemen 3: Just Say Gulp". Gerard Cosloy.

New Musical Express, Summer 1988, "Alien Trips". Ian Gittins.

New Musical Express, Autumn 1988, "Spiral Scratch", *Fade Out* review. Jack Barron.

Music Week, October 22, 1988, "Smiley's people". Martin Ashton.

Melody Maker, December 10, 1988, "Single Of The Week", 'Revolution' review.

New Musical Express, December 10, 1988, "Single Of The Day", 'Revolution' review. Sarah Champion.

Record Mirror, December 10, 1988, "The Urbane Spaceman".

Sounds, December 5, 1988, "We're Leading The Revolution – which way did it go?". Ron Rom.

Sounds, February 1989, "A Cosmic Launch".

New Musical Express, March 18, 1989, "Spaced In".

Melody Maker, Spring 1989, "Spacemen 3: Baptism Of Fire". Paul Oldfield.

Sounds, Spring 1989, Spacemen 3 concert review. John Robb.

Melody Maker, Spring 1989, Spacemen 3 concert review. Paul Lester.

Melody Maker, November 19, 1989, "Hallucinating Light". Chris Roberts.

Lime Lizard, April 1989, "Spectrum Is Green". Dan and Julian Kitchen.

Sounds, March 11, 1989, "Spacemen 3: God Only Knows". Ralph Traitor.

Hot Press, Spring 1989, *Playing With Fire* review.

Music Week, Spring 1989, *Playing With Fire* review.

Record Mirror, Spring 1989, *Playing With Fire* review. Geoff Zeppelin.

Q, Spring 1989, *Playing With Fire* review. Martin Ashton.

Sounds, Spring 1989, *Playing With Fire* review. David Cavanagh.

Melody Maker, Spring 1989, "Burning In Heaven". Chris Roberts.

Ripple, Spring 1989, *Playing With Fire* review. Joseph Banks.

Regionals, Spring 1989, *Playing With Fire* review. Andrew Perry.

Record Mirror, Spring 1989, "1989: A Stereo Spacemen Odyssey".

New Musical Express, Spring 1989, *Playing With Fire* review. Danny Kelly.

Offbeat, March 1989, *Playing With Fire* review. Lance Johnson.

Melody Maker, Spring 1989, *Threebie3* review. Simon Reynolds.

Regionals, March 1989, Spacemen 3 concert review.

New Musical Express, March 18, 1989, Spacemen 3 concert review.

OffBEAT, Spring 1989, Issue 7, "The New Wave Out Of Spaced-Psyche-Rock". Helen Togneri.

Music Week, July 1989, 'Hypnotized' review.

Melody Maker, July 15, 1989, "Spacemen: Altered States". Simon Reynolds.

Melody Maker, July 1989, "Sonic Boom". Spacemen 3 concert review. Chris Roberts.

Sounds, July 29, 1989, "The Final Frontier". Spacemen 3 concert review. Ron Rom.

New Musical Express, July 1989, Spacemen 3 concert review. Ian Gittins.

New Musical Express, July 29, 1989, "Spacemen E". Jack Barron.

Sounds, July 15, 1989, "Mama We're All Hazy Now". Roy Wilkinson.

New Musical Express, January 27, 1990, "Spacemen-Free". Andrew Collins.

The Catalogue, February 1991, Full-length interview. Martin Ashton.

Sounds, February 9, 1991, "Rock'n'Roll Suicide". John Robb.

New Musical Express, February 23, 1991, "Spacemen Free Zone". John Mulvey.

Select, April 1991, "To The Power Of 3". Chris Marlowe.

New Musical Express, February 16, 1991, "Get Out Of My Space, Man". Mary Anne Hobbs.

Vox, April 1991, "Two Into 3 Won't Go". Stephen Dalton.

Melody Maker, Spring 1991, "Twin Piques". David Stubbs.

Vox, Spring 1991, *Recurring* review. Steve Malins.

Sonic Boom interview, May 1991. Chris Peck.

Vox, Autumn 1991, "Give Pierce A Chance". Stephen Dalton.

Melody Maker, Summer 1991, "Single Of The Week", 'Feel So Sad' review.

Melody Maker, September 7, 1991, "Control Zone: Spiritualized". Effects interview. Tom Doyle.

Melody Maker, August 17, 1991, "Spiritualized: Young, Gifted And Tongue-Tied". Jim Arundel and Sally Margaret Joy.

Lime Lizard, 1991, "Spiritualised".

"Nessun Dormant", Ian Watson, 1991.

Melody Maker, 1991, "Spiritualized: Holy Ghosts". David Stubbs.

Rapido TV show, 1991. Television interview with Jason Pierce and Pete Kember.

Outer Limits Spacemen 3 fanzine, Summer 1991, Issue 1. Edited by Charlie Pritchard.

Outer Limits Spacemen 3 fanzine, Autumn 1991, Issue 2. Edited by Charlie Pritchard.

Lime Lizard, 1993, "Spiritualized: Ghosts In The Machine". Tony Morley.

Melody Maker, June 13, 1992, "Spectrum: Prism Sells". David Stubbs.

Lime Lizard, Summer 1992, "Spectrum: Life On The Refractory Floor". Julian Carrera.

New Musical Express, Spring 1992, "Single Of The Week", 'How You Satisfy Me' review.

Articles

Melody Maker, Summer 1992, "Sonic: The Edge Hodge". Simon Price.

Melody Maker, March 1992, "The 'Ized Of March". Simon Reynolds.

New Musical Express, March 1992, "Pierce De Resistance". John Mulvey.

Select, 1993, "The Far Side". David Cavanagh.

The Wire, 1994, "Shaking The Rock Narcotic". Simon Reynolds.

The Wire, June 1995, Issue 136, "Motor City Burning". Edwin Pouncey.

Resonance, 1995, Issue 5. Interview with Jason Pierce.

The Wire, April 1996, Issue 146, "Low End Theories". Simon Reynolds.

Ptolemaic Terrascope, 1996, "Sonic Boom". Carrie Hourihan.

Mondo, 1996, "Ground Control To Sonic Boom". Cedric Puleston.

Utne Reader, July 1996, "The Post-Rock Phenomenon". Scot Hacker.

Magnet, Winter 1996, Issue 26, "Things Will Never Be The Same". Fred Mills.

Suk Music, 1997. Interview with Bobby Gillespie. Shaun Phillips.

New Musical Express, May 24, 1997, "Jason And The Astronauts". James Oldham and John Mulvey.

Option, April 1997, "Sound Salvation: On The Boards With Spiritualized's Jason Pierce". Dan Epstein.

New Musical Express, December 20, 1997. Interview with Jason Pierce. James Oldham.

Mojo, February 1998, "The Mile High Club". Barney Hoskyns.

The Wire, 1998, "Dream Encounters". Mark Webber.

Unknown, Sonic Boom interview, February 2001. Markie Cola.

The Guardian, September 14, 2001. Interview with Jason Pierce. Alexis Petridis.

CMJ, September 17, 2001. Interview with Jason Pierce.

Entertainment Weekly, October 5, 2001, "High Powered". David Browne.

LA Weekly, November 2001. Interview with Jason Pierce. Jay Babcock.

The Wessex Scene, 2002, "From The Edge: Jason Pierce Reveals All". Paul Cornwell.

3 AM, October 2002, "Taking Drugs To Make Music To Take Drugs To: An Interview With Sonic Boom". Andrew Stevens.

The New York Times, September 16, 2003, "Two Soul Mates, Souls Ablaze". Neil Strauss.

Swizzle Stick, Neil Halstead interview. Chip Midnight.

Excerpts from Fred Mills' interview with Pete Bain, March 10, 1996.

Excerpts from Fred Mills' phone conversations with Jason Pierce, June 2, 1992, and September 27, 1996.

Excerpts from Fred Mills' phone conversations with Pete Kember, October 8, 1996.

INTERNET WEBSITES

Ian Edmond's Spacemen 3 website, www.spacemen3.co.uk

Spiritualized Official website, www.spiritualized.com

Chris Barrus' Spacemen 3-related websites, www.spacemen3.info, www.sonicboommusic.info, and spiritualized.quartzcity.net

Marco Fleischhut's Spiritualized website, www.spiritualized.biz

Sonic Boom/Spectrum/EAR official website, www.sonic-boom.info

Will Carruthers' website, www.willcarruthers.com

Rosco Roswell's website, www.jungle-records.demon.co.uk

Pete Bain's website, www.alphastone.co.uk

Bomp Records website (including a detailed history of Bomp and Greg Shaw), www.bomp.com

Creation Records website, www.creation-records.com

Vox website (including detailed history of the company and its gear), www.voxshowroom.com

EMS website (with background and specifications of said synthesizers), www.ems-synthi.demon.co.uk

The Wire Magazine's website, www.thewire.co.uk

Simon Reynold's website, members.aol.com/blissout

Magnet Magazine's website, www.magnetmagazine.com

All Music Guide, www.allmusic.com

DISCOGRAPHY

U.K. SINGLES

Glass   GLAEP105   WALKIN' WITH JESUS (SOUND OF CONFUSION) / ROLLERCOASTER / FEEL SO GOOD (12″, p/s, 1st 1,300 with numbered insert, 11/86)

Glass   GLAEP108   TRANSPARENT RADIATION / ECSTASY SYMPHONY / TRANSPARENT RADIATION (FLASHBACK) / THINGS'LL NEVER BE THE SAME / STARSHIP (12″, p/s, 7/87)

Glass   GLAEP12054   TAKE ME TO THE OTHER SIDE / SOUL 1 / THAT'S JUST FINE (INSTRUMENTAL) (12″, p/s, 7/88)

Fire   BLAZE29S   REVOLUTION / CHE (7″, Fire Records die-cut sleeve, 11/88)

Fire   BLAZE29T   REVOLUTION / CHE / MAY THE CIRCLE BE UNBROKEN (12″, p/s, 11/88)

Fire   BLAZE29CD   REVOLUTION / CHE / MAY THE CIRCLE BE UNBROKEN (3″ CD, later reissued as 5″ CD, 11/88)

Fire   BLAZE36S   HYPNOTIZED / JUST TO SEE YOU SMILE (HONEY PT. 2) (7″, Fire Records die-cut sleeve, 7/89)

Fire   BLAZE36T   HYPNOTIZED / JUST TO SEE YOU SMILE (HONEY PT. 2) / THE WORLD IS DYING (12″, p/s, 1st 2,000 with poster, 7/89)

Fire   BLAZE36CD   HYPNOTIZED / JUST TO SEE YOU SMILE (HONEY PT. 2) / THE WORLD IS DYING (3″ CD, later reissued as 5″ CD, 7/89)

Fire   BLAZE41   BIG CITY (EDIT) / DRIVE (7″, p/s, 1/91)

Fire   BLAZE41T   BIG CITY (EVERYBODY I KNOW CAN BE FOUND HERE) / BIG CITY (WAVES OF JOY) DEMO / DRIVE (12″, p/s, 1/91)

Fire   BLAZE41CD   BIG CITY (EVERYBODY I KNOW CAN BE FOUND HERE) / DRIVE / BIG CITY (WAVES OF JOY) DEMO / DRIVE (DEMO) (CD, 1/91)

Fire   BLAZE41TR   BIG CITY (REMIX) / DRIVE (REMIX) (12″, p/s, 2/91)

Fire   BLAZE41TR   BIG CITY (REMIX) / I LOVE YOU (REMIX) (12″, white label, 50 copies, 2/91)

U.K. LPs

Glass   GLALP018   SOUND OF CONFUSION (7/86)
1. Losing Touch With My Mind [Kember/Pierce]
2. Hey Man [Kember/Pierce]
3. Rollercoaster [Hall/Erickson]
4. Mary Anne [Glen Campbell]
5. Little Doll [J. Osterberg]
6. 2.35 [Kember/Pierce]
7. OD Catastrophe [Kember/Pierce]

Glass   GLALP026   THE PERFECT PRESCRIPTION (Gold/silver or bronze/silver sleeve, 9/87)
1. Take Me To The Other Side [Kember/Pierce]
2. Walkin' With Jesus [Kember/Pierce]
3. Ode To Street Hassle [Kember/Pierce]
4. Ecstasy Symphony [Kember/Pierce]/Transparent Radiation (Flashback) [Thompson/Cunningham/Barthhelp] arranged [Kember/Pierce]
5. Feel So Good [Kember/Pierce]
6. Things'll Never Be The Same [Kember/Pierce]
7. Come Down Easy [Kember/Pierce]
8. Call The Doctor [Kember/Pierce]

Glass   GLALP030   PERFORMANCE Recorded live at the Melkweg in Amsterdam, February 6, 1988   (7/88)
1. Mary Anne
2. Come Together
3. Things'll Never Be The Same
4. Take Me To The Other Side
5. Rollercoaster
6. Starship
7. Walkin' With Jesus

Fire   FIRELP16   PLAYING WITH FIRE (1st issue in embossed sleeve, later issues in plain glossy sleeve, 2/89)
1. Honey [Kember]
2. Come Down Softly To My Soul [Pierce]
3. How Does It Feel? [Kember]
4. I Believe It [Kember]
5. Revolution [Kember]
6. Let Me Down Gently [Kember]
7. So Hot (Wash Away All Of My Tears) [Pierce]
8. Suicide [Kember/Pierce]
9. Lord Can You Hear Me? [Pierce]

Fire   THREEBIE3   LIVE (Mail order with first 2,000 copies of *Playing With Fire*, numbered, 6/89)
1. Starship
2. Revolution
3. Suicide
4. Repeater
5. Live Intro Theme (Xtacy)

Fire   REFIRE5   SOUND OF CONFUSION (Reissue, some with photographic inner sheet, 9/89)

Fire   REFIRE6   THE PERFECT PRESCRIPTION (Reissue, some with insert, 11/89)

Fire   FIRELP23   RECURRING (2/91)
1. Big City (Everybody I Know Can Be Found Here) [Kember]
2. Just To See You Smile (Orchestral Mix) [Kember]
3. I Love You [Kember]
4. Set Me Free/I've Got The Key [Kember]
5. Set Me Free (Reprise) [Kember]
6. Feel So Sad (Reprise) [Pierce]
7. Hypnotized [Pierce]
8. Sometimes [Pierce]
9. Feelin' Just Fine (Head Full Of Shit) [Pierce]
10. Billy Whizz/Blue 1 [Pierce]

Fire   FIRELP23S   RECURRING (Limited gold sleeve from Chain With No Name shops, 2/91)

Fire   REFIRE11   PERFORMANCE (Reissue, 4/91)

Fire   FLIPDLP003   TRANSLUCENT FLASHBACKS (THE GLASS SINGLES) (DBLP, 4/95)
1. Rollercoaster
2. Feel So Good
3. Walkin' With Jesus
4. Things'll Never Be The Same
5. Starship
6. Transparent Radiation
7. Ecstasy Symphony
8. Transparent Radiation (Flashback)
9. Take Me To The Other Side
10. Soul 1
11. That's Just Fine

Space Age   ORBIT001   DREAMWEAPON (DBLP, 11/95)
1. Dreamweapon (An Evening Of Contemporary Sitar Music)
2. Ecstasy Live Intro Theme

Space Age   ORBIT002   LIVE IN EUROPE 1989 (DBLP, 11/95)
1. Rollercoaster
2. Mary Anne
3. Bo Diddley Jam
4. 2.35
5. Walkin' With Jesus
6. I Believe It
7. Lord Can You Hear Me?
8. Things'll Never Be The Same
9. Starship
10. Revolution
11. Suicide
12. Take Me To The Other Side
13. Suicide (Version 2)

U.K. CDs

Glass   GLACD030   PERFORMANCE (8/88)

Fire   FIRECD16   PLAYING WITH FIRE (2/89)
1. Honey [Kember]
2. Come Down Softly To My Soul [Pierce]
3. How Does It Feel? [Kember]
4. I Believe It [Kember]

5. Revolution [Kember]
6. Let Me Down Gently [Kember]
7. So Hot (Wash Away All My Tears) [Pierce]
8. Suicide [Kember/Pierce]
9. Lord Can You Hear Me? [Pierce]
10. Suicide (live) [Kember/Pierce]
11. Repeater (How Does It Feel?) (live) [Kember]

Fire   REFIRECD5   SOUND OF CONFUSION (9/89)

Fire   REFIRECD6   THE PERFECT PRESCRIPTION (11/89)
1. Take Me To The Other Side [Kember/Pierce]
2. Walkin' With Jesus [Kember/Pierce]
3. Ode To Street Hassle [Kember/Pierce]
4. Ecstasy Symphony [Kember/Pierce]
5. Transparent Radiation [Thompson/Cunningham/Barthhelp] arranged
[Kember/Pierce]
6. Feel So Good [Kember/Pierce]
7. Things'll Never Be The Same [Kember/Pierce]
8. Come Down Easy [Kember/Pierce]
9. Call The Doctor [Kember/Pierce]
10. Soul 1 [Kember/Pierce]
11. That's Just Fine [Kember/Pierce]

Fire   FIRECD23   RECURRING (2/91)
1. Big City (Everybody I Know Can Be Found Here) [Kember]
2. Just To See You Smile (Orchestral Mix) [Kember]
3. I Love You [Kember]
4. Set Me Free/I've Got The Key [Kember]
5. Set Me Free (Reprise) [Kember]
6. Why Couldn't I See? [Kember]
7. Just To See You Smile (Instrumental) [Kember]
8. When Tomorrow Hits [Arm/Turner/Peters/Lukin]
9. Feel So Sad (Reprise) [Pierce]
10. Hypnotized [Pierce]
11. Sometimes [Pierce]
12. Feelin' Just Fine (Head Full Of Shit) [Pierce]
13. Billy Whizz/Blue 1 [Pierce]
14. Drive/Feel So Sad [Pierce]
15. Feelin' Just Fine (Alternative Mix) [Pierce]

Fire   REFIRECD11   PERFORMANCE (Reissue, 4/91)

Fire   FLIPCD003   TRANSLUCENT FLASHBACKS (THE GLASS SINGLES) (4/95)
1. Walkin' With Jesus (Sound Of Confusion)
2. Rollercoaster
3. Feel So Good
4. Transparent Radiation
5. Ecstasy Symphony
6. Transparent Radiation (Flashback)
7. Starship
8. Take Me To The Other Side
9. Soul 1
10. That's Just Fine

Space Age   ORBIT001CD   DREAMWEAPON (11/95)
1. Dreamweapon (An Evening Of Contemporary Sitar Music)
2. Ecstasy Live Intro Theme
3. Ecstasy In Slow Motion
4. Spacemen Jam

Space Age   ORBIT002CD   LIVE IN EUROPE 1989 (11/95)

Space Age   ORBIT011CD   PLAYING WITH FIRE (Reissue with bonus CD, 3/99)
1. Honey [Kember]
2. Come Down Softly To My Soul [Pierce]
3. How Does It Feel? [Kember]
4. I Believe It [Kember]
5. Revolution [Kember]
6. Let Me Down Gently [Pierce]
7. So Hot (Wash Away All Of My Tears) [Pierce]
8. Suicide [Kember/Pierce]
9. Lord Can You Hear Me? [Pierce]
10. Suicide (live) [Kember/Pierce]
11. Repeater (How Does It Feel?) (live) [Kember]
12. Che [Rev/Vega] arr. [Kember]
13. May The Circle Be Unbroken [traditional] arr. [Pierce]

1. Honey (demo)
2. Let Me Down Gently (drum mix)
3. How Does It Feel? (alternate version)
4. Suicide (alternate mix)
5. Lord Can You Hear Me? (demo vocal)
6. I Believe (alternate mix)

7. Che (maracas mix)
8. Anyway That You Want Me (demo)
9. Girl On Fire (demo)

Space Age   ORBIT020CD   LIVE (1,000 only, mail order, 3/99)

Space Age   ORBIT023CD   TAKING DRUGS TO MAKE MUSIC TO
TAKE DRUGS TO (5/00)
1. Sound Of Confusion
2. 2.35
3. Losing Touch With My Mind
4. Amen
5. That's Just Fine (Vocal Version)
6. Come Down Easy
7. Mary Anne
8. Feel So Good
9. 2.35 (Feedback Version)
10. Hey Man
11. It's Alright
12. 2.35
13. Things'll Never Be The Same
14. Transparent Radiation (Organ Version)

Space Age   ORBIT006CD   FORGED PRESCRIPTIONS (2-CD,
Perfect Prescription demos and out-takes, 6/03)
1. Things'll Never Be The Same
2. Walkin' With Jesus
3. Come Down Easy (demo version)
4. Transparent Radiation (single version)
5. Ode To Street Hassle
6. Call The Doctor
7. Ecstasy Symphony
8. Feel So Good
9. Soul 1

1. Transparent Radiation
2. Come Down Easy
3. Walkin' With Jesus (demo version)
4. Things'll Never Be The Same (demo version)
5. We Sell Soul
6. Starship (demo version)
7. Take Me To The Other Side (demo version)
8. Velvet Jam
9. I Want You Right Now

Important Appearances On Compilations

Glass   GLALP019   50,000 GLASS FANS CAN'T BE WRONG (LP, includes 2.35 (DEMO), initial pressings on clear vinyl, later pressings on black vinyl, '86)

Munster   TFOSR7001   MUNSTER DANCE HALL FAVOURITES VOLUME 1 (7″ p/s, includes TAKE ME TO THE OTHER SIDE (DEMO), free with the Spanish La Herencia de los Munster fanzine, several issues, 1st issue in pink/green sleeve, '87)

SHELTER4   TAKE 5 (Shelter compilation LP, includes ROLLERCOASTER, 7/88)

Munster   MR003   MUNSTER DANCE HALL FAVOURITES VOLUME 3 (LP, includes BIG CITY (HYPNOBEAT MIX), '90)

Space Age   ORBIT004CD   THE NEW ATLANTIS (Space Age sampler CD, includes X-TACY (LIVE INTRO THEME), TRANSPARENT RADIATION (DEMO) and REPEATER (DEMO), 5/96)

U.S./Overseas Releases

Genius   GENILP001   THE PERFECT PRESCRIPTION (U.S. LP, some in purple/white sleeve, some in die-cut sleeve on purple "pyramid" vinyl, '88)

Genius   GENICD001   THE PERFECT PRESCRIPTION (U.S. CD, with extra tracks, purple/white / orange/white / silver/white sleeve, also a "50th Anniversary Edition")
1. Take Me To The Other Side [Kember/Pierce]
2. Walkin' With Jesus [Kember/Pierce]
3. Ode To Street Hassle [Kember/Pierce]
4. Ecstasy Symphony [Kember/Pierce]/Transparent Radiation (Flashback) [Thompson/Cunningham/Barthhelp] arranged [Kember/Pierce]
5. Feel So Good [Kember/Pierce]
6. Things'll Never Be The Same [Kember/Pierce]
7. Come Down Easy [Kember/Pierce]
8. Call The Doctor [Kember/Pierce]
9. Rollercoaster [Hall/Erickson]
10. Starship (Sun Ra/MC5)

Discography

Genius   GENICD006   PERFORMANCE (U.S. CD, '89)
1. Mary Anne
2. Come Together
3. Things'll Never Be The Same
4. Take Me To The Other Side
5. Rollercoaster
6. Starship
7. Walkin' With Jesus
8. OD Catastrophe
9. Feel So Good

Vogue   VOGUE506203   PLAYING WITH FIRE (French LP, '89)

Hitchhyke   LIFT022   PLAYING WITH FIRE (Greek LP, '89)

BOMP!   BLP4032   PLAYING WITH FIRE (U.S. LP, black vinyl, '89)

BOMP!   BLP4032   PLAYING WITH FIRE (U.S. LP, several different coloured vinyls, '90)

BOMP!   BOMPCD4032   PLAYING WITH FIRE (U.S. CD, '90)

Forced Exposure   FE017   TRANSPARENT RADIATION / HONEY (7″, p/s, demo versions, available to subscribers of U.S. Forced Exposure magazine, '90)

Dedicated   ZL74917   RECURRING (German LP, fluorescent sleeve)
1. Big City (Everybody I Know Can Be Found Here) [Kember]
2. Why Couldn't I See? [Kember]
3. I Love You [Kember]
4. Just To See You Smile [Kember]
5. Set Me Free/I've Got The Key [Kember]
6. When Tomorrow Hits [Arm, Turner, Peters, Lukin]
7. Feel So Sad [Pierce]
8. Hypnotized [Pierce]
9. Sometimes [Pierce]
10. Feelin' Just Fine (Head Full Of Shit) [Pierce]
11. Billy Whizz/Blue 1 [Pierce]

Dedicated   ZD74917   RECURRING (German CD, fluorescent sleeve, different tracks to UK issue)

Dedicated   3047-2-R   RECURRING (U.S. CD)

BMG BVCP131 RECURRING (Japanese CD)

BOMP! BCD4047 TAKING DRUGS TO MAKE MUSIC TO TAKE DRUGS TO (U.S. CD, different sleeve, '94)

BOMP! BCD4044 SPACEMEN ARE GO! (CD, 5/95)

TAANG! TAANG!93 SOUND OF CONFUSION (U.S. CD, different sleeve, 4 bonus tracks, 9/95)

TAANG! TAANG!94 THE PERFECT PRESCRIPTION (U.S. CD, different sleeve, 2/96)
1. Take Me To The Other Side [Kember/Pierce]
2. Walkin' With Jesus [Kember/Pierce]
3. Ode To Street Hassle [Kember/Pierce]
4. Ecstasy Symphony [Kember/Pierce]/Transparent Radiation (Flashback) [Thompson/Cunningham/Barthhelp] arranged [Kember/Pierce]
5. Feel So Good [Kember/Pierce]
6. Things'll Never Be The Same [Kember/Pierce]
7. Come Down Easy [Kember/Pierce]
8. Call The Doctor [Kember/Pierce]
10. Soul 1 [Kember/Pierce]
11. That's Just Fine [Kember/Pierce]
12. Starship [Sun Ra/MC5]
13. Ecstasy [Kember/Pierce]

TAANG! TAANG!95 PERFORMANCE (U.S. CD, different sleeve, 2/96)
1. Mary Anne
2. Come Together
3. Things'll Never Be The Same
4. Take Me To The Other Side
5. Rollercoaster
6. Walkin' With Jesus
7. Repeater
8. Starship
9. Revolution
10. Suicide

TAANG! TAANG!96 THE SINGLES (U.S. CD, '95)

TAANG! TAANG!97 PLAYING WITH FIRE (U.S. CD, different sleeve, '95)

TAANG!   TAANG!97   PLAYING WITH FIRE (U.S. double orange vinyl / black vinyl 10″ LP, different sleeve, '95)

Other Important Releases

Cheree   CHEREEF5   EXTRACT FROM AN EVENING OF CONTEMPORARY SITAR MUSIC (7″ flexi p/s, insert,'88)

Sniffin' Rock   SR008   WHEN TOMORROW HITS (7″ with Sniffin' Rock magazine / without fanzine, '89)

Father Yod   FYP-L25   TAKING DRUGS (TO MAKE MUSIC TO TAKE DRUGS TO) (LP, '90)
1. 2.35
2. Mary Anne
3. Losing Touch With My Mind
4. Amen
5. That's Just Fine
6. Come Down Easy
7. Sound Of Confusion

Fierce   FRIGHT040   DREAMWEAPON (CD, '90)

Fierce   FRIGHT42   DREAMWEAPON (LP, '90)
1. Dreamweapon (An Evening Of Contemporary Sitar Music)
2. Ecstasy In Slow Motion

WHEN TOMORROW HITS / Revolution (Mudhoney) (7″, p/s, 500 copies, '90)

Catalogue CAT 089   THE CATALOGUE NO. 89 (magazine, contains article and 2 flexis of I LOVE YOU and SOMETIMES, 2/91)

MR011   LOSING TOUCH WITH YOUR MIND (LP, 1st 2,000 numbered with gatefold insert and printed inner sleeve, some later pressings on coloured vinyl, '91)
1. Honey (Alternative Mix)
2. Walkin' With Jesus (Alternative Mix)
3. Repeater (Alternative Mix)
4. X-Tacy Symphony (Alternative Mix)
5. Transparent Radiation (Alternative Mix)
6. Losing Touch With My Mind (Northampton Demo)

7. Suicide (Heavy Drum Mix)
8. Things'll Never Be The Same (Drum Mix)
9. Why Couldn't I See? (Alternate Mix)

MRCD011   LOSING TOUCH WITH YOUR MIND (CD, 1st 2,000 numbered, insert, '91)

Sympathy For The Record Industry   SFTRI211   DREAMWEAPON (CD reissue, different sleeve, 11/93)
1. Dreamweapon (An Evening Of Contemporary Sitar Music)
2. Ecstasy In Slow Motion
3. Spacemen Jam

Oblivious Participant   WALKIN' WITH JESUS / TRANSPARENT RADIATION (CD, compilation of first two Glass EPs, 12/93)

Quiver At Dawn Entertainment   ODT21   FOR ALL THE FUCKED-UP CHILDREN OF THIS WORLD WE GIVE YOU SPACEMEN 3 (CD, pre-release of 500, 1/95)
1. Things'll Never Be The Same
2. 2.35
3. Walkin' With Jesus
4. Fixin' To Die
5. T.V. Catastrophe
6. Things'll Never Be The Same (Alternate Mix)
7. Walkin' With Jesus (Alternate Mix)

Sympathy For The Record Industry   SFTRI368   FOR ALL THE FUCKED-UP CHILDREN OF THIS WORLD WE GIVE YOU SPACEMEN 3 (CD, 4/95)

Sympathy For The Record Industry   SFTRI368   FOR ALL THE FUCKED-UP CHILDREN OF THIS WORLD WE GIVE YOU SPACEMEN 3 (LP, 1,500 copies, 4/95)

Moroccan Mayhem   MM002   TAKE ME TO THE OTHER SIDE (DEMO) / Set Me Free (Spectrum) / I LOVE YOU (REMIX) (7", p/s, 500 copies, orange vinyl, 4/95)

COME DOWN EASY (DEMO) / TRANSPARENT RADIATION (DEMO) (7", p/s, 500 copies, clear vinyl, 5/95)

Fierce   FRIGHT063   REVOLUTION OR HEROIN (CD, 6/95)
1. Sound Of Confusion
2. Take Me To The Other Side
3. Rollercoaster
4. Things'll Never Be The Same
5. Starship/Revolution
6. Suicide

SCRIPT1   ALL FUCKED UP (CD, 11/02)
1. Come Together
2. Rollercoaster
3. Take Me To The Other Side
4. Things'll Never Be The Same
5. Starship / Revolution
6. Little Doll
7. OD Catastrophe

Reproduced with kind permission from Ian Edmond, *Record Collector*, Issue 285, May 2003, and with special thanks to Mark Lascelles and Chris Barrus.